METABOLIC SYNDROME RESEARCH TRENDS

METABOLIC SYNDROME RESEARCH TRENDS

THOMAS E. BATONE
EDITOR

Nova Science Publishers, Inc.
New York

For permission to use material from this book please contact us:
Telephone 631-231-7269; Fax 631-231-8175
Web Site: http://www.novapublishers.com

Library of Congress Cataloging-in-Publication Data

Metabolic syndrome research trends / Thomas E. Batone, editor.
p. ; cm.
Includes bibliographical references and index.
ISBN 978-1-60456-224-8 (hardcover)
1. Metabolic syndrome. I. Batone, Thomas E.
[DNLM: 1. Metabolic Syndrome X. WK 820 M5869 2007]
RC662.4.M522 2007
362.196'3990072--dc22 2007051516

Published by Nova Science Publishers, Inc. ✦ New York

Contents

Preface		**vii**
Chapter I	Genetic Endocrinology of the Metabolic Syndrome: Networks of Genotype-Determined Feedback Loop Setpoints *Santiago Rodríguez, Tom R. Gaunt, Mohammad Reza Abdollahi, Sabine Sonnenberg and Ian N.M. Day*	**1**
Chapter II	Metabolic Syndrome in Hypertensive Subjects: Amplifying Effect on Target Organ Damage *Giuseppe Mulè and Giovanni Cerasola*	**65**
Chapter III	Prevalence of the Metabolic Syndrome and Its Relation to Risks for Cardiovascular Disease *Zhijie Yu and Gang Hu*	**89**
Chapter IV	Associations Between Carbohydrate Intake and Risk for Coronary Heart Disease, Insulin Resistance and the Metabolic Syndrome *Maria Luz Fernandez and Marcela Vergara-Jimenez*	**105**
Chapter V	Diets for Weight Reduction: The Recommended Diets and the Popular Diets *Annie Ferland and Paul Poirier*	**121**
Chapter VI	Metabolic Syndrome Treatment: Therapeutic Lifestyle Change *David Alexander Leaf, Ronald W. Deitrick and Nancy D. Harada*	**153**
Chapter VII	The Emerging Role of Inflammatory Markers in the Metabolic Syndrome *Ali A. Rizvi*	**171**
Chapter VIII	Obesity, Metabolic Syndrome, and Weight Management *Jian Huang and Donna Carden*	**191**

Chapter IX Comparing the Definitions of WHO and ATPIII Metabolic Syndrome (MS) in School Children **225**
V. Hirschler, C. Aranda, G. Maccalini, C. Gonzalez and M. Jadzinsky

Index **235**

Preface

Since cardiovascular (heart and blood vessel) disease is the leading cause of death for adults in developed countries, many medical studies focus on treating or preventing heart disease and stroke. The metabolic syndrome, a collection of unhealthy body measurements and abnormal laboratory test results, may identify persons at high risk for developing cardiovascular disease. Aggressive lifestyle modification and possible use of medications to treat the conditions that make up the metabolic syndrome may reduce a person's chances of developing heart disease or stroke. This new book presents the latest research in the field from around the world.

Chapter I - Cardiovascular disease and mortality risk are significantly increased in people with metabolic syndrome, a cluster of interrelated metabolic disorders including obesity, insulin resistance, glucose intolerance, dyslipidemia and hypertension. A complex interplay between predisposing and protective factors ultimately determines whether an individual will develop this set of disorders or not. Genetic factors are one of the significant contributors that predispose to, or protect against, each component of the metabolic syndrome. As in other complex diseases and traits, such genetic factors are likely to be multiple and interacting, with individual polymorphisms producing only a moderate effect. The identification of genetic variants influencing the metabolic syndrome is of great importance to understanding pathogenesis, identifying groups of individuals with different relative risk, and developing or improving therapies against this cluster of metabolic disorders. This has greatly stimulated both theoretical and applied genetic research in recent years. A range of new analytical tools has been developed for the dissection of complex traits. Applied genetic analyses have identified large numbers of candidate markers and chromosomal regions (more than 600 for obesity, which represents only one of the disorders of this cluster). In this chapter, the authors present a basic overview of the genetic approaches currently used for the identification of candidate genetic factors involved in the metabolic syndrome. They also summarise current evidence suggesting that genetic variants within elements of the endocrine system are directly involved in the risk of the metabolic syndrome. They focus attention on endocrine pathways for which candidate genetic variants have been identified, and introduce the foundations of a new hypothesis which postulates the involvement of a network of endocrine genetic setpoints as a combined contributor to the risk of the metabolic syndrome.

Chapter II - For many years, it has been recognized that hypertension tends to cluster with various metabolic abnormalities including abdominal obesity, elevated triglycerides, reduced high-density lipoprotein cholesterol, glucose intolerance and insulin resistance. This constellation of various conditions has a long list of colorful aliases, including polymetabolic syndrome, syndrome X, insulin resistance syndrome, dysmetabolic syndrome, deadly quartet and most recently metabolic syndrome (MS). The prevalence and the consequences of the MS have been difficult to assess without a commonly accepted definition. For this reason, in recent years, some scientific organizations proposed working definitions for MS. Among these definitions, the one suggested by NCEP-ATPIII is the simplest and the most commonly applied.

The incidence of the MS has been increasing worldwide in parallel with an increase in overweight and obesity. The epidemic proportion reached by the metabolic syndrome represents a major public health challenge, because several lines of evidence showed that the MS, even without type 2 diabetes, confers an increased risk of cardiovascular morbidity and mortality in the general population. Recently it has been demonstrated that the adverse prognostic impact of MS may also be extended to hypertensive patients.

It is likely that the enhanced cardiovascular risk associated with MS in patients with high blood pressure may be partly mediated through an increased prevalence of preclinical cardiovascular and renal changes, such as left ventricular hypertrophy, early carotid atherosclerosis, impaired aortic elasticity, hypertensive retinopathy and microalbuminuria. Indeed, some recent reports support this notion, showing that hypertensive patients with MS exhibit, more often than those without it, these early signs of end-organ damage, most of which are recognized as significant independent predictors of adverse cardiovascular outcomes.

Chapter III - There are five definitions of the metabolic syndrome that have been recommended by the World Health Organization (WHO), the European Group for Study of Insulin Resistance (EGIR), the National Cholesterol Education Program Expert Panel (NCEP), the International Diabetes Federation (IDF), and the American Association of Clinical Endocrinologists (AACE) separately since 1998. The prevalence of the metabolic syndrome reported from different studies has varied widely, mainly because of differences in the definitions of the syndrome and in the characteristics of the populations studied. Prospective studies on the relationship between the metabolic syndrome and cardiovascular risk are still scanty. Results from several studies including a large population-based Italian study, the Framingham Offspring Study, the Botnia Study, the Kuopio Ischemic Heart Disease Study, the National Health and Nutrition Examination Survey II Mortality Study, the San Antonio Heart Study, the Hoorn Study, the British Regional Heart Study, the Swedish Study in Uppsala, and the DECODE study have shown that the presence of metabolic syndrome using different definitions is associated with a significantly increased risk of total mortality and cardiovascular morbidity and mortality.

Clustering of some metabolic and physiological abnormalities was first described in 1923 by Kylin who published a report on a syndrome comprising hypertension, hyperglycaemia and hyperuricaemia. The coining of the term "syndrome X" in 1988 by Reaven renewed the impetus to conduct research concerning this syndrome. In his description of syndrome X, Reaven considered the following abnormalities: resistance to insulin-stimulated glucose uptake, glucose intolerance, hyperinsulinaemia, an increased plasma concentration of VLDL triglyceride, a decreased plasma concentration of high-density lipoprotein (HDL) cholesterol, and high blood pressure. Subsequently, several new components to the syndrome, such as obesity and its central distribution, mircoalbuminuria, hyperuricaemia, abnormalities in haemostatic factors, have been suggested. Characterized by insulin resistance, this syndrome is also sometimes called the insulin resistance syndrome, or the metabolic syndrome. The metabolic syndrome has a specific code in the International Classification of Diseases at least in Finland (ICD-10: E66.00). More recently, a term of "dysmetabolic syndrome" has been launched by the American Association of Clinical Endocrinologists (AACE) with a specific ICD-9 code 277.7.

The pathogenesis of the syndrome is complex and so far incompletely understood, but obesity, sedentary lifestyle, dietary factors and genetic factors are known to contribute and interact in its development. It has been proposed that the metabolic syndrome is a powerful determinant of type 2 diabetes and atherosclerotic cardiovascular disease (CVD).

Chapter IV - Because the incidence of obesity has increased dramatically over the past 20 years, finding the most appropriate diets for losing weight has become a major issue. It is also well established that overweight individuals have a higher risk of developing insulin resistance, coronary heart disease (CHD) and diabetes type II. The amount of carbohydrate in the diet may play a significant role in the maintenance of body weight and in reducing the risk factors for chronic disease.

Dietary carbohydrates are indeed at the core of the debate regarding healthy diets that promote weight loss and decrease biomarkers for heart disease and the metabolic syndrome. Very low, moderate or high carbohydrate diets have been studied in their effects on body weight, dyslipidemias, insulin sensitivity, plasma glucose, leptin levels, inflammatory cytokines and adhesive molecules. Very low carbohydrate diets have been reported to effectively reduce body weight and improve plasma lipids and insulin sensitivity in studies of short duration between 4 to 24 weeks. Moderate and high carbohydrate diets have also been shown to have beneficial effects on anthropometrics and other cardiovascular risk factors depending on the duration of the study and the investigated population. Overall the controversies of the findings depend on the type of study (parallel versus randomized crossover) the duration of the intervention, the assessed subjects (normal versus diabetic or hyperlipidemic) and the retention of subjects, which appeared to be poor in the majority of the cases. All these factors still continue to make it difficult to interpret the available data and to reach conclusive statements regarding the relationship between dietary carbohydrate and chronic disease.

It is the purpose of ths review to evaluate a variety of clinical interventions conducted in the past 5 years in which dietary carbohydrate was one of the main variables under investigation. The effects of different dietary interventions varying in the amount of dietary carbohydrate on symptoms associated with the metabolic syndrome, insulin resistance and increased risk for CHD are discussed.

Chapter V - It is well recognized that the prevalence of metabolic abnormalities found in the presence of obesity is increasing within our sedentary population. In fact, obesity is a growing epidemic that is primarily due to environmental influences. There has been a rapid increase in obesity over the past 30 years in North America, whereas the recent prevalence estimations from self-reported data in Canada indicated that 15 % of the adult population is obese and 33 % is classified in the overweight category, while in the US nearly 1/3 of adults are obese, corresponding to almost 20 % of the US population [1-3]. This highlights the importance of environmental factors and lifestyle choices since obesity cannot be totally explained by genetic factors alone [4]. Unfortunately, sedentary lifestyle and increased energy intake predispose to high fat and high calorie food choices, and refined diet seems to be adopted by an increasing proportion of our population. This is leading to weight gain, positive energy balance, obesity and health-related complications. Thus, "at risk" obesity (abdominal obesity) is an important cause of metabolic complications, such as cardiovascular disease (CVD), type 2 diabetes and hypertension[5-7]. Indeed, the American Heart Association (AHA) has classified obesity as a modifiable risk factor for coronary heart disease (CHD) [8]. A variety of therapies may help to reduce the incidence of obesity, including diet, physical exercise, and pharmacological treatments. Weight loss is an essential component in the management of the metabolic complications of obesity. Low-fat diets have been advocated for weight loss for many years. However, some popular diets such as the very low-carbohydrate (ketogenic) diets have challenged the effectiveness of conventional low-fat diets, partly because of there rapid efficiency in contrast to the continuing increased prevalence of obesity despite reductions of fat intake. Thus, several authors have compared the effectiveness of various weight loss approaches, such as those proposed by the official guidelines, to the "popular" diets (as Atkins, Ornish, The Zone, South Beach diet, Weight Watchers) in the management of obesity and its related complications. Although there is a need to perform well-designed clinical trials showing long-term safety and efficacy of low-carbohydrate diets, several studies have showed effective short-term weight loss and improved metabolic disturbances compared to low-fat diets. The major targets of intervention for proper treatment of the epidemic of obesity remain weight loss and active lifestyle. Even if different types of diet or diet/exercise combinations can produce weight loss, if this treatment is stopped, weight is regained. The current review underlines the clinical and the experimental evidence of the different dietary approaches for weight loss regarding obesity treatment and related metabolic complications. Despite numerous researches, there is still controversy regarding the optimal macronutrient content, and the authors also overview the issue of carbohydrate restriction versus fat restriction on weight loss and weight control in order to achieve effective weight loss and better health. Indeed, modest weight reduction (5 % to 10 % of body weight) can decrease total cholesterol, improve glucose tolerance and decrease blood pressure in overweight and obese patients [6;9-12]. The authors also briefly discuss the role of several dietary interventions, which can lower CHD risk and improve lipid profile.

Chapter VI – Background - During the past two decades, Metabolic Syndrome (MetS) in the U.S. has increased to the point of being 'epidemic', primarily due to the increased prevalence of obesity. MetS is associated with increased coronary artery disease (CAD) risk. Although dietary interventions are a fundamental component of therapeutic lifestyle change (TLC), programs aimed at weight reduction, physical activity and exercise play a pivotal in reinforcing and sustaining long-term weight loss.

Methods - This article reviews and describes MetS including approaches for implementing physical activity in the context of TLC interventions. These include center- and phone-based programs as well as provider-based intervention settings.

Results and Conclusions - While TLC interventions aimed at reducing MetS are a public imperative, the most effective intervention remains to be elucidated. The various approaches used can be described as effective and having common characteristics. Further research is needed to determine the best method for reducing the risk of MetS.

Chapter VII - The metabolic syndrome consists of a constellation of risk factors including obesity, glucose intolerance, hypertension, and dyslipidemia in the setting of insulin resistance that confers an increased risk of cardiovascular disease and type 2 diabetes. Although the major pathophysiologic mechanisms are still in the process of being elucidated, the possible role of inflammation, cytokines, and atherogenic markers has received attention lately. Recent studies suggest that inflammatory markers like C-reactive protein (CRP), Interleukin (IL)-6, and Tumor Necrosis Factor (TNF)-α mirror oxidative stress and may be instrumental in the final pathway of adverse vascular outcomes in the metabolic syndrome. Other adipocytokines produced by fatty tissue are also altered, with lower levels of adiponectin and increased leptin and resistin. Elevated Plasminogen Activator Inhibitor (PAI)-1 and fibrinogen levels, and derangement in clotting factors, correlate with the degree of insulin resistance and may contribute to the prothrombotic tendency. Taken together, these abnormalities shift the balance of endothelial function towards an abnormal state that heightens the risk of atherothrombosis. Lifestyle factors and medications can have a profound effect in modifying these parameters. The phenomenal increase in the prevalence of obesity has accentuated the various clinical manifestations and pathopysiologic underpinnings of this epidemic. Continued research looking at the role of inflammation and cytokines in the genesis and propagation of the metabolic syndrome should provide a window into its pathogenesis at the cellular and humoral level, improve the understanding of disease mechanisms, and open up possibilities for effective therapeutic interventions in the future.

Chapter VIII - The metabolic syndrome (MS) describes a cluster of cardiovascular risk factors, including central adiposity, insulin resistance or overt type 2 diabetes mellitus (DM2), atherogenic dyslipidemia, and elevated blood pressure or overt hypertension. Obesity, especially central adiposity, is associated with insulin resistance, the central feature of MS. Predictably, the incidence of MS increases with increasing body mass index (BMI) but also occurs with weight gain, even at normal weight. MS predisposes individuals to the development of DM2 and is responsible for increased all cause and coronary artery disease (CAD) mortality. MS, therefore, likely represents a latent disease process that may be viewed as preclinical diabetes or preclinical atherosclerosis. Because transitional conditions are more amenable to therapeutic intervention than late-stage disease, it is becoming increasingly recognized that early identification and treatment of MS is necessary to prevent CAD mortality. Recent clinical trials have demonstrated that weight loss through lifestyle modification with or without pharmacologic intervention can improve all components of MS. Although the exact mechanisms underlying MS remain undefined, physicians can contribute to improved long-tem clinical outcome by endorsing a healthy lifestyle that promotes weight loss or maintenance and physical activity. This may lead to the reduction in morbidity and mortality associated with obesity, DM2, and MS.

Chapter IX - Studies indicate that MS starts in children. The purpose was to determine: a) the prevalence of MS among children using ATPIII defined MS and WHO defined MS, as well as b) the agreement between both definitions. The authors evaluated 478 (221M) school children aged 9.62 years between April and July 2005. Data for BMI, waist circumference (WC), blood pressure (BP), Tanner, OGTT, lipid profile and insulinemia were obtained. The presence of MS was determined using two different criteria: a) analogous to ATPIII (de Ferranti Circulation 110: 2494-97, 2004) and b) analogous to WHO guidelines. WHO guidelines were defined as insulin resistance (>=HOMA-IR III quartile) or fasting glucose >100 mg/dL and at least two of the following criteria: WC 75%ile , BP>95%ile; HDL<5%ile; triglycerides>95%ile , urinary albumin excretion (UAE) III quartile was assessed. Of 478 children examined, 87 (18.2%) were OW (BMI>95%ile, z-BMI=2.0.3), 126 (26%) at risk of OW (BMI>85<95%ile; z-BMI=1.31) and 265 (55.4%) non-OW (BMI<85%ile; z-BMI= -0.03). Two hundred forty eight (57.6%) were Tanner 1. There was a higher (p<0.01) prevalence of WHO-defined MS (10.8%; n=52) than ATPIII-defined MS (5.3%; n=26). However, mean values for HOMA-IR (4.3 vs 3.9), systolic BP (99 vs 97 mmHg), TG (144 vs 158 mg/dl), HDL-C (42 vs 40mg/dl), fasting glucose (89 vs 91mg/dl), and UAE (1.1 vs 1.5mg/l) were not significantly different by either definition. No age or sex differences were found either. Agreement between definitions was poor (Kappa 0.34; 95% CI 0.19-0.48 $p<0.001$). Results indicate that there was a higher prevalence of WHO-defined MS and agreement between both definitions was poor. These differences suggest that the concept of a common MS defined by these two guidelines may be flawed.

In: Metabolic Syndrome Research Trends
Editor: Thomas E. Batone, pp. 1-63
ISBN: 978-1-60456-224-8

Chapter I

Genetic Endocrinology of the Metabolic Syndrome: Networks of Genotype-Determined Feedback Loop Setpoints

***Santiago Rodríguez*[1*], *Tom R. Gaunt*[1], *Mohammad Reza Abdollahi*[2], *Sabine Sonnenberg*[1] *and Ian N.M. Day*[1]**

[1] Human Genetics Division, University of Southampton, School of Medicine, Duthie Building (MP 808), Southampton General Hospital, Tremona Road, Southampton, SO16 6YD, UK

[2] Bristol Genetic Epidemiology Laboratory, University of Bristol, No. 24 Tyndall Avenue, Bristol, BS8 1TQ, UK

Abstract

Cardiovascular disease and mortality risk are significantly increased in people with metabolic syndrome, a cluster of interrelated metabolic disorders including obesity, insulin resistance, glucose intolerance, dyslipidemia and hypertension. A complex interplay between predisposing and protective factors ultimately determines whether an individual will develop this set of disorders or not. Genetic factors are one of the significant contributors that predispose to, or protect against, each component of the metabolic syndrome. As in other complex diseases and traits, such genetic factors are likely to be multiple and interacting, with individual polymorphisms producing only a moderate effect. The identification of genetic variants influencing the metabolic syndrome is of great importance to understanding pathogenesis, identifying groups of individuals with different relative risk, and developing or improving therapies against this cluster of metabolic disorders. This has greatly stimulated both theoretical and applied genetic research in recent years. A range of new analytical tools has been developed for the dissection of complex traits. Applied genetic analyses have identified large numbers of candidate markers and chromosomal regions (more than 600 for obesity, which represents only one of the disorders of this cluster). In this chapter, we present

* E-mail address: santi@soton.ac.uk. Tel.: +44 (0) 23 8079 8731 Fax: +44 (0) 23 8079 4264; Correspondence: Dr. Santiago Rodríguez, Human Genetics Division, University of Southampton, School of Medicine, Duthie Building (MP 808), Southampton General Hospital, Tremona Road, Southampton, SO16 6YD, UK.

a basic overview of the genetic approaches currently used for the identification of candidate genetic factors involved in the metabolic syndrome. We also summarise current evidence suggesting that genetic variants within elements of the endocrine system are directly involved in the risk of the metabolic syndrome. We focus our attention on endocrine pathways for which candidate genetic variants have been identified, and we introduce the foundations of a new hypothesis which postulates the involvement of a network of endocrine genetic setpoints as a combined contributor to the risk of the metabolic syndrome.

1. Introduction

Unraveling the genetic basis of complex traits is one of the greatest challenges of science and medicine in the 21st century (Dean, 2003). Complex traits (also known as multifactorial or non-Mendelian traits) influence the normal and abnormal function of all body systems, and are directly involved in the diseases that account for most of the mortality and morbidity in humans (Sankaranarayanan et al., 1999). Most phenotypes for which there is a continuous variation at the population level are complex traits. Examples span all kinds of human features, including skin colour, weight, hormone levels, blood pressure, intelligence, etc. The genetic dissection of complex traits is relevant to improving our basic knowledge of mechanisms for life. In particular, it is key for understanding pathogenesis and potentially for disease prediction. It is hoped that advances in this field will fuel the development or improvement of therapeutic approaches, diagnostics and risk assessment for common diseases such as cardiovascular disease, diabetes and cancer.

However, multifactorial traits are doubly complex. Firstly, they have a complex genetic basis. Their phenotypic expression is the result of the action and interaction of both genetic and non-genetic factors (Chakravarti and Little, 2003). A large number of genes are involved in the determination of complex traits, but none of them is necessary or sufficient to explain all phenotypic variation. On the contrary, most of these "polygenes" have a small effect and contribute in a quantitative manner (Sankaranarayanan et al., 1999). Polygenes may interact with each other and with multiple environmental factors in unpredictable ways. As a result, the mode of inheritance of complex traits is far more complex than that imposed by the laws of classical Mendelian inheritance. And secondly, at present, the analysis of the genetic basis of multifactorial traits is also complex. A number of approaches have been developed and implemented in recent years to identify and disentangle the role of such genetic factors. But the fact that the inheritance of multifactorial traits follows non-Mendelian patterns, together with the existence of genetic heterogeneity, polygenic effects and interactions, uncontrollable development-environmental variability, etc., (Risch, 2000) has resulted in a low rate of independently confirmed findings (Sillanpaa and Auranen, 2004).

The metabolic syndrome is one of the paradigms in the genetic analysis of complex traits. In this chapter we summarise recent advances in the genetic analysis of the metabolic syndrome, focusing the emphasis on the endocrine factors involved.

2. The Metabolic Syndrome: Concept, Definition, Effect and Prevalence

The scientific community has known for many decades that different (but interrelated) metabolic abnormalities (including glucose intolerance, insulin resistance, central obesity, dyslipidaemia and hypertension) occur simultaneously in some individuals with a frequency higher than might be expected by chance, and that this condition increases considerably the risk of cardiovascular disease and type 2 diabetes (Eckel et al., 2005). This concept has been recognised for many years and the syndrome was formally first labelled by Reaven in 1988 as syndrome X (Reaven, 1988). Today, this syndrome is widely known as metabolic syndrome, but also called insulin resistance syndrome, dysmetabolic syndrome and Reaven syndrome.

Recently, the International Diabetes Federation (IDF) has published a new definition of the metabolic syndrome aiming to provide a better prediction in the identification of individuals at high risk for cardiovascular disease and type 2 diabetes. This new definition considers that five complex traits can behave as risk factors for the metabolic syndrome, namely central obesity, triglyceride levels, cholesterol levels, blood pressure and plasma glucose levels. Each trait is considered to be a risk factor for the metabolic syndrome in a given individual according to established thresholds (Table 1). The metabolic syndrome is defined as the simultaneous ocurrence, in a given individual, of central obesity plus at least any two of the other risk factors (raised triglyceride levels, reduced HDL-cholesterol levels, raised blood pressure or raised fasting plasma glucose levels). Controversy exists, however, in the criteria followed to define individuals with the syndrome. Other definitions exist (Table 1), but given that all definitions to date are arbitrary, there can be no "correct" definition, merely good or bad predictors of outcome.

The negative effect of the metabolic syndrome on human health and its prevalence [ranging from 22% to 39% of the adult population in developed countries (Khunti and Davies, 2005)] has fuelled and justified a huge effort by the scientific community in order to disentangle all the aspects of the syndrome.

3. Pathophysiology of the Metabolic Syndrome

The precise pathogenesis and the pathophysiological sequence of metabolic abnormalities resulting in metabolic syndrome remain uncertain, although it is widely accepted that both insulin resistance and obesity are central components.

Table 1. Definitions of the metabolic syndrome proposed by different organisations [adapted from Magliano et al., 2006]

WHO (1999)	EGIR (1999)	ATPIII (2001)	IDF (2005)
Insulin resistance	**Insulin resistance**	**Three or more of:**	**Central obesity**
Plus two or more of:	**Plus two or more of:**	a) Central obesity: waist circumference>102 cm in M (>88 cm in F)	**Plus any two of:**
a) Obesity: BMI>30 kg/m^2 or WHR>0.9 in M (>0.85 in F)	a) Central obesity: waist circumference≥94 cm in M (≥80 cm in F)	b) Hypertriglyceridaemia: triglycerides≥1.7 mmol/L	a) Raised triglycerides≥1.7 mmol/L or specific treatment for this abnormality.
b) Dyslipidaemia: triglycerides≥1.7 mmol/L or HDL-C<0.9 mmol/L in M (<1.0 mmol/L in F)	b) Dyslipidaemia: triglycerides>2.0 mmol/L or HDL-C<1.0mmol/L	c) Low HDL-C:<1.03 mmol/L in M (<1.29 mmol/L in F)	b) Reduced HDL-C<1.03 mmol/L in M (1.29 mmol/L in F) or specific treatment for this abnormality
c) Hypertension: blood pressure≥140/90 mmHg or medication	c) Hypertension: blood pressure≥140/90 mmHg or medication	d) Hypertension: blood pressure≥130/85 mmHg or medication	c) Hypertension: blood pressure≥ 130/85 mmHg or medication.
d) Microalbuminuria: albumin excretion≥20 μg/min or albumin:creatinine ratio≥30 mg/g	d) Fasting plasma glucose≥6.1 mmol/L	e) Fasting plasma glucose≥6.1 mmol/L	d) Fasting plasma glucose≥5.6 mmol/L) or previously diagnosed type 2 diabetes

WHO = World Health Organization; EGIR = the European Group for the Study of Insulin Resistance; the American college of Endocrinology Task Force on the Insulin Resistance Syndrome; ATPIII = National Cholesterol Education Program Expert Panel on Detection, Evaluation, and Treatment of High Blood Cholesterol in Adults (Adult Treatment Panel III); IDF = International Diabetes Association; F = female; M = male.

Some authors have suggested that insulin resistance, in both adipose tissue and muscle, is the main underlying factor leading to the metabolic syndrome (Eckel et al., 2005). Insulin resistance is an impaired metabolic response of the body to insulin action (Schinner et al., 2005). In a normal physiological condition, insulin exerts an anabolic role on glucose metabolism by lowering blood glucose levels, both by facilitating glucose uptake mainly into skeletal muscle and fat tissue and by inhibiting endogenous glucose production by the liver. In an insulin resistance state, the actions of insulin are impaired. In the initial stages of insulin resistance, there is a hypersecretion of insulin from pancreatic β cells. This compensates temporarily for insulin resistance, keeping normal glucose tolerance and glucose fasting levels. When insulin hypersecretion cannot compensate for insulin resistance, glucose intolerance manifests, leading ultimately to β cell failure and type 2 diabetes.

Insulin resistance is therefore causally related to glucose intolerance, dyslipidemia, high blood pressure and vascular dysfunction. However, it has been suggested that insulin resistance alone is insufficient to cause these anomalies (Ferrannini, 2006). In fact there is increased recognition that abdominal obesity is the most prevalent form of the metabolic syndrome, which has led some authors to suggest obesity as the primary cause of the metabolic syndrome (Despres, 2006). In an obesity state, free fatty acids (FFA) are released in abundance from the expanded adipose tissue mass. FFA stimulate the production of glucose and triglycerides in the liver, and alterations in lipoprotein balance. Overabundance of circulating FFA is a major contributor in the development of insulin resistance in muscle. It also contributes to the proinflammatory state characteristic of the metabolic syndrome (Eckel et al., 2005).

It has been suggested that the interaction between obesity and defects in insulin signalling is so complex that it is not yet possible to disentangle the two. For example, obesity causes insulin resistance, whereas insulin resistance seemingly exacerbates the adverse effects of obesity (Grundy, 2004).

There is increasing evidence showing the involvement of various mechanisms such as increased sympathetic activity, disorders of hypothalamo-pituitary-adrenal axis, proinflammatory cytokines and adipocytokines or psychoemotional stress, in complex pathophysiology of the metabolic syndrome. In addition, there is a considerable amount of research confirming the role of neurotrophins and mastocytes in pathophysiology of this syndrome. Based on these and considering the lower level of (brain-derived neurotrophic factor (BDNF) in the metabolic syndrome, (Hristova and Aloe, 2006) suggested the hypothesis of neuro-immune-endocrine interaction in its pathophysiology. This seems to be a relatively new window into the events happening in the metabolic syndrome, (and might be a confirmation of our own thought of considering counter-regulatory hormones in studying of this cluster of metabolic abnormalities).

4. Causes of the Metabolic Syndrome: Genetics and Environment

Despite the complexity of its pathogenesis, it is widely accepted that the underlying cause of the metabolic syndrome results from the action of many susceptibility genes, the influence of many environmental exposures and the interactions between both. This complex interplay influences all metabolic syndrome features, from the primary events to the final health consequences (Figure 1).

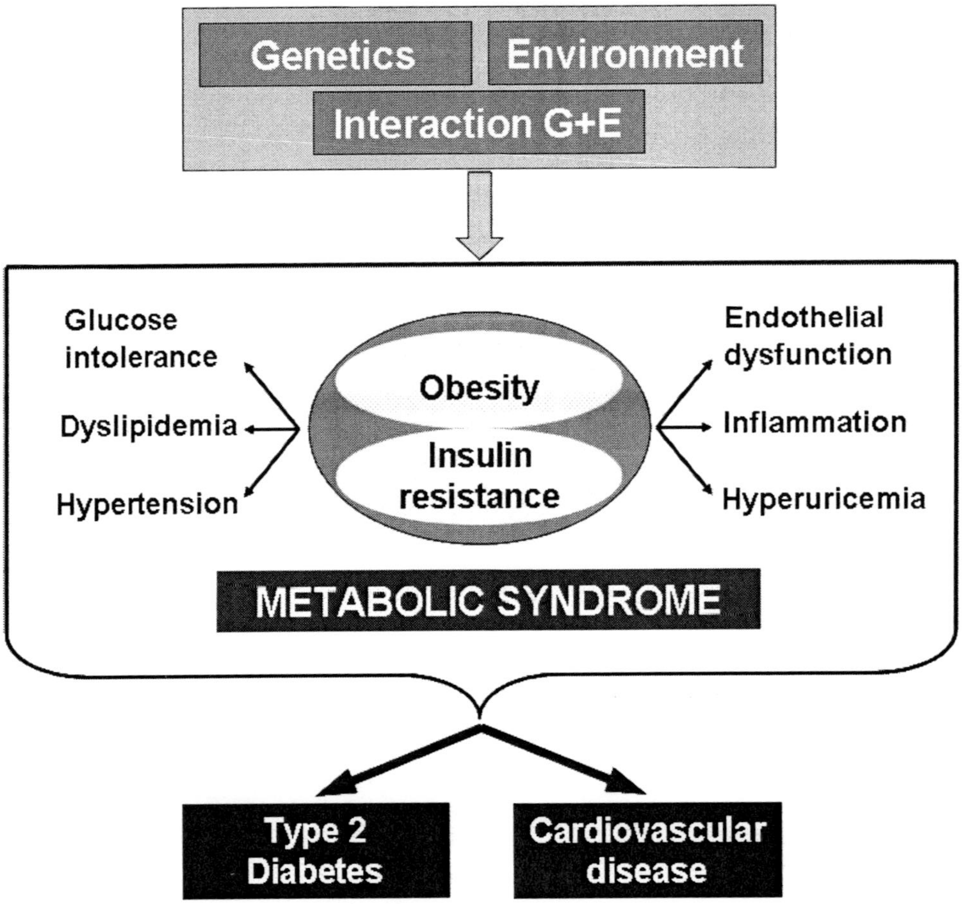

Figure 1. Simplified diagram of the metabolic syndrome. The two central components of the metabolic syndrome (obesity and insulin resistance) are caused by a combination of effects produced by genes, by environmental factors and by the interactions between genes and environment. Also shown are a number of other core components of the metabolic syndrome. Type 2 diabetes and cardiovascular disease are end-stage consequences of the syndrome.

The relative importance of hereditary and environmental influences on metabolic syndrome risk traits has been studied in detail. There is evidence suggesting that metabolic syndrome risk phenotypes aggregate within families. The percentage of phenotypic variation attributed to genetic factors (as measured by heritability) has been estimated in many studies. Table 2 shows the values observed in two of these studies, one of them based on elderly Danish twins (Poulsen et al., 2001), and the other on healthy European families (Freeman et al., 2002). Differences in study design, ethnic origin, and other factors have a direct impact on the heritability estimates observed. Table 2 illustrates that, within a given study, heritability estimates differ among each of the components of the metabolic syndrome. In addition, for a given metabolic syndrome risk trait, there are differences between men and women. Overall, these studies show that a considerable proportion of the phenotypic variation of metabolic syndrome risk traits is attributable to genetic factors.

Table 2. Heritabilities (h^2) observed for each of the features of the metabolic syndrome in two independent studies

	Danish twins[a]			Unrelated Europeans[b]
Trait	h^2	h^2 (men)	h^2 (women)	h^2
BMI	0.80	0.58	0.90	0.36
WHR*	0.06*	0.22	0.10	0.15*
Fasting insulin	0.26	0.36	0.14	0.29
Triglycerides	0.40	0.50	0.34	0.18
Systolic BP	0.76	1.00	0.58	0.11
HDL cholesterol	0.70	0.56	0.84	0.50

[a] (Poulsen et al., 2001) and [b] (Freeman et al., 2002)

*For WHR, the heritability estimates range from 0.30 to 0.60 in other studies (Selby et al., 1990; Rose et al., 1998)

On the other hand, environmental exposures related with lifestyle such as diet, physical activity, alcohol intake and alcoholism strongly influence the development of the metabolic syndrome. Importantly, phenotypic variation is also influenced by complex interactions between genes and environment. Under gene-environment interaction, the joint effect of both a genetic factor and an environmental exposure differs from the additive effects of each of them (Stephens and Humphries, 2003). In an extreme situation, gene-environment interaction could lead the same gene to behave either as a predisposing risk factor (when interacting with a given environmental exposure), or as a protective factor (if interacting with a different environmental exposure). This idea forms the basis of the thrifty genotype hypothesis, which was postulated by Neel (Neel, 1962) to explain the greater incidence of the metabolic syndrome in societies with an urban lifestyle as compared with societies with a rural lifestyle. It is widely accepted today that the pandemic of obesity is caused by a profound mismatch between humanity's present environmental circumstances and those that have moulded evolutionary selection (Prentice et al., 2005). According to the thrifty genotype hypothesis, genotypes promoting energy conservation confer a survival advantage during periods of starvation. However, these same genotypes would act detrimentally if exposed to the abundance of food typical in Western societies (Groop, 2000). This hypothesis has been supported by a number of observations both in animal models and in humans (Coleman, 1973;Ravussin et al., 1994).

More recently, a new hypothesis has introduced the concept of a 'thrifty phenotype'. The fetal origins of adult disease hypothesis (FOAD) (Barker et al., 2002) proposes that a malnourished fetus would lead to low birth weight and increased risk of the metabolic syndrome in adult life, as exemplified by several published works (Barker et al., 1989;Ravelli et al., 1998;Ravelli et al., 1999). However, there is an alternative possibility that birthweight and later life traits are covariates of the same genotype, or that birthweight and genotype interact or become canalised to an outcome in later life (Day et al., 2004a).

Disentangling the genetic chain of causality for the metabolic syndrome and the genetic variation accounting for a differential predisposition/risk of this cluster of disorders requires and will require the use and development of a wide range of genetic approaches and tools.

5. Genetic Analysis of the Metabolic Syndrome

Many different approaches have been used to analyse the genetic basis of the metabolic syndrome. Here we briefly review the most commonly used. We arbitrarily group them into three separate categories: 1) direct methods based on molecular biology approaches; 2) indirect methods based on statistical genetic approaches including genetic epidemiology and formal population genetics; and 3) mixed methods combining molecular biology and statistical genetic approaches.

5.1. Direct Methods (Based on Molecular Biology)

We briefly show here some of the existent strategies that provide evidence of the effect of genetic variation of genes potentially influencing metabolic syndrome risk traits, based on direct analyses of their function.

5.1.1. Comparative Genomics

The study of animal models enables possible predictive inferences in humans due to the existence of synteny (evolutionary conservation of genomic regions between species) and homology (sequence conservation between species), although this does not apply to all genomic regions and sequences. Direct methods used in animal models to study gene function are mainly based on genetic modification. The most widely used techniques include disruption of the function of a given gene (knock-outs), and introduction of exogenous genetic information in the germline of the animal model (transgenics). Further advantages of animal studies include the possibility of conducting controlled experimental crosses. There are a number of congenic, recombinant inbred, advanced intercross, and chromosome substitution strains available, which allow the design of powerful analyses (due to the larger number of offspring and the possibility of reducing the effect of environmental factors) (Brockmann and Bevova, 2002).

Knock-outs, transgenics and controlled experimental crosses have been widely and successfully used in the study of the metabolic syndrome (Brockmann and Bevova, 2002;Takahashi and Smithies, 2004;Biddinger and Kahn, 2006). Examples of successful findings in animal models leading to the identification of genes involved in the metabolic syndrome in humans include the discovery of leptin and leptin receptor as the human homologues of the mouse *ob* and *db* mutants respectively (Zhang et al., 1994;Tartaglia et al., 1995;Chen et al., 1996;Lee et al., 1996).

5.1.2. Pharmacological Methods and Pharmacogenetics

The use of drugs known to act as agonists (or antagonists) of a specific gene allows testing the phenotypic effect resulting from the enhancement (or inhibition) of such gene. For example, pharmacological inhibition of *11βHSD1* in humans increases insulin sensitivity

(Schupp et al., 2004), *AGTR1* pharmacological blockade lowers the risk of type 2 diabetes and promotes insulin sensitivity (Walker et al., 1995), etc.

Importantly, there is variation among individuals in drug response. This variation has, at least in part, a genetic basis. Pharmacogenetics is a discipline that studies the variability in drug responses attributed to genetic factors and aims to identify genetic variants responsible for such variation in order to design more effective personalised medicine (Roses, 2001;Goldstein et al., 2003). The combination of pharmacological analyses and pharmacogenetics is a powerful direct method to gain knowledge of gene function in relation with the effect of genetic variation on metabolic syndrome risk traits.

5.1.3. Other Functional Studies

Many other functional study designs have been applied to the study of the metabolic syndrome. For example, it is possible to test for intraindividual differences in mRNA expression. We have developed an approach combining TaqMan® assays and intraindividual gel-fluorimaging allelic ratiometry of single nucleotide polymorphisms (SNPs) and haplotypes (on quantitative-gel image analysis of restriction digests of cDNA) that enables comparison of mRNA levels for the two alleles in heterozygote individuals. We have applied this new approach to determine relative allelic expression from haplotypes of the angiotensin II type I receptor in relation to metabolic syndrome traits (Abdollahi et al., 2004).

5.2. Indirect Methods (Based on Statistical Genetics)

Indirect methods can be grouped into two strategies, based on different philosophies. Both aim to determine the genetic basis of a complex phenotype, but while one uses genotypic information, the other does not. The approaches that do not require genotypic information make inferences about the influence of genetic factors on phenotypes following classical genetic analyses of the distribution of phenotypes among related individuals. This strategy, has been defined as the "top-down" strategy, and includes complex segregation analyses and heretability analyses. On the other hand, inferences about the influence of genetic factors on phenotypes can be done by studying directly DNA variations and their effect on the phenotype, a strategy known as the "bottom-up" approach. This is the most widely used strategy in the dissection of complex traits in general and includes linkage analyses and association analyses. In this section we will focus the attention only on the approaches based on the "bottom-up" philosophy.

Study design and genetic models

The power of statistical genetic approaches for unraveling the effects of genes influencing human complex traits, such as metabolic syndrome risk traits, is highly dependent on the study design (Terwilliger and Goring, 2000). A variety of genetic epidemiological approaches offer considerable potential to examine the contribution of genetic variants or genes to the population burden of disease (Day et al., 2001). The scope of genetic epidemiology includes every aspect of population genetics that is not concerned primarily with evolution (Morton, 2000). In addition, there has been an emphasis on the key role of population genetics in the study design of genetic epidemiological studies, both in general (Schork et al., 1998;Chakravarti, 1999;Morton, 2000;Jorde et al., 2001;Risch, 2005) and in the context of complex cardiovascular risk traits (Schork, 1997). The Shifting Balance of Evolution theory by Sewall Wright (Wright, 1982), among other seminal works, detailed the importance of stochastic (i.e. random) factors, gene interactions, migration, population size, subdivision and inbreeding (together with mutation and selection) in the emergence and maintenanance of novel phenotypes and diseases. These population-level complexities may also obscure the detection of gene effects if not accounted for through factors such as random and non-random mating and assortative mating (Schork et al., 1998). Ignorance of the evolutionary history of populations can hamper mapping efforts based on the analysis of linkage disequilibrium (LD) and haplotypes (Schork et al., 1998).

There are two classical genetic models for the molecular basis of common diseases. The prevailing model is based on the hypothesis that common polymorphic alleles exert small individual effects but with significant population attributable risk (common disease/ common variant, CD/CV hypothesis) (Lander, 1996). A contrasting model (rare disease/ rare variant, RD/RV hypothesis) assumes that rare but severe single gene mutations can cause a phenotype which shows strong familial clustering (Pritchard, 2001). Examples supporting both models have been described in the literature. In addition, an intermediate genetic model has been proposed: sequence changes at an intermediate frequency [termed "paucimorphisms" (Day et al., 2004b)] may exist and may have a moderate effect. Theoretical and observational evidence supporting the paucimorphism hypothesis has also been published recently (Day et al., 2004b;Alharbi et al., 2005).

Appropriate genetic models and careful study designs integrating knowledge derived from different disciplines (including genetic epidemiology, classical population genetics, statistics, medicine, molecular biology, etc.) are crucial for the interpretation of the statistical and biological reliability of results obtained in statistical genetic analyses.

5.2.1. Linkage Analysis

The linkage approach can be used to localize genes of unknown function from family data. Linkage analyses are based on the lod score method proposed by Morton in 1955 (Morton, 1955). Many variants of this method exist, including parametric and non-parametric approaches. Linkage analyses enable testing cosegregation of a trait and marker loci in pedigrees. Different variants enable analysis of different family information, ranging from sib pairs to extended pedigrees.

Linkage analyses are mostly performed using microsatellites. They have been very successful in the mapping of Mendelian disorders, and have produced convincing evidence showing links between several chromosomal regions and metabolic syndrome risk traits. For example the human obesity gene map (http://obesitygene.pbrc.edu/, which is being updated every year) lists more than 100 chromosomal regions that have been linked to obesity risk phenotypes (Perusse et al., 2005).

5.2.2. Association Analysis

Genetic association studies are better suited than linkage for the localization of genes involved in complex traits because they are based on linkage disequilibrium (LD), which provides historic recombination events over many generations and hence higher resolution (Morton, 2003). Genetic association is usually limited to candidate genes or candidate regions and generally uses information from unrelated individuals (either cohort or case-control association studies), although there are genetic association approaches based on related individuals (Spielman and Ewens, 1996). These approaches are based on establishing a significantly increased or decreased occurrence of a marker allele in correlation with a disease trait (Zak et al., 2001). A statistically significant association between the marker locus and the trait is usually considered to imply close physical linkage with the disease locus, although associations can also be spurious due to a number of reasons including population stratification, sample size, allele frequencies, linkage disequilibrium, etc. (Zondervan and Cardon, 2004). Replication of findings in independent samples is therefore important in order to provide further validation of association results (Cardon and Bell, 2001).

The most widely used genetic markers for association mapping at present are SNPs (analysed both as single markers or as SNP haplotypes). However, any type of genetic marker can be used in an association study. There is extensive literature on the advantages and disadvantages of each type of marker, which need to be taken into account in the design of each association study. For example, we and others have shown that the multiallelism of microsatellites and their high density across genomes may be suitable to tag haplotypes for association studies and/or to identify different allele lineages, thus resulting in an increase of power in association mapping of candidate genes (Burgner et al., 2003; Stefansson et al., 2003; Newton et al., 2004; Rodríguez et al., 2004; Day et al., 2004a; Tanaka et al., 2005; Rodríguez et al., 2006a; Rodríguez et al., 2006b).

Hundreds of associations between genetic variants and metabolic syndrome risk traits have been published in the literature. Some of them are listed in the Genetic Association Database http://geneticassociationdb.nih.gov/, which includes published scientific papers of human genetic association studies of complex diseases and disorders (Becker et al., 2004).

5.2.3. Genome-Wide Scans

Genome-wide scans apply both to linkage and association studies. Their principle is performing whole genome screens using a large number of markers representative of the entire genome, and then conducting appropriate linkage (or association) analyses.

Usually, the number of chromosomal regions found to be significantly linked to a complex trait in genome-wide linkage scans is low (from 0 to 4 in most instances), and the length of the chromosomal region, large. However, at least 19 genome-wide linkage scans were performed in 2004 for obesity risk phenotypes (Perusse et al., 2005).

There is a great interest at present in optimising the design for genome-wide association scans, based on the hope that they will provide more power and more resolution than genome-wide linkage studies for the identification of complex disease genetic factors (Hirschhorn and Daly, 2005). Recent evidence seems to confirm these expectations (Evans and Cardon, 2006). There are however many theoretical and practical variables, including models of the allelic architecture of common diseases, sample size, map density, sample-collection biases and multiple testing, that need to be taken into account in order to design optimal genome-wide association studies (Wang et al., 2005).

5.2.4. Meta-analysis

Meta-analyses are study designs based on combining the results of other published studies. The aim of meta-analyses is integrating findings and producing a conclusion that is supported by an increased statistical power (Munafo and Flint, 2004). Like in other approaches, the design of meta-analyses is crucial for the finding of reliable conclusions. One of the main drawbacks of meta-analyses is publication bias (published articles may not be representative of all analyses performed due to the tendency to publish positive results). Other biases are produced by differences among studies in variables such as sample sizes, ethnic origin of population samples, etc. Despite all these limitations, there are examples of meta-analyses that have provided additional evidence on the influence of genetic factors on metabolic syndrome risk traits (Sookoian et al., 2005b).

5.2.5. From Candidate Variants to Causal Variants

A genetic variant significantly linked (or associated) to a metabolic syndrome risk trait may not be *per se* causal, but in linkage disequilibrium with the actual causal variant. In addition to functional analyses, other approaches have been developed in order to provide further evidence of causality.

One of these is a multiple pairwise method to identify causal sites and their support intervals through high resolution mapping by maps in LD units (LDU) under the composite likelihood framework (Maniatis et al., 2004). This method has been recently refined for association mapping of quantitative traits, and applied to the estimation of the location and the 95% confidence and support intervals of causal variants influencing weight in the human *H19-IGF2-INS-TH* chromosomal region (Zhang et al., 2006).

Other approaches based on a different philosophy exist, including the so-called method of Mendelian randomisation. This method is based on testing the association of a genetic variant with both an intermediate phenotype, and a trait known to be influenced by such intermediate phenotype. The Mendelian randomisation approach has the potential of supporting or excluding evidence for causality because the association between a trait and a polymorphism that mimics the biological link between the intermediary phenotype and the trait is not generally susceptible to reverse causation or confounding (Davey-Smith and Ebrahim, 2003). The application of this approach has provided recent evidence suggesting that there is no causal association between variation in the C-reactive protein gene and metabolic syndrome phenotypes (Timpson et al., 2005).

5.2.6. Multilocus Approaches and Network Analyses

New statistical methods that capture the simultaneous effects of multiple genes are becoming available. These include neural networks, sums of single-marker statistics, combinatorial partitioning method, multifactor-dimensionality reduction method, bump hunting, logical analysis of data, mining association rules, special approaches for microarray data, etc. (Hoh and Ott, 2003).

Similarly, approaches enabling analysis of gene networks are being developed. A method for the reconstruction of a functional human gene network has been recently developed and applied for prioritizing positional candidate genes (Franke et al., 2006).

Both multilocus approaches and statistical network analyses represent complementary alternatives to single gene analyses and have the potential of providing a more global view of gene action and interaction than analyses based on single genes.

5.3. Mixed Methods (Combining Molecular Biology and Statistical Genetics)

It has been suggested that integration of recent advances in microarray expression profiling, marker-based fingerprinting of each individual in a segregating population, and available statistical tools for gene mapping (the so-called genetical genomics approach) would represent a more powerful approach for the genetic dissection of complex disease traits than either approach alone (Jansen and Nap, 2001). The increasing number of published articles based on analysis of gene expression microarrays (more than 5,000 in 2005), the development of sophisticated mathematical methods for the analysis of such information and the development of software packages facilitating integrative analyses (Reich et al., 2006), is paving the way for new advances in genetical genomics.

Such approaches have already been applied to the metabolic syndrome. For example, an approach integrating genome-wide expression profiling and linkage analysis recently applied to the analysis of the regulation of gene expression in fat and kidney tissue in a panel of rat recombinant inbred strains (used as a model system for the metabolic syndrome) has identified a set of 73 candidate genes for hypertension (Hubner et al., 2005).

6. Genetic Variants in Endocrine Pathways Influencing Metabolic Syndrome

Application of the above genetic approaches has led to the identification of a large number of candidate genes and variants influencing the metabolic syndrome. In this section we present strong evidence demonstrating that interindividual variation in hormones and related pathways accounts for a differential predisposition to develop this cluster of metabolic abnormalities. We have focused our attention on the central components of the metabolic syndrome, i.e., obesity and insulin resistance, with some additional discussion on the other features of the syndrome.

Variants in other genes encoding proteins that are not endocrine factors have been found to have a significant influence on the metabolic syndrome. However, these genes are not within the scope of the present chapter. On the other hand, our intention is not to present here a detailed review of the genetic evidence available for each of the endocrine pathways listed. Detailed specific reviews exist for most of the endocrine factors mentioned here (some of which are cited in this book chapter). In addition, a number of databases providing exhaustive and specific genetic and endocrine information are freely available online. Table 3 lists some useful websites that provide more detailed information on genes encoding factors involved in endocrine pathways that have been identified to date as significant contributors to metabolic syndrome risk traits.

In the following sections, we have grouped genes according to the endocrine pathway in which they are involved, and endocrine pathways according to the main endocrine gland involved in their control. Brain, pancreas, adipose tissue and adrenal glands are arguably the key elements involved in the endocrine control of the metabolic syndrome, with genes expressed in other glands also influencing features of the syndrome.

Table 3. List of various websites with detailed information relevant to the genetic endocrinology of the metabolic syndrome.

Genetic Epidemiology	**Online Encyclopedia for Genetic Epidemiology studies** - information and links about and for genetic research studies relevant to population genetics and health: http://www.oege.org/
Literature	**Entrez-PubMed** - journal search: http://www.ncbi.nlm.nih.gov/entrez/query.fcgi?db=PubMed **OMIM** - Online Mendelian Inheritance in Man: http://www.ncbi.nlm.nih.gov/entrez/query.fcgi?db=OMIM **Google** - general web search: http://www.google.co.uk/ **Google Scholar** – web search for scholar literature: http://scholar.google.com/ **Medical Subject Headings (MeSH)**: http://www.nlm.nih.gov/mesh/meshhome.html **Scirus** - for scientific information - web and journal search (full text): http://www.scirus.com/srsapp/
Pathways	**BioCarta** - pathways: http://www.biocarta.com/ **Biochemical pathways at Humboldt State University**: http://www.humboldt.edu/~rap1/BiochSupp/PathwayDiagrams/PathIndex.html **EndoNet** - http://endonet.bioinf.med.uni-goettingen.de/ **SNPs3D database** - http://www.snps3d.org/
Genome	**Ensembl Genome Browser**: http://www.ensembl.org/ **H-Invitational Database** - search database of genes with structure, function etc.: http://www.jbirc.aist.go.jp/hinv/top.html **UCSC Genome Bioinformatics Site** - http://genome.ucsc.edu/
Genes	**NCBI Entrez Gene** - http://www.ncbi.nlm.nih.gov/entrez/query.fcgi?db=gene **Genew Searchgenes** - search for gene names: http://www.gene.ucl.ac.uk/cgi-bin/nomenclature/searchgenes.pl **PubGene** - literature and sequence relationships between genes: http://www.pubgene.org/ **OMIM** - Online Mendelian Inheritance in Man: http://www.ncbi.nlm.nih.gov/entrez/query.fcgi?db=OMIM **LocusLink** - access multiple NCBI resources for a gene: http://www.ncbi.nlm.nih.gov/LocusLink/ **iHOP** - http://www.ihop-net.org/UniPub/iHOP/ **GeneCards** - http://www.genecards.org/index.shtml
SNPs	**DbSNP** - http://www.ncbi.nlm.nih.gov/projects/SNP/ **Ensembl Human SNPView** - http://www.ensembl.org/Homo_sapiens/snpview **GeneSNPs** at The National Institute of Environmental Health Sciences, University of Utah: http://www.genome.utah.edu/genesnps/ **HGMD** the Human Gene Mutation Database at Cardiff - with associations: http://archive.uwcm.ac.uk/uwcm/mg/hgmd0.html **HGVBase** annotated database of human genetic variation: http://hgvbase.cgb.ki.se/cgi-bin/main.pl?page=index_new1.htm **SNPper** - search for SNPs, by frequency, validation, submitter etc with spacing: http://snpper.chip.org/ **The SNP Consortium Ltd**.: http://snp.cshl.org/ **HapMap** - Haplotype map of the human genome: http://www.hapmap.org/ **UW-FHCRC** - Fred Hutchinson Cancer Research Center, University of Washington: http://pga.gs.washington.edu/finished_genes.html **CGAP-GAI** - CGAP Genetic Annotation Initiative at the National Cancer Institute: http://gai.nci.nih.gov/ **FESD** - Functional Element SNPs Database: http://combio.kribb.re.kr/FESD/
Associations	**Genetic Association Database**: http://geneticassociationdb.nih.gov/cgi-bin/index.cgi

6.1. Central Nervous System Pathways

It is well known that the brain harbours neuronal systems sensing and regulating energy intake, energy expenditure and endogenous glucose production (Schwartz and Porte, Jr., 2005). The brain receives information about the metabolic status of the individual both by hormonal and neuronal signals, and influences metabolism by adjusting behaviour, the endocrine system and the autonomic nervous system. Key central nervous system (CNS) elements directly involved in the regulation of metabolic syndrome risk traits include the hypothalamic arcuate nucleus (which produces bioactive peptides of the melanocortin/agouti system), the pituitary (involved in the synthesis of elements of the GH-IGF axis) and the pineal gland (with a direct control of the circadian phenomenon).

6.1.1. Melanocortin/Agouti System

Two different types of neurons contained in the hypothalamic arcuate nucleus exert potent effects on metabolism: the NPY/AgRP neurons, and the POMC/CART neurons (van Dijk et al., 2003;Schwartz and Porte, Jr., 2005;Broberger, 2005). NPY/AgRP neurons coexpress two anabolic peptides, neuropeptide Y (NPY) and agouti-related peptide (AgRP), both increasing food intake and decreasing energy expenditure. POMC/CART neurons coexpress CART (cocaine and amphetamine-regulated transcript) and the neuropeptide precursor pro-opiomelanocortin (POMC) which is processed to several bioactive peptides. All CART and POMC-derived peptides have a catabolic role with opposite effects to NPY and AgRP, i.e., inhibition of food intake and stimulation of energy expenditure. Activation of the NPY/AgRP neurons therefore promote weight gain, whereas activation of the POMC/CART neurons promote weight reduction.

POMC (Pro-opiomelanocortin)

POMC encodes a large precursor protein which undergoes posttranslational processing to give rise to several bioactive peptides. Two enzymes are involved in such processing: prohormone convertase 1 (PC1) and PC2. PC1 is expressed in the corticotroph of the anterior pituitary and leads to the production of N-terminal peptide, joining peptide, ACTH and β-lipotropin. In contrast, the action of PC2, which is expressed in neurons originating from the hypothalamic arcuate nucleus, results in three different types of melanocortin peptides α-, β- and γ-melanocyte-stimulating hormones (MSH). ACTH and α-MSH are known to control adrenal steroidogenesis and skin pigmentation, respectively. However, recent work has established that melanocortin peptides play a central role in the control of energy homeostasis. In particular, both α- and γ-MSH, have been shown to exert potent anorexigenic effects when administered intracerebroventricularly (Fan et al., 1997). Melanocortin effects are mediated by five melanocortin receptors (MC1R to MC5R), central effects being mainly mediated by MC3R and MC4R (both highly expressed in the CNS).

Knock-out mice for either *POMC*, *MC3R* or *MC4R* show an obese phenotype (Broberger 2005). This applies also to mutations disrupting the human homologues, which indicates a highly conserved role of these genes in the control of energy homeostasis and adrenal function (Coll et al., 2004). At least five congenital human cases lacking *POMC* gene products have been described (Krude et al., 2003). They include a compound heterozygote for two nonsense mutations in exon 3, a homozygote for a mutation in the 5'-UTR introducing an additional out-of-frame start site for translation initiation, and other nonsense and frameshift mutations. On the other hand, more than 50 heterozygous mutations in *MC4R* have been reported in obese humans [for details, see table 1 of (Perussc et al., 2005)], these mutations representing the commonest known monogenic cause of obesity (Coll et al., 2004). In some studies, nearly 5% of patients with a BMI > 40 Kg/m^2 have been reported to be heterozygous for mutations in *MC4R*. However, not all individuals with *MC4R* mutations in the general population are obese, suggesting other interacting components influencing the expression of such mutations (Leibel et al., 2001).

Linkage results suggest also that genetic variation in key elements of the POMC pathway influence metabolic syndrome risk traits. At least two independent studies have linked the *POMC* gene with plasma leptin levels (Comuzzie et al., 1997;Hager et al., 1998). On the other hand, the Quebec family study (Chagnon et al., 2000) has reported significant linkage between *MC5R* and a variety of metabolic syndrome traits (including BMI, fat mass, percentage of body fat and resting metabolic rate) and between *MC4R* and respiratory quotient. Finally, several studies have tested for association between genetic variants of the POMC pathway and metabolic syndrome traits (Delplanque et al., 2000;Suviolahti et al., 2003).

CART (Cocaine and Amphetamine-Regulated Transcript)

CART has also been linked to plasma leptin levels (LOD~3) (Hager et al., 1998). Infusion of CART peptide inhibits feeding in the dark phase of the circadian cycle, during fasting and during NPY-induced feeding (Leibel et al., 2001). Like POMC, CART is also anorexigenic and is regulated by the metabolic state within the arcuate nucleus (Kristensen et al., 1998).

NPY (Neuropeptide Y)

NPY has known functions on stimulation of appetite, inhibition of thermogenesis and lipolysis and as one of the most potent vasoconstrictor peptides. These roles place it among the candidate genes in humans for blood-pressure homeostasis, hypertension and obesity related phenotypes (Pesonen, 2006). Up to five genes encode NPY receptors, among which NPY1R, NPY2R and NPY5R probably mediate the effects of NPY on food intake, psychomotor activity and vasoactivity (Leibel et al., 2001). Lean mice homozygous for the *Npy* gene knockout exhibit a normal weight phenotype. In contrast, knocking out *Npy* ameliorates the obesity syndrome of *ob/ob* mice (obese mice caused by leptin deficiency, see section 6.4.1), which suggests NPY as a mediator of leptin actions. Disruption of NPY Y1 and Y5 receptor genes in mice results in mild late-onset obesity (Perusse et al., 2005).

Both *NPY* and a neighbouring microsatellite (D7S1808) have been linked to several obesity phenotypes in linkage studies based on Mexican American (Bray et al., 1999) and Quebec families (Chagnon et al., 2000). In addition, a number of studies have reported associations between *NPY* gene variants and metabolic syndrome traits including waist-to-hip ratio (Bray et al., 2000), hyperlipidaemia (Karvonen et al., 1998), higher birth weight (Karvonen et al., 2000), alcohol dependence (Lappalainen et al., 2002), enhanced rate of atherosclerosis (Niskanen et al., 2000;Karvonen et al., 2001), etc. The most studied *NPY* variant to date has been L7P, a common nonsynonymous coding polymorphism located in the signal sequence part of *NPY* (Pesonen, 2006). This is as T to C variant which changes amino acid seven of the prepro NPY from leucine to proline. This amino acid change causes a significant change in the tertiary structure of the signal peptide, and has been suggested to cause altered synthesis, processing and release of the active, mature NPY (Pesonen, 2006).

The frequency of allele P7 varies from 6% to 15% in Caucasian populations, but is extremely low or absent in African-Americans, Mexican-Americans and oriental populations. This suggests that the effects of the L7P substitution on metabolic syndrome traits may only be relevant in populations of European descent (Pesonen, 2006).

Another possible functional sequence variant within *NPY* has been described (GenBank AC004485:154841C>T). This variant putatively destroys the SP1 consensus motif of the *NPY* promoter. *In vitro* studies have shown that this alteration changes the transcriptional activity of the gene by more than five-fold, although the implications of this variant on metabolic syndrome risk traits have not been described to date.

Variants at NPY receptors have also been associated with metabolic syndrome traits including decreased TG and increased HDL, obesity, etc.) (Pesonen, 2006).

Brain-derived Neurotrophic Factor (BDNF)

BDNF has been implicated in the regulation of food intake and body weight in rodents (Lyons et al., 1999; Kernie et al., 2000; Rios et al., 2001). In diabetic transgenic mice (obese, non-insulin-dependent diabetic C57BLKS-Lepr(*db*)/lepr(*db*) (*db*/*db*) mice), BDNF administration normalised fasting blood glucose and decreased body weight. This was perhaps performed by BDNF action on liver because hepatomegaly, liver glycogen and liver enzyme activity in serum were also reduced in these animals (Tonra et al., 1999).

Genetic variants of *BDNF* have recently been studied in relation to different phenotypes including eating disorders. Met66 allele of Val66Met in BDNF has been associated with anorexia nervosa restrictive type in Spanish people (Ribases et al., 2003) and C allele of –270C>T with all eating disorder subtypes in people from five European countries (Ribases et al., 2004).

Involvement of BDNF, nerve growth factor (NGF) and mast cells in coronary atherosclerosis and metabolic syndrome with significant decrease in plasma level of NGF and BDNF in metabolic syndrome have been reported (Chaldakov et al., 2001;Chaldakov et al., 2004). Reduction of BDNF serum level in the metabolic syndrome has also been reported in other investigations (Geroldi et al., 2006;Hristova and Aloe, 2006).

Considering that *BDNF* associations have recently been discovered, one might expect to see more findings in the future.

AgRP (Agouti-Related Peptide)

The agouti locus in mice encodes the agouti signalling protein (ASP). ASP inhibits the activation of melanocortin receptors mediated by melanocortin peptides. Expression in the hair follicle inhibits MC1R and affects hair pigmentation, while ectopic expression in the hypothalamus blocks the action of melanocortin peptides on MC4R and produces pleiotropic effects including a dominantly inherited form of late onset obesity, type 2 diabetes and increased somatic growth (Klebig et al., 1995;Wilson et al., 1999). Homology searches of the agouti sequence in brain cDNA libraries and sequence databases identified an agouti-related gene (AgRP) normally expressed in the hypothalamus of mice and humans. Overexpression of AGRP in transgenic mice causes hyperphagia and obesity. It has been determined that AGRP acts as an antagonist of MC4R (Ollmann et al., 1997).

6.1.2. GH-IGF axis

The GH-IGF axis includes the hypothalamic-pituitary axis (responsible for synthesis and secretion of growth hormone, GH), GH receptors (mediating the production of insulin-like growth factors, IGF), IGF binding proteins (IGFBP, involved in transport of IGF), and IGF receptors (controlling IGF action) (Menon, 2006). It is well established that the GH-IGF axis is involved in the control of several physiologic processes including somatic growth and metabolic processes. In recent years, our group has published evidence mutually consistent with an increasing body of literature showing that genetic variants in the GH-IGF axis are strong candidates for metabolic syndrome risk traits.

GH (Growth hormone)

GH is a hormone of major importance both for linear growth in childhood, and for metabolism in adulthood. GH impacts directly on protein, glucose and lipid metabolism. Simplistically, GH is a diabetogenic hormone which antagonises the effects of insulin on lipid and glucose metabolism. GH treatment thus induces a number of metabolic syndrome conditions including insulin resistance, hyperinsulinemia, increased lipolysis and lipid oxidation into ketone bodies (Norrelund, 2005).

A number of mutations (in pituitary-specific transcription factors and in other genes of the GH-IGF axis) leading to deficiency in GH secretion and action have been identified (Lopez-Bermejo et al., 2000;Lee and Menon, 2005).

In 2004, we described for the first time, the relationship between genetic variation in the *GH* gene cluster and its interaction with the fetal origins of adult disease (FOAD) hypothesis. We found associations between common diversity in the *GH* gene cluster (as defined by allele categories of a highly polymorphic microsatellite, *CSH1.01*) and both low one year weight and features of the metabolic syndrome in later life in men (Day et al., 2004a). Categorising the microsatellite into D2 and T allele groups on the basis of lineage, we demonstrated that the T category of alleles associated with significantly lower weight at one year (implying lower early growth), higher systolic and diastolic blood pressure, higher fasting triglycerides, higher fasting and 30 minute insulin and higher 30 minute glucose levels (Day et al., 2004a). These results are the endogenous equivalent of published findings on the effect of exogeneous growth hormone on adiposity and other ageing traits in later life (Rudman et al., 1990), and support a significant and important role for the growth hormone gene cluster in the relationship between early growth and cardiovascular disease risk.

IGF (Insulin-like growth factors)

Two major forms of IGF have been described, IGF-I and IGF-II. IGF-I can mimic some, but not all of the metabolic actions of GH (Mauras and Haymond, 2005). Indeed, hepatic IGF-I synthesis is mainly regulated by GH (Heald et al., 2006). IGFs produce rapid metabolic changes and play a key role both in pre-adolescent growth and as autocrine regulators of cell proliferation, with long-term growth promoting effects (O'Dell and Day, 1998). In the context of the metabolic syndrome, IGF deficiency appears to increase the risk of conditions such as obesity, diabetes and heart disease (Heald et al., 2006). In particular, increasing evidence indicates that IGF-I protects against the metabolic syndrome, endothelial dysfunction, atherosclerotic plaque development, clinical instability and ischaemic myocardial damage (Conti et al., 2004).

Both IGF-I and IGF-II circulate in plasma bound to a family of six binding proteins (IGFBP-1 through 6), and interact with three distinct cell receptors (type 1 IGF receptor, type 2 IGF receptor and insulin receptor) (O'Dell and Day, 1998). IGFBPs are key modulators of the effects of IGFs, and can either inhibit or promote IGF actions (Clemmons, 1997;Heald et al., 2006). There are a number of genetic variants described across both IGF genes, the six IGFBPs and the IGF receptors, with several reports of significant associations with metabolic syndrome traits. Among those, *IGF2* is by far, the gene better examined and understood genetically in relation to phenotype (Heald et al., 2006).

IGF2

Since the first reports showing evidence of association between low weight in adult men and *IGF2* SNPs (O'Dell et al., 1997;Gaunt et al., 2001), our group has conducted a number of genetic studies of the *IGF2* gene and its surrounding genomic region (which includes the closely linked genes insulin, *INS*, and tyrosine hydroxylase, *TH*) in relation to metabolic syndrome risk traits.

In 2004, we published the first broad analysis of the haplotypes of the *IGF2-INS-TH* region and their effects on cardiovascular risk traits (Rodríguez et al., 2004). Characterisation of patterns of interallelic LD between the *TH01* microsatellite and *IGF2* haplotypes constituted by 11 SNPs permitted us the identification of genetic factors that modify the risk for CV disease. Their effects were independent of other covariates including smoking. One extended tagging haplotype (*IGF2-INS-TH**5) protected against obesity, whereas two others (*IGF2-INS-TH**4 and *IGF2-INS-TH**6) conferred increased risk for cardiovascular disease.

Based on the analysis of various large epidemiological surveys, we have also shown evidence suggesting that the *IGF2-INS-TH**5 haplotype may have a pleiotropic effect on different metabolic syndrome risk traits including BMI, fat mass, visceral obesity, plasma insulin levels, plasma glucose levels and age of first regular smoking in current adult smokers, by influencing both independent chain of events and interrelated intermediary phenotypes (Rodríguez et al., 2004;Rodríguez et al., 2006a;Rodríguez et al., 2006b). The main effect of this haplotype seems to be on obesity risk traits. The significant weight-lowering association of *5 that we found (-2.5kg) represents a ~10% decrease in the rate of coronary events (Rodríguez et al., 2004). This effect is relevant given that this is a common haplotype observed in more than 25% of individuals from two independent samples representative of the general UK population (Northwick Park Heart Study II, NPHSII and Hertfordshire Cohort Study, HCS). In a follow-up study, we have provided stronger evidence of the protective effect of *5 against obesity by replicating the significant association in an independent cohort (Rodríguez et al., 2006a). The results obtained suggest that the weight effect conferred by this haplotype occurs mainly via reduction of visceral obesity.

Using a refined association mapping approach to identify causal variants we have demonstrated for the first time in humans that at least one causal variant for weight locates within a narrowed interval of the *IGF2* gene (Zhang et al., 2006)(Figure 2).

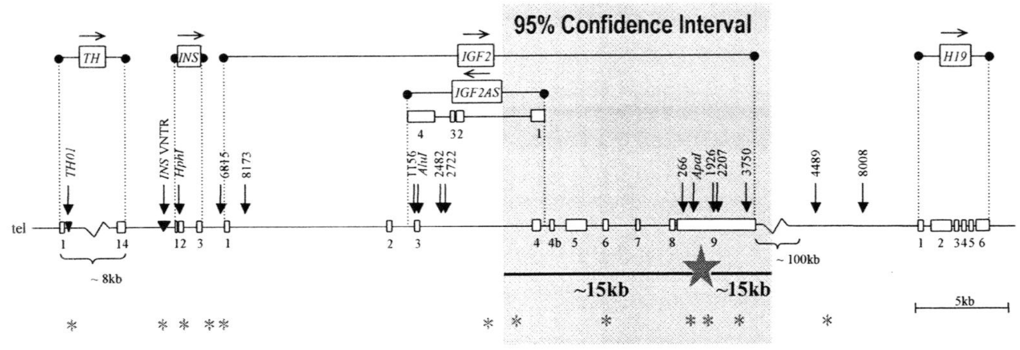

Figure 2. Genetic map of the *H19-IGF2-INS-TH* region on human chromosome 11p15. Exons of *H19*, *IGF2*, *IGF2AS*, *INS* and *TH* are numbered and represented by boxes, and the transcription direction, by arrows. Also shown are the DNA markers analysed in our group (Gaunt et al., 2001;Rodríguez et al., 2004; Zhang et al., 2006). The star marks the estimated location of a candidate causal site for low weight in men (Zhang et al., 2006). Asterisks indicate the location of published potential functional sites with effects on gene expression.

IGF15

There is also strong evidence for the role of IGF-I in the metabolic syndrome. Deletion of the *IGF1* gene in the liver of adult mice resulted in reduced circulating IGF-I levels which caused insulin resistance (due to secondary elevation of circulating GH levels), pancreatic islet enlargement, and hyperinsulinemia, whereas, in a different mouse model, inhibition of IGF-I and insulin receptor function in skeletal muscle also resulted in severe insulin resistance (Yakar et al., 2005). IGF-I deficiency can be caused by a number of established and hypothetical genetic defects, including primary defects of IGF-I synthesis, IGF-I transport/clearance and in the type I IGF receptor (Lopez-Bermejo et al., 2000). Common genetic polymorphisms in the *IGF1* gene have been associated with metabolic syndrome risk traits such as small birth size, post-natal growth and future diabetes risk, but with inconsistent results (Dunger et al., 2004).

6.1.3. Metabolic Syndrome and Circadian Phenomenon

The phenomenon of diurnal rhythmicity or circadian pattern of many physiological events e.g. sleep/wake cycle, has already been described in the literature. Plasma cholesterol (high and low density lipoprotein), triglycerides and coagulation factors (fibrinogen and platelets) (Bremner et al., 2000), and also blood pressure (Millar-Craig et al., 1978) show circadian variations. In addition, the incidence of cardiovascular diseases such as myocardial infarction, sudden cardiac death, stroke, unstable angina and high blood pressure seem to happen at higher frequency at specific times of the day (Bremner et al., 2000). This phenomenon is governed by a system of clocks composed of a main central master oscillator (clock), the master clock, which is located within the suprachiasmatic nucleus (SCN) of the anterior hypothalamus, orchestrating daily cycles of these rhythms and peripheral clocks (Reppert and Weaver, 2002). Understanding the molecular clock would help us develop our knowledge of behavioural and metabolic changes, and manipulation of the clock would enable us to find new treatments for various disorders such as psychiatric sleep disorders or perhaps metabolic and cardiovascular traits.

The molecular aspects of the circadian oscillator as a transcriptional-translational feedback loop have been studied in *Drosophila* and mammals. A group of genes are involved in this pathway in mammals: *Clock (Circadian locomotor output cycles kaput)*, *Bmal1*, *Period* (*Per1*, *Per2* and *Per3*), *Casein Kinase 1ε* (*CK1ε*), *Timeless* (*Tim*) and *Cryptochrome* (*Cry1* and *Cry2*). *Bmal1* and *Clock* genes are positive, while *Period* and *Timeless* are negative components of the loop. *Clock* and *Bmal1* encode proteins which dimerise through the HLH (helix loop helix) and PAS (PER-ARNT-SIM) domains, and then bind to DNA regulatory sequences (E-boxes) and activate transcription of *Per* and *Cry*. These genes are widely expressed in central and peripheral tissues: CNS, eye, cerebellum, hippocampus, olfactory bulbs, heart, lung, liver, kidney, testis and ovary (King and Takahashi, 2000; Young and Kay, 2001).

Physiologically, nutrient, especially glucose, metabolism, is not only under influence of insulin and other processors in the liver and muscles, but is also regulated by other components of counterregulatory hormones such as glucocorticoid, growth hormone and glucagon which are secreted from adrenal, hypophysis, and pancreas. Plasma glucose and insulin also have daily rhythms (Bolli et al., 1984; Van, 1990), which are entrained by the SCN (La Fleur et al., 1999; La Fleur et al., 2001).

Further evidence comes from *in vitro* experiments showing the regulatory effect of clock genes on circadian rhythmicity in central and peripheral tissues, especially those involved in nutrient homeostasis, e.g. liver, muscle and pancreas (Lavery and Schibler, 1993; Balsalobre et al., 1998; Yagita et al., 2001; Yoo et al., 2004).

(Oishi et al., 2005) studied glucocorticoid as a circadian time cue for mammalian peripheral clocks using DNA microarrays in mice. They tried to identify the influence of glucocorticoid on circadian expression of genes. Of 169 genes with daily fluctuations in the liver of the sham-operated mice, 100 lost circadian rhythmicity in adrenalectomized (ADX) mice. These included genes with metabolic functions such as glucokinase, HMG-CoA reductase and glucose-6-phosphatase.

A recent report (Turek et al., 2005) showed that homozygous *Clock* mutant mice fed a regular diet gained body weight similar in magnitude to wild-type mice on a high-fat diet. These homozygous *Clock* mutant mice suffered from attenuated diurnal feeding rhythm, hyperphagia, obesity, and developed a metabolic syndrome composed of hyperleptinemia, hyperlipidemia, hyperglycemia, hepatic steatosis, and hypoinsulinemia. This report also demonstrated down-regulation of genes involved in appetite and energy balance in mediobasal hypothalamus (MBH): *orexin*, *ghrelin*, and *Per2*.

These data evidence the role of the *Clock* gene, and perhaps other components of this system, in a broad spectrum of mammalian energy balance and metabolism.

6.2. Adrenocortical Pathways

Hormones produced in the adrenal glands are actively involved in the primary control of a variety of cardiac, vascular, pulmonary and metabolic functions. While the inner region (adrenal medulla) produces catecholamines, the outer region (adrenal cortex) produces mainly glucocorticoids and mineralocorticoids, acting also as a secondary site for the synthesis of sex hormones.

6.2.1. Catecholamines

Catecholamines (dopamine, noradrenaline and adrenaline), are adrenomedullary hormones which also act as central and sympathetic neurotransmitters (Nagatsu, 1995). Catecholamines have a direct effect on cardiovascular functions such as systemic blood pressure, myocardial contractility and cardiac output by actions on the central and peripheral nervous systems, vascular smooth muscle, the heart and the kidney (Jose et al., 1999; Contreras et al., 2002). Indeed, many of the available dopamine agonists and antagonists, have a range of indirect cardiovascular effects (Ziegler et al., 1985; Schindler et al., 2002; Volkow et al., 2003). Cathecolamines also influence a number of other functions relevant to the metabolic syndrome including lipid metabolism and weight (Groop, 2000; Camp et al., 2002). Key genetic elements involved in such actions are the enzyme tyrosine hydroxylase (TH), which catalyses the rate-limiting step in the biosynthesis of catecholamines (Nagatsu, 1995), dopaminergic receptors and adrenergic receptors, both mediating catecholamine actions in several tissues including lung, fat tissue, kidney, the adrenals and pancreatic β-cells (Groop, 2000; Pijl and Romijn, 2006).

TH (Tyrosine Hydroxylase)

There is a growing body of literature relating *TH* gene variants with traits influencing risk of metabolic syndrome such as blood pressure (Sharma et al., 1998; Jindra et al., 2000; Rodríguez et al., 2004 ;Zhang et al., 2004), insulin resistance (Chiba et al., 2000), left ventricular structure (Linhart et al., 2002), haemodynamic response to stress (Barbeau et al., 2003), obesity-related traits (Rodríguez et al., 2004), plasma triglycerides (Rodríguez et al., 2004), smoking (Olsson et al., 2004;Anney et al., 2004; Rodríguez et al., 2006b) and alcoholism (Dahmen et al., 2005). Most of the genetic analyses conducted to date have focussed on the study of a single tetranucleotide-repeat microsatellite (*TH01*) located in the first intron of the *TH* gene. It has been suggested that this microsatellite has a role in the transcription of *TH*, transcription appearing to be inhibited in proportion to the number of repeats from 3 to 8 and with a counteracted effect for alleles above eight repeats (Albanese et al., 2001). This raises the possibility of functional effects in relation to metabolic syndrome traits, but no conclusive evidence has been published to date.

DR (Dopaminergic receptors)

Dopamine is involved in the control of food intake, energy expenditure, glucose and lipid metabolism, blood pressure and insulin release (Pijl and Romijn, 2006). Dopaminergic transmission is mediated through at least two receptor families, known as D1-like (D1 and D5) and D2-like (D2, D3 and D5) (Neve et al., 2004). Recent findings from physiological and pharmacological studies in animal models, non-diabetic obese individuals and obese humans with type 2 diabetes suggest that reduction in DRD2 signal transduction contribute to various components of the metabolic syndrome (Pijl and Romijn, 2006).

AR (Adrenergic receptors)

There are nine AR subtypes originating from different genes, *α1A, α1B, α1D, α2A, α2B, α2C, β1, β2* and *β3*. β-AR antagonists (known as β-blockers) have a direct effect on metabolic syndrome traits [they effectively reduce hypertension, but have potential adverse effects on carbohydrate and lipid metabolism, including insulin resistance, glucose intolerance and dyslipidemia (Jacob and Henriksen, 2004)], which suggest a possible role of genetic variation in these genes in relation to metabolic syndrome risk. Indeed, a number of nonsynonymous polymorphisms, both in β- and in α-ARs, have been shown to have functional effects *in vitro* and pathophysiological effects in human studies in relation to metabolic syndrome traits, mostly related to hypertension and other cardiovascular phenotypes (Small et al., 2003; Zaugg and Schaub, 2005).

6.2.2. Corticoids

Both glucocorticoids and mineralocorticoids are steroid hormones synthetized from cholesterol. Glucocorticoids (GC) are stress hormones involved in metabolic, inflammatory, cardiovascular and behavioural processes, cortisol being the principal active GC in humans. The main mineralocorticoid hormone is aldosterone, which is involved in the control of blood pressure and homeostasis. Recent evidence suggests an important role of GC action in the aetiology of the metabolic syndrome, with genetic variation in the GC pathway influencing many features of the metabolic syndrome, especially obesity and insulin resistance (Wang, 2005). Similarly, the renin-angiotensin-aldosterone system is a major regulator of cardiovascular function, and has been causally implicated in obesity-associated hypertension (Engeli et al., 2005).

GC pathway

Studies in animal models and clinical evidence from humans have demonstrated the association of abnormal GC metabolism and the metabolic syndrome. Genetic epidemiologic studies from a cohort of individuals of the general population (Fraser et al., 1999) and from an elderly cohort of metabolic syndrome patients (Andrew et al., 2002) have shown that increased levels of cortisol are positively correlated with increased systolic blood pressure, fasting glucose and insulin and obesity. Two isozymes of 11β-hydroxysteroid dehydrogenase (11β-HSD1 and 11β-HSD2) are responsible for the conversion of cortisol into cortisone (the inert GC). Association studies in humans have shown a relationship between polymorphisms in the *11β-HSD1* gene (*CYP11B1*) and adiposity (Wang, 2005).

Renin-angiotensin-aldosterone (RAS) system

The influence of the RAS system on adipose-tissue physiology:

Substances with cardiovascular and metabolic characteristics are found in adipocytes, and angiotensinogen receptor 1 (*AGTR1*) is a mediator of the secretion of some of these, such as prostacyclin, leptin, plasminogen activator inhibitor I (PAI-1), and nitric oxide (NO). It has also been shown that adipose tissue is a source of metabolically active elements of the RAS such as angiotensinogen (*AGT*), angiotensin converting enzyme (*ACE*) and angiotensin II (*AGT II*) (Cassis et al., 1988;Engeli et al., 1999).

AGT and AGT II have lipogenic characteristics (Darimont et al., 1994;Jones et al., 1997). Through stimulation of prostacyclin (PGI2) release and formation, AGT II triggers the final differentiation of pre-adipocytes to adipocytes, mediated by *AGTR2* (Darimont et al., 1994). The complete set of RAS elements occurs in adipose tissue: (Mallow et al., 2000) reported that *AGTR1* could be detected throughout the whole adipocyte differentiation period, while expression of *AGTR2* is inversely correlated to adipocyte differentiation period.

AGT formation is increased in situations reflecting obesity-associated insulin resistance; e.g. *AGT* expression is increased by free fatty acids (Safonova et al., 1997), while insulin has a negative effect on its expression and secretion. This down-regulation effect of insulin on *AGT* is inhibited by TNF-alpha (Aubert et al., 1998), and decreases by fasting and increases after re-feeding in epididymal fat pads of *Sprague-Dawley rats*, which is in a tissue specific manner because AGT serum concentration and liver expression are unaffected (Frederich, Jr. et al., 1992). Besides, the binding of AGT II to receptors on adipocyte plasma membrane and pre-synaptic nerve endings and blood vessels may further reflect its effect on adipose-tissue metabolism directly or through perfusion or local sympathetic nervous system (SNS) (Crandall et al., 1997).

In human, normotensive individuals, *AGT* and *AGTR1* mRNA levels are higher in visceral adipose tissue compared with subcutaneous adipose tissue, while *ACE* and *AGTR2* mRNA levels were not significantly different in these tissues (Giacchetti et al., 2002).

However, there is not a consensus over the pattern of RAS gene expression in adipose tissue, as (Davis et al., 2002) reported lower *AGT* mRNA in subcutaneous adipose tissue of hypertensives compared with normotensive individuals, and (Faloia et al., 2002) reported no difference in *AGT* mRNA in adipose tissue of obese, hypertensives and controls, and interestingly, *AGTR1* was found more expressed in subcutaneous adipose tissue from obese patients with hypertension than in those without hypertension and controls. In female abdominal subcutaneous adipose tissue, *AGT* is down-regulated in obesity, renin and *AGTR1* are up-regulated exclusively in obese hypertensives and *ACE* is up-regulated in obesity with highest expression levels in obese hypertensive women (Gorzelniak et al., 2002). These differences might be due to gender differences or different adipose tissues or methods of biopsy (needle or surgery) or perhaps clinical background (drug treatment or concomitant disease).

If different elements of the RAS are expressed in adipose tissue, it would then be sensible to hypothesise the plausible effect of their genetic variants on aspects of adipose tissue. (Li et al., 2006) showed the involvement of a promoter haplotype of *AGT* in its higher expression in adipocyte and liver. Prat-Larquemin L et al. (2004) (Prat-Larquemin et al., 2004) reported that well replicated *AGT* M235T is associated with adipocyte size but not AGT secretion in adipose tissue.

We have recently reported the association of CC genotype of A1166C in the 3' UTR of *AGTR1*, which is associated with lower mRNA abundance (unpublished data), with a wide range of metabolic traits, including lower BMI, WHR and waist circumference in men and stayed significant in combined analysis (Abdollahi et al., 2005). D (DD & ID) allele of an insertion/deletion polymorphism in *ACE* is associated with the metabolic syndrome (based on WHO definition) in Chinese (Lee and Tsai, 2002) and Caucasian (Stephens et al., 2005) patients with type 2 diabetes, while it was the I allele which had previously been reported in Hong Kong Chinese (Thomas et al., 2001); however, these associations were not replicated in Brazilians (Costa et al., 2002).

In spite of conflicting results about RAS regulation in obesity, it seems that there is an activation of local adipose-tissue RAS which may result in higher *AGT II* formation and increased susceptibility of adipocytes to *AGTR1* mediated effects.

Gender effect on RAS function

It might seem apparent, from our knowledge of physiology and epidemiology of various disorders, to expect that gender matters in different ways and influences many if not all aspects of our body. This effect exists at molecular e.g. imprinting and X- inactivation or sex influenced gene expression (Stahlberg et al., 2004) (female specific secretion of GH and hepatic fuel metabolism); and cellular levels e.g. sex-specific receptors and signaling, production of hormones, and metabolism.

The rate of cardiovascular mortality in men is much higher than in pre-menopausal women of the same age group, and generally, the prevalence of atherosclerotic disease in men differs largely from that of women. It seems that estrogen is responsible for this protective effect, though the mechanism has not been completely understood. This protective effect might be more beneficial in the context of primary rather than secondary prevention (Hulley et al., 1998), i.e. pre-menopausal physiological conditions compared with post-menopausal hormone replacement therapy.

RAS is not an exception to this complexity and sex difference, especially after epidemiological observations showing different associations in males and females. There is a large body of evidence in the literature that various associations of *ACE* I/D such as hypertension, diastolic blood pressure, over-weight and abdominal obesity may be male-specific (Schunkert et al., 1996; O'Donnell et al., 1998; Strazzullo et al., 2003). In mice also, the blood pressure effect of *ACE* I/D predominates in males, although the mechanism remains obscure (Krege et al., 1995). In transgenic mice, human *AGT* expression has been detected in white and brown adipose tissue (WAT & BAT), which is higher in males (Yang et al., 1994), and is decreased by castration and restored by testosterone in *Sprague Dawley* rats (Serazin-Leroy et al., 2000).

The point that the expression of the first element of RAS, *AGT*, is under a sex hormone influence suggests that it is possible that distal elements and the whole pathway might behave in a sexually influenced manner.

The presence of an estrogen response element in the promoter of *AGT* explains the higher circulating level in women compared to men (Clauser et al., 1989; Feldmer et al., 1991). Estrogen replacement therapy in post-menopausal women increases AGT concentration in the circulation (Schunkert et al., 1997).

Estrogen up-regulates *AGT* and down-regulates renin, *ACE* and *AGTR1*, but its net effect is suppression of the pathway. This effect might be modulated by mode of administration or experimental context, for example, trans-dermal estrogen has different levels of effect compared to oral consumption because the former would not go through the portal vein; however, the latter might still suppress renin and ACE though lacks AGT stimulation (Schunkert et al., 1997). Besides, pharmacological doses such as contraceptives might behave differently from physiologic conditions.

Testosterone increases plasma renin activity (Ellison et al., 1989), and up-regulates *AGT* in male rats (Ellison et al., 1989; Chen et al., 1992).

AGTR1 is up-regulated in vascular smooth muscle cells in hypercholesterolemia and estrogen deficit conditions, which might augment the effect of menopause on the cardiovascular system (Nickenig et al., 1997; Nickenig et al., 1998; Strehlow et al., 2000; Nickenig et al., 2000).

The effect of *AGT II* in CNS might be influenced by gender, as pressor and dipsogenic effects were observed in male dogs (Doursout et al., 1990). Similarly, in human the half life of pressor effect of *AGT I* after its discontinuation is longer in men than women (Gandhi et al., 1998).

To address this issue comprehensively, one needs to bear in mind the complex relationship between different elements of physiological cascades e.g. counter-regulatory hormones in this case, especially that the net effect of the interactions of various components of these multi-factorial systems is hard and perhaps impossible to predict and measure with today's technology. Moreover, the epistatic effect of nearby genes might be another explanation for some observations e.g. *ACE* and *GH* proximity, which suggests a possible alternative explanation of *ACE* I/D effects.

6.3. Pancreatic Pathways

Islet cells in the pancreas produce two types of hormones, insulin and glucagon. Both are directly implicated in the control of the cellular use of glucose and in the control of glucose levels in blood. Insulin and glucagon have opposite effects on glucose metabolism, the first acting as an anabolic hormone and the latter with catabolic functions.

6.3.1. Insulin Signalling Pathway

The insulin signalling pathway is central in many features of the metabolic syndrome, with special relevance to insulin resistance. Strong evidence relates several elements of this pathway with this syndrome both at the physiological and genetic levels. Key elements are the insulin gene encoding the pre-pro-insulin polypeptide, insulin receptors (IR) and insulin receptor substrates (IRS).

INS (Insulin)

INS is a key hormone which regulates metabolism and plays a principal role in the maintenance of normoglycemia and normolipidemia levels (Pirola et al., 2004). At the cellular level, INS actions encompass control of carbohydrate, lipid and amino acid metabolism and mRNA transcription and translation (Wilcox, 2005). Deregulation of INS actions ultimately leads to hyperglycemia, insulin resistance and type 2 diabetes (Pirola et al., 2004).

There is strong genetic evidence (whole genome linkage scans, functional studies) suggesting that a susceptibility locus for type 1 diabetes risk (*IDDM2*) maps to the *INS* gene. The risk conferred by *IDDM2* has been attributed to, although never formally proven to be determined by, a minisatellite (*VNTR*) upstream of *INS* in the proximal promoter region (Bennett and Todd, 1996;Barratt et al., 2004). We have recently shown that the *INS* RFLP "-23*HphI*" (commonly used as a convenient genotyping tag in perfect linkage disequilibrium with the *VNTR*, but previously considered to be without functional importance) is an important *INS* variant affecting pre-mRNA splicing, and secondarily exerting major effect on translation efficiency (Kralovicova et al., 2006). It is possible that splicing and translation, instead of or as well as promoter function, represent the important functional aspect of *IDDM2* disease associated haplotypes.

A number of associations studies between variants in the *INS* gene and metabolic syndrome traits have been published (Genetic Association Database, http://geneticassociationdb.nih.gov/cgi-bin/index.cgi), but there is no conclusive evidence identifying *INS* causal variants and their possible functional role on intermediary phenotypes.

INSR (INS receptors)

Genetic variation in *INSR* accounts for monogenic forms of insulin resistance. Specifically, a number of mutations in *INSR* have been shown to cause several syndromes (including leprechaunism or Donahue syndrome, Rabson–Mendenhall syndrome and type A insulin resistance) characterised by profound insulin-resistant diabetes (Hegele, 2003). Besides these rare genetically determined cases, a number of associations have been found relating *INSR* variants with metabolic syndrome risk traits (Genetic Association Database, http://geneticassociationdb.nih.gov/cgi-bin/index.cgi).

IRS (insulin receptor substrates).

The *IRS* gene family has been implicated in the pathogenesis of insulin resistance (White, 1998). Analysis of the *IRS1* gene has shown one polymorphism (Gly972Arg) to be more prevalent in type 2 diabetes, to predispose obese individuals to glucose intolerance and to associate with both altered insulin action and secretion (Almind et al., 1993;Sigal et al., 1996;Porzio et al., 1999). Similarly, a common variant (Gly1057Asp) of the *IRS2* gene also seems to influence metabolic syndrome risk traits, with opposite effects according to the obesity state of the individuals [protective effect in lean subjects, and increased risk for obese individuals (Mammarella et al., 2000)]. A haplotypic association analysis has shown that IRS2 haplotypes influence severe obesity and glucose intolerance (Lautier et al., 2003).

6.4. Adipose Tissue Pathways

The adipose tissue has been traditionally considered as a passive reservoir for energy storage. However, since the discovery of leptin in 1994, evidence has demonstrated that the white adipose tissue has a very important role as endocrine organ both responding to CNS and endocrine signals, and secreting a growing number of peptides in response to a variety of stimuli. Bioactive peptides secreted by the adipose tissue are known as adipokines and include key elements involved in glucose and fat metabolism including leptin, adiponectin, resistin, tumour necrosis factor-α and interleukin-6 (Guerre-Millo, 2002;Jazet et al., 2003;Kershaw and Flier, 2004).

6.4.1. Leptin Pathway

Leptin is secreted by the adipose tissue into plasma in direct proportion to adipose tissue mass and to nutritional status, and has a crucial role on energy homeostasis through effects mediated both via hypothalamic pathways and via direct action on peripheral tissues including muscle and pancreas (Kershaw and Flier, 2004). Genetic variation in the gene encoding leptin and in the genes encoding leptin receptors has a significant impact on genetic predisposition to the metabolic syndrome.

LEP (Leptin)

The leptin gene (*LEP*) was first discovered in 1994 by positional cloning in obese mice carrying the recessive mutation *ob* (*ob*/*ob* mice) and in humans (Zhang et al., 1994). This study also showed that the *ob* mutation caused disruption of *LEP* leading to absence of this hormone and an extreme obesity phenotype. Since then, a large body of evidence has demonstrated that leptin potently inhibits food intake and stimulates energy expenditure, and that defects in leptin production cause severe hereditary obesity in rodents and humans.

Linkage studies and meta-analyses have provided strong evidence linking *LEP* with obesity phenotypes (Duggirala et al., 1996;Reed et al., 1996;Allison and Heo, 1998). In addition, a number of mutations and allelic variants of the human leptin gene have been proven to cause obesity (OMIM*164160 http://www.ncbi.nlm.nih.gov/entrez/dispomim.cgi?id=164160)

LEPR (Leptin Receptor)

Evidence from mice showed that, like the *ob/ob* strain, mice carrying a different recessive mutation (diabetes, *db*) present an extreme obesity phenotype. Studies of *db/db* mice, led to the identification of the leptin receptor and to establish that the recessive mutation *db* results in disruption of the LEPR leading to a reduction of leptins effect (Tartaglia et al., 1995;Chen et al., 1996;Lee et al., 1996). Recent analyses have shown that the *LEPR* gene generates six different isoforms via alternative splicing, from which the Ob-Rb isoform (the long isoform) is present at high levels in the hypothalamus, where it plays a vital role in regulating obesity (Harvey and Ashford, 2003).

6.4.2. Adiponectin Pathway

Adiponectin is the most abundant gene product in adipose tissue and accounts for 0.01% of total plasma protein (Gil-Campos et al., 2004). This hormone participates in the regulation of energy balance and insulin action, with additional anti-inflammatory and anti-atherogenic properties (Jazet et al., 2003). Indeed, both plasma adiponectin levels and adiponectin gene transcription are decreased in obese and diabetic humans and rodents (Jazet et al., 2003).

There is strong evidence (replicated associations in different ethnic groups) suggesting a direct influence of genetic variation in the adiponectin gene on metabolic syndrome risk traits, including body weight, glucose metabolism, insulin sensitivity, and the risk of type 2 diabetes and coronary artery disease (Yang and Chuang, 2006). These associations involve several common polymorphisms spanning the adiponectin gene, many of which have been shown to associate with differential adiponectin expression, at the levels of both mRNA expression and plasma protein levels (Yang and Chuang, 2006).

6.4.3. Resistin

Initial findings related the increased serum levels of a newly discovered protein in obese mice with insulin resistance, and suggested that this protein (called resistin) potentially links obesity to diabetes (Steppan et al., 2001). Current studies seem to confirm the role of this hormone on glucose homeostasis in rodent systems, but the possible involvement of resistin in the regulation of glucose homeostasis in humans has not been confirmed (McTernan et al., 2006). In fact, there are important differences between rodents and humans with regard to resistin structure and expression. Overall, human resistin is only 53% identical with its murine counterpart (Banerjee and Lazar, 2003). In addition, while resistin is predominantly expressed in the adipose tissue in mice, the higher levels of expression in humans are localised to bone marrow and mononuclear cells (Koerner et al., 2005). Results from genetic studies are controversial, some of them suggesting associations with metabolic syndrome risk traits, and others reporting no association (Banerjee and Lazar, 2003; Koerner et al., 2005). However, there is evidence suggesting a functional role for a SNP located within a DNA element of the promoter region of resistin that binds the Sp1 and Sp3 transcription factors.

Epidemiological and functional evidence has shown that GG genotype at this SNP increases promoter activity of the resistin gene via Sp1 and Sp3, leading to enhanced serum resistin levels, thereby inducing human T2DM (Osawa et al., 2004). A number of other studies have found associations between this SNP and metabolic syndrome risk traits in different populations (Koerner et al., 2005).

6.4.4. Cytokines (TNF, interleukin 6)

Cytokines are non-antibody proteins that act as intercellular mediators. They generally act locally in a paracrine or autocrine manner. Interleukin 6 (IL-6) and Tumor Necrosis Factor-alpha (TNF-α) are the two key cytokines associated with metabolic syndrome. They are produced by a variety of tissues and cells, including adipose tissue. Both IL-6 and TNF-α have been implicated in the development of obesity and insulin resistance.

6.4.4.1. Interleukin 6

High circulating levels of IL-6 have been demonstrated in subjects with features of metabolic syndrome and it has been suggested that Interleukin 6 plays a pathogenetic role in the two main features of this disease complex: insulin resistance and obesity (Pickup et al., 1997).

IL6 Pathways

Recent data shows that IL-6 may influence body weight by participating in the control of feeding behaviour (Plata-Salaman, 1998). IL-6 may be involved in signalling the amount of fat mass and its variation to the brain (Cancello et al., 2004). Up to one third of the circulating IL-6 originates from adipose tissue and IL-6 production increases with increased adiposity (Mohamed-Ali et al., 1997; Tsigos et al., 1999; Berthier et al., 2003). This could provide a negative feedback mechanism by which energy homeostasis is maintained, as increasing IL-6 levels in the brain lead to a decrease in food intake and enhance energy expenditure (Cancello et al., 2004). However, this theory assumes that peripherally produced IL-6 can act as a hormone, affecting organs remote from its site of production such as the brain. There is some evidence to support this (Papanicolaou and Vgontzas, 2000), but further studies are necessary.

Besides an indirect role in adipogenesis by modulating feeding behaviour, IL-6 may play a more immediate role in cellular lipid metabolism via induction of Signal Transducer and Activator of Transcription STAT3. IL-6 acts via the IL6 receptor complex, containing at least one subunit of the signal transducing protein gp130 (Bihl et al., 2002; McLoughlin et al., 2004). Signal transduction via the gp130 receptor subunit results in activation of the Janus kinase/STAT3 pathway (Huber et al., 1999;Chen et al., 2006). Data exists that shows increased STAT3 expression in cultured human cells early in adipocyte formation. It has therefore been suggested that STAT3 plays a role in human adipogenesis and lipid metabolism (Harp et al., 2001; Deng et al., 2006).

IL-6 also plays a role in the development of insulin resistance. In human hepatocytes Insulin receptor signal transduction is impaired by IL-6. It has also been shown that IL-6 may promote insulin resistance in fat cells via induction of suppressor of cytokine signalling (SOCS)-3 (Senn et al., 2002; Fasshauer et al., 2004).

The existence of these pathways indicates a likely role for IL-6 in the development of obesity and insulin resistance. Inter-individual genetic variations, which can affect the levels of *IL6* gene expression, will therefore influence the susceptibility of an individual to develop metabolic syndrome.

IL6 Gene

The gene for IL-6 was first mapped to chromosome 7 in 1986 (Sehgal et al., 1986). Subsequent studies further localised the gene to position 7p21 (Bowcock et al., 1988;Ferguson-Smith et al., 1988). Multiple single nucleotide polymorphisms (SNP) have been described in this gene, but interest has focused on a promoter polymorphism, that is thought to influence gene expression (SNP -174).

The *IL6* promoter SNP (-174) genotype has been shown to be associated with increased insulin resistance. In Spanish subjects the G-allele was associated with lower insulin resistance than the C-allele (Fernandez-Real et al., 2000). A study on French Canadian men showed the C allele to be associated with higher insulin or glucose levels following insulin load (Berthier et al., 2003). However some of the evidence is conflicting as the G-allele for SNP -174 appears to be more common in Spanish Caucasians and Pima Indians with Type II diabetes (Vozarova et al., 2003). A study on Italian subjects also found the G-allele to be associated with reduced insulin sensitivity (Cardellini et al., 2005).

The causal role of IL-6 in the development of obesity is supported by a study on French-Canadian men showing that the G/G genotype for the -174 promoter polymorphism was associated with a lower waist circumference (Berthier et al., 2003). In support of this an association of the C-allele with obesity was also found in other studies (Wernstedt et al., 2004; Klipstein-Grobusch et al., 2006). However these findings are put into question by other studies, that found associations between markers of obesity and the G-allele of the promoter variant (Roth et al., 2004;Dedoussis et al., 2004).

In part these discrepant observations may be due to interethnic variation, as the allelic frequency varies widely between different populations (Cardellini et al., 2005). In addition some of the studies were carried out on a relatively small sample size. It is also possible that *IL6* promoter haplotypes play a more important role than individual polymorphisms. This is supported by a study comparing the population based inter99study cohort (n=4,568) of middle aged people and a group of type II diabetic patients (n=1,389). This larger study demonstrated that *IL6* promoter haplotypes (-174,-597,-592) were associated with several features of the metabolic syndrome (Hamid et al., 2005).

6.4.4.2. Tumor Necrosis Factor-alpha (TNF-α)

TNF-α is a pro-inflammatory cytokine that is synthesised in a variety of tissues, including adipose tissue. It has been implicated in the main features of metabolic syndrome: obesity and insulin resistance.

Pathways

TNF-α production is elevated in the obese state and it is likely that this increased production arises from the adipose tissue itself (Hotamisligil et al., 1993; Winkler et al., 1998; Coppack, 2001; Moon et al., 2004). TNF-α is thought to have an anti-adipogenic effect (Hube and Hauner, 1999). It has been suggested that TNF-α production is induced by increasing obesity and acts in a negative feed-back mechanism to halt its progression (Spiegelman and Hotamisligil, 1993). The anti-adipogenic effects of TNF-α range from actions within the adipose tissue itself to remote effects on appetite (Coppack, 2001). Actions within the adipose tissue itself include stimulating apoptosis and lipolysis as well as inhibiting differentiation of adipocytes (Coppack, 2001).

A further route by which TNF-α may indirectly influence lipid metabolism is through modulating the expression of other adipokines such as Interleukin 6 and leptin (Fernandez-Real et al., 1997b).

There is a significant body of evidence to suggest that TNF-α is a major mediator in the insulin resistance of obesity, both from experiments in knock-out mice and human studies (Hotamisligil et al., 1995; Saghizadeh et al., 1996; Uysal et al., 1997; Hotamisligil, 2003). It has been suggested that TNF-alpha can disrupt the insulin signalling pathway in pancreatic-β cells, hepatocytes and adipocytes (Greenberg and McDaniel, 2002). In cultured cells TNF-α induces insulin resistance through increased serine phosphorylation of insulin receptor subrate 1 (IRS-1) and converts IRS-1 in to an inhibitor of insulin receptor tyrosine kinase activity *in vitro* (Hotamisligil et al., 1996). A further mechanism by which TNF-α may influence systemic insulin action is by modulating systemic levels of free fatty acids (Uysal et al., 1997) and by down-regulating the expression of insulin sensitive glucose transporter Glut4 (Stephens and Pekala, 1991;Hotamisligil et al., 1993). In addition TNF-α may indirectly affect insulin resistance by modulating the expression of adiponectin, an insulin-sensitising hormone.

Gene

The *TNF-α* gene is located on the short arm of chromosome 6 (Gene map locus 6p21.3). A SNP in the promoter region of the gene G-308A has been described (Wilson et al., 1992) which may cause an increase in the transcriptional activity of the gene (Wilson et al., 1997).

It has been shown that the promoter polymorphism G-308A is associated with features of the metabolic syndrome supporting the view that *TNF-α* is causally involved in the development of this disease complex.

The SNP -308 promoter allele-A was shown to convey an increased risk of developing insulin resistance in obese subjects (Dalziel et al., 2002) and a study in adolescents found the A-allele to be associated with an elevated HOMA index (measure of insulin resistance) (Sookoian et al., 2005a). A study on Finnish subjects demonstrated that the A-allele of the *TNF-α* -308 SNP carried an increased risk of converting from impaired glucose tolerance to type II diabetes (Kubaszek et al., 2003). However not all studies were able to demonstrate an association between SNP-308 and insulin resistance (Fernandez-Real et al., 1997a;Romeo et al., 2001).

There is evidence from several studies of an association between the promoter polymorphism G-308A and obesity (Fernandez-Real et al., 1997b; Herrmann et al., 1998; Hoffstedt et al., 2000; Pihlajamaki et al., 2003). A study in Korean women found no association between the SNP and BMI, but did find an association with waist-hip ratio (Um et al., 2004). There is a growing body of evidence to support an association of the G-308A SNP with indices such as BMI/WHR and thus indicate a causal role of *TNF-α* in the development of obesity. However further studies are needed to clarify this association as some studies found no association between markers of obesity and -308 genotype (Walston et al., 1999; Romeo et al., 2001).

IL 6, TNF-α, metabolic syndrome and atherosclerosis

Atherosclerosis is the most common cause of death in the western world. All features of the metabolic syndrome constitute risk factors for arteriosclerosis. It is likely that the rising prevalence of metabolic syndrome in westernised countries will bring an associated increase in cardiovascular morbidity. The evidence suggests that *IL6* and *TNF-α* represent two of the candidate genes that may be important in the development of metabolic syndrome. In addition both genes play a role in the pathogenesis of cardiovascular disease itself.

Atherosclerosis is thought to represent a chronic inflammatory process with characteristic associated increases in levels of circulating pro-inflammatory cytokines (IL-6, IL-1β, TNFα) (Huber et al., 1999). The earliest manifestation of the atherosclerotic lesion is the 'fatty streak' (Glass and Witztum, 2001). Fatty streaks are characterized by the presence of macrophages and T-cells in the intima. Cell adhesion molecules are implicated in leukocyte recruitment into the fatty streak and have been shown to be upregulated in lesion prone sites in the arterial tree (Nakashima et al., 1998). These include VCAM-1, ICAM-1 and e-selectin (Cybulsky and Gimbrone, Jr., 1991;Dong et al., 1998). Both Interleukin 6 and TNF-α can induce expression of these adhesion molecules in endothelial cells (Romano et al., 1997; Modur et al., 1997; Huber et al., 1999). VCAM-1, ICAM-1 and e-selectin interact with specific ligands on circulating Leukocytes to facilitate their adhesion to the vessel wall (Huber et al., 1999). After binding to the endothelium, leukocytes migrate into the subendothelial space. This migration is driven by chemoattractants such as oxLDL, Lp(α), MCP-1, IL-1 and TNF-α (Fan and Watanabe, 2003). Within the intima, monocytes differentiate into macrophages. This process is partially controlled by IL-6 and ultimately leads to the formation of lipid laden cells called foam cells. Foam cells are one of the characteristic components of the atherosclerotic plaque. The transition of macrophages into foam cells through lipid uptake is mediated by TNF-α, IL-1β and IFNγ. These cytokines activate monocyte-macrophages to increase their mobility, phagocytosis and enzyme levels (Huber et al., 1999). The large number of T-cells seen in the arterial plaque may be the result of cell migration but could in part be caused by clonal expansion. IL-6 is a potent lymphocyte growth factor and could lead to clonal expansion of pathogenic T-cells in atherosclerotic lesions (Huber et al., 1999).

The more advanced arteriosclerotic lesion contains macrophages, T-cells, smooth muscle cells (SMC), extracellular lipid and matrix deposits (Stary et al., 1995). The cellular components of the advanced plaque contribute to the ongoing inflammatory process that drives plaque progression by expressing a variety of mediators involved in intercellular signalling. These mediators are for example involved in the proliferation of smooth muscle cells, a characteristic histological feature of a mature arteriosclerotic lesion. Interleukin 6 and its soluble receptor have been shown to be released from human macrophages. The ensuing IL6/sIL6 receptor complex stimulates upregulation of gp130 in cultured human SMC and ultimately drives these cells into a proliferative state (Klouche et al., 2000).

IL-6 and TNF-α have effects which are closely interconnected. In addition to this they are each able to influence one others expression. Transcriptional activity of *IL6* is increased in response to TNF-α, whereas IL-6 down regulates *TNF-α* (Huber et al., 1999;Terry et al., 2000). Both TNF-α and IL-6 have an effect on the expression of other mediators of atherosclerosis. IL-6 and TNF-alpha induce, among others, MCP-1, a powerful chemoattractant involved in leukocyte adhesion and migration.

In addition to the autocrine and paracrine effects of IL-6 within the arterial lesion itself, IL-6 also induces hepatic acute phase response proteins such as fibrinogen. Increased levels of fibrinogen lead to a more pro-thrombotic state which favours plaque formation (Ernst and Resch, 1993).

It has been shown that circulating levels of TNF-α and IL-6 are elevated in patients with metabolic syndrome. These cytokines are likely to represent part of the causal chain that links metabolic syndrome and atherosclerosis.

Though some controversy remains, it seems plausible that Interleukin 6 and TNF-α play a causal role in the development of metabolic syndrome. IL6 and TNF-α genotypes/haplotypes appear to be associated with predisposition to this disease, complex and possible pathways by which this may occur have been demonstrated. The conflicting evidence (see above) will in part be related to the multifactorial nature of disease. It underscores the need to delineate a panel of endocrine genetic setpoints which act as a combined contributor to the risk of the metabolic syndrome. In addition these cytokines also play a role in atherosclerosis, one of the main sequelae of metabolic syndrome. Predisposing factors leading to variation in cytokine gene expression will therefore influence both primary disease development as well as secondary complications.

Gene expression is regulated at four levels. The first and most important is the primary control of transcription. Subsequent levels of regulation are alternative splicing, RNA editing and post translational changes of the protein substrate. RNA expression assays with regards to promoter genotype/haplotype are the most likely approach to shed light on the role of IL-6 and TNF-alpha in metabolic syndrome. Variations within the promoter of the gene exert their control at the level of transcription. Therefore RNA expression studies looking at the primary transcript (unspliced RNA) will allow the greatest insight into the most important regulatory mechanisms of gene expression.

6.4.5. Other Adipokines

There are a number of other adipocyte-derived proteins with endocrine functions related to metabolic control. These include lipoprotein lipase, hormone sensitive lipase, adipsin, acylation-stimulating protein, plasminogen activator inhibitor-1, apolipoprotein E, hydroxysteroid dehydrogenases, visfatin, vaspin, etc. There is molecular and genetic evidence suggesting the involvement of these adipokines in metabolic syndrome risk. For the sake of brevity, we are not presenting here this evidence, some of which has been reviewed previously (Groop, 2000; Jazet et al., 2003; Kershaw and Flier, 2004; Jackson and Ahima, 2006).

6.4.5. PPARs as Key Regulators of the Adipocyte Endocrine Function

Peroxisome Proliferator-Activated Receptors (PPARs) are not hormones, but transcription factors belonging to the nuclear receptor superfamily. We briefly mention here molecular and genetic evidence showing that PPARs are key elements regulating adipogenesis and adipose tissue endocrine pathways, and hence, primary elements in metabolism control.

There are three forms of PPAR (α, β and γ), each one encoded by a different gene. All PPARs heterodimerize with retinoic X receptor to induce transcription of a number of genes expressed in the adipose tissue including those that code for lipoprotein lipase, fatty acid transporter protein, adipocyte fatty acid binding protein, fatty acyl-synthase, malic enzyme, glucokinase and the glucose transporter *GLUT4* (Groop, 2000;Hauner, 2002). PPARs are activated mainly by free fatty acids, and this activation is a critical step in adipogenesis (Leibel et al., 2001). Chronic exposure to high levels of dietary fatty acids might thus promote the development of obesity, insulin resistance and metabolic dysfunction (Gurnell, 2005).

A number of mutations disrupting PPARs function have been described in association with the metabolic syndrome and related clinical phenotypes (Gurnell, 2005). A large number of association studies have implicated variants in PPARs with obesity phenotypes (Perusse et al., 2005). One of the most widely studied polymorphisms has been a Pro12Ala variant in PPARγ. It has been suggested that this polymorphism is associated with overall adiposity, apparently in interaction with adiponectin (Tanko et al., 2005). It is known that thiazolidinediones (a new class of oral antidiabetic drugs that improve metabolic control in patients with type 2 diabetes through the improvement of insulin sensitivity), exert their antidiabetic effects through a mechanism that involves activation of PPARγ (Hauner, 2002).

6.5. Other Endocrine Pathways

In addition to the pathways already discussed, there are a number of other endocrine factors and hormones secreted by organs different than those described in previous sections, also involved in the regulation of metabolism. Some of the most important ones identified to date include ghrelin (produced in the stomach) and PYY (produced in the gut).

6.5.1. Ghrelin

Ghrelin is as an appetite-stimulating hormone, involved also in the regulation of body weight, that acts as an endogenous ligand for the growth hormone secretagogue receptor (Cummings and Schwartz, 2003). Ghrelin circulating in the bloodstream is originally secreted from the stomach under the control of feeding, plasma ghrelin concentration being increased during fasting conditions and decreased after food intake (Kojima et al., 2004).

Several studies have suggested a relationship between obesity and variants in the ghrelin gene, including a polymorphism that changes the C-terminal processing site of ghrelin, resulting in posttranslational variation of the protein (Kojima et al., 2004).

6.5.2. PYY

The gut hormone fragment peptide YY (PYY) has opposite effects to ghrelin. PYY is known to reduce appetite and food intake both in humans and in rodents (Batterham and Bloom, 2003). PYY is released into the circulation following a meal, and acts as an important feedback signal from the gut to the hypothalamus (Broberger, 2005). Genetic studies conducted in order to test the association between obesity and variants both in the gene encoding PYY and in genes encoding receptors that mediate PYY effects, have reported some evidence of association that need to be replicated in further studies (Hung et al., 2004).

7. Gender Differences in Genetic Factors Influencing Metabolic Syndrome Risk

Individual abnormalities comprising the metabolic syndrome, and the metabolic syndrome as a whole, have a different frequency between sexes. The metabolic syndrome is more prevalent in men, who generally have higher rates of impaired fasting glucose, hypertriglyceridemia and hypertension. In contrast, women usually have comparatively higher rates of impaired glucose tolerance, cardiovascular risk associated with inflammation and lower HDL cholesterol (McCarthy et al., 2003; Regitz-Zagrosek et al., 2006). Indeed, current definitions for the metabolic syndrome take into account gender as a variable influencing metabolic syndrome risk, and define men-specific and women-specific thresholds for some risk traits (Table 1).

In addition to this, there is evidence in the literature suggesting that there may be differences between men and women in the genetic factors that influence variation in metabolic syndrome risk. In section 6.2.2, we have presented detailed evidence illustrating the effect of gender on a particular endocrine pathway (the RAS system). Gender differences in genetic factors influencing metabolic syndrome risk seem to be a common scenario. As previously illustrated in section 4, there are gender differences in heretability within given metabolic syndrome risk traits. For example, a comparative study of results from twin studies in eight countries (representing approximately 37,000 complete twin pairs) revealed both sex differences in heritability and evidence of sex-specific effects for BMI, suggesting that there may be differences between men and women in the genetic factors that influence variation of this trait (Schousboe et al., 2003). In this respect, we have replicated an association between weight and the *IGF2-INS-TH**5 haplotype in men in two independent UK cohorts, but no significant association was found in women (Rodríguez et al., 2004;Rodríguez et al., 2006a). Indeed, most metabolic effects that our group has seen in the growth hormone and growth factor pathways are sex-specific (Rodríguez et al., 2004;Day et al., 2004a;Rodríguez et al., 2006a). Similar observations have been published by other groups in relation to other genes, including *LRPAP1, THBS1, ACAT2, ITGB3, F2, SELP* and *PRCP* genes (McCarthy et al., 2003), and in relation to endocrine pathways like the hypothalamic-pituitary-adrenal axis (Vicennati et al., 2006).

Differences in sex chromosomes constitute the main genetic difference between men and women. It has been suggested a factor that could contribute to the sexual dimorphism of a metabolic syndrome risk trait (blood pressure) is the presence of one or more genes influencing this trait on the Y chromosome (Charchar et al., 2003). Some positive findings have suggested association between a polymorphism on the Y chromosome and blood pressure in humans (Ellis et al., 2000; Charchar et al., 2002)., although other studies could not replicate such findings (Kang et al., 2003; Garcia et al., 2003; Rodríguez et al., 2005;Russo et al., 2006).

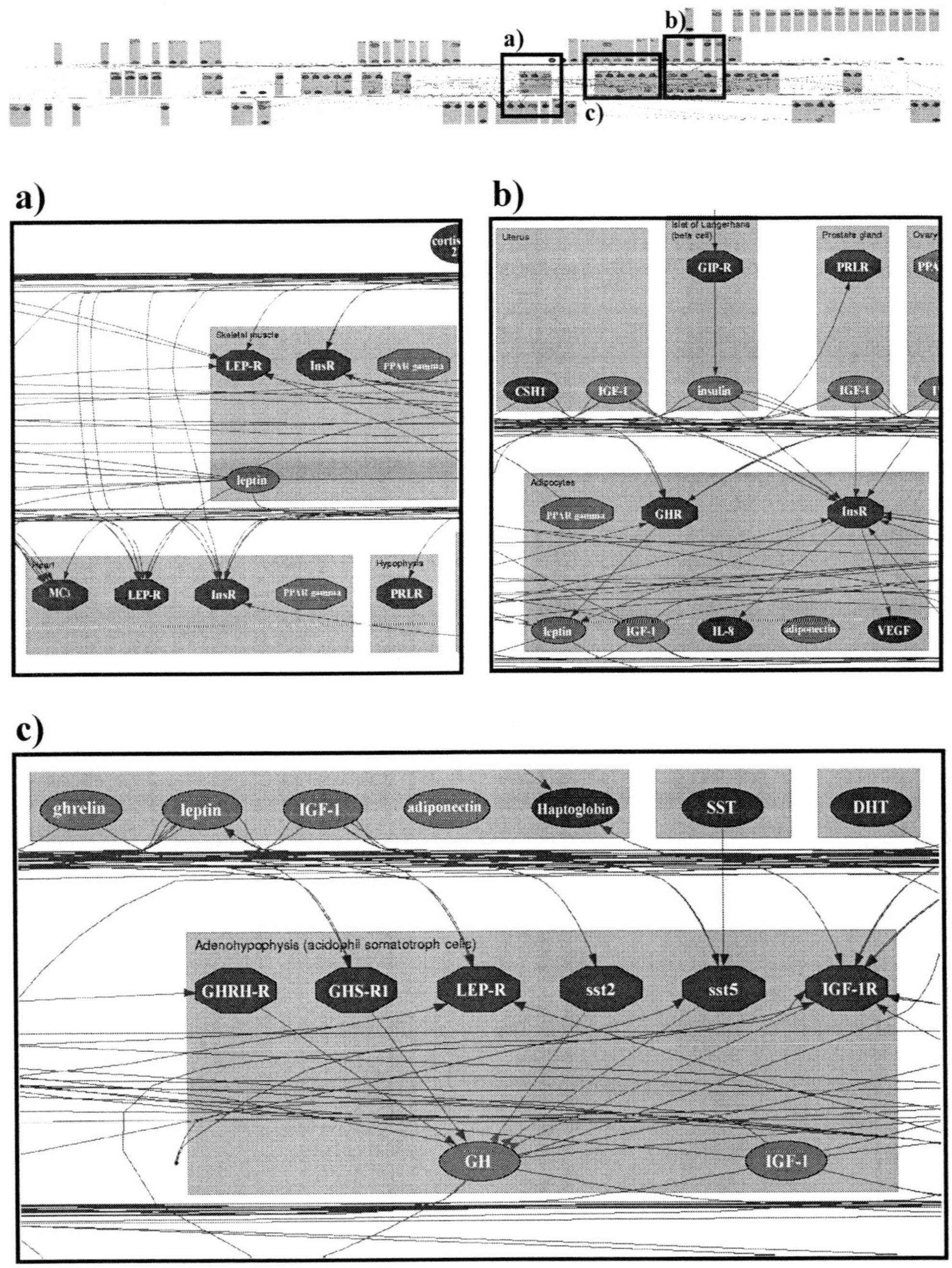

Figure 3. Complex network of interactions at the cellular level between endocrine factors involved in the metabolic syndrome. Boxes a), b) and c) show zoomed details of the overall network of relations generated in the database EndoNet (http://endonet.bioinf.med.uni-goettingen.de/) in March 2006.

8. Interaction among Elements Influencing Metabolic Syndrome Risk

In the previous sections of this chapter, we have shown a simplistic overview of several of the most important endocrine factors known to influence the metabolic syndrome. From this brief overview, it is evident that both the pathophysiology and the genetic basis of this syndrome are very complex, even when considering each of the factors involved as independent. The challenge of identifying genetic factors predisposing or protecting individuals from developing metabolic syndrome is however far more complex due to the existence of higher levels of physiological and genetic complexity. One challenge is imposed by the effect of, and interaction with, environmental factors. Another is the existence of an intricate network of molecular interactions among most of the mentioned endocrine factors. These interactions have been discussed in detail in many publications and reviews, and there are a number of online databases that provide detailed and integrated information. We only present here two selective schematic figures for the sake of illustration of the actual complexity. Figure 3 shows some of the cellular relations between a number of components (hormones and hormone receptors) of endocrine networks generated in the database EndoNet (http://endonet.bioinf.med.uni-goettingen.de/) (Potapov et al., 2006). Complex inter-regulations exist both among elements expressed within a given endocrine gland (e.g. leptin, INSR, IGF-1 and IL-8 in adipocytes), among elements across different endocrine glands (insulin interaction with INSR on heart, skeletal muscle and adipocytes), etc.

Figure 4 illustrates the enormous complexity of the network of genetic interactions among candidate genes for obesity. These have been generated in the SNPs3D database (http://www.snps3d.org/) from a wide range of data and literature (Yue et al., 2006).

It follows that an Occam's razor (reductionist) approach is not enough to fully understand the genetic basis of the metabolic syndrome. On the contrary, more holistic genetic analyses (such as gene-environment interaction analyses, haplotypic analyses, multilocus analyses, network analyses) are required.

9. Network of Endocrine Setpoints as a Combined Contributor to Metabolic Syndrome Risk

In this section, we introduce the foundations of a new hypothesis which postulates the involvement of a network of endocrine genetic setpoints collectively defining interindividual variation of metabolic syndrome phenotypes under endocrine control. In our view, the optimal design of holistic approaches dealing with the genetic dissection of such a network will require taking into account different levels of genetic variation, including interactions involving single genes, haplotypic analyses, multilocus analyses and ultimately the whole network of genetic setpoints.

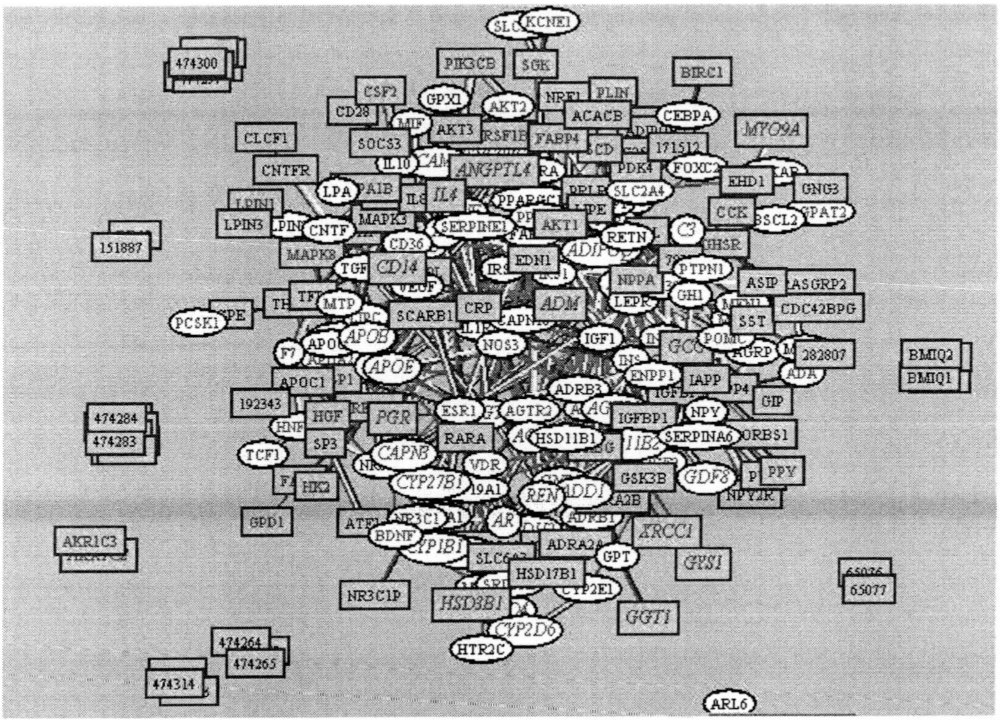

Figure 4. Complex network of interactions at the genetic level between endocrine factors involved in the metabolic syndrome. The diagram was generated in the SNPs3D database (http://www.snps3d.org/) in March 2006.

9.1. Interactions Involving One Single Gene

Variants at a given common gene influencing a complex trait such as the metabolic syndrome usually have complex interactions with other genes and with the environment. For example, it is known that the genetic effects of *TH* in a given individual, and hence the interindividual variation in a population, are influenced by many factors such as age, sex, tobacco smoking and interaction with other genes and pathways (Table 3).

As discussed previously, TH influences several interrelated biochemical and physiological responses. This raises the possibility of the existence of pleiotropic effects for *TH* (i.e., this single gene may influence many phenotypes). This hypothesis has recently been supported by results showing that allelic variation at *TH01* exerts widespread determination of a number of autonomic traits (plasma epinephrine concentration, renal norepinephrine excretion, and basal pulse interval) (Zhang et al., 2004). The fact that biochemical traits (such as norepinephrine secretion) and more distal physiological traits (such as heart rate or blood pressure) flow from the action of the same disease predisposition alleles reinforces the necessity of conducting holistic genetic analyses to fully understand the effects mediated by the *TH* gene.

Table 4. Published evidence demonstrating interaction between a single gene (*TH*) and a number of environmental and genetic factors.

Factor	Finding	Reference
Age	Loss of plasticity in catecholamine biosynthesis with age (*TH* expression is increased)	(Tümer et al., 2002)
Sex	Gender differences in hypothalamic *TH* expression in cafeteria diet-induced hypertension in rats	(Plut et al., 2002)
Sex	The Y *Sry* locus regulates *TH* transcription in rats *[The ability of Sry to increase TH transcription could be a primary cause of the increased blood pressure associated with the Y chromosome in spontaneously hypertensive rats (Charchar et al., 2003), and might also be related to gender specific differences in susceptibility to several catecholamine related disorders, including cardiovascular disease (Milsted et al., 2004)]*	(Milsted et al., 2004)
Sex	Sex-specific longevity associations defined by haplotypes including *TH01*	(De Luca et al., 2001)
Smoking	Nicotine induces *TH* mRNA by interacting with nicotinic acetylcholine receptors in cultured adrenal medullary cell systems	(Yoshimura et al., 2004)
Other genes	Dopaminergic D1-like receptor-dependent inhibition of *TH* mRNA expression in human lymphocytes	(Ferrari et al., 2004)
Other genes	Stimulating effect of angiotensin II in the biosynthesis of TH in the rat adrenal medulla	(Dogan et al., 2004)
Other genes	TH participates in the paracrine control of insulin secretion.	(Borelli et al., 2003)

9.2. Haplotypic Analyses

Genetic variants within a gene are linked in a chromosome. Similarly, many human chromosomal regions harbour different genes and exhibit high levels of LD. It is known that haplotypes are intrinsic attributes of population genetic variation, and define functional units of genes and chromosomal regions (Clark, 2004). Haplotypic analyses are thus useful tools for the combined analysis of the role of different gene variants.

There are haplotypes in the human genome which represent a genetic bridge between different endocrine pathways. Haplotypes spanning the *IGF2-INS-TH* gene cluster in human chromosome 11 are one example. Haplotypic, phenotypic and functional evidence recently published by our group has shown that the *IGF2*, *INS* and *TH* genes (representing key elements of the *GH-IGF* axis, the insulin signalling pathway and the catecholaminergic pathway, respectively) are evolutionarily coupled and functionally coupled in their effects on gene expression and on intermediate traits influencing diseases of the heart and circulation (Rodríguez et al., 2004; Kralovicova et al., 2006; Rodríguez et al., 2006a; Rodríguez et al., 2006b). These observations apply to other chromosomal regions and endocrine pathways in humans (Fullerton et al., 2000; Day et al., 2004a).

It is therefore likely that the intricate network of molecular interactions leading to the metabolic syndrome is also influenced by a no less intricate network of genetic interactions. Any of the genetic changes of this extremely complex cascade of inter-regulations among factors influencing the metabolic syndrome may be either insufficient or have a significant effect on the metabolic syndrome. However, the final outcome (presence or absence of metabolic syndrome) depends on the combined effect of all factors involved.

This idea is illustrated in Figure 5 taking as an example the *IGF2-INS-TH* region. An effect on a quantitative trait observed from a candidate region including more than one gene can be due to the action of only one of the genes, which would confer an independent effect higher than the minimum threshold that is required for the expression of the effect (Figure 5a). Alternatively, it is possible that the independent effect of each of the genes is not sufficient for the final outcome, but the combinations of effects exceeds the minimum threshold required (Figure 5b).

There are molecular mechanisms that can account for combined effects across different genes. Following the *IGF2-INS-TH* example, evidence has shown that *INS* and *IGF2* interact at the genetic and molecular levels. It is known that IGF-II can exert its functions also through the INS receptor. In addition, recent evidence has demonstrated the existence of two novel combined *INSIGF2* transcripts. Both use the *INS* promoter and alternative splice to downstream *IGF2* exons, and are expressed in restricted human tissues including pancreas (Monk et al., 2006).

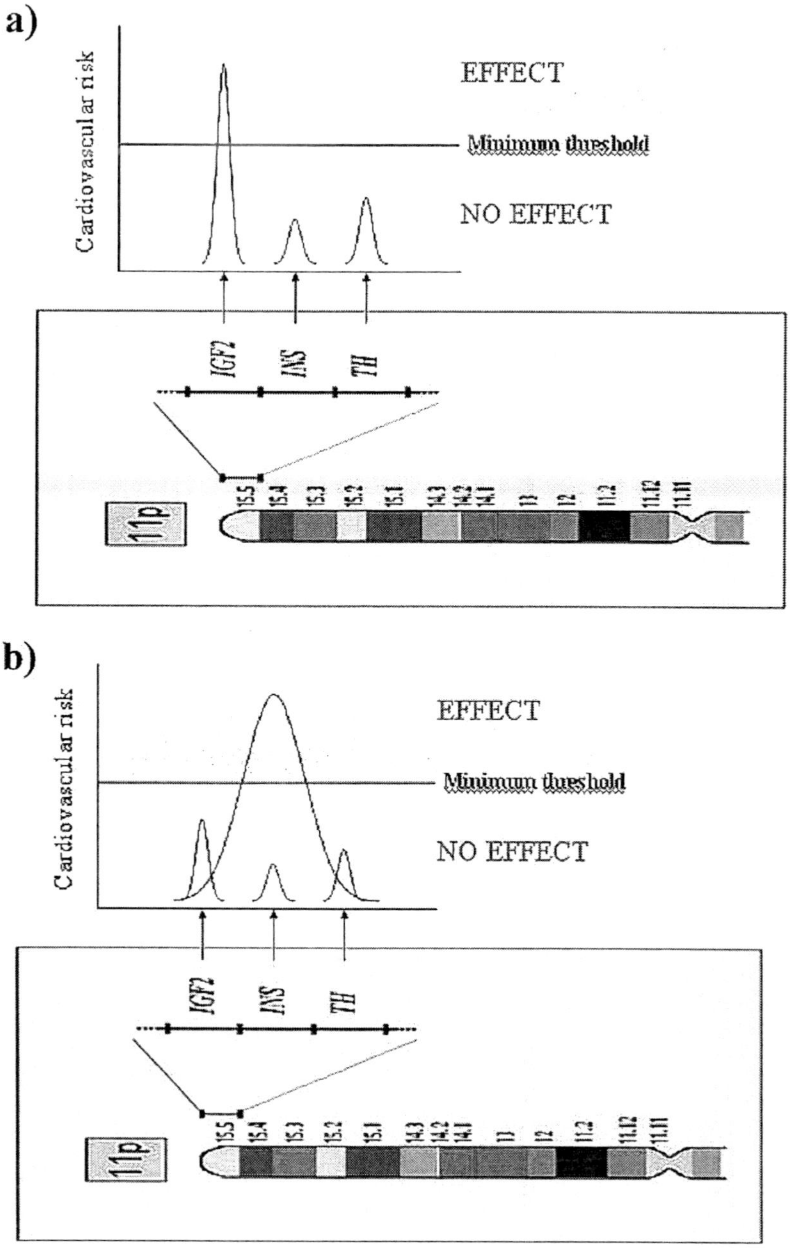

Figure 5. Schematic diagram illustrating two potential explanations accounting for a possible genetic effect of the *IGF2-INS-TH* region on cardiovascular risk. a) Only one of the genes in the cluster is sufficient to produce the effect. b) Although neither of the genes is sufficient to produce the effect, the joint contribution of them does influence the cardiovascular risk.

9.3. Holistic Analysis of Genetic Setpoints

Intensive work of the scientific community in recent years has contributed and will continue to contribute crucial information on genetic factors influencing the metabolic syndrome at the levels of individual genes and haplotypes (involving one or more genes).

Our hypothesis is that this research is defining at present, and will define in the future, genetic setpoints including not only single variants shown to account for the highest percentages of phenotypic variation but, importantly, also new variables accounting for gene-environment interactions and gene-gene interactions. Fully informative analyses of genetic interaction between genes require consideration of both interallelic and overall genetic associations (Zapata et al., 2001). These analyses are being facilitated with the development of new software tools, such as MIDAS (multiallelic interallelic disequilibrium analysis software) (Gaunt et al., 2006). Recent evidence indicates the existence of a greater genetic complexity in genetic interaction than previously thought, with reports demonstrating the existence of interactions between functionally related genes located in different chromosomes or completely unlinked (Zapata et al., 2002; Spilianakis et al., 2005; Kioussis, 2005; Ling et al., 2006; Spilianakis and Flavell, 2006).

The combined analysis of such genetic setpoints (defined from population genetic variation) in each individual using existing or new genetic holistic approaches should contribute to a better understanding of the genetic basis of the metabolic syndrome (and complex diseases in general) and the influence of individual genetic variation on this cluster of interrelated metabolic disorders.

References

[1] Abdollahi, Gaunt TR, Rodríguez S, Syddall HE, Aihie Sayer A, Cooper C, Phillips DIW, Cameron IT, Day IN (2004) *Quantitative Studies of AGTR1 mRNA Haplotypes and Metabolic Syndrome Traits*. Supplement edn p A1342

[2] Abdollahi MR, Gaunt TR, Syddall HE, Cooper C, Phillips DI, Ye S, Day IN (2005) Angiotensin II type I receptor gene polymorphism: anthropometric and metabolic syndrome traits. *J Med Genet* 42:396-401

[3] Albanese V, Biguet NF, Kiefer H, Bayard E, Mallet J, Meloni R (2001) Quantitative effects on gene silencing by allelic variation at a tetranucleotide microsatellite. *Hum Mol Genet* 10:1785-1792

[4] Alharbi KK, Aldahmesh MA, Spanakis E, Haddad L, Whittall RA, Chen XH, Rassoulian H, Smith MJ, Sillibourne J, Ball NJ, Graham NJ, Briggs PJ, Simpson IA, Phillips DI, Lawlor DA, Ye S, Humphries SE, Cooper C, Smith GD, Ebrahim S, Eccles DM, Day IN (2005) Mutation scanning by meltMADGE: validations using BRCA1 and LDLR, and demonstration of the potential to identify severe, moderate, silent, rare, and paucimorphic mutations in the general population. *Genome Res* 15:967-977

[5] Allison DB, Heo M (1998) Meta-analysis of linkage data under worst-case conditions: a demonstration using the human OB region. *Genetics* 148:859-865

[6] Almind K, Bjorbaek C, Vestergaard H, Hansen T, Echwald S, Pedersen O (1993) Aminoacid polymorphisms of insulin receptor substrate-1 in non-insulin-dependent diabetes mellitus. *Lancet* 342:828-832

[7] Andrew R, Gale CR, Walker BR, Seckl JR, Martyn CN (2002) Glucocorticoid metabolism and the Metabolic Syndrome: associations in an elderly cohort. *Exp Clin Endocrinol Diabetes* 110:284-290

[8] Anney RJ, Olsson CA, Lotfi-Miri M, Patton GC, Williamson R (2004) Nicotine dependence in a prospective population-based study of adolescents: the protective role of a functional tyrosine hydroxylase polymorphism. *Pharmacogenetics* 14:73-81

[9] Aubert J, Safonova I, Negrel R, Ailhaud G (1998) Insulin down-regulates angiotensinogen gene expression and angiotensinogen secretion in cultured adipose cells. *Biochem Biophys Res Commun* 250:77-82

[10] Balsalobre A, Damiola F, Schibler U (1998) A serum shock induces circadian gene expression in mammalian tissue culture cells. *Cell* 93:929-937

[11] Banerjee RR, Lazar MA (2003) Resistin: molecular history and prognosis. *J Mol Med* 81:218-226

[12] Barbeau P, Litaker MS, Jackson RW, Treiber FA (2003) A tyrosine hydroxylase microsatellite and hemodynamic response to stress in a multi-ethnic sample of youth. *Ethn Dis* 13:186-192

[13] Barker DJ, Eriksson JG, Forsen T, Osmond C (2002) Fetal origins of adult disease: strength of effects and biological basis. *Int J Epidemiol* 31:1235-1239

[14] Barker DJ, Osmond C, Golding J, Kuh D, Wadsworth ME (1989) Growth in utero, blood pressure in childhood and adult life, and mortality from cardiovascular disease. *BMJ* 298:564-567

[15] Barratt BJ, Payne F, Lowe CE, Hermann R, Healy BC, Harold D, Concannon P, Gharani N, McCarthy MI, Olavesen MG, McCormack R, Guja C, Ionescu-Tirgoviste C, Undlien DE, Ronningen KS, Gillespie KM, Tuomilehto-Wolf E, Tuomilehto J, Bennett ST, Clayton DG, Cordell HJ, Todd JA (2004) Remapping the insulin gene/IDDM2 locus in type 1 diabetes. *Diabetes* 53:1884-1889

[16] Batterham RL, Bloom SR (2003) The gut hormone peptide YY regulates appetite. *Ann N Y Acad Sci* 994:162-168

[17] Becker KG, Barnes KC, Bright TJ, Wang SA (2004) The genetic association database. *Nat Genet* 36:431-432

[18] Bennett ST, Todd JA (1996) Human type 1 diabetes and the insulin gene: principles of mapping polygenes. *Annu Rev Genet* 30:343-370

[19] Berthier MT, Paradis AM, Tchernof A, Bergeron J, Prud'homme D, Despres JP, Vohl MC (2003) The interleukin 6-174G/C polymorphism is associated with indices of obesity in men. *J Hum Genet* 48:14-19

[20] Biddinger SB, Kahn CR (2006) FROM MICE TO MEN: Insights into the Insulin Resistance Syndromes. *Annu Rev Physiol* 68:123-158

[21] Bihl MP, Heinimann K, Rudiger JJ, Eickelberg O, Perruchoud AP, Tamm M, Roth M (2002) Identification of a novel IL-6 isoform binding to the endogenous IL-6 receptor. *Am J Respir Cell Mol Biol* 27:48-56

[22] Bolli GB, De FP, De CS, Perriello G, Ventura MM, Calcinaro F, Lolli C, Campbell P, Brunetti P, Gerich JE (1984) Demonstration of a dawn phenomenon in normal human volunteers. *Diabetes* 33:1150-1153

[23] Borelli MI, Rubio M, Garcia ME, Flores LE, Gagliardino JJ (2003) Tyrosine hydroxylase activity in the endocrine pancreas: changes induced by short-term dietary manipulation. *BMC Endocr Disord* 3:2

[24] Bowcock AM, Kidd JR, Lathrop GM, Daneshvar L, May LT, Ray A, Sehgal PB, Kidd KK, Cavalli-Sforza LL (1988) The human "interferon-beta 2/hepatocyte stimulating factor/interleukin-6" gene: DNA polymorphism studies and localization to chromosome 7p21. *Genomics* 3:8-16

[25] Bray MS, Boerwinkle E, Hanis CL (1999) Linkage analysis of candidate obesity genes among the Mexican-American population of Starr County, Texas. *Genet Epidemiol* 16:397-411

[26] Bray MS, Boerwinkle E, Hanis CL (2000) Sequence variation within the neuropeptide Y gene and obesity in Mexican Americans. *Obes Res* 8:219-226

[27] Bremner WF, Sothern RB, Kanabrocki EL, Ryan M, McCormick JB, Dawson S, Connors ES, Rothschild R, Third JL, Vahed S, Nemchausky BM, Shirazi P, Olwin JH (2000) Relation between circadian patterns in levels of circulating lipoprotein(a), fibrinogen, platelets, and related lipid variables in men. *Am Heart J* 139:164-173

[28] Broberger C (2005) Brain regulation of food intake and appetite: molecules and networks. *J Intern Med* 258:301-327

[29] Brockmann GA, Bevova MR (2002) Using mouse models to dissect the genetics of obesity. *Trends Genet* 18:367-376

[30] Burgner D, Rockett K, Ackerman H, Hull J, Usen S, Pinder M, Kwiatkowski DP (2003) Haplotypic relationship between SNP and microsatellite markers at the NOS2A locus in two populations. *Genes Immun* 4:506-514

[31] Camp HS, Ren D, Leff T (2002) Adipogenesis and fat-cell function in obesity and diabetes. *Trends Mol Med* 8:442-447

[32] Cancello R, Tounian A, Poitou C, Clement K (2004) Adiposity signals, genetic and body weight regulation in humans. *Diabetes Metab* 30:215-227

[33] Cardellini M, Perego L, D'Adamo M, Marini MA, Procopio C, Hribal ML, Andreozzi F, Frontoni S, Giacomelli M, Paganelli M, Pontiroli AE, Lauro R, Folli F, Sesti G (2005) C-174G polymorphism in the promoter of the interleukin-6 gene is associated with insulin resistance. *Diabetes Care* 28:2007-2012

[34] Cardon LR, Bell JI (2001) Association study designs for complex diseases. *Nat Rev Genet* 2:91-99

[35] Cassis LA, Saye J, Peach MJ (1988) Location and regulation of rat angiotensinogen messenger RNA. *Hypertension* 11:591-596

[36] Chagnon YC, Borecki IB, Perusse L, Roy S, Lacaille M, Chagnon M, Ho-Kim MA, Rice T, Province MA, Rao DC, Bouchard C (2000) Genome-wide search for genes related to the fat-free body mass in the Quebec family study. *Metabolism* 49:203-207

[37] Chakravarti A (1999) Population genetics--making sense out of sequence. *Nat Genet* 21:56-60

[38] Chakravarti A, Little P (2003) Nature, nurture and human disease. Nature 421:412-414

[39] Chaldakov GN, Fiore M, Stankulov IS, Hristova M, Antonelli A, Manni L, Ghenev PI, Angelucci F, Aloe L (2001) NGF, BDNF, leptin, and mast cells in human coronary atherosclerosis and metabolic syndrome. *Arch Physiol Biochem* 109:357-360

[40] Chaldakov GN, Fiore M, Stankulov IS, Manni L, Hristova MG, Antonelli A, Ghenev PI, Aloe L (2004) Neurotrophin presence in human coronary atherosclerosis and metabolic syndrome: a role for NGF and BDNF in cardiovascular disease? *Prog Brain Res* 146:279-289

[41] Charchar FJ, Tomaszewski M, Padmanabhan S, Lacka B, Upton MN, Inglis GC, Anderson NH, McConnachie A, Zukowska-Szczechowska E, Grzeszczak W, Connell JM, Watt GC, Dominiczak AF (2002) The Y chromosome effect on blood pressure in two European populations. *Hypertension* 39:353-356

[42] Charchar FJ, Tomaszewski M, Strahorn P, Champagne B, Dominiczak AF (2003) Y is there a risk to being male? *Trends Endocrinol Metab* 14:163-168

[43] Chen H, Charlat O, Tartaglia LA, Woolf EA, Weng X, Ellis SJ, Lakey ND, Culpepper J, Moore KJ, Breitbart RE, Duyk GM, Tepper RI, Morgenstern JP (1996) Evidence that the diabetes gene encodes the leptin receptor: identification of a mutation in the leptin receptor gene in db/db mice. *Cell* 84:491-495

[44] Chen SC, Chang YL, Wang DL, Cheng JJ (2006) Herbal remedy magnolol suppresses IL-6-induced STAT3 activation and gene expression in endothelial cells. *Br J Pharmacol*

[45] Chen YF, Naftilan AJ, Oparil S (1992) Androgen-dependent angiotensinogen and renin messenger RNA expression in hypertensive rats. *Hypertension* 19:456-463

[46] Chiba M, Suzuki S, Hinokio Y, Hirai M, Satoh Y, Tashiro A, Utsumi A, Awata T, Hongo M, Toyota T (2000) Tyrosine hydroxylase gene microsatellite polymorphism associated with insulin resistance in depressive disorder. *Metabolism* 49:1145-1149

[47] Clark AG (2004) The role of haplotypes in candidate gene studies. *Genet Epidemiol* 27:321-333

[48] Clauser E, Gaillard I, Wei L, Corvol P (1989) Regulation of angiotensinogen gene. *Am J Hypertens* 2:403-410

[49] Clemmons DR (1997) Insulin-like growth factor binding proteins and their role in controlling IGF actions. *Cytokine Growth Factor Rev* 8:45-62

[50] Coleman DL (1973) Effects of parabiosis of obese with diabetes and normal mice. *Diabetologia* 9:294-298

[51] Coll AP, Farooqi IS, Challis BG, Yeo GS, O'Rahilly S (2004) Proopiomelanocortin and energy balance: insights from human and murine genetics. *J Clin Endocrinol Metab* 89:2557-2562

[52] Comuzzie AG, Hixson JE, Almasy L, Mitchell BD, Mahaney MC, Dyer TD, Stern MP, MacCluer JW, Blangero J (1997) A major quantitative trait locus determining serum leptin levels and fat mass is located on human chromosome 2. *Nat Genet* 15:273-276

[53] Conti E, Carrozza C, Capoluongo E, Volpe M, Crea F, Zuppi C, Andreotti F (2004) Insulin-like growth factor-1 as a vascular protective factor. *Circulation* 110:2260-2265

[54] Contreras F, Fouillioux C, Bolivar A, Simonovis N, Hernandez-Hernandez R, Armas-Hernandez MJ, Velasco M (2002) Dopamine, hypertension and obesity. *J Hum Hypertens* 16 Suppl 1:S13-S17

[55] Coppack SW (2001) Pro-inflammatory cytokines and adipose tissue. *Proc Nutr Soc* 60:349-356

[56] Costa LA, Canani LH, Maia AL, Gross JL (2002) The ACE insertion/deletion polymorphism is not associated with the metabolic syndrome (WHO Definition) in Brazilian type 2 diabetic patients. *Diabetes Care* 25:2365-2366

[57] Crandall DL, Hausman GJ, Kral JG (1997) A review of the microcirculation of adipose tissue: anatomic, metabolic, and angiogenic perspectives. *Microcirculation* 4:211-232

[58] Cummings DE, Schwartz MW (2003) Genetics and pathophysiology of human obesity. *Annu Rev Med* 54:453-471

[59] Cybulsky MI, Gimbrone MA, Jr. (1991) Endothelial expression of a mononuclear leukocyte adhesion molecule during atherogenesis. *Science* 251:788-791

[60] Dahmen N, Volp M, Singer P, Hiemke C, Szegedi A (2005) Tyrosine hydroxylase Val-81-Met polymorphism associated with early-onset alcoholism. *Psychiatr Genet* 15:
13-16

[61] Dalziel B, Gosby AK, Richman RM, Bryson JM, Caterson ID (2002) Association of the TNF-alpha -308 G/A promoter polymorphism with insulin resistance in obesity. *Obes Res* 10:401-407

[62] Darimont C, Vassaux G, Ailhaud G, Negrel R (1994) Differentiation of preadipose cells: paracrine role of prostacyclin upon stimulation of adipose cells by angiotensin-II. *Endocrinology* 135:2030-2036

[63] Davey-Smith G, Ebrahim S (2003) 'Mendelian randomization': can genetic epidemiology contribute to understanding environmental determinants of disease? *Int J Epidemiol* 32:1-22

[64] Davis D, Liyou N, Lockwood D, Johnson A (2002) Angiotensinogen genotype, plasma protein and mRNA concentration in isolated systolic hypertension. *Clin Genet* 61: 363-368

[65] Day IN, Chen XH, Gaunt TR, King TH, Voropanov A, Ye S, Rodriguez S, Syddall HE, Sayer AA, Dennison EM, Tabassum F, Barker DJ, Cooper C, Phillips DI (2004a) Late life metabolic syndrome, early growth, and common polymorphism in the growth hormone and placental lactogen gene cluster. *J Clin Endocrinol Metab* 89:5569-5576

[66] Day IN, Gu D, Ganderton RH, Spanakis E, Ye S (2001) Epidemiology and the genetic basis of disease. *Int J Epidemiol* 30:661-667

[67] Day INM, Al-Harbi K, Smith M, Al Dahmesh M, Zhang B, Lotery A, Cross NCP, Ye S, Eccles D, Fox K, Rodríguez S (2004b) Paucimorphic alleles versus polymorphic alleles in disease causation: theory, observation and detection. *Curr Genomics* 5: 431-438

[68] De Luca M, Rose G, Bonafe M, Garasto S, Greco V, Weir BS, Franceschi C, De Benedictis G (2001) Sex-specific longevity associations defined by Tyrosine Hydroxylase-Insulin-Insulin Growth Factor 2 haplotypes on the 11p15.5 chromosomal region. *Exp Gerontol* 36:1663-1671

[69] Dean M (2003) Approaches to identify genes for complex human diseases: lessons from Mendelian disorders. *Hum Mutat* 22:261-274

[70] Dedoussis GV, Manios Y, Choumerianou DM, Yiannakouris N, Panagiotakos DB, Skenderi K, Zampelas A (2004) The IL-6 gene G-174C polymorphism related to health indices in Greek primary school children. *Obes Res* 12:1037-1041

[71] Delplanque J, Barat-Houari M, Dina C, Gallina P, Clement K, Guy-Grand B, Vasseur F, Boutin P, Froguel P (2000) Linkage and association studies between the proopiomelanocortin (POMC) gene and obesity in caucasian families. *Diabetologia* 43:1554-1557

[72] Deng J, Hua K, Caveney EJ, Takahashi N, Harp JB (2006) Protein inhibitor of activated STAT3 inhibits adipogenic gene expression. *Biochem Biophys Res Commun* 339:923-931

[73] Despres JP (2006) Is visceral obesity the cause of the metabolic syndrome? *Ann Med* 38:52-63

[74] Dogan MD, Sumners C, Broxson CS, Clark N, Tumer N (2004) Central angiotensin II increases biosynthesis of tyrosine hydroxylase in the rat adrenal medulla. *Biochem Biophys Res Commun* 313:623-626

[75] Dong ZM, Chapman SM, Brown AA, Frenette PS, Hynes RO, Wagner DD (1998) The combined role of P- and E-selectins in atherosclerosis. *J Clin Invest* 102:145-152

[76] Doursout MF, Chelly JE, Wouters P, Lawrence C, Liang YY, Buckley JP (1990) Effect of gender in centrally induced angiotensin II hypertension in dogs. *Hypertension* 15:I117-I120

[77] Duggirala R, Stern MP, Mitchell BD, Reinhart LJ, Shipman PA, Uresandi OC, Chung WK, Leibel RL, Hales CN, O'Connell P, Blangero J (1996) Quantitative variation in obesity-related traits and insulin precursors linked to the OB gene region on human chromosome 7. *Am J Hum Genet* 59:694-703

[78] Dunger D, Yuen K, Ong K (2004) Insulin-like growth factor I and impaired glucose tolerance. *Horm Res* 62 Suppl 1:101-107

[79] Eckel RH, Grundy SM, Zimmet PZ (2005) The metabolic syndrome. *Lancet* 365:1415-1428

[80] Ellis JA, Stebbing M, Harrap SB (2000) Association of the human Y chromosome with high blood pressure in the general population. *Hypertension* 36:731-733

[81] Ellison KE, Ingelfinger JR, Pivor M, Dzau VJ (1989) Androgen regulation of rat renal angiotensinogen messenger RNA expression. *J Clin Invest* 83:1941-1945

[82] Engeli S, Bohnke J, Gorzelniak K, Janke J, Schling P, Bader M, Luft FC, Sharma AM (2005) Weight loss and the renin-angiotensin-aldosterone system. *Hypertension* 45:356-362

[83] Engeli S, Gorzelniak K, Kreutz R, Runkel N, Distler A, Sharma AM (1999) Co-expression of renin-angiotensin system genes in human adipose tissue. *J Hypertens* 17:555-560

[84] Ernst E, Resch KL (1993) Fibrinogen as a cardiovascular risk factor: a meta-analysis and review of the literature. *Ann Intern Med* 118:956-963

[85] Evans DM, Cardon LR (2006) Genome-wide association: a promising start to a long race. *Trends Genet*

[86] Faloia E, Gatti C, Camilloni MA, Mariniello B, Sardu C, Garrapa GG, Mantero F, Giacchetti G (2002) Comparison of circulating and local adipose tissue renin-angiotensin system in normotensive and hypertensive obese subjects. *J Endocrinol Invest* 25:309-314

[87] Fan J, Watanabe T (2003) Inflammatory reactions in the pathogenesis of atherosclerosis. *J Atheroscler Thromb* 10:63-71

[88] Fan W, Boston BA, Kesterson RA, Hruby VJ, Cone RD (1997) Role of melanocortinergic neurons in feeding and the agouti obesity syndrome. *Nature* 385:165-168

[89] Fasshauer M, Kralisch S, Klier M, Lossner U, Bluher M, Klein J, Paschke R (2004) Insulin resistance-inducing cytokines differentially regulate SOCS mRNA expression via growth factor- and Jak/Stat-signaling pathways in 3T3-L1 adipocytes. *J Endocrinol* 181:129-138

[90] Feldmer M, Kaling M, Takahashi S, Mullins JJ, Ganten D (1991) Glucocorticoid- and estrogen-responsive elements in the 5'-flanking region of the rat angiotensinogen gene. *J Hypertens* 9:1005-1012

[91] Ferguson-Smith AC, Chen YF, Newman MS, May LT, Sehgal PB, Ruddle FH (1988) Regional localization of the interferon-beta 2/B-cell stimulatory factor 2/hepatocyte stimulating factor gene to human chromosome 7p15-p21. *Genomics* 2:203-208

[92] Fernandez-Real JM, Broch M, Vendrell J, Gutierrez C, Casamitjana R, Pugeat M, Richart C, Ricart W (2000) Interleukin-6 gene polymorphism and insulin sensitivity. *Diabetes* 49:517-520

[93] Fernandez-Real JM, Gutierrez C, Ricart W, Casamitjana R, Broch M, Vendrell J, Richart C (1997a) The TNF-beta gene Nco I polymorphism is not associated with hypertriglyceridemia or insulin resistance in lean and obese subjects. *Biochem Biophys Res Commun* 236:829-832

[94] Fernandez-Real JM, Gutierrez C, Ricart W, Casamitjana R, Fernandez-Castaner M, Vendrell J, Richart C, Soler J (1997b) The TNF-alpha gene Nco I polymorphism influences the relationship among insulin resistance, percent body fat, and increased serum leptin levels. *Diabetes* 46:1468-1472

[95] Ferrannini E (2006) Is insulin resistance the cause of the metabolic syndrome? *Ann Med* 38:42-51

[96] Ferrari M, Cosentino M, Marino F, Bombelli R, Rasini E, Lecchini S, Frigo G (2004) Dopaminergic D1-like receptor-dependent inhibition of tyrosine hydroxylase mRNA expression and catecholamine production in human lymphocytes. *Biochem Pharmacol* 67:865-873

[97] Franke L, Bakel H, Fokkens L, de Jong ED, Egmont-Petersen M, Wijmenga C (2006) Reconstruction of a functional human gene network, with an application for prioritizing positional candidate genes. *Am J Hum Genet* 78:1011-1025

[98] Fraser R, Ingram MC, Anderson NH, Morrison C, Davies E, Connell JM (1999) Cortisol effects on body mass, blood pressure, and cholesterol in the general population. *Hypertension* 33:1364-1368

[99] Frederich RC, Jr., Kahn BB, Peach MJ, Flier JS (1992) Tissue-specific nutritional regulation of angiotensinogen in adipose tissue. *Hypertension* 19:339-344

[100] Freeman MS, Mansfield MW, Barrett JH, Grant PJ (2002) Heritability of features of the insulin resistance syndrome in a community-based study of healthy families. *Diabet Med* 19:994-999

[101] Fullerton SM, Clark AG, Weiss KM, Nickerson DA, Taylor SL, Stengard JH, Salomaa V, Vartiainen E, Perola M, Boerwinkle E, Sing CF (2000) Apolipoprotein E variation at the sequence haplotype level: implications for the origin and maintenance of a major human polymorphism. *Am J Hum Genet* 67:881-900

[102] Gandhi SK, Gainer J, King D, Brown NJ (1998) Gender affects renal vasoconstrictor response to Ang I and Ang II. *Hypertension* 31:90-96

[103] Garcia EC, Gonzalez P, Castro MG, Alvarez R, Reguero JR, Batalla A, Cortina A, Alvarez V (2003) Association between genetic variation in the Y chromosome and hypertension in myocardial infarction patients. *Am J Med Genet* 122A:234-237

[104] Gaunt TR, Cooper JA, Miller GJ, Day IN, O'Dell SD (2001) Positive associations between single nucleotide polymorphisms in the IGF2 gene region and body mass index in adult males. *Hum Mol Genet* 10:1491-1501

[105] Gaunt TR, Rodriguez S, Zapata C, Day IN (2006) MIDAS: software for analysis and visualisation of interallelic disequilibrium between multiallelic markers. *BMC Bioinformatics* 7:227

[106] Geroldi D, Minoretti P, Emanuele E (2006) Brain-derived neurotrophic factor and the metabolic syndrome: More than just a hypothesis. *Med Hypotheses* 67:195-196

[107] Giacchetti G, Faloia E, Mariniello B, Sardu C, Gatti C, Camilloni MA, Guerrieri M, Mantero F (2002) Overexpression of the renin-angiotensin system in human visceral adipose tissue in normal and overweight subjects. *Am J Hypertens* 15:381-388

[108] Gil-Campos M, Canete RR, Gil A (2004) Adiponectin, the missing link in insulin resistance and obesity. *Clin Nutr* 23:963-974

[109] Glass CK, Witztum JL (2001) Atherosclerosis. the road ahead. *Cell* 104:503-516

[110] Goldstein DB, Tate SK, Sisodiya SM (2003) Pharmacogenetics goes genomic. *Nat Rev Genet* 4:937-947

[111] Gorzelniak K, Engeli S, Janke J, Luft FC, Sharma AM (2002) Hormonal regulation of the human adipose-tissue renin-angiotensin system: relationship to obesity and hypertension. *J Hypertens* 20:965-973

[112] Greenberg AS, McDaniel ML (2002) Identifying the links between obesity, insulin resistance and beta-cell function: potential role of adipocyte-derived cytokines in the pathogenesis of type 2 diabetes. *Eur J Clin Invest* 32 Suppl 3:24-34

[113] Groop L (2000) Genetics of the metabolic syndrome. *Br J Nutr* 83 Suppl 1:S39-S48

[114] Grundy SM (2004) Obesity, metabolic syndrome, and cardiovascular disease. *J Clin Endocrinol Metab* 89:2595-2600

[115] Guerre-Millo M (2002) Adipose tissue hormones. *J Endocrinol Invest* 25:855-861

[116] Gurnell M (2005) Peroxisome proliferator-activated receptor gamma and the regulation of adipocyte function: lessons from human genetic studies. *Best Pract Res Clin Endocrinol Metab* 19:501-523

[117] Hager J, Dina C, Francke S, Dubois S, Houari M, Vatin V, Vaillant E, Lorentz N, Basdevant A, Clement K, Guy-Grand B, Froguel P (1998) A genome-wide scan for human obesity genes reveals a major susceptibility locus on chromosome 10. *Nat Genet* 20:304-308

[118] Hamid YH, Rose CS, Urhammer SA, Glumer C, Nolsoe R, Kristiansen OP, Mandrup-Poulsen T, Borch-Johnsen K, Jorgensen T, Hansen T, Pedersen O (2005) Variations of the interleukin-6 promoter are associated with features of the metabolic syndrome in Caucasian Danes. *Diabetologia* 48:251-260

[119] Harp JB, Franklin D, Vanderpuije AA, Gimble JM (2001) Differential expression of signal transducers and activators of transcription during human adipogenesis. *Biochem Biophys Res Commun* 281:907-912

[120] Harvey J, Ashford ML (2003) Leptin in the CNS: much more than a satiety signal. *Neuropharmacology* 44:845-854

[121] Hauner H (2002) The mode of action of thiazolidinediones. *Diabetes Metab Res Rev* 18 Suppl 2:S10-S15

[122] Heald A, Stephens R, Gibson JM (2006) The insulin-like growth factor system and diabetes--an overview. *Diabet Med* 23 Suppl 1:19-24

[123] Hegele RA (2003) Monogenic forms of insulin resistance: apertures that expose the common metabolic syndrome. *Trends Endocrinol Metab* 14:371-377

[124] Herrmann SM, Ricard S, Nicaud V, Mallet C, Arveiler D, Evans A, Ruidavets JB, Luc G, Bara L, Parra HJ, Poirier O, Cambien F (1998) Polymorphisms of the tumour necrosis factor-alpha gene, coronary heart disease and obesity. *Eur J Clin Invest* 28: 59-66

[125] Hirschhorn JN, Daly MJ (2005) Genome-wide association studies for common diseases and complex traits. *Nat Rev Genet* 6:95-108

[126] Hoffstedt J, Eriksson P, Hellstrom L, Rossner S, Ryden M, Arner P (2000) Excessive fat accumulation is associated with the TNF alpha-308 G/A promoter polymorphism in women but not in men. *Diabetologia* 43:117-120

[127] Hoh J, Ott J (2003) Mathematical multi-locus approaches to localizing complex human trait genes. *Nat Rev Genet* 4:701-709

[128] Hotamisligil GS (2003) Inflammatory pathways and insulin action. *Int J Obes Relat Metab Disord* 27 Suppl 3:S53-S55

[129] Hotamisligil GS, Arner P, Caro JF, Atkinson RL, Spiegelman BM (1995) Increased adipose tissue expression of tumor necrosis factor-alpha in human obesity and insulin resistance. *J Clin Invest* 95:2409-2415

[130] Hotamisligil GS, Peraldi P, Budavari A, Ellis R, White MF, Spiegelman BM (1996) IRS-1-mediated inhibition of insulin receptor tyrosine kinase activity in TNF-alpha- and obesity-induced insulin resistance. *Science* 271:665-668

[131] Hotamisligil GS, Shargill NS, Spiegelman BM (1993) Adipose expression of tumor necrosis factor-alpha: direct role in obesity-linked insulin resistance. *Science* 259:87-91

[132] Hristova M, Aloe L (2006) Metabolic syndrome--neurotrophic hypothesis. *Med Hypotheses* 66:545-549

[133] Hube F, Hauner H (1999) The role of TNF-alpha in human adipose tissue: prevention of weight gain at the expense of insulin resistance? *Horm Metab Res* 31:626-631

[134] Huber SA, Sakkinen P, Conze D, Hardin N, Tracy R (1999) Interleukin-6 exacerbates early atherosclerosis in mice. *Arterioscler Thromb Vasc Biol* 19:2364-2367

[135] Hubner N, Wallace CA, Zimdahl H, Petretto E, Schulz H, Maciver F, Mueller M, Hummel O, Monti J, Zidek V, Musilova A, Kren V, Causton H, Game L, Born G, Schmidt S, Muller A, Cook SA, Kurtz TW, Whittaker J, Pravenec M, Aitman TJ (2005) Integrated transcriptional profiling and linkage analysis for identification of genes underlying disease. *Nat Genet* 37:243-253

[136] Hulley S, Grady D, Bush T, Furberg C, Herrington D, Riggs B, Vittinghoff E (1998) Randomized trial of estrogen plus progestin for secondary prevention of coronary heart disease in postmenopausal women. Heart and Estrogen/progestin Replacement Study (HERS) Research Group. *JAMA* 280:605-613

[137] Hung CC, Pirie F, Luan J, Lank E, Motala A, Yeo GS, Keogh JM, Wareham NJ, O'Rahilly S, Farooqi IS (2004) Studies of the peptide YY and neuropeptide Y2 receptor genes in relation to human obesity and obesity-related traits. *Diabetes* 53:2461-2466

[138] Jackson MB, Ahima RS (2006) Neuroendocrine and metabolic effects of adipocyte-derived hormones. *Clin Sci (Lond)* 110:143-152

[139] Jacob S, Henriksen EJ (2004) Metabolic properties of vasodilating beta blockers: management considerations for hypertensive diabetic patients and patients with the metabolic syndrome. *J Clin Hypertens (Greenwich)* 6:690-696

[140] Jansen RC, Nap JP (2001) Genetical genomics: the added value from segregation. *Trends Genet* 17:388-391

[141] Jazet IM, Pijl H, Meinders AE (2003) Adipose tissue as an endocrine organ: impact on insulin resistance. *Neth J Med* 61:194-212

[142] Jindra A, Jachymova M, Horky K, Peleska J, Umnerova V, Bultas J, Savlikova J (2000) Association analysis of two tyrosine hydroxylase gene polymorphisms in normotensive offspring from hypertensive families. *Blood Press* 9:250-254

[143] Jones BH, Standridge MK, Moustaid N (1997) Angiotensin II increases lipogenesis in 3T3-L1 and human adipose cells. *Endocrinology* 138:1512-1519

[144] Jorde LB, Watkins WS, Bamshad MJ (2001) Population genomics: a bridge from evolutionary history to genetic medicine. *Hum Mol Genet* 10:2199-2207

[145] Jose PA, Eisner GM, Felder RA (1999) Role of dopamine in the pathogenesis of hypertension. *Clin Exp Pharmacol Physiol Suppl* 26:S10-S13

[146] Kang BY, Kim SJ, Lee KO (2003) No association of the human Y chromosome with blood pressure in korean male population. *J Toxicol Pub Health* 19:29-31

[147] Karvonen MK, Koulu M, Pesonen U, Uusitupa MI, Tammi A, Viikari J, Simell O, Ronnemaa T (2000) Leucine 7 to proline 7 polymorphism in the prepronouropeptide Y is associated with birth weight and serum triglyceride concentration in preschool aged children. *J Clin Endocrinol Metab* 85:1455-1460

[148] Karvonen MK, Pesonen U, Koulu M, Niskanen L, Laakso M, Rissanen A, Dekker JM, Hart LM, Valve R, Uusitupa MI (1998) Association of a leucine(7)-to-proline(7) polymorphism in the signal peptide of neuropeptide Y with high serum cholesterol and LDL cholesterol levels. *Nat Med* 4:1434-1437

[149] Karvonen MK, Valkonen VP, Lakka TA, Salonen R, Koulu M, Pesonen U, Tuomainen TP, Kauhanen J, Nyyssonen K, Lakka HM, Uusitupa MI, Salonen JT (2001) Leucine7 to proline7 polymorphism in the prepronouropeptide Y is associated with the progression of carotid atherosclerosis, blood pressure and serum lipids in Finnish men. *Atherosclerosis* 159:145-151

[150] Kernie SG, Liebl DJ, Parada LF (2000) BDNF regulates eating behavior and locomotor activity in mice. *EMBO J* 19:1290-1300

[151] Kershaw EE, Flier JS (2004) Adipose tissue as an endocrine organ. *J Clin Endocrinol Metab* 89:2548-2556

[152] Khunti K, Davies M (2005) Metabolic syndrome. *BMJ* 331:1153-1154

[153] King DP, Takahashi JS (2000) Molecular genetics of circadian rhythms in mammals. *Annu Rev Neurosci* 23:713-742

[154] Kioussis D (2005) Gene regulation: kissing chromosomes. *Nature* 435:579-580

[155] Klebig ML, Wilkinson JE, Geisler JG, Woychik RP (1995) Ectopic expression of the agouti gene in transgenic mice causes obesity, features of type II diabetes, and yellow fur. *Proc Natl Acad Sci U S A* 92:4728-4732

[156] Klipstein-Grobusch K, Mohlig M, Spranger J, Hoffmann K, Rodrigues FU, Sharma AM, Klaus S, Pfeiffer AF, Boeing H (2006) I*nterleukin-6 g.-174G>C promoter polymorphism is associated with obesity in the EPIC-Potsdam Study. Obesity (Silver Spring)* 14:14-18

[157] Klouche M, Rose-John S, Schmiedt W, Bhakdi S (2000) Enzymatically degraded, nonoxidized LDL induces human vascular smooth muscle cell activation, foam cell transformation, and proliferation. *Circulation* 101:1799-1805

[158] Koerner A, Kratzsch J, Kiess W (2005) Adipocytokines: leptin--the classical, resistin--the controversical, adiponectin--the promising, and more to come. *Best Pract Res Clin Endocrinol Metab* 19:525-546

[159] Kojima M, Hosoda H, Kangawa K (2004) Clinical endocrinology and metabolism. Ghrelin, a novel growth-hormone-releasing and appetite-stimulating peptide from stomach. *Best Pract Res Clin Endocrinol Metab* 18:517-530

[160] Kralovicova J, Gaunt TR, Rodriguez S, Wood PJ, Day IN, Vorechovsky I (2006) Variants in the Human Insulin Gene That Affect Pre-mRNA Splicing: Is -23HphI a Functional Single Nucleotide Polymorphism at IDDM2? *Diabetes* 55:260-264

[161] Krege JH, John SW, Langenbach LL, Hodgin JB, Hagaman JR, Bachman ES, Jennette JC, O'Brien DA, Smithies O (1995) Male-female differences in fertility and blood pressure in ACE-deficient mice. *Nature* 375:146-148

[162] Kristensen P, Judge ME, Thim L, Ribel U, Christjansen KN, Wulff BS, Clausen JT, Jensen PB, Madsen OD, Vrang N, Larsen PJ, Hastrup S (1998) Hypothalamic CART is a new anorectic peptide regulated by leptin. *Nature* 393:72-76

[163] Krude H, Biebermann H, Schnabel D, Tansek MZ, Theunissen P, Mullis PE, Gruters A (2003) Obesity due to proopiomelanocortin deficiency: three new cases and treatment trials with thyroid hormone and ACTH4-10. *J Clin Endocrinol Metab* 88:4633-4640

[164] Kubaszek A, Pihlajamaki J, Komarovski V, Lindi V, Lindstrom J, Eriksson J, Valle TT, Hamalainen H, Ilanne-Parikka P, Keinanen-Kiukaanniemi S, Tuomilehto J, Uusitupa M, Laakso M (2003) Promoter polymorphisms of the TNF-alpha (G-308A) and IL-6 (C-174G) genes predict the conversion from impaired glucose tolerance to type 2 diabetes: the Finnish Diabetes Prevention Study. *Diabetes* 52:1872-1876

[165] La Fleur SE, Kalsbeek A, Wortel J, Buijs RM (1999) A suprachiasmatic nucleus generated rhythm in basal glucose concentrations. *J Neuroendocrinol* 11:643-652

[166] La Fleur SE, Kalsbeek A, Wortel J, Fekkes ML, Buijs RM (2001) A daily rhythm in glucose tolerance: a role for the suprachiasmatic nucleus. *Diabetes* 50:1237-1243

[167] Lander ES (1996) The new genomics: global views of biology. *Science* 274:536-539

[168] Lappalainen J, Kranzler HR, Malison R, Price LH, Van DC, Rosenheck RA, Cramer J, Southwick S, Charney D, Krystal J, Gelernter J (2002) A functional neuropeptide Y Leu7Pro polymorphism associated with alcohol dependence in a large population sample from the United States. *Arch Gen Psychiatry* 59:825-831

[169] Lautier C, El Mkadem SA, Renard E, Brun JF, Gris JC, Bringer J, Grigorescu F (2003) Complex haplotypes of IRS2 gene are associated with severe obesity and reveal heterogeneity in the effect of Gly1057Asp mutation. *Hum Genet* 113:34-43

[170] Lavery DJ, Schibler U (1993) Circadian transcription of the cholesterol 7 alpha hydroxylase gene may involve the liver-enriched bZIP protein DBP. *Genes Dev* 7:1871-1884
[171] Lee GH, Proenca R, Montez JM, Carroll KM, Darvishzadeh JG, Lee JI, Friedman JM (1996) Abnormal splicing of the leptin receptor in diabetic mice. *Nature* 379:632-635
[172] Lee J, Menon RK (2005) Molecular defects in the growth hormone-IGF axis. *Indian J Pediatr* 72:145-148
[173] Lee YJ, Tsai JC (2002) ACE gene insertion/deletion polymorphism associated with 1998 World Health Organization definition of metabolic syndrome in Chinese type 2 diabetic patients. *Diabetes Care* 25:1002-1008
[174] Leibel, Chua SC, Rosenbaum M (2001) Obesity. In: Scriver CR, Beaudet AL, Sly WS, Valle D, Childs B, Kinzler KW, Vogelstein B (eds) *The metabolic & molecular bases of inherited disease,* 8th edn. McGraw-Hill, New York, pp 3965-4028
[175] Li Y, Jain S, Patil S, Kumar A (2006) A haplotype of angiotensinogen gene that is associated with essential hypertension increases its promoter activity in adipocytes. *Vascul Pharmacol* 44:29-33
[176] Ling JQ, Li T, Hu JF, Vu TH, Chen HL, Qiu XW, Cherry AM, Hoffman AR (2006) CTCF mediates interchromosomal colocalization between Igf2/H19 and Wsb1/Nf1. *Science* 312:269-272
[177] Linhart A, Jindra A, Golan L, Jachymova M, Sedlacek K, Peleska J, Umnerova V, Bultas J, Horky K, Aschermann M (2002) Association between tyrosine hydroxylase polymorphisms and left ventricular structure in young normotensive men. *Br J Biomed Sci* 59:90-94
[178] Lopez-Bermejo A, Buckway CK, Rosenfeld RG (2000) Genetic defects of the growth hormone-insulin-like growth factor axis. *Trends Endocrinol Metab* 11:39-49
[179] Lyons WE, Mamounas LA, Ricaurte GA, Coppola V, Reid SW, Bora SH, Wihler C, Koliatsos VE, Tessarollo L (1999) Brain-derived neurotrophic factor-deficient mice develop aggressiveness and hyperphagia in conjunction with brain serotonergic abnormalities. *Proc Natl Acad Sci U S A* 96:15239-15244
[180] Magliano DJ, Shaw JE, Zimmet PZ (2006) How to best define the metabolic syndrome. *Ann Med* 38:34-41
[181] Mallow H, Trindl A, Loffler G (2000) Production of angiotensin II receptors type one (AT1) and type two (AT2) during the differentiation of 3T3-L1 preadipocytes. Horm *Metab Res* 32:500-503
[182] Mammarella S, Romano F, Di VA, Creati B, Esposito DL, Palmirotta R, Capani F, Vitullo P, Volpe G, Battista P, Della LF, Mariani-Costantini R, Cama A (2000) Interaction between the G1057D variant of IRS-2 and overweight in the pathogenesis of type 2 diabetes. *Hum Mol Genet* 9:2517-2521
[183] Maniatis N, Collins A, Gibson J, Zhang W, Tapper W, Morton NE (2004) Positional cloning by linkage disequilibrium. *Am J Hum Genet* 74:846-855
[184] Mauras N, Haymond MW (2005) Are the metabolic effects of GH and IGF-I separable? *Growth Horm IGF Res* 15:19-27
[185] McCarthy JJ, Meyer J, Moliterno DJ, Newby LK, Rogers WJ, Topol EJ (2003) Evidence for substantial effect modification by gender in a large-scale genetic association study of the metabolic syndrome among coronary heart disease patients. *Hum Genet* 114:87-98

[186] McLoughlin RM, Hurst SM, Nowell MA, Harris DA, Horiuchi S, Morgan LW, Wilkinson TS, Yamamoto N, Topley N, Jones SA (2004) Differential regulation of neutrophil-activating chemokines by IL-6 and its soluble receptor isoforms. *J Immunol* 172:5676-5683

[187] McTernan PG, Kusminski CM, Kumar S (2006) Resistin. *Curr Opin Lipidol* 17: 170-175

[188] Menon PS (2006) Editorial--Growth and its disorders. Indian J Pediatr 73:65-66

[189] Millar-Craig MW, Bishop CN, Raftery EB (1978) Circadian variation of blood-pressure. Lancet 1:795-797

[190] Milsted A, Serova L, Sabban EL, Dunphy G, Turner ME, Ely DL (2004) Regulation of tyrosine hydroxylase gene transcription by Sry. *Neurosci Lett* 369:203-207

[191] Modur V, Li Y, Zimmerman GA, Prescott SM, McIntyre TM (1997) Retrograde inflammatory signaling from neutrophils to endothelial cells by soluble interleukin-6 receptor alpha. *J Clin Invest* 100:2752-2756

[192] Mohamed-Ali V, Goodrick S, Rawesh A, Katz DR, Miles JM, Yudkin JS, Klein S, Coppack SW (1997) Subcutaneous adipose tissue releases interleukin-6, but not tumor necrosis factor-alpha, in vivo. *J Clin Endocrinol Metab* 82:4196-4200

[193] Monk D, Sanches R, Arnaud P, Apostolidou S, Hills FA, bu-Amero S, Murrell A, Friess H, Reik W, Stanier P, Constancia M, Moore GE (2006) Imprinting of IGF2 P0 transcript and novel alternatively spliced INS-IGF2 isoforms show differences between mouse and human. *Hum Mol Genet* 15:1259-1269

[194] Moon YS, Kim DH, Song DK (2004) Serum tumor necrosis factor-alpha levels and components of the metabolic syndrome in obese adolescents. *Metabolism* 53:863-867

[195] Morton NE (2000) Unsolved problems in genetic epidemiology. *Hum Hered* 50:5-13

[196] Morton NE (1955) Sequential tests for the detection of linkage. *Am J Hum Genet* 7:277-318

[197] Morton NE (2003) Genetic epidemiology, genetic maps and positional cloning. *Philos Trans R Soc Lond B Biol Sci* 358:1701-1708

[198] Munafo MR, Flint J (2004) Meta-analysis of genetic association studies. *Trends Genet* 20:439-444

[199] Nagatsu T (1995) Tyrosine hydroxylase: human isoforms, structure and regulation in physiology and pathology. *Essays Biochem* 30:15-35

[200] Nakashima Y, Raines EW, Plump AS, Breslow JL, Ross R (1998) Upregulation of VCAM-1 and ICAM-1 at atherosclerosis-prone sites on the endothelium in the ApoE-deficient mouse. *Arterioscler Thromb Vasc Biol* 18:842-851

[201] Neel JV (1962) Diabetes mellitus: a "thrifty" genotype rendered detrimental by "progress"? *Am J Hum Genet* 14:353-362

[202] Neve KA, Seamans JK, Trantham-Davidson H (2004) Dopamine receptor signaling. *J Recept Signal Transduct Res* 24:165-205

[203] Newton JL, Harney SM, Timms AE, Sims AM, Rockett K, Darke C, Wordsworth BP, Kwiatkowski D, Brown MA (2004) Dissection of class III major histocompatibility complex haplotypes associated with rheumatoid arthritis. *Arthritis Rheum* 50:2122-2129

[204] Nickenig G, Baumer AT, Grohe C, Kahlert S, Strehlow K, Rosenkranz S, Stablein A, Beckers F, Smits JF, Daemen MJ, Vetter H, Bohm M (1998) Estrogen modulates AT1 receptor gene expression in vitro and in vivo. *Circulation* 97:2197-2201

[205] Nickenig G, Sachinidis A, Michaelsen F, Bohm M, Seewald S, Vetter H (1997) Upregulation of vascular angiotensin II receptor gene expression by low-density lipoprotein in vascular smooth muscle cells. *Circulation* 95:473-478

[206] Nickenig G, Strehlow K, Wassmann S, Baumer AT, Albory K, Sauer H, Bohm M (2000) Differential effects of estrogen and progesterone on AT(1) receptor gene expression in vascular smooth muscle cells. *Circulation* 102:1828-1833

[207] Niskanen L, Karvonen MK, Valve R, Koulu M, Pesonen U, Mercuri M, Rauramaa R, Toyry J, Laakso M, Uusitupa MI (2000) Leucine 7 to proline 7 polymorphism in the neuropeptide Y gene is associated with enhanced carotid atherosclerosis in elderly patients with type 2 diabetes and control subjects. *J Clin Endocrinol Metab* 85:2266-2269

[208] Norrelund H (2005) The metabolic role of growth hormone in humans with particular reference to fasting. *Growth Horm IGF Res* 15:95-122

[209] O'Dell SD, Day IN (1998) Insulin-like growth factor II (IGF-II). *Int J Biochem Cell Biol* 30:767-771

[210] O'Dell SD, Miller GJ, Cooper JA, Hindmarsh PC, Pringle PJ, Ford H, Humphries SE, Day IN (1997) Apal polymorphism in insulin-like growth factor II (IGF2) gene and weight in middle-aged males. *Int J Obes Relat Metab Disord* 21:822-825

[211] O'Donnell CJ, Lindpaintner K, Larson MG, Rao VS, Ordovas JM, Schaefer EJ, Myers RH, Levy D (1998) Evidence for association and genetic linkage of the angiotensin-converting enzyme locus with hypertension and blood pressure in men but not women in the Framingham Heart Study. *Circulation* 97:1766-1772

[212] Oishi K, Amagai N, Shirai H, Kadota K, Ohkura N, Ishida N (2005) Genome-wide Expression Analysis Reveals 100 Adrenal Gland-dependent Circadian Genes in the Mouse Liver. *DNA Res* 12:191-202

[213] Ollmann MM, Wilson BD, Yang YK, Kerns JA, Chen Y, Gantz I, Barsh GS (1997) Antagonism of central melanocortin receptors in vitro and in vivo by agouti-related protein. *Science* 278:135-138

[214] Olsson C, Anney R, Forrest S, Patton G, Coffey C, Cameron T, Hassett A, Williamson R (2004) Association between dependent smoking and a polymorphism in the tyrosine hydroxylase gene in a prospective population-based study of adolescent health. *Behav Genet* 34:85-91

[215] Osawa H, Yamada K, Onuma H, Murakami A, Ochi M, Kawata H, Nishimiya T, Niiya T, Shimizu I, Nishida W, Hashiramoto M, Kanatsuka A, Fujii Y, Ohashi J, Makino H (2004) The G/G genotype of a resistin single-nucleotide polymorphism at -420 increases type 2 diabetes mellitus susceptibility by inducing promoter activity through specific binding of Sp1/3. *Am J Hum Genet* 75:678-686

[216] Papanicolaou DA, Vgontzas AN (2000) Interleukin-6: the endocrine cytokine. *J Clin Endocrinol Metab* 85:1331-1333

[217] Perusse L, Rankinen T, Zuberi A, Chagnon YC, Weisnagel SJ, Argyropoulos G, Walts B, Snyder EE, Bouchard C (2005) The human obesity gene map: the 2004 update. *Obes Res* 13:381-490

[218] Pesonen U (2006) *Human NPY gene variants in cardiovascular and metabolic diseases*. EXS247-267

[219] Pickup JC, Mattock MB, Chusney GD, Burt D (1997) NIDDM as a disease of the innate immune system: association of acute-phase reactants and interleukin-6 with metabolic syndrome X. *Diabetologia* 40:1286-1292

[220] Pihlajamaki J, Ylinen M, Karhapaa P, Vauhkonen I, Laakso M (2003) The effect of the -308A allele of the TNF-alpha gene on insulin action is dependent on obesity. *Obes Res* 11:912-917

[221] Pijl H, Romijn JA (2006) Obesity, dopamine and the metabolic syndrome: potential of dopaminergic agents in the control of metabolism. *Current Opinion in Endocrinology & Diabetes* 13:179-184

[222] Pirola L, Johnston AM, Van OE (2004) Modulation of insulin action. *Diabetologia* 47:170-184

[223] Plata-Salaman CR (1998) Cytokines and Feeding. *News Physiol Sci* 13:298-304

[224] Plut C, Ribiere C, Giudicelli Y, Dausse JP (2002) Gender differences in hypothalamic tyrosine hydroxylase and alpha(2)-adrenoceptor subtype gene expression in cafeteria diet-induced hypertension and consequences of neonatal androgenization. *J Pharmacol Exp Ther* 302:525-531

[225] Porzio O, Federici M, Hribal ML, Lauro D, Accili D, Lauro R, Borboni P, Sesti G (1999) The Gly972-->Arg amino acid polymorphism in IRS-1 impairs insulin secretion in pancreatic beta cells. *J Clin Invest* 104:357-364

[226] Potapov A, Liebich I, Donitz J, Schwarzer K, Sasse N, Schoeps T, Crass T, Wingender E (2006) EndoNet: an information resource about endocrine networks. *Nucleic Acids Res* 34:D540-D545

[227] Poulsen P, Vaag A, Kyvik K, Beck-Nielsen H (2001) Genetic versus environmental aetiology of the metabolic syndrome among male and female twins. Diabetologia 44:537-543

[228] Prat-Larquemin L, Oppert JM, Clement K, Hainault I, Basdevant A, Guy-Grand B, Quignard-Boulange A (2004) Adipose angiotensinogen secretion, blood pressure, and AGT M235T polymorphism in obese patients. *Obes Res* 12:556-561

[229] Prentice AM, Rayco-Solon P, Moore SE (2005) Insights from the developing world: thrifty genotypes and thrifty phenotypes. *Proc Nutr Soc* 64:153-161

[230] Pritchard JK (2001) Are rare variants responsible for susceptibility to complex diseases? *Am J Hum Genet* 69:124-137

[231] Ravelli AC, Van Der Meulen JH, Michels RP, Osmond C, Barker DJ, Hales CN, Bleker OP (1998) Glucose tolerance in adults after prenatal exposure to famine. *Lancet* 351:173-177

[232] Ravelli AC, Van Der Meulen JH, Osmond C, Barker DJ, Bleker OP (1999) Obesity at the age of 50 y in men and women exposed to famine prenatally. *Am J Clin Nutr* 70:811-816

[233] Ravussin E, Valencia ME, Esparza J, Bennett PH, Schulz LO (1994) Effects of a traditional lifestyle on obesity in Pima Indians. *Diabetes Care* 17:1067-1074

[234] Reaven GM (1988) Banting lecture 1988. Role of insulin resistance in human disease. *Diabetes* 37:1595-1607

[235] Reed DR, Ding Y, Xu W, Cather C, Green ED, Price RA (1996) Extreme obesity may be linked to markers flanking the human OB gene. *Diabetes* 45:691-694

[236] Regitz-Zagrosek V, Lehmkuhl E, Weickert MO (2006) Gender differences in the metabolic syndrome and their role for cardiovascular disease. *Clin Res Cardiol* 95: 136-147

[237] Reich M, Liefeld T, Gould J, Lerner J, Tamayo P, Mesirov JP (2006) GenePattern 2.0. *Nat Genet* 38:500-501

[238] Reppert SM, Weaver DR (2002) Coordination of circadian timing in mammals. *Nature* 418:935-941

[239] Ribases M, Gratacos M, Armengol L, de CR, Badia A, Jimenez L, Solano R, Vallejo J, Fernandez F, Estivill X (2003) Met66 in the brain-derived neurotrophic factor (BDNF) precursor is associated with anorexia nervosa restrictive type. *Mol Psychiatry* 8: 745-751

[240] Ribases M, Gratacos M, Fernandez-Aranda F, Bellodi L, Boni C, Anderluh M, Cavallini MC, Cellini E, Di BD, Erzegovesi S, Foulon C, Gabrovsek M, Gorwood P, Hebebrand J, Hinney A, Holliday J, Hu X, Karwautz A, Kipman A, Komel R, Nacmias B, Remschmidt H, Ricca V, Sorbi S, Wagner G, Treasure J, Collier DA, Estivill X (2004) Association of BDNF with anorexia, bulimia and age of onset of weight loss in six European populations. *Hum Mol Genet* 13:1205-1212

[241] Rios M, Fan G, Fekete C, Kelly J, Bates B, Kuehn R, Lechan RM, Jaenisch R (2001) Conditional deletion of brain-derived neurotrophic factor in the postnatal brain leads to obesity and hyperactivity. *Mol Endocrinol* 15:1748-1757

[242] Risch N (2005) 2004 Curt Stern Award Address. The SNP endgame: a multidisciplinary approach. *Am J Hum Genet* 76:221-226

[243] Risch NJ (2000) Searching for genetic determinants in the new millennium. *Nature* 405:847-856

[244] Rodríguez S, Chen XH, Miller GJ, Day IN (2005) Non-recombining chromosome Y haplogroups and centromeric HindIII RFLP in relation to blood pressure in 2,743 middle-aged Caucasian men from the UK. *Hum Genet* 116:311-318

[245] Rodríguez S, Gaunt TR, Dennison E, Chen XH, Syddall HE, Phillips DI, Cooper C, Day IN (2006a) Replication of IGF2-INS-TH*5 haplotype effect on obesity in older men and study of related phenotypes. *Eur J Hum Genet* 14:109-116

[246] Rodríguez S, Gaunt TR, O'Dell SD, Chen XH, Gu D, Hawe E, Miller GJ, Humphries SE, Day IN (2004) Haplotypic analyses of the IGF2-INS-TH gene cluster in relation to cardiovascular risk traits. *Hum Mol Genet* 13:715-725

[247] Rodríguez S, Huang S, Chen XH, Gaunt TR, Syddall HE, Gilg JA, Miller GJ, Cooper CC, Cook DG, Whincup PH, Day IN (2006b) A study of TH01 and IGF2-INS-TH haplotypes in relation to smoking initiation in three independent surveys. *Pharmacogenet Genomics* 16:15-23

[248] Romano M, Sironi M, Toniatti C, Polentarutti N, Fruscella P, Ghezzi P, Faggioni R, Luini W, van H, V, Sozzani S, Bussolino F, Poli V, Ciliberto G, Mantovani A (1997) Role of IL-6 and its soluble receptor in induction of chemokines and leukocyte recruitment. *Immunity* 6:315-325

[249] Romeo S, Sentinelli F, Capici F, Arca M, Berni A, Vecci E, Di MU, Baroni MG (2001) The G-308A variant of the Tumor Necrosis Factor-alpha (TNF-alpha) gene is not associated with obesity, insulin resistance and body fat distribution. *BMC Med Genet* 2:10

[250] Rose KM, Newman B, Mayer-Davis EJ, Selby JV (1998) Genetic and behavioral determinants of waist-hip ratio and waist circumference in women twins. *Obes Res* 6:383-392

[251] Roses AD (2001) Pharmacogenetics. *Hum Mol Genet* 10:2261-2267

[252] Roth J, Qiang X, Marban SL, Redelt H, Lowell BC (2004) The obesity pandemic: where have we been and where are we going? *Obes Res* 12 Suppl 2:88S-101S

[253] Rudman D, Feller AG, Nagraj HS, Gergans GA, Lalitha PY, Goldberg AF, Schlenker RA, Cohn L, Rudman IW, Mattson DE (1990) Effects of human growth hormone in men over 60 years old. *N Engl J Med* 323:1-6

[254] Russo P, Venezia A, Lauria F, Strazzullo P, Cappuccio FP, Iacoviello L, Barba G, Siani A (2006) HindIII(+/-) polymorphism of the Y chromosome, blood pressure, and serum lipids: no evidence of association in three White populations. *Am J Hypertens* 19:331-338

[255] Safonova I, Aubert J, Negrel R, Ailhaud G (1997) Regulation by fatty acids of angiotensinogen gene expression in preadipose cells. *Biochem J* 322 (Pt 1):235-239

[256] Saghizadeh M, Ong JM, Garvey WT, Henry RR, Kern PA (1996) The expression of TNF alpha by human muscle. Relationship to insulin resistance. *J Clin Invest* 97:1111-1116

[257] Sankaranarayanan K, Chakraborty R, Boerwinklc EA (1999) Ionizing radiation and genetic risks. VI. Chronic multifactorial diseases: a review of epidemiological and genetical aspects of coronary heart disease, essential hypertension and diabetes mellitus. *Mutat Res* 436:21-57

[258] Schindler CW, Gilman JP, Bergman J, Mello NK, Woosley RL, Goldberg SR (2002) Interactions between cocaine and dopamine agonists on cardiovascular function in squirrel monkeys. J *Pharmacol Exp Ther* 300:180-187

[259] Schinner S, Scherbaum WA, Bornstein SR, Barthel A (2005) Molecular mechanisms of insulin resistance. *Diabet Med* 22:674-682

[260] Schork NJ (1997) Genetically complex cardiovascular traits. Origins, problems, and potential solutions. *Hypertension* 29:145-149

[261] Schork NJ, Cardon LR, Xu X (1998) The future of genetic epidemiology. *Trends Genet* 14:266-272

[262] Schousboe K, Willemsen G, Kyvik KO, Mortensen J, Boomsma DI, Cornes BK, Davis CJ, Fagnani C, Hjelmborg J, Kaprio J, De Lange M, Luciano M, Martin NG, Pedersen N, Pietilainen KH, Rissanen A, Saarni S, Sorensen TI, Van Baal GC, Harris JR (2003) Sex differences in heritability of BMI: a comparative study of results from twin studies in eight countries. *Twin Res* 6:409-421

[263] Schunkert H, Danser AH, Hense HW, Derkx FH, Kurzinger S, Riegger GA (1997) Effects of estrogen replacement therapy on the renin-angiotensin system in postmenopausal women. *Circulation* 95:39-45

[264] Schunkert H, Hense HW, Muscholl M, Luchner A, Riegger GA (1996) Association of angiotensin converting enzyme activity and arterial blood pressure in a population-based sample. *J Hypertens* 14:571-575

[265] Schupp M, Janke J, Clasen R, Unger T, Kintscher U (2004) Angiotensin type 1 receptor blockers induce peroxisome proliferator-activated receptor-gamma activity. *Circulation* 109:2054-2057

[266] Schwartz MW, Porte D, Jr. (2005) Diabetes, obesity, and the brain. *Science* 307: 375-379

[267] Sehgal PB, Zilberstein A, Ruggieri RM, May LT, Ferguson-Smith A, Slate DL, Revel M, Ruddle FH (1986) Human chromosome 7 carries the beta 2 interferon gene. *Proc Natl Acad Sci U S A* 83:5219-5222

[268] Selby JV, Newman B, Quesenberry CP, Jr., Fabsitz RR, Carmelli D, Meaney FJ, Slemenda C (1990) Genetic and behavioral influences on body fat distribution. *Int J Obes* 14:593-602

[269] Senn JJ, Klover PJ, Nowak IA, Mooney RA (2002) Interleukin-6 induces cellular insulin resistance in hepatocytes. *Diabetes* 51:3391-3399

[270] Serazin-Leroy V, Morot M, de MP, Giudicelli Y (2000) Androgen regulation and site specificity of angiotensinogen gene expression and secretion in rat adipocytes. *Am J Physiol Endocrinol Metab* 279:E1398-E1405

[271] Sharma P, Hingorani A, Jia H, Ashby M, Hopper R, Clayton D, Brown MJ (1998) Positive association of tyrosine hydroxylase microsatellite marker to essential hypertension. *Hypertension* 32:676-682

[272] Sigal RJ, Doria A, Warram JH, Krolewski AS (1996) Codon 972 polymorphism in the insulin receptor substrate-1 gene, obesity, and risk of noninsulin-dependent diabetes mellitus. *J Clin Endocrinol Metab* 81:1657-1659

[273] Sillanpaa MJ, Auranen K (2004) Replication in genetic studies of complex traits. *Ann Hum Genet* 68:646-657

[274] Small KM, McGraw DW, Liggett SB (2003) Pharmacology and physiology of human adrenergic receptor polymorphisms. *Annu Rev Pharmacol Toxicol* 43:381-411

[275] Sookoian S, Garcia SI, Gianotti TF, Dieuzeide G, Gonzalez CD, Pirola CJ (2005a) The G-308A promoter variant of the tumor necrosis factor-alpha gene is associated with hypertension in adolescents harboring the metabolic syndrome. *Am J Hypertens* 18:1271-1275

[276] Sookoian SC, Gonzalez C, Pirola CJ (2005b) Meta-analysis on the G-308A tumor necrosis factor alpha gene variant and phenotypes associated with the metabolic syndrome. *Obes Res* 13:2122-2131

[277] Spiegelman BM, Hotamisligil GS (1993) Through thick and thin: wasting, obesity, and TNF alpha. *Cell* 73:625-627

[278] Spielman RS, Ewens WJ (1996) The TDT and other family-based tests for linkage disequilibrium and association. *Am J Hum Genet* 59:983-989

[279] Spilianakis CG, Flavell RA (2006) Molecular biology. Managing associations between different chromosomes. *Science* 312:207-208

[280] Spilianakis CG, Lalioti MD, Town T, Lee GR, Flavell RA (2005) Interchromosomal associations between alternatively expressed loci. *Nature* 435:637-645

[281] Stahlberg N, Rico-Bautista E, Fisher RM, Wu X, Cheung L, Flores-Morales A, Tybring G, Norstedt G, Tollet-Egnell P (2004) Female-predominant expression of fatty acid translocase/CD36 in rat and human liver. *Endocrinology* 145:1972-1979

[282] Stary HC, Chandler AB, Dinsmore RE, Fuster V, Glagov S, Insull W, Jr., Rosenfeld ME, Schwartz CJ, Wagner WD, Wissler RW (1995) A definition of advanced types of atherosclerotic lesions and a histological classification of atherosclerosis. A report from the Committee on Vascular Lesions of the Council on Arteriosclerosis, American Heart Association. *Arterioscler Thromb Vasc Biol* 15:1512-1531

[283] Stefansson H, Sarginson J, Kong A, Yates P, Steinthorsdottir V, Gudfinnsson E, Gunnarsdottir S, Walker N, Petursson H, Crombie C, Ingason A, Gulcher JR, Stefansson K, St Clair D (2003) Association of neuregulin 1 with schizophrenia confirmed in a Scottish population. *Am J Hum Genet* 72:83-87

[284] Stephens JM, Pekala PH (1991) Transcriptional repression of the GLUT4 and C/EBP genes in 3T3-L1 adipocytes by tumor necrosis factor-alpha. *J Biol Chem* 266:21839-21845

[285] Stephens JW, Dhamrait SS, Cooper JA, Acharya J, Miller GJ, Hurel SJ, Humphries SE (2005) The D allele of the ACE I/D common gene variant is associated with Type 2 diabetes mellitus in Caucasian subjects. *Mol Genet Metab* 84:83-89

[286] Stephens JW, Humphries SE (2003) The molecular genetics of cardiovascular disease: clinical implications. *J Intern Med* 253:120-127

[287] Steppan CM, Bailey ST, Bhat S, Brown EJ, Banerjee RR, Wright CM, Patel HR, Ahima RS, Lazar MA (2001) The hormone resistin links obesity to diabetes. *Nature* 409:307-312

[288] Strazzullo P, Iacone R, Iacoviello L, Russo O, Barba G, Russo P, D'Orazio A, Barbato A, Cappuccio FP, Farinaro E, Siani A (2003) Genetic variation in the renin-angiotensin system and abdominal adiposity in men: the Olivetti Prospective Heart Study. *Ann Intern Med* 138:17-23

[289] Strehlow K, Wassmann S, Bohm M, Nickenig G (2000) Angiotensin AT1 receptor over-expression in hypercholesterolaemia. *Ann Med* 32:386-389

[290] Suviolahti E, Ridderstrale M, Almgren P, Klannemark M, Melander O, Carlsson E, Carlsson M, Hedenbro J, Orho-Melander M (2003) Pro-opiomelanocortin gene is associated with serum leptin levels in lean but not in obese individuals. *Int J Obes Relat Metab Disord* 27:1204-1211

[291] Takahashi N, Smithies O (2004) Human genetics, animal models and computer simulations for studying hypertension. *Trends Genet* 20:136-145

[292] Tanaka G, Matsushita I, Ohashi J, Tsuchiya N, Ikushima S, Oritsu M, Hijikata M, Nagata T, Yamamoto K, Tokunaga K, Keicho N (2005) Evaluation of microsatellite markers in association studies: a search for an immune-related susceptibility gene in sarcoidosis. *Immunogenetics* 56:861-870

[293] Tanko LB, Siddiq A, Lecoeur C, Larsen PJ, Christiansen C, Walley A, Froguel P (2005) ACDC/adiponectin and PPAR-gamma gene polymorphisms: implications for features of obesity. *Obes Res* 13:2113-2121

[294] Tartaglia LA, Dembski M, Weng X, Deng N, Culpepper J, Devos R, Richards GJ, Campfield LA, Clark FT, Deeds J, Muir C, Sanker S, Moriarty A, Moore KJ, Smutko JS, Mays GG, Wool EA, Monroe CA, Tepper RI (1995) Identification and expression cloning of a leptin receptor, OB-R. *Cell* 83:1263-1271

[295] Terry CF, Loukaci V, Green FR (2000) Cooperative influence of genetic polymorphisms on interleukin 6 transcriptional regulation. *J Biol Chem* 275:18138-18144

[296] Terwilliger JD, Goring HH (2000) Gene mapping in the 20th and 21st centuries: statistical methods, data analysis, and experimental design. *Hum Biol* 72:63-132

[297] Thomas GN, Tomlinson B, Chan JC, Sanderson JE, Cockram CS, Critchley JA (2001) Renin-angiotensin system gene polymorphisms, blood pressure, dyslipidemia,

and diabetes in Hong Kong Chinese: a significant association of tne ACE insertion/deletion polymorphism with type 2 diabetes. *Diabetes Care* 24:356-361

[298] Timpson NJ, Lawlor DA, Harbord RM, Gaunt TR, Day IN, Palmer LJ, Hattersley AT, Ebrahim S, Lowe GD, Rumley A, Davey SG (2005) C-reactive protein and its role in metabolic syndrome: mendelian randomisation study. *Lancet* 366:1954-1959

[299] Tonra JR, Ono M, Liu X, Garcia K, Jackson C, Yancopoulos GD, Wiegand SJ, Wong V (1999) Brain-derived neurotrophic factor improves blood glucose control and alleviates fasting hyperglycemia in C57BLKS-Lepr(db)/lepr(db) mice. *Diabetes* 48:588-594

[300] Tsigos C, Kyrou I, Chala E, Tsapogas P, Stavridis JC, Raptis SA, Katsilambros N (1999) Circulating tumor necrosis factor alpha concentrations are higher in abdominal versus peripheral obesity. *Metabolism* 48:1332-1335

[301] Tümer, Broxson CS, Demirel HA, Serova L, Sabban EL, Scarpace PJ (2002) Mechanisms of tyrosine hyroxylase with age. In: Nagatsu T, Nabeshima T, McCarty R, Goldstein DS (eds) Catecholamine Research: From *Molecular Insights to Clinical Medicine.* Kluwer Academic/Plenum Publisher, New York, pp 123-126

[302] Turek FW, Joshu C, Kohsaka A, Lin E, Ivanova G, McDearmon E, Laposky A, Losee-Olson S, Easton A, Jensen DR, Eckel RH, Takahashi JS, Bass J (2005) Obesity and metabolic syndrome in circadian Clock mutant mice. *Science* 308:1043-1045

[303] Um JY, Kang BK, Lee SH, Shin JY, Hong SH, Kim HM (2004) Polymorphism of the tumor necrosis factor alpha gene and waist-hip ratio in obese Korean women. *Mol Cells* 18:340-345

[304] Uysal KT, Wiesbrock SM, Marino MW, Hotamisligil GS (1997) Protection from obesity-induced insulin resistance in mice lacking TNF-alpha function. *Nature* 389:610-614

[305] van Dijk G, de Vries K, Benthem L, Nyakas C, Buwalda B, Scheurink AJ (2003) Neuroendocrinology of insulin resistance: metabolic and endocrine aspects of adiposity. *Eur J Pharmacol* 480:31-42

[306] Van CE (1990) Diurnal and ultradian rhythms in human endocrine function: a minireview. *Horm Res* 34:45-53

[307] Vicennati V, Ceroni L, Genghini S, Patton L, Pagotto U, Pasquali R (2006) Sex Difference in the Relationship between the Hypothalamic-pituitary-adrenal Axis and Sex Hormones in Obesity. *Obes Res* 14:235-243

[308] Volkow ND, Wang GJ, Fowler JS, Molina PE, Logan J, Gatley SJ, Gifford A, Ding YS, Wong C, Pappas NR, Zhu W, Swanson JM (2003) Cardiovascular effects of methylphenidate in humans are associated with increases of dopamine in brain and of epinephrine in plasma. *Psychopharmacology (Berl)* 166:264-270

[309] Vozarova B, Fernandez-Real JM, Knowler WC, Gallart L, Hanson RL, Gruber JD, Ricart W, Vendrell J, Richart C, Tataranni PA, Wolford JK (2003) The interleukin-6 (-174) G/C promoter polymorphism is associated with type-2 diabetes mellitus in Native Americans and Caucasians. *Hum Genet* 112:409-413

[310] Walker BR, Connacher AA, Lindsay RM, Webb DJ, Edwards CR (1995) Carbenoxolone increases hepatic insulin sensitivity in man: a novel role for 11-oxosteroid reductase in enhancing glucocorticoid receptor activation. *J Clin Endocrinol Metab* 80:3155-3159

[311] Walston J, Seibert M, Yen CJ, Cheskin LJ, Andersen RE (1999) Tumor necrosis factor-alpha-238 and -308 polymorphisms do not associated with traits related to obesity and insulin resistance. *Diabetes* 48:2096-2098

[312] Wang M (2005) The role of glucocorticoid action in the pathophysiology of the Metabolic Syndrome. *Nutr Metab (Lond)* 2:3

[313] Wang WY, Barratt BJ, Clayton DG, Todd JA (2005) Genome-wide association studies: theoretical and practical concerns. *Nat Rev Genet* 6:109-118

[314] Wernstedt I, Eriksson AL, Berndtsson A, Hoffstedt J, Skrtic S, Hedner T, Hulten LM, Wiklund O, Ohlsson C, Jansson JO (2004) A common polymorphism in the interleukin-6 gene promoter is associated with overweight. *Int J Obes Relat Metab Disord* 28:1272-1279

[315] White MF (1998) The IRS-signaling system: a network of docking proteins that mediate insulin and cytokine action. *Recent Prog Horm Res* 53:119-138

[316] Wilcox G (2005) Insulin and insulin resistance. *Clin Biochem Rev* 26:19-39

[317] Wilson AG, di Giovine FS, Blakemore AI, Duff GW (1992) Single base polymorphism in the human tumour necrosis factor alpha (TNF alpha) gene detectable by NcoI restriction of PCR product. *Hum Mol Genet* 1:353

[318] Wilson AG, Symons JA, McDowell TL, McDevitt HO, Duff GW (1997) Effects of a polymorphism in the human tumor necrosis factor alpha promoter on transcriptional activation. *Proc Natl Acad Sci U S A* 94:3195-3199

[319] Wilson BD, Ollmann MM, Barsh GS (1999) The role of agouti-related protein in regulating body weight. *Mol Med Today* 5:250-256

[320] Winkler G, Lakatos P, Nagy Z, Speer G, Salamon F, Szekeres O, Kovacs M, Cseh K (1998) Elevated serum tumor necrosis factor-alpha and endothelin 1 levels correlate with increased C-peptide concentration in android type obesity. *Diabetes Care* 21:1778-1779

[321] Wright S (1982) The shifting balance theory and macroevolution. *Annu Rev Genet* 16:1-19

[322] Yagita K, Tamanini F, van Der Horst GT, Okamura H (2001) Molecular mechanisms of the biological clock in cultured fibroblasts. *Science* 292:278-281

[323] Yakar S, Pennisi P, Kim CH, Zhao H, Toyoshima Y, Gavrilova O, Leroith D (2005) Studies involving the GH-IGF axis: Lessons from IGF-I and IGF-I receptor gene targeting mouse models. *J Endocrinol Invest* 28:19-22

[324] Yang G, Merrill DC, Thompson MW, Robillard JE, Sigmund CD (1994) Functional expression of the human angiotensinogen gene in transgenic mice. *J Biol Chem* 269:32497-32502

[325] Yang WS, Chuang LM (2006) Human genetics of adiponectin in the metabolic syndrome. *J Mol Med* 84:112-121

[326] Yoo SH, Yamazaki S, Lowrey PL, Shimomura K, Ko CH, Buhr ED, Siepka SM, Hong HK, Oh WJ, Yoo OJ, Menaker M, Takahashi JS (2004) PERIOD2::LUCIFERASE real-time reporting of circadian dynamics reveals persistent circadian oscillations in mouse peripheral tissues. *Proc Natl Acad Sci U S A* 101:5339-5346

[327] Yoshimura R, Xu L, Sun B, Tank AW (2004) Nicotinic and muscarinic acetylcholine receptors are essential for the long-term response of tyrosine hydroxylase gene

expression to chronic nicotine treatment in rat adrenal medulla. *Brain Res Mol Brain Res* 126:188-197

[328] Young MW, Kay SA (2001) Time zones: a comparative genetics of circadian clocks. *Nat Rev Genet* 2:702-715

[329] Yue P, Melamud E, Moult J (2006) SNPs3D: candidate gene and SNP selection for association studies. *BMC Bioinformatics* 7:166

[330] Zak NB, Shifman S, Shalom A, Darvasi A (2001) Population-based gene discovery in the post-genomic era. *Drug Discov Today* 6:1111-1115

[331] Zapata C, Nunez C, Velasco T (2002) Distribution of nonrandom associations between pairs of protein loci along the third chromosome of Drosophila melanogaster. *Genetics* 161:1539-1550

[332] Zapata C, Rodríguez S, Visedo G, Sacristán F (2001) Spectrum of nonrandom associations between microsatellite loci on human chromosome 11p15. *Genetics* 158:1235-1251

[333] Zaugg M, Schaub MC (2005) Genetic modulation of adrenergic activity in the heart and vasculature: implications for perioperative medicine. *Anesthesiology* 102:429-446

[334] Zhang L, Rao F, Wessel J, Kennedy BP, Rana BK, Taupenot L, Lillie EO, Cockburn M, Schork NJ, Ziegler MG, O'Connor DT (2004) Functional allelic heterogeneity and pleiotropy of a repeat polymorphism in tyrosine hydroxylase: prediction of catecholamines and response to stress in twins. *Physiol Genomics* 19:277-291

[335] Zhang W, Maniatis N, Rodriguez S, Miller GJ, Day IN, Gaunt TR, Collins A, Morton NE (2006) Refined Association Mapping for a Quantitative Trait: Weight in the H19-IGF2-INS-TH Region. *Ann Hum Genet* 70:in press

[336] Zhang Y, Proenca R, Maffei M, Barone M, Leopold L, Friedman JM (1994) Positional cloning of the mouse obese gene and its human homologue. *Nature* 372:425-432

[337] Ziegler MG, Kennedy B, Holland OB, Murphy D, Lake CR (1985) The effects of dopamine agonists on human cardiovascular and sympathetic nervous systems. Int J Clin Pharmacol *Ther Toxicol* 23:175-179

[338] Zondervan KT, Cardon LR (2004) The complex interplay among factors that influence allelic association. *Nat Rev Genet* 5:89-100

In: Metabolic Syndrome Research Trends
Editor: Thomas E. Batone, pp. 65-87
ISBN: 978-1-60456-224-8

Chapter II

Metabolic Syndrome in Hypertensive Subjects: Amplifying Effect on Target Organ Damage

Giuseppe Mulè[*] and Giovanni Cerasola
Dipartimento di Medicina Interna, Malattie Cardiovascolari e Nefrourologiche, Cattedra di Medicina Interna e Centro Ipertensione, Università di Palermo, Italy

Abstract

For many years, it has been recognized that hypertension tends to cluster with various metabolic abnormalities including abdominal obesity, elevated triglycerides, reduced high-density lipoprotein cholesterol, glucose intolerance and insulin resistance. This constellation of various conditions has a long list of colorful aliases, including polymetabolic syndrome, syndrome X, insulin resistance syndrome, dysmetabolic syndrome, deadly quartet and most recently metabolic syndrome (MS). The prevalence and the consequences of the MS have been difficult to assess without a commonly accepted definition. For this reason in recent years, some scientific organizations proposed working definitions for MS. Among these definitions, the one suggested by NCEP-ATPIII is the simplest and the most commonly applied.

The incidence of the MS has been increasing worldwide in parallel with an increase in overweight and obesity. The epidemic proportion reached by the metabolic syndrome represents a major public health challenge, because several lines of evidence showed that the MS, even without type 2 diabetes, confers an increased risk of cardiovascular morbidity and mortality in the general population. Recently it has been demonstrated that the adverse prognostic impact of MS may also be extended to hypertensive patients.

It is likely that the enhanced cardiovascular risk associated with MS in patients with high blood pressure may be partly mediated through an increased prevalence of preclinical cardiovascular and renal changes, such as left ventricular hypertrophy, early carotid atherosclerosis, impaired aortic elasticity, hypertensive retinopathy and microalbuminuria. Indeed, some recent reports support this notion, showing that hypertensive patients with MS exhibit, more often than those without it, these early signs of end-organ damage, most of

[*] E-mail address: giusemme@unipa.it. Phone Italy - 91- 6554345. Fax Italy - 91 – 6554331. Address for correspondence: Giuseppe Mulè, M.D., Via Monte San Calogero, 29, 90146 Palermo, Italy

which are recognized as significant independent predictors of adverse cardiovascular outcomes.

Introduction

For many years, it has been recognized that high blood pressure is often associated with various anthropometric and metabolic abnormalities including abdominal (or truncal) obesity, elevated triglycerides, reduced high-density lipoprotein (HDL) cholesterol, glucose intolerance, insulin resistance, and hyperuricemia.

Several lines of evidence support the notion that these traits occur simultaneously to a greater degree than would be expected by chance alone. This evidence supports the existence of a discrete disorder meriting in recent years the appellation as a "metabolic syndrome."

As early as 1923, Kylin recognized that hypertension, hyperuricemia, and hyperglycemia tended to occur together [1] and in 1967, Avogaro and Crepaldi described a new syndrome (plurimetabolic syndrome) characterized by an association of hyperlipidemia, obesity, and diabetes. Interestingly, the Italian authors also pointed out the frequent presence of hypertension in association with these abnormalities, as well as the high risk of coronary artery disease in subjects with this syndrome [2].

This early conceptualization of the metabolic syndrome has evolved considerably since that time and in 1985 Modan and colleagues [3] proposed that hyperinsulinaemia could be the common element accounting for the relationship between obesity, type 2 diabetes and hypertension. Ferrannini et al [4] proposed that essential hypertension per se was an insulin resistance state. He proposed that insulin resistance involved glucose but not lipid or potassium metabolism, that it was observed in peripheral tissues but not in the liver and that it was directly correlated with the degree of hypertension.

The concept of a constellation of abnormalities linked to insulin resistance as a key component was really pioneered, however, by Reaven [5] at the Banting lecture of the American Diabetes Association annual meeting in 1988. Reaven introduced the concept that an impaired in vivo insulin action was a central component of a cluster of metabolic abnormalities that did not necessarily include classical risk factors such as raised LDL-cholesterol but rather included elevated triglyceride concentrations, low HDL-cholesterol, fasting hyperinsulinaemia and elevated blood pressure. Obesity was not included as a feature of his "insulin resistance syndrome", since Reaven argued that he could find insulin resistant subjects among nonobese individuals. Reaven referred to this agglomeration of metabolic complications as Syndrome X.

Subsequently, Kaplan defined the presence of a Deadly Quartet as the concurrent association of upper body obesity, glucose intolerance, hypertriglyceridemia, and hypertension [6].

In an effort to provide uniformity in the description of this phenomenon, in recent years some scientific organizations proposed working definitions for MS.

Table 1. Comparison of definitions of the metabolic syndrome

Criteria	WHO 1999	EGIR 1999	ATP III 2001*	AACE 2003	IDF 2005
A) Glucose intolerance	Type 2 diabetes or IFG or IGT	Fasting glucose: 6.1 -6.94 mmol/L	Fasting glucose: ≥ 5.6 mmol/L	IFG or IGT	Fasting glucose: ≥ 5.6 mmol/L or Type 2 diabetes
B) Insulin resistance	Hyperinsulinaemic, euglycaemic clamp: glucose uptake in lowest 25%	Hyperinsulinaemia: top 25% of fasting insulin values from nondiabetic population			
C) High blood pressure	> 140/90 mmHg	≥140/90 mmHg and/or medication	≥130/85 mmHg or medication	≥130/85 mmHg	≥130/85 mmHg or medication
D) High triglycerides	≥ 1.7 mmol/L	≥ 2 mmol/L	≥ 1.7 mmol/L	≥ 1.7 mmol/L	≥ 1.7 mmol/L or specific treatment
E) Low HDL	< 0.9 (male) or <1.0 (female) mmol/L	<1.0 mmol/L	<1.0 mmol/L (male), <1.3 mmol/L (female)	<1.0 mmol/L (male), <1.3 mmol/L (female)	<1.0 mmol/L (male), <1.3 mmol/L (female) or specific treatment
F) Obesity	BMI >30 Kg/m^2 or waist-to-hip ratio > 0.9 (male) or >0.85 (female)	Waist circumference ≥ 94 cm (male) or ≥80 cm (female)	Waist circumference > 102 cm (male) or > 88 cm (female)		Waist circumference ≥ 94 cm (male) or ≥80 cm (female) for Europid subjects (with ethnicity specific values for other groups)
G)Microalbuminuria	Albumin excretion rate ≥ 20 µg/min or albumin:creatinine ratio ≥ 30 mg/g				

* revised in 2005

WHO (World Health Organization): MS is diagnosed when criteria A and/or B are associated with 2 or more of C, D, E, F; G.

EGIR (European Group for the Study of Insulin Resistance): MS is diagnosed when criterion B is associated with 2 or more of A, C, D, E, F.

ATP III (Third Report of the National Cholesterol Education Program Expert Panel on Detection, Evaluation, and Treatment of High Blood Cholesterol in Adults): MS is diagnosed when concur 3 or more criteria among A, C, D, E, F .

AACE (American Association of Clinical Endocrinologists): Diagnosis of MS depends on clinical judgement based on the criteria A, C, D, E and some risk factors such as family history of type 2 diabetes, hypertension, or cardiovascular disease, polycystic ovary syndrome, sedentary lifestyle, nonalcoholic hepatic steatosis, acanthosis nigricans, history of gestational diabetes or glucose intolerance, non-Caucasian ethnicity, BMI >25.0 kg/m^2 or waist circumference >40 inches in men, >35 inches in women, age >40 years.

IDF (International Diabetes Federation): MS is diagnosed when criterion F is associated with 2 or more of A, C, D, E.

IFG: *impaired fasting glucose, that is fasting glucose ≥ 5.6 mmol/L and < 6.94 mmol/L*

IGT: impaired glucose tolerance, that is fasting glucose < 6.94 mmol/L and 2-hour post-glucose challenge > 7.77 mmol/L and < 11 mmol/L

In 1998 the World Health Organization (WHO) endorsed the concept of MS and published a working definition of this syndrome [7] that was slightly revised in 1999 [8]. Alternative definitions have been proposed subsequently by the European Group for the Study of Insulin Resistance (EGIR) [9], the Third Report of the National Cholesterol Education Program Expert Panel on Detection, Evaluation, and Treatment of High Blood Cholesterol in Adults (ATP III) [10-11], the American Association of Clinical Endocrinologists (AACE) [12], and very recently the International Diabetes Federation (IDF) [13] (Table 1). All definitions include a measure of blood pressure, triglycerides, HDL cholesterol, and fasting glucose. They differ with respect to the selection of cutoff points and a measure of obesity. In contrast to the WHO and EGIR definition, in which the presence of insulin resistance is the starting point, the ATPIII definition is based on the number of abnormalities only, whereas the AACE definition considers the number of abnormalities in selected subjects with high risk of insulin resistance. The ATP III and WHO definitions implicitly include type 2 diabetes as syndrome traits. Not all experts agree that type 2 diabetes should be part of the definition, as the importance of the syndrome is that it identifies patients at increased risk for the development of diabetes [14].

The most applicable set of criteria in everyday clinical practice is that of the NCEP-ATPIII. In the ATP III definition [10], that was recently slightly revised [11], MS is diagnosed when at least three or more of the following abnormalities are present: blood pressure ≥ 130/85 mmHg (or drug treatment for hypertension), HDL < 1.0 mmol/l (40 mg/dl) in men or < 1.3 mmol/l (50 mg/dl) in women (or drug treatment for reduced HDL); fasting glucose ≥ 5.6 mmol/l (100 mg/dl) (or drug treatment for elevated glucose) ; triglycerides > 1.7 mmol/l (150 mg/dl) (or drug treatment for elevated triglycerides); and waist circumference > 102 cm in men or > 88 cm in women [11].

Very recently, the IDF has proposed a set of clinical criteria that are similar to those of the updated ATP III criteria. In fact, thresholds are identical for triglycerides, HDL-C, blood pressure, and plasma glucose. The major difference is that the IDF considered central obesity, as assessed by waist circumference, essential for diagnosis. Moreover, in this definition the waist circumference cutoffs were adjusted for different ethnic groups. In Europids (white people of European origin, regardless of where they live in the world) waist circumference thresholds were the same as that used by the EGIR, and lower than the main ATPIII recommendations [13] (Table 1).

Two major health organizations in Europe (the European Association for the Study of Diabetes -EASD) and the United States (American Diabetes Association -ADA) are calling for closer examination of the MS, questioning whether it has been appropriately defined and whether it is in fact a syndrome at all [15]. We believe, together with IDF [13] and with many experts on cardiovascular risk, that this clustering of interrelated metabolic risk factors is indeed a good basis for calling this as a syndrome. Moreover, the label of metabolic syndrome seems to be an important way to educate patients about the connection between their lifestyle, health risks, and medical outcomes. The increasing burden of type 2 diabetes and cardiovascular disease worldwide seem to justify the identification and treatment of people with MS.

Prevalence of Metabolic Syndrome in General Population and in Hypertensive Patients

The prevalence of the MS is at least in part dependent on the definition of the syndrome and its omponents and on the population studied. However, there is a strong epidemiological evidence that, regardless of the definition used, MS has reached epidemic proportions.

Using the WHO definition on participants in the Botnia Project, Isomaa et al assessed the prevalence of the syndrome and its components in a Scandinavian population in relation to glucose tolerance. The prevalence was low in middle-aged women with normal glucose tolerance (6 %) rising to about 80% in patients with type 2 diabetes [16].

Data from the US NHANES III survey indicate a high prevalence of components of the metabolic syndrome as defined by ATP III. Among 8814 adults, abdominal obesity was present in 38.6%, elevated triglycerides in 30.0%, low HDL-C in 37.1%, elevated blood pressure in 34.0% and hyperglycemia/diabetes in 12.6% [8]. Overall, the age-adjusted prevalence of the metabolic syndrome among adults aged 20 years and older in the NHANES III survey was 23.7%. However, its prevalence increases with age, affecting 7% of Americans in their 20s, and up to 44% of those in their 60s. Applied on the U.S. population in the year 2000, about 47 million US residents have the metabolic syndrome. The NHANES also showed the MS varies by sex and ethnicity, such that Mexican-Americans had the highest age-adjusted prevalence and African American the lowest. Among African-Americans and Mexican-Americans, the prevalence was higher in women than in men (57 and 26 percent higher prevalence, respectively) [17]. Other factors associated with an increased risk of metabolic syndrome included postmenopausal status, higher body mass index, smoking, low household income, high carbohydrate diet, no alcohol consumption, and physical inactivity [18].

In other US studies, 24% of subjects met the ATP III criteria and an equal proportion met the WHO criteria in the Framingham Offspring Study; 23% and 21%, respectively, in a non-Hispanic white population in the San Antonio Heart Study; and 31% and 30%, respectively, in a population of Mexican Americans [19]. Pooled data from 11 European study cohorts in subjects aged 30–89 years showed that 15.7 % of nondiabetic men and 14.2 % of nondiabetic women had the metabolic syndrome as defined by a modified WHO definition [20].

A very consistent finding in all of these studies is that the prevalence of the metabolic syndrome is highly age-dependent.

In patients with hypertension MS is highly prevalent.

Cuspidi et al found an overall prevalence of the MS of 30.2% in 447 hypertensive patients [21] and in another study of Leoncini et al a total of 25 % of 353 nondiabetic hypertensive subjects fulfilled the criteria for the MS [22].

Moreover, in the PIUMA (Progetto Ipertensione Umbria Monitoraggio Ambulatoriale) study, a prospective observational investigation of 1742 Italian adult subjects with essential hypertension, MS defined according to ATPIII criteria was diagnosed in 34% of the population [23].

An identical figure was reported in a wide group of Kuwaiti hypertensive patients attending a primary care clinic [24].

Similar data were obtained in our cross-sectional study conducted in 353 essential hypertensives and 37 % of whom had MS [25]. In our study population prevalence of MS was higher in women than it was in men (Figure 1). This greater proportion of women with MS was explained by a higher prevalence of visceral obesity and of low HDL values in females when compared to males. The over-representation of women in the MS group may appear surprising in the light of the higher percentage of males reported in MS in previous papers, such as in the Botnia study [16], in which the modified WHO criteria [7] were used to diagnose MS. These criteria require very different limits and modalities to define obesity and low HDL values, from those proposed by the NCEP-ATPIII. Indeed, when the latter definition was used it was frequently observed that there was no gender difference (17, 21-23) or there was a greater proportion of women in the MS group (26-30), as was the case in our study.

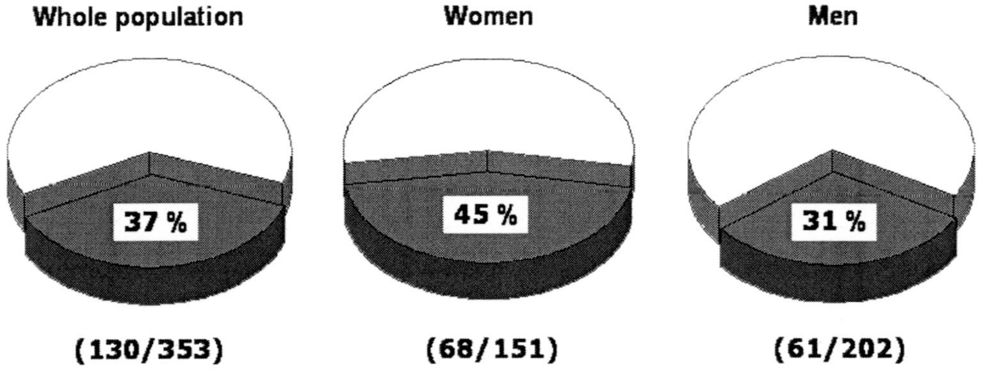

Figure 1. Prevalence of metabolic syndrome, as defined by NCEP-ATPIII criteria, among 353 nondiabetic subjects with essential hypertension and among women and men of the same population [25]

Pathophysiology of Hypertension in Metabolic Syndrome

There is general agreement that insulin resistance (IR) is the underlying cause of most cases of MS [5, 11-14]. Although the precise reason for IR is not well understood, it is widely believed that a combination of genetic and environmental factors are responsible [14]. Resistance to insulin-mediated glucose disposal determines a compensatory hyperinsulinemia, which serves to maintain glucose homeostasis. However, this initially adaptive mechanism ultimately becomes maladaptive, as the combination of IR and hyperinsulinemia eventually results in hypertension, hyperlipidemia, visceral fat distribution, pro-thrombotic tendencies, and inflammation. It is only after the pancreas is unable to meet the increased demand for insulin necessary to overcome IR that glucose control becomes abnormal. Thus hyperglycemia occurs relatively late, often many years after these other pro-atherosclerotic factors have been in place. More significantly, the earliest abnormalities in plasma glucose levels occur postprandially, at a time when fasting glucose concentrations may still be within normal limits. Therefore fasting hyperglycemia signifies a more advanced stage in the loss of normal glucose homeostasis [5, 14]. To help improve the diagnostic accuracy of fasting glucose levels in this regard, the American Diabetes Association recently revised its definition for impaired fasting glucose to include values as low as 100 mg/dL [31].

Hypertension is a major component of the metabolic syndrome. About 50% of patients with essential hypertension are insulin-resistant [4, 32], lending epidemiologic proof that high blood pressure and insulin resistance may be causally related. Independently of body mass index (BMI) or body fat distribution, hypertensive individuals, when compared with healthy normotensive controls, have higher fasting and postprandial insulin levels, and greater reductions in insulin sensitivity [33-35]. This raises the possibility of a role for insulin and/or insulin resistance in the pathogenesis of essential hypertension. Several mechanisms have been hypothesized.

Insulin, in response to states of over-nutrition, stimulates the sympathetic nervous system (SNS) to promote thermogenesis or facultative heat production, a protective mechanism to minimize weight gain and maintain lean body mass. The insulin-mediated hyperadrenergic state, however, leads to an overall increase in metabolism, heart rate, and eventually, blood pressure [36].

Other factors may contribute to the sympathetic activation occurring in MS. They include leptin, which increases in obesity and has been shown to act as a powerful sympathostimulator [37]. Sleep apnoea, which frequently occurs in obesity, may also play a role because its sympathoexcitatory effect via the hypoxic activation of the chemoreceptor reflex [38].

The enhanced SNS activity and insulin *per se* [39] stimulate renal sodium absorption leading to volume expansion and further elevation of blood pressure [36].

Moreover, insulin can cause an upregulation of angiotensin II type I receptors by post-transcriptional mechanisms such as stabilization of receptor mRNA and prolongation of its half life [40]. The increase in angiotensin II type I receptors potentiates the physiologic actions of angiotensin II that include peripheral vasoconstriction and plasma volume expansion. Furthermore, overexpression of systemic as well as local adipose tissue renin-angiotensin-aldosterone system (RAAS) has been documented in obese persons [37,41-42], and evidence suggests that it may, in part, contribute to hypertension in the insulin-resistant state [42].

In some studies elevated plasma levels of aldosterone have been reported in obese subjects [43-44]. Recent reports suggest that an adipocyte-derived factor (presumably a fatty acid) enhances the release of a hepatic stimulator of aldosterone synthesis [44-45]. Also, elevated leptin levels, associated with increased adipose tissue mass, are thought to contribute to elevated aldosterone levels [46]. Similarly, there are now several reports suggesting a positive correlation between plasma angiotensinogen (AGT) levels [47–49], plasma renin activity (PRA) [43, 50], plasma ACE activity [48], and angiotensin II type 1 receptor [49] with BMI in different human populations. It has been postulated that the elevation of AGT levels is partially a result of overexpression of tumor necrosis factor-α (TNF- α), which is documented in obese persons and animals [48]. On the other hand, increased intrarenal pressure accompanying perirenal fat deposition in obesity contributes to the increased activity of RAAS [51]. These positive correlations between RAAS activity and BMI are also true in some animal models [52], but not in obese Zucker (ob-/ob) rats with genetic leptin deficiency [53], suggesting a role for leptin in RAAS overexpression [37].

Insulin resistance/hyperinsulinemia and visceral obesity appear to predispose patients to impaired peripheral glucose utilization and nitric oxide production. Indeed, insulin is a mediator of important vasodilatory functions on the vasculature. In obese individuals with insulin resistance, these functions are lost or even reversed leading to impaired vascular relaxation and hypertension [54]. The underlying mechanism may be an impairment of nitric oxide (NO)-mediated vasodilation and a relative increase in the activity of endothelins [55]. To understand this, it is best to consider insulin action under both normal and insulin-resistant circumstances. Cellular response to insulin is mediated by means of 2 pathways: phosphatidylinositol (PI3) 3-kinase and mitogen-activated protein (MAP) kinase [56]. Activation of the PI3 kinase pathway is associated with the metabolic effects of insulin, including glucose transport, glycogen synthesis, lipid metabolism, and NO-synthesis, whereas MAP kinase activation is associated with mitogenic effects, such as cell growth and proliferation. It has been demonstrated that in the setting of insulin resistance or type 2 diabetes, insulin had reduced effects on PI3 kinase–mediated pathways, while maintaining MAP kinase activity [56-57].

Furthermore, the increased peripheral vascular resistance that often accompanies insulin resistance may be due in part to altered divalent cation metabolism ("cation inbalance") of vascular smooth muscle cells (VSMC) [4,58]. One mechanism by which insulin, and its omologous peptide insulin-like growth factor –1 (IGF-1), attenuate vascular contractility is through effects on VSMC divalent cation metabolism [58–61]. These hormones reduce Ca 2+ influx into VSMCs by attenuating both voltage- and receptor-operated Ca 2+ channels in conjunction with reductions in VSMC contractile responses. It is thought that the mechanism by which insulin and IGF-1 decreases VSMC intracellular Ca 2+ vasoconstriction is through stimulation of the Na + ,K + -ATPase pump. Recently, it has been demonstrated that insulin/IGF-I activation of the PI3-kinase pathway is critical for the ability of these peptides to stimulate the pump [62]. Thus, altered PI3-kinase responses to insulin/IGF-I, described in insulin resistance state, may explain the decreased ability of those peptides to mediate vasodilation in insulin-resistant patients. As angiotensin II has been shown to interfere with PI3 activation in VSMC and cardiomyocytes, overexpression of the tissue renin-angiotensin system (RAS) may be one of the major factors in cardiovascular insulin/IGF-I resistance [58,63].

Other factors may contribute to reduce the activity of Na + ,K + -ATPase pump in patients with MS, such as the increased production of the endogenous digoxin-like factor (EDLF) [64]. Elevated plasma levels of this substance have been documented in obese hypertensives with glucose intolerance [65] and in several circumstances characterized by volume expansion [64, 66]. This Na + ,K + -ATPase inhibitor promotes natriuresis but also produces accumulation of intracellular sodium, reducing in turn the sodium-calcium exhange system, and increasing cytosolic free calcium [65-66]. The cation imbalance may lead to enhanced VSMC contraction and to an elevation of peripheral vascular resistance. Moreover, reducing the sodium pump activity may exaggerate neural stimulation and norepinephrine overflow which might contribute to increase BP [65, 67].

On the other hand, the low levels of plasma natriuretic peptides observed in obese and overweight individuals [68] may also predispose to salt retention and increased activation of the sympathetic and renin-angiotensin systems, leading to persistent BP elevations in patients with MS [52] (Fig. 2).

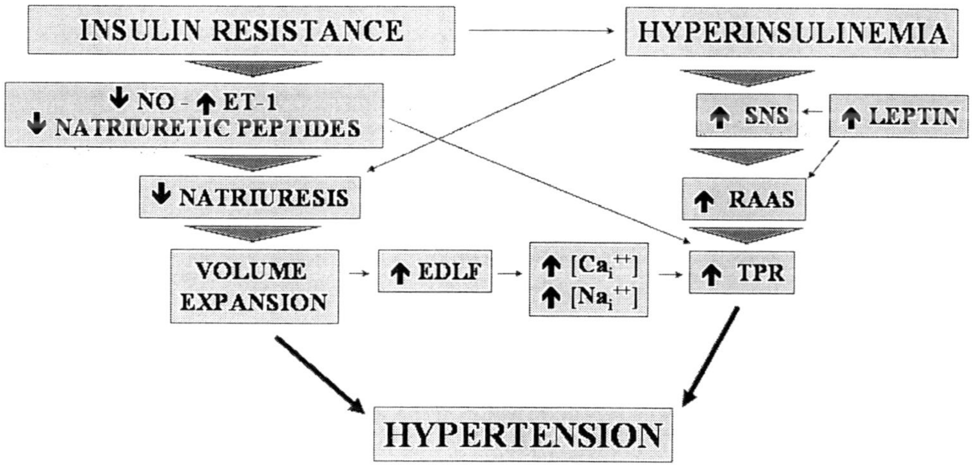

Figure 2. Hypothetical mechanisms by which insulin and/or insulin resistance may lead to high blood pressure in patients with metabolic syndrome. NO: nitric oxide; ET1: Endothelin-1; SNS: sympathetic nervous system; RAAS: Renin-angiotensin-aldosterone system; TPR: total peripheral resistance; EDLF: endogenous digoxin-like factor; [Ca_i^{++}]: intracellular concentration of calcium; [Na_i^{++}]: intracellular concentration of sodium.

Metabolic Syndrome and Cardiovascular Risk

The high prevalence of the MS is of considerable concern because several studies suggest that people with the MS are at increased risk for developing diabetes mellitus [69-74] and cardiovascular disease and dying prematurely [16, 20, 23, 73-79].

The cardiovascular risk associated with the metabolic syndrome, according to the WHO definition, has been firstly reported from the Botnia Study in a Scandinavian population. The prevalence of coronary heart disease and stroke was increased threefold in subjects with the syndrome. During a 6.9 year prospective follow-up the cardiovascular mortality was markedly increased in subjects with the syndrome (12.2 vs. 2.2%) [16]. Subsequently, the results from a Finnish prospective study have been published [75]. A cohort of 1209 men (42–60 years old and without cardiovascular disease or diabetes at baseline) was followed for 11.4 years. Both the WHO and the NCEP criteria of the metabolic syndrome were applied to the study cohort. The highest risk (3 to 4-fold) associated with the MS (both definitions) was for coronary heart disease mortality [75]. Overall mortality was also increased in men with the metabolic syndrome but this risk was lower, indicating that the impact on overall mortality was mediated mainly by CHD mortality.

Using a modified ATP-III definition with BMI in place of waist circumference, the MS was found to predict cardiovascular morbidity in hypercholesterolemic men [73], in apparently healthy women [76], and in 10,384 patients with previous myocardial infarction [74].

Very recently, Ford summarized the estimates of relative risk for cardiovascular disease and diabetes reported from prospective studies in samples from the general population using definitions of the MS developed by the NCEP-ATPIII and WHO. For studies that used the exact NCEP definition of the MS, random-effects estimates of combined relative risk were

2.99 (1.96–4.57) for diabetes and 1.65 (1.38–1.99) for cardiovascular disease. For studies that used the most exact WHO definition of the metabolic syndrome, the fixed-effects estimates of relative risk were 1.93 (1.39–2.67) for cardiovascular disease; the fixed-effects estimate was 2.60 (1.55–4.38) for coronary heart disease [79].

The adverse prognostic impact of the MS, has also been confirmed in hypertensive patients [23].

In the aforementioned PIUMA study, hypertensive participants with MS had an increased risk of developing cardiac and cerebrovascular events, independently of traditional cardiovascular risk factors, including left ventricular hypertrophy and 24-h blood pressure. Most notably, the association between the metabolic syndrome and future cardiovascular morbidity also held in patients without diabetes mellitus at the baseline examination [23].

It is conceivable that the increased cardiovascular risk conferred by MS in hypertensive subjects may in part be mediated through preclinical cardiac and renal organ damage. Indeed, major cardiovascular events in most hypertensive patients are preceded by the development of asymptomatic cardiovascular and renal structural and functional abnormalities [80]; these abnormalities, such as left ventricular hypertrophy, carotid atherosclerosis, arterial stiffness and microalbuminuria, are recognized as significant independent predictors of adverse cardiovascular outcomes [81-85].

Metabolic Syndrome and Hypertensive Target Organ Damage

Recently we performed a cross-sectional study to assess the impact of MS, defined according to the NCEP-ATPIII criteria, on some cardiac, renal and retinal markers of target organ damage, in 353 nondiabetic young and middle aged essential hypertensives without clinical or laboratory evidence of cardiovascular and renal diseases [25].

In a subset of untreated subjects of the same population we also explored the carotid-femoral pulse wave velocity (PWV), a measure of aortic stiffness, in patients with and without MS [86].

Hypertensive patients with MS exhibited higher left ventricular (LV) mass on echocardiography [either normalized by body surface area (BSA) or by height elevated by a power of 2.7] (Figure 3), relative wall thickness (0.43 ± 0.08 vs 0.39 ± 0.07; $p = 0.0002$), left atrial size (36.4 ± 4.6 vs 33.9 ± 4.4; $p < 0.00001$), and greater prevalence of LV hypertrophy (Figure 4), lower mid-wall fractional shortening (16.8 ± 1.7 % vs 17.5 ± 1.6 % ; $p < 0.002$) and a longer E-wave deceleration time (226.8 ± 50.1 % vs 201.8 ± 30.8 % ; $p < 0.0001$) than subjects without MS [25]. These results were maintained even after correction for several confounding variables, such as age, gender distribution, severity and duration of hypertension and previous antihypertensive therapy. In particular, after adjustment for these covariates, the likelihood of LV hypertrophy was 2.89- fold (95 % interval, 1.68 to 4.98) higher in subjects with MS than in those without it, when LV mass was indexed by $height^{2.7}$ ($LVMH^{2.7}$) (Figure 5) . Moreover, the higher the number of components of the MS, the greater the $LVMH^{2.7}$ (Figure 6). It is noteworthy that the relationship between MS and LV mass was confirmed in multivariate regression models including MS together with its individual components, as independent variables [25]; this suggests that MS may have a deleterious effect on cardiac structure over and above the potential contribution of each single component of this syndrome, and that the confluence of abnormalities that comprise MS may have a synergistic negative impact on LV mass.

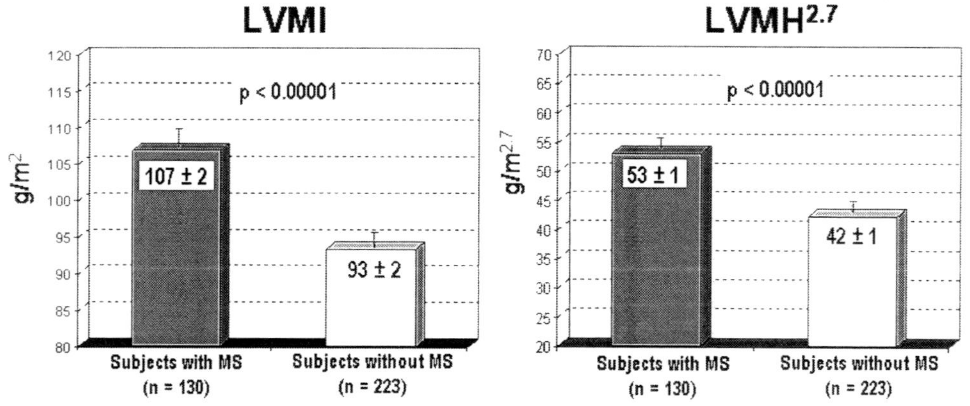

Figure 3. Left ventricular mass indexed by body surface area (LVMI) and by height elevated by a power of 2.7 (LVMH2.7) in hypertensive subjects with and without metabolic syndrome (MS). Data are given as means ± SEM [25]

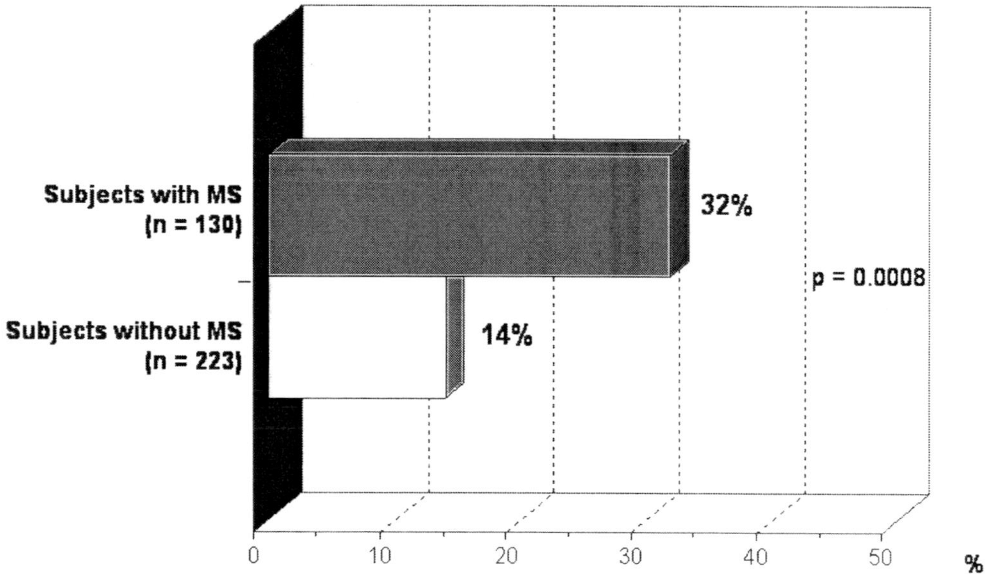

Figure 4. Prevalence of left ventricular hypertrophy (LVH), defined as LVMI ≥ 125 g/m2 for men and ≥ 110 g/m2 for women, in hypertensive subjects with and without metabolic syndrome. When LVH was defined as LVMH2.7 ≥ 49.2 g/ m2.7 for men and ≥ 46.7 g/ m2.7 for women (B), the prevalence of LVH was 58% in patients with MS and 25% in those whithout MS (p< 0.00001) [25].

The data of our study, obtained from a wide sample of Caucasian hypertensive patients, are in agreement with the results of four other investigations conducted on the general population [26, 87] and in hypertensive subjects [21-22].

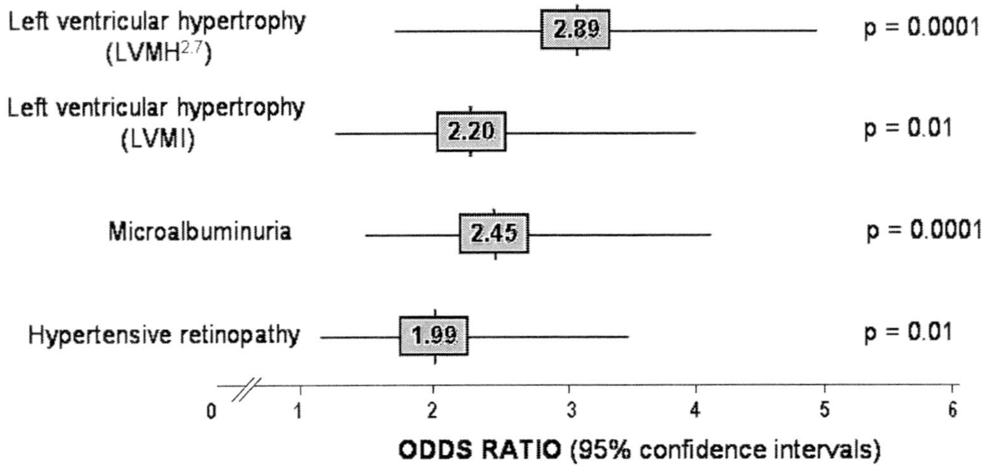

Figure 5. Adjusted risk associated with metabolic syndrome of left ventricular hypertrophy (defined as LVMH2.7 ≥ 49.2/46.7 g/m2.7 M/W or as LVMI ≥ 125/110 g/m2 M/W), of microalbuminuria (albumin excretion rate ≥ 20 mcg/min) and of hypertensive retinopathy (all grades of Keith-Wagener classification ≥ 1). Adjustment was made for age, sex, 24-h systolic BP, 24-h diastolic BP, duration of hypertension and previous antihypertensive therapy [25].

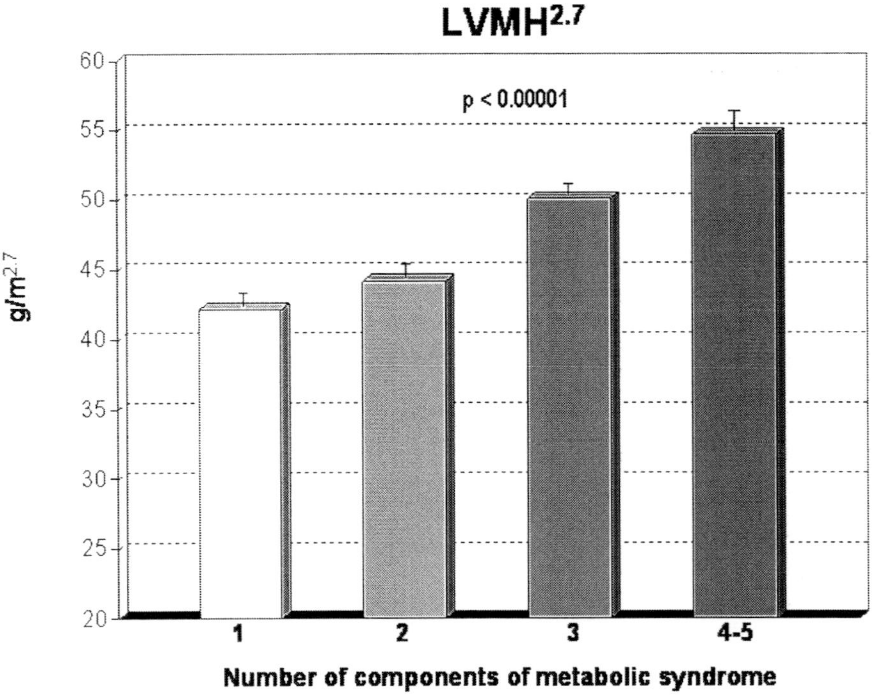

Figure 6. Age and gender-adjusted left ventricular mass, indexed by height elevated by a power of 2.7 (LVMH2.7), among 354 hypertensive subjects grouped by number of components of the metabolic syndrome. Data are given as means ± SEM. P refers to ANOVA for intergroup comparison. Subjects with 4 and 5 characteristics of metabolic syndrome were included in the same group, because only 8 patients had all five components of MS.

In the Strong Heart Study, a longitudinal investigation performed in American Indian communities, a subset of the study population, including 1436 nondiabetic participants without cardiovascular disease (61.2 % of whom had high BP), was examined to analyze the impact of the MS on cardiac structure and function. Subjects with MS showed greater LV dimension, mass and relative wall thickness, and left atrial diameter, and a higher prevalence of LV hypertrophy, with lower mid-wall shortening than individuals who did not have MS [26].

More recently, in a group of 1572 black adults participating to the Atherosclerosis Risk in Communities (ARIC) Study, it has been demonstrated that age-adjusted LV mass indexed by height increased in a stepwise gradient with increasing number of MS components [87]. Associations were diminished slightly by adjustment for smoking, alcohol intake, and education; additional adjustment for waist circumference resulted in some attenuation, but associations remained statistically significant. Analyses focusing on components of LV mass revealed that posterior wall and interventricular septal thickness, but not LV chamber size, were significantly and independently associated in general with the number of MS disorders [87].

Furthermore, Cuspidi et al. in 447 untreated middle-aged hypertensives, found that patients with MS had a more pronounced cardiac and extra-cardiac involvement than those without it [21].

Leoncini et al. in 354 nondiabetic patients with primary hypertension, observed that subjects with MS exhibited higher LV mass index, and a greater prevalence of LV hypertrophy [22].

Interestingly, they also found that the presence of MS entailed a twofold greater risk for microalbuminuria and carotid structural abnormalities (intima-media thickening and atherosclerotic plaques) [22].

Several potential mechanisms may be responsible for these findings.

The association of MS with cardiac hypertrophy might be explained by insulin resistance and the accompanying compensatory hyperinsulinemia, which are regarded as the pathophysiological key features underlying the MS [5, 11-14]. Trophic effects of insulin on myocardial tissue have been demonstrated in cell cultures and animal models [88] and could be mediated, at least in part, by the insulin-like growth factor-1 (IGF-1) receptors [89-90]. However, the in vivo studies that have sought an association between insulin and LV mass have yielded conflicting results [90-93] and therefore a direct relationship between hyperinsulinemia and LV hypertrophy in humans remains still to be clarified.

In addition, insulin may affect LV mass indirectly by increasing sodium retention [39] therefore coupling another important (although not unanimously considered) stimulus for LV growth. Sodium intake has been shown to be a potent determinant of LV growth in hypertensive as well as in normotensive experimental animal models, through complex mechanisms that involve circulating volume expansion and possible activation of the tissue renin-angiotensin system [94-95].

A potential mechanism linking MS to cardiac hypertrophy may be also sympathetic activation induced by elevated insulin levels [96]. Direct growth-stimulating effect on myocardial cells of catecholamines has long been suggested on the basis of several experimental and animal studies [97-98] and it has been recently confirmed in humans by using microneurography and radiotracer dilution methods [99].

Another possible biological mediator of the association between MS and LV mass may be endothelin-1 (ET-1). A positive relationship between insulin and endothelin-1 has been demonstrated in vitro and vivo [55, 100] and several studies reported that ET-1 levels in obese subjects are increased [101-102]. Mounting evidence from both clinical and animal studies shows that ET-1 plays an important role in the development of cardiac hypertrophy [103-104].

It is now widely accepted that white adipose tissue is an active endocrine gland, that secretes a number of peptide hormones, including components of the renin-angiotensin-system [42]. Apart from expressing angiotensin peptides locally, it has been suggested that adipose tissue may contribute to circulating angiotensin II, a potent growth factor in myocardial tissue [50]. Among the other adipocyte-derived peptides, leptin, whose plasma concentrations are strongly related to the principal components of the MS [105], has been recently evaluated for its potential mitogenic effect in cardiomyocytes, with discrepant results [93, 106-107].

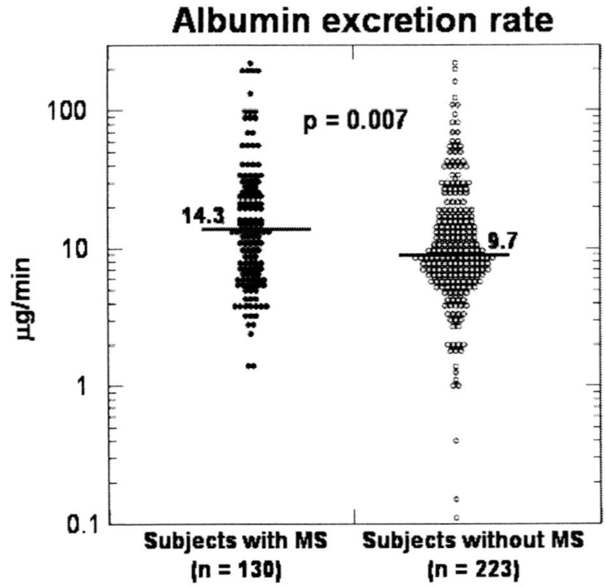

Figure 7. Albumin excretion rate, in logarithmic scale, in hypertensive subjects with and in those without metabolic syndrome. Horizontal lines and the numbers above the lines indicate median values [25].

There are other important findings from our study that deserve special mention: the greater level of albumin excretion rate (Figure 7) and the consequent higher prevalence of microalbuminuria (36.2 % vs 19.3 %; $p = 0.002$) observed in hypertensive subjects with MS in comparison to those without it (Figure 5) [25].

These results concur with the abovementioned studies of Cuspidi [21] and Leoncini [22] and with a cross-sectional evaluation of the NANHES III (Third National Health and Nutrition Examination Survey) data in 5360 US civilian non-institutionalized subjects, in whom a close association was found between microalbuminuria and MS (defined according to NCEP-ATPIII criteria) [27].

The relationship between albumin excretion rate (AER) and MS is so close that WHO recommendations include microalbuminuria among the criteria for diagnosing MS [7-8]. However, the inclusion of microalbuminuria as part of the metabolic syndrome has been controversial because its association with insulin resistance has been described in several, but not all, reports [35, 108-11].

The value of microalbuminuria as a marker of target organ damage [84, 112] and powerful predictor of cardiovascular events and total mortality is well-established [16, 85, 113-115]. In the previously quoted Botnia study, Isomaa et al found that microalbuminuria, among the individual components of the metabolic syndrome (WHO definition), conferred the strongest risk of cardiovascular disease death when compared to obesity, hypertension, and dyslipidemia [16].

The finding of microalbuminuria along with other components of the metabolic syndrome may increase the specificity of this risk prediction tool, and may explain the increased cardiovascular disease risk seen with this syndrome.

Another finding from our study merits a comment: the increased prevalence of grade I and grade II hypertensive retinopathy observed in subjects with MS when compared to persons without MS (Figure 5) [25]. This result is in keeping with a recent cross-sectional investigation involving 11,265 participants in the ARIC Study (Atherosclerosis Risk in Communities Study), in which associations were noted between MS and arterio-venous nicking, focal arteriolar narrowing and generalized arteriolar narrowing, even in people without diabetes or hypertension [116].

However, the prognostic significance of this finding is unclear, because studies exploring the association between the first two degrees of hypertensive retinopathy and cardiovascular outcomes have shown inconsistent results [117].

Unlike eye ground examination, the clinical and prognostic value of increased aortic stiffness seems to be more consistently demonstrated; there is a growing awareness that large artery stiffening is a powerful predictor of cardiovascular morbidity and mortality [83].

Pulse wave velocity (PVW) is the most widely used measure of arterial stiffness. The basic principle of PWV assessment is that the pulse wave runs along the arterial tree at a speed which depends upon the elasticity of the wall itself: the stiffer (i.e. less elastic) the wall, the higher the velocity of propagation. PWV measured along the aortic and aortoiliac pathway is the most clinically relevant since the aorta and its first branches are responsible for most of the pathophysiological effects of arterial stiffness [83].

When we assess the influence of MS on carotid-femoral PWV, an index of aortic stiffness, in a sample of never treated nondiabetic patients with essential hypertension, we found faster carotid-femoral PWV in subjects with MS when compared to those without it (10.2 $\pm$ 1.6 vs 9.2 $\pm$1.5 m/sec; $p= 0.005$). [86]. This difference held after controlling by ANCOVA for age, 24-h mean BP and gender and lost its statistical significance after further adjustment for albumin excretion rate. This latter finding may be explained since microalbuminuria may reflect impaired endothelial function [84, 113] and evidence from several studies suggests that the endothelium is an important regulator of arterial stiffness [83]. In addition, a relationship between AER and carotid-femoral PWV has been previously documented [118]. Similar results were obtained when MS was defined using the WHO modified criteria (Figure 8).

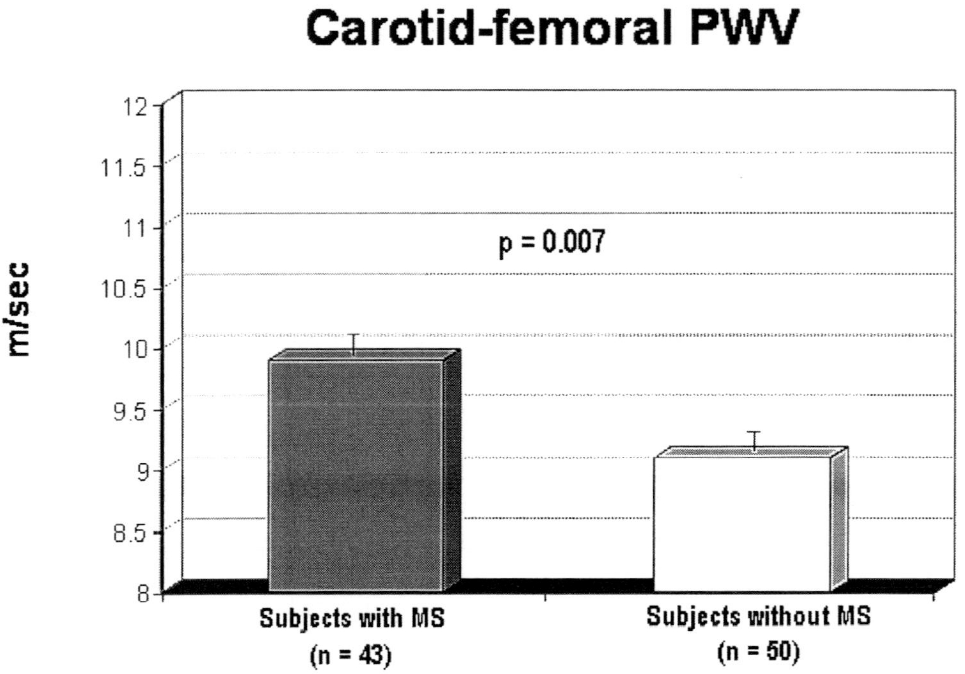

Figure 8. Age-adjusted carotid-femoral pulse wave velocity (PWV) in never treated essential hypertensive patients with and without metabolic syndrome, defined using World Health Organization criteria (modified). Data are given as mean ± SEM [25].

Our data are in agreement with the results of Schillaci et al that, in 169 newly diagnosed nondiabetic hypertensive subjects, observed a greater aortic PWV in the subgroup with MS, whereas upper limb PWV did not differ in the groups with and without MS [119].

Moreover, an independent relationship has been reported of MS, defined according to NCEP-ATPIII, with increased stiffness of the carotid artery in subjects participating in the Baltimore Longitudinal Study on Aging [120].

In conclusion, several lines of evidence suggest that MS may amplify hypertension-related cardiovascular and renal changes, over and above the potential contribution of each single component of this syndrome. This may partly explain the enhanced cardiovascular risk associated with MS, since these markers of target organ damage are well-known predictors of cardiovascular events. Therefore, the simple search for the metabolic syndrome in hypertensive patients may enable the clinician to better assess the absolute cardiovascular risk. Once this syndrome is properly identified, aggressive implementation of therapeutic lifestyle change and appropriate medication can greatly reduce its adverse prognostic impact.

Acknowledgments

This work was supported in part by a grant from the Italian Ministry for University and Scientific Research (MURST).

References

[1] Kylin E. Studien ueber das hypertonie-hyperglykämie-hyperurikämiesyndrom. *Zentralblatt fuer Innere Medizin* 1923; 44:105–127.

[2] Avogaro P, Crepaldi G, Enzi G, et al . Associazione di iperlipidemia, diabete mellito e obesità di medio grado. *Acta Diabetol Lat* 1967; 4:36-41.

[3] Modan M, Halkin H, Almog S, et al. Hyperinsulinemia. A link between hypertension obesity and glucose intolerance. *J Clin Invest* 1985;75:809-817.

[4] Ferrannini E, Buzzigoli G, Bonadonna R, et al. Insulin resistance in essential hypertension. *N Engl J Med* 1987;317:350-357.

[5] Reaven GM. Banting lecture 1988. Role of insulin resistance in human disease. *Diabetes* 1988; 37:1595-1607.

[6] Kaplan NM. The deadly quartet. Upper body adiposity, glucose intolerance, hypertriglyceridemia and hypertension. *Arch Intern Med* 1989; 149: 1514-1520.

[7] Alberti KG, Zimmet PZ. Definition, diagnosis and classification of diabetes mellitus and its complications. Part 1: diagnosis and classification of diabetes mellitus: provisional report of a WHO consultation. *Diabet Med* 1998;15: 539–553.

[8] World Health Organization. Definition, diagnosis and classification of diabetes mellitus and its complications: report of a WHO Consultation. Part 1: diagnosis and classification of diabetes mellitus. Geneva, Switzerland: World Health Organization; 1999. Available at: http://whqlibdoc.who.int/hq/1999/WHO_NCD_NCS_99.2.pdf. Accessed October 12, 2005.

[9] Balkau B, Charles MA: Comment on the provisional report from the WHO consultation. European Group for the Study of Insulin Resistance. *Diabet Med* 1999; 16: 442-443.

[10] Executive Summary of The Third Report of The National Cholesterol Education Program (NCEP) Expert Panel on Detection, Evaluation, And Treatment of High Blood Cholesterol In Adults (Adult Treatment Panel III). *JAMA* 2001;285:2486-2497.

[11] Grundy SM, Cleeman JI, Daniels SR, et al. Diagnosis and Management of the Metabolic Syndrome. An American Heart Association/ National Heart, Lung, and Blood Institute Scientific Statement. *Circulatio*n 2005 112: 2735 - 2752.

[12] Einhorn D, Reaven GM, Cobin RH, et al. American College of Endocrinology position statement on the insulin resistance syndrome. *Endocr Pract* 2003; 9:237–252.

[13] Alberti KGMM, Zimmet P, Shaw J for the IDF Epidemiology Task Force Consensus Group. The metabolic syndrome – a new worldwide definition. *Lancet* 2005; 366: 1059–1062

[14] Eckel RH, Grundy SM, Zimmet PZ. The metabolic syndrome. *Lancet* 2005; 365: 1415–1428

[15] Kahn R, Buse J, Ferrannini E, et al.: The metabolic syndrome: Time for a critical appraisal: Joint statement from the American Diabetes Association and the European Association for the Study of Diabetes. *Diabetes Care* 28:2289–2304, 2005

[16] Isomaa B, Almgren P, Tuomi T, et al Cardiovascular morbidity and mortality associated with the metabolic syndrome. *Diabetes Care* 2001; 24: 683 – 689.

[17] Ford ES, Giles WH, Dietz WH. Prevalence of metabolic syndrome among US adults: findings from the Third National Health and Nutrition Examination Survey. JAMA 2002;287:356– 359

[18] Park YW, Zhu S, Palaniappan L, et al. The metabolic syndrome: prevalence and associated risk factor findings in the US population from the Third National Health and Nutrition Examination Survey, 1988–1994. *Arch Intern Med.* 2003;163: 427–436

[19] Meigs JB, Wilson PWF, Nathan DM, et al. Prevalence and characteristics of the metabolic syndrome in the San Antonio Heart and Framingham Offspring Studies. *Diabetes* 2003; 52: 2160–2167.

[20] Hu G, Qiao Q, Tuomilehto J, et al. Prevalence of the metabolic syndrome and its relation to all-cause and cardiovascular mortality in nondiabetic European men and women. *Arch Intern Med* 2004; 164: 1066–1076.

[21] Cuspidi C, Meani S, Fusi V et al. Metabolic syndrome and target organ damage in untreated essential hypertensives. *J Hypertens* 2004, 22; 1991-1998.

[22] Leoncini G, Ratto E, Viazzi F, et al Metabolic syndrome is associated with early signs of organ damage in nondiabetic, hypertensive patients. *J Intern Med* 2005; 257: 454–460

[23] Schillaci G, Pirro M, Vaudo G, et al. Prognostic value of the metabolic syndrome in essential hypertension. *J Am Coll Cardiol.* 2004; 43:1817-1822.

[24] Sorkhou EI, Al-Qallaf B, Al-Namash HA, et al . Prevalence of metabolic syndrome among hypertensive patients attending a primary care clinic in Kuwait. *Med Princ Pract* 2004;13: 39-42.

[25] Mule' G, Nardi E, Cottone S, et al. Influence of metabolic syndrome on hypertension-related target organ damage. *J Intern Med* 2005; 257: 503–513.

[26] Chinali M, Devereux RB, Howard BW, et al. Comparison of cardiac structure and function in American Indians with and without the metabolic syndrome. (The Strong Heart Study). *Am J Cardiol* 2004; 93: 40–44.

[27] Palaniappan L, Carnethon M, and Fortmann SP. Association between microalbuminuria and the metabolic syndrome: NHANES III. *Am J Hypertens* 2003; 16: 952-958.

[28] Miccoli R, Bianchi C, Odoguardi L et al. Prevalence of the metabolic syndrome among Italian adults according to ATP III definition. *Nutr Metab Cardiovasc Dis* 2005, 15: 250-254

[29] Jørgensen ME, Bjerregaard P, Gyntelberg F, and the Greenland Population Study. Prevalence of the metabolic syndrome among the Inuit in Greenland. A comparison between two proposed definitions. *Diabet Med* 2004; 21: 1237–1242.

[30] Gupta R, Deedwania PC, Gupta A, et al. Prevalence of metabolic syndrome in an Indian urban population. *Int J Cardiol* 2004; 97: 257– 261.

[31] Genuth S, Alberti KG, Bennett P, et al. Expert Committee on the Diagnosis and Classification of Diabetes Mellitus. Follow-up report on the diagnosis of diabetes mellitus. *Diabetes Care.* 2003; 26: 3160 –3167.

[32] Bonora E, Kiechl S, Willeit J, et al. Prevalence of insulin resistance in metabolic disorders: the Bruneck Study. *Diabetes* 1998; 47: 1643–1649.

[33] Dengel DR, Pratley RE, Hagberg JM, et al. Impaired insulin sensitivity and maximal responsiveness in older hypertensive men. *Hypertension* 1994, 23: 320–324

[34] Shen DC, Shieh SM, Fuh MM, et al.: Resistance to insulin-stimulated-glucose uptake in patients with hypertension. *J Clin Endocrinol Metab* 1988, 66:580–583.

[35] Andronico G, Ferrara L, Mulè G, et al Insulin, sodium-lithium countertransport, and microalbuminuria in hypertensive patients. *Hypertension* 1998; 31:110-113.

[36] Reaven GM, Lithell H, Landsberg L. Hypertension and associated metabolic abnormalities--the role of insulin resistance and the sympathoadrenal system. *N Engl J Med* 1996, 334: 374–381.

[37] Hall JE, Hildebrandt DA, Kuo J. Obesity hypertension: role of leptin and sympathetic nervous system. *Am J Hypertens* 2001, 14: 103S–115S.

[38] Wolk R, Shamsuzzaman ASM, Somers VK. Obesity, sleep apnea, and hypertension *Hypertension* 2003; 42: 1067-1074.

[39] DeFronzo RA, Cooke CR, Andres R, et al. The effect of insulin on renal handling of sodium, potassium, calcium, and phosphate in man. *J Clin Invest* 1975;55: 845– 855.

[40] Nickenig G, Roling J, Strehlow K, *et al.*: Insulin induces upregulation of vascular AT1 receptor gene expression by posttranscriptional mechanisms. *Circulation* 1998, 98: 2453–2460.

[41] Mark AL, Correia M, Morgan DA, et al. State-of-the-art-lecture: Obesity-induced hypertension: new concepts from the emerging biology of obesity. *Hypertension* 1999, 3: 537–541.

[42] Engeli S, Negrel R, Sharma AM. Physiology and pathophysiology of the adipose tissue renin-angiotensin system. *Hypertension* 2000;35: 1270–1277.

[43] Andronico G, Cottone S, Mule' G et al. Insulin, renin-aldosterone system and blood pressure in obese people. *Int J Obes* 2001: 25, 239-242

[44] Goodfriend TL, Egan BM, Kelley DE. Aldosterone in obesity. *Endocr Res* 1998, 24:789–796.

[45] Goodfriend TL, Egan BM, Kelley DE. Plasma aldosterone, plasma lipoproteins, obesity and insulin resistance in humans. *Prostaglandins Leukot Essent Fatty Acids* 1999, 60:401–405.

[46] Suter PM, Locher R, Hasler E, et al. Is there a role for the ob gene product leptin in essential hypertension? *Am J Hypertens* 1998, 11:1305–1311.

[47] Schorr U, Blaschke K, Turan S, et al. Relationship between angiotensinogen, leptin and blood pressure levels in young normotensive men. *J Hypertens* 1998, 16:1475–1480.

[48] Cooper R, McFarlane Anderson N, et al. ACE, angiotensinogen and obesity: a potential pathway leading to hypertension. *J Hum Hypertens* 1997, 11:107–111.

[49] Cooper R, Forrester T, Ogunbiyi O, et al. Angiotensinogen levels and obesity in four black populations. ICSHIB investigators. *J Hypertens* 1998, 16:571–575.

[50] Uckaya G, Ozata M, Sonmez A, et al. Plasma leptin levels strongly correlate with plasma renin activity in patients with essential hypertension. *Horm Metab Res* 1999, 31:435–438.

[51] Engeli S, Sharma AM. The renin-angiotensin system and natriuretic peptides in obesity-associated hypertension. *J Mol Med* 2001, 79: 21–29.

[52] Hall JE, Brands MW, Dixon WN, et al. Obesity-induced hypertension: renal function and systemic hemodynamics. *Hypertension* 1993, 22:292–299.

[53] Alonso-Galicia M, Brands MW, Zappe DH, et al Hypertension in obese Zucker rats. Role of angiotensin II and adrenergic activity. *Hypertension* 1996, 28:1047–1054.

[54] Steinberg HO, Chaker H, Leaming R, et al. Obesity/insulin resistance is associated with endothelial dysfunction. Implications for the syndrome of insulin resistance. *J Clin Invest* 1996, 97: 2601–2610.

[55] Andronico G, Mangano M, Mulè G, et al *In vivo* relationship between insulin and endothelin role of insulin-resistance. *J Hum Hypertens* 1997; 11: 63–66

[56] Cusi K, Maezono K, Osman A, et al. Insulin resistance differentially affects the PI 3-kinase– and MAP kinase–mediated signaling in human muscle. *J Clin Invest* 2000;105: 311–320.

[57] Montagnani M, Golovchenko I, Kim I, et al . Inhibition of phosphatidylinositol 3-kinase enhances mitogenic actions of insulin in endothelial cells. *J Biol Chem* 2002; 277:1794–1799.

[58] Sowers JR, Epstein M. Diabetes mellitus and associated hypertension, vascular disease, and nephropathy: an update. *Hypertension* 1995, 26: 869–879.

[59] Standley PR, Zhang F, Ram JL, et al. Insulin attenuates vasopressin-induced calcium transient and voltage-dependent calcium response in rat vascular smooth muscle cells. *J Clin Invest* 1991, 88:1230–1236.

[60] Kahn AM, Seidel CL, Allen JC, et al. Insulin reduces contraction and intracellular calcium concentration in vascular smooth muscle. *Hypertension* 1993, 22:735–742.

[61] Sowers JR. Effects of insulin and IGF-I on vascular smooth muscle glucose and cation metabolism. *Diabetes* 1996; 45:S47–S51

[62] Li D, Sweeney G, Wang Q, Klip A: Participation of PI3K and atypical PKC in Na+-K+-pump stimulation by IGF-I in VSMC. *Am J Physiol* 1999; 276: H2109–H2116.

[63] McFarlane SI, Banerji M, Sowers JR. Insulin resistance and cardiovascular disease. *J Clin Endocrinol Metab* 2001, 86:713–718.

[64] Haddy FG. Endogenous digitalis-like factor or factors. *N Engl J Med* 1987; 361: 621-623.

[65] Andronico G, Mulè G, Mangano MT, et al. Insulin resistance and endogenous digoxin-like factor in obese hypertensive patients with glucose intolerance. *Acta Diabetol* 1992: 28: 203-205.

[66] Panmani MB, Burris JF, Jemionek JF, et al. Humoral Na + ,K + pump inhibitory activity in essential hypertension and in normotensive subjects after acute volume expansion. *Am J Hypertens* 1989; 2: 524-531.

[67] Tsuda K, Tsuda S, Shima H, et al. Facilitatory effects of ouabain and digitalis-like substances on adrenergic trasmission in hypertension. *Am J Hypertens* 2: 465-467, 1989

[68] Wang TJ, Larson MG, Daniel D, et al. Impact of Obesity on Plasma Natriuretic Peptide Levels. *Circulation.* 109:594-600, 2004.

[69] Laaksonen DE, Lakka HM, Niskanen LK et al Metabolic syndrome and development of diabetes mellitus: application and validation of recently suggested definitions of the metabolic syndrome in a prospective cohort study. *Am J Epidemiol* 2002; 156:1070–1077.

[70] Resnick HE, Jones K, Ruotolo G, et al. Insulin resistance, the metabolic syndrome, and risk of incident cardiovascular disease in nondiabetic american indians: the Strong Heart Study. *Diabetes Care* 2003; 26: 861– 867.

[71] Lorenzo C, Okoloise M, Williams K, the San Antonio Heart Study. The metabolic syndrome as predictor of type 2 diabetes: the San Antonio Heart Study. *Diabetes Care* 2003; 26:3153–3159.

[72] Stern MP, Williams K, Gonzalez-Villalpando C, et al. Does the metabolic syndrome improve identification of individuals at risk of type 2 diabetes and/or cardiovascular disease? *Diabetes Care* 2004; 27:2676–2681.

[73] Sattar N, Gaw A, Scherbakova O, et al. Metabolic syndrome with and without C-reactive protein as a predictor of coronary heart disease and diabetes in the West of Scotland Coronary Prevention Study. *Circulation* 2003;108:414–419.

[74] Levatesi G, Macchia A, Marfisi RM. Metabolic syndrome and risk of cardiovascular events after myocardial infarction. *J Am Coll Cardiol* 2005; 46:277– 283)

[75] Lakka HM, Laaksonen DE, Lakka TA, et al. The metabolic syndrome and total and cardiovascular disease mortality in middle-aged men. *JAMA* 2002; 288: 2709–2716.

[76] Ridker PM, Buring JE, Cook NR, Rifai N. C-reactive protein, the metabolic syndrome, and risk of incident cardiovascular events: an 8-year follow-up of 14,719 initially healthy American women. *Circulation* 2003;107:391–397.

[77] Malik S, Wong ND, Franklin SS. Impact of the metabolic syndrome on mortality from coronary heart disease, cardiovascular disease, and all causes in United States adults. *Circulation* 2004;110:1239-1244.

[78] Dekker JM, Girman C, Rhodes T et al. Metabolic syndrome and 10-year cardiovascular disease risk in the Hoorn study. *Circulation* 2005;112:666-673.

[79] Ford ES. Risks for all-cause mortality, cardiovascular disease, and diabetes associated with the metabolic syndrome. A summary of the evidence. *Diabetes Care* 2005; 28:1769–1778

[80] Devereux RB, Alderman MH. Role of preclinical cardiovascular disease in the evolution from risk factor exposure to development of morbid events. *Circulation* 1993; 88: 1444–1455.

[81] Vakili BA, Okin PM, and Devereux RB. Prognostic implications of left ventricular hypertrophy. *Am Heart J* 2001;141: 334-341.

[82] O'Leary DH, Polak JF, Kronmal RA, et al. Carotid-artery intima and media thickness as a risk factor for myocardial infarction and stroke in older adults. Cardiovascular Health Study Collaborative Research Group. *N Engl J Med* 1999; 340: 14–22.

[83] Oliver JJ, Webb DJ. Noninvasive assessment of arterial stiffness and risk of atherosclerotic events. *Arterioscler Thromb Vasc Biol* 2003; 23:554-566.

[84] Karalliedde J and Viberti G. Microalbuminuria and cardiovascular risk *Am J Hypertens* 2004;17: 986-893.

[85] Cerasola G, Mulè G, Nardi E et al. Usefulness of microalbuminuria in cardiovascular risk stratification of essential hypertensive patients. *Nephron Clin Pract* 2004; 96: 123-130.

[86] Mule' G, Cottone S, Mongiovì R, et al. Influence of metabolic syndrome on aortic stiffness in never treated hypertensive patients. Nutr Metab Cardiovasc Dis 2005, in press

[87] Burchfiel CM, Skelton TN, Andrew ME et al. Metabolic syndrome and echocardiographic left ventricular mass in blacks. The Atherosclerosis Risk in Communities (ARIC) Study. *Circulation* 2005;112: 819-827

[88] Strauss DS. Growth-stimulatory actions of insulin in vitro and in vivo. *Endocr Rev* 1984; 5: 356 –367.

[89] Andronico G, Mangano MT, Mulè G, et al. Insulin-like growth factor 1 and sodium-lithium countertransport in essential hypertension and in hypertensive left ventricular hypertrophy. *J Hypertens*. 1993;11:1097–1101.

[90] Verdecchia P, Reboldi G, Schillaci G, et al. Circulating insulin and insulin growth factor-1 are independent determinants of left ventricular mass and geometry in essential hypertension. *Circulation* 1999;100:1802-1807.

[91] Kamide K, Nagano M, Nakano N, et al. Insulin resistance and cardiovascular complications in patients with essential hypertension. *Am J Hypertens.* 1996;9:1165–1171.

[92] Quiñones Galvan A, Galetta F, Natali A et al. Insulin resistance and hyperinsulinemia no independent relation to left ventricular mass in humans. *Circulation* 2000;102: 2233-2238

[93] Malmqvist K, K. P. Ohman KP, Lind L et al Relationships between left ventricular mass and the renin–angiotensin system, catecholamines, insulin and leptin *J Intern Med* 2002; 252: 430–439.

[94] Frohlich ED, Chien Y, Sesoko S, et al. Relationship between dietary sodium intake, hemodynamics, and cardiac mass in SHR and WKY rats. *Am J Physiol.* 1993; 264(1 pt 2): R30–R34.

[95] de Simone G, Devereux RB, Camargo MJ, et al. Influence of sodium intake on in vivo left ventricular anatomy in experimental renovascular hypertension. *Am J Physiol.* 1993; 264(6 pt 2): H2103–H2110.

[96] Rowe JW, Young JB, Minaker KL, et al. Effects of insulin and glucose infusions on sympathetic nervous system activity in normal man. *Diabetes* 1981; 30: 219-225.

[97] Simpson P. Norepinephrine-stimulated hypertrophy of cultured rat myocardial cells is an alpha 1 adrenergic response. *J Clin Invest* 1983; 72: 732–738.

[98] Patel MB, Stewart JM, Loud AV, et al. Altered function and structure of the heart in dogs with chronic elevation in plasma norepinephrine. *Circulation* 1991; 84:2091–2100.

[99] Schlaich MP, Kaye DM, Lambert E, et al. Relation between cardiac sympathetic activity and hypertensive left ventricular hypertrophy. *Circulation.* 2003;108:560-565.

[100] Ferri C, Pittoni V, Piccoli A, et al. Insulin stimulates endothelin-1 secretion from human endothelial cells and modulates its circulating levels *in vivo*. *J Clin Endocrinol Metab* 1995; 80: 829–835.

[101] Mather KJ, Mirzamohammadi B, Lteif A, et al. Endothelin contributes to basal vascular tone and endothelial dysfunction in human obesity and type 2 diabetes. *Diabetes.* 2002;51:3517–3523.

[102] Ferri C, Bellini C, Desideri G, et al. Plasma endothelin-1 levels in obese hypertensive and normotensive men. *Diabetes.* 1995;44:431–436.

[103] Yamazaki T, Komuro I, Kudoh S, et al. Endothelin-1 is involved in mechanical stress-induced cardiomyocyte hypertrophy. *J Biol Chem* 1996;271:3221–3228.

[104] Sugden PH. An overview of endothelin signaling in the cardiac myocyte. *J Mol Cell Cardiol.* 2003;35:871–886.

[105] Leyva F, Godsland IF, Ghatei M, et al. Hyperleptinemia as a component of a metabolic syndrome of cardiovascular risk *Arterioscler Thromb Vasc Biol* 1998;18:928-933.

[106] Rajapurohitam V, Gan XT, Kirshenbaum LA, et al. The obesity associated peptide leptin induces hypertrophy in neonatal rat ventricular myocytes. *Circ Res* 2003; 93:277–279.

[107] Barouch LA, Berkowitz DE, Harrison RW, et al. Disruption of leptin signaling contributes to cardiac hypertrophy independently of body weight in mice. *Circulation* 2003;108:754–759.

[108] Mykkanen L, Zaccaro DJ, Wagenknecht LE, et al Microalbuminuria is associated with insulin resistance in nondiabetic subjects: the Insulin Resistance Atherosclerosis Study. *Diabetes* 1998;47:793– 800.

[109] Bianchi S, Bigazzi R, Quiñones Galvan A, et al. Insulin resistance in microalbuminuric hypertension: sites and mechanisms. *Hypertension* 1995;26:789–95.

[110] Srinivasan SR, Myers L, Berenson GS. Risk variables of insulin resistance syndrome in African American and Caucasian young adults with microalbuminuria: the Bogalusa Heart Study. *Am J Hypertens* 2000;13:1274 –9.

[111] Borch-Johnsen K, Feldt-Rasmussen B, Strandgaard S, et al: Microalbuminuria is strongly associated with NIDDM and hypertension, but not with the insulin resistance syndrome: the Hoorn Study. *Diabetologia* 1998;41:694–700.

[112] Cerasola G, Cottone S, Mulè G, et al. Microalbuminuria, renal dysfunction and cardiovascular complication in essential hypertension. *J Hypertens* 1996;14: 915-920.

[113] Campese VM, Bianchi S, Bigazzi R. Microalbuminuria in Essential Hypertension: Significance, Pathophysiology, and Therapeutic Implications *Am J Kidney Diseases* 1999; 34:973-995.

[114] Gerstein HC, Mann JF, Yi Q, et al HOPE Study Investigators. Albuminuria and risk of cardiovascular events, death, and heart failure in diabetic and nondiabetic individuals. *JAMA* 2001 286: 421-426.

[115] Hillege HL, Fidler V, Diercks GFH, et al for the Prevention of Renal and Vascular End Stage Disease (PREVEND) Study Group. Urinary Albumin Excretion Predicts Cardiovascular and Noncardiovascular Mortality in General Population. *Circulation* 2002;106:1777-1782.

[116] Wong TY, Duncan BB, Golden SH, et al. Associations between the Metabolic Syndrome and Retinal Microvascular Signs: The Atherosclerosis Risk in Communities Study. *Invest Ophthalmol Vis Sci* 2004; 45: 2949-2954.

[117] Wong TY, Mitchell P. Hypertensive Retinopathy. *N Engl J Med* 2004; 351:2310-2317.

[118] Mulè G, Cottone S, Vadalà A, et al. Relationship between albumin excretion rate and aortic stiffness in untreated essential hypertensive patients. *J Intern Med* 2004; 256: 22-29.

[119] Schillaci G, Pirro M, Vaudo G, et al. Metabolic syndrome is associated with aortic stiffness in untreated essential hypertension. *Hypertension* 2005; 45: 1078-1082.

[120] Scuteri A, Najjar SS, Muller DC, et al. Metabolic syndrome amplifies the age-associated increases in vascular thickness and stiffness. *J Am Coll Cardiol* 2004; 43:1388-1395.

In: Metabolic Syndrome Research Trends
Editor: Thomas E. Batone, pp. 89-103
ISBN: 978-1-60456-224-8

Chapter III

Prevalence of the Metabolic Syndrome and Its Relation to Risks for Cardiovascular Disease

Zhijie Yu and Gang Hu*

Institute for Nutritional Sciences, Shanghai Institutes for Biological Sciences, Chinese Academy of Sciences, Shanghai, China; Department of Health Promotion and Chronic Diseases Prevention, National Public Health Institute, Helsinki, and Department of Public Health, University of Helsinki, Finland

Abstract

There are five definitions of the metabolic syndrome that have been recommended by the World Health Organization (WHO), the European Group for Study of Insulin Resistance (EGIR), the National Cholesterol Education Program Expert Panel (NCEP), the International Diabetes Federation (IDF), and the American Association of Clinical Endocrinologists (AACE) separately since 1998. The prevalence of the metabolic syndrome reported from different studies has varied widely, mainly because of differences in the definitions of the syndrome and in the characteristics of the populations studied. Prospective studies on the relationship between the metabolic syndrome and cardiovascular risk are still scanty. Results from several studies including a large population-based Italian study, the Framingham Offspring Study, the Botnia Study, the Kuopio Ischemic Heart Disease Study, the National Health and Nutrition Examination Survey II Mortality Study, the San Antonio Heart Study, the Hoorn Study, the British Regional Heart Study, the Swedish Study in Uppsala, and the DECODE study have shown that the presence of metabolic syndrome using different definitions is associated with a significantly increased risk of total mortality and cardiovascular morbidity and mortality.

Clustering of some metabolic and physiological abnormalities was first described in 1923 by Kylin [1] who published a report on a syndrome comprising hypertension, hyperglycaemia and hyperuricaemia. The coining of the term "syndrome X" in 1988 by Reaven renewed the

* E-mail address: hu.gang@ktl.fi. Tel: +358 9 19127366, Fax: +358 9 19127313, Correspondence to: Gang. Hu, MD, PhD, Department of Health Promotion and Chronic Diseases Prevention, National Public Health Institute, Mannerheimintie 166, FIN-00300 Helsinki, Finland

impetus to conduct research concerning this syndrome [2]. In his description of syndrome X, Reaven considered the following abnormalities: resistance to insulin-stimulated glucose uptake, glucose intolerance, hyperinsulinaemia, an increased plasma concentration of VLDL triglyceride, a decreased plasma concentration of high-density lipoprotein (HDL) cholesterol, and high blood pressure. Subsequently, several new components to the syndrome, such as obesity and its central distribution, mircoalbuminuria, hyperuricaemia, abnormalities in haemostatic factors, have been suggested [3-6]. Characterized by insulin resistance, this syndrome is also sometimes called the insulin resistance syndrome, or the metabolic syndrome [2,3,7]. The metabolic syndrome has a specific code in the International Classification of Diseases at least in Finland (ICD-10: E66.00). More recently, a term of "dysmetabolic syndrome" has been launched by the American Association of Clinical Endocrinologists (AACE) with a specific ICD-9 code 277.7 [8].

The pathogenesis of the syndrome is complex and so far incompletely understood, but obesity, sedentary lifestyle, dietary factors and genetic factors are known to contribute and interact in its development [2,7,9]. It has been proposed that the metabolic syndrome is a powerful determinant of type 2 diabetes [10-17] and atherosclerotic cardiovascular disease (CVD) [16-26].

The Definition of the Metabolic Syndrome

Clinical practice and epidemiological research on the metabolic syndrome have suffered from the lack on an unequivocal definition of the syndrome and from the diversity in the cut-offs proposed for its components. To overcome these problems, five international or national bodies have recently formulated definitions for the metabolic syndrome. These definitions are presented in Table 1. The World Health Organization (WHO) Consultation [27] and the European Group for Study of Insulin Resistance (EGIR) [28], have been proposed to improve uniformity in the research, whereas three other definitions given by the National Cholesterol Education Program Expert Panel (NCEP)/the American Heart Association(AHA)/National Heart, Lung, and Blood Institute (NHLBI) [29,30], the International Diabetes Federation (IDF) [31], and the American Association of Clinical Endocrinologists (AACE) [8,32], have been proposed for clinical use, for the identification of high-risk individuals. The components of the syndrome and the positive diagnostic values of each component vary between different definitions. The AACE recommendation, deviating from other three, does not include obesity among the core components of the syndrome but rather views it as a characteristic that increases insulin resistance [32]. Cut-off levels used for the definition of central obesity, blood pressure and plasma lipid levels differ in some instances substantially [27-32]. Because assessment of insulin sensitivity by the euglycaemic clamp or other alternative methods is not feasible in clinical practice and the use of the fasting insulin as a surrogate measurement for insulin resistance is problematic due to lack of standardisation of methods and large intra-individual variability, the insulin resistance is not required by either the NCEP, the IDF or the AACE definitions [8,29-32].

Table 1. WHO, EGIR, NCEP and AACE definitions of the metabolic syndrome

World Health Organisation (WHO) Definition [27]
Diabetes (FPG ≥7.0 mmol/l and/or 2- hour PG ≥11.1 mmol/l) or impaired glucose regulation (FPG 6.1-6.9 mmol/l or 2-hour PG 7.8-11.0 mmol/l) and/or insulin resistance (below lowest quartile of glucose uptake in the euglycaemic clamp) and, in addition, 2 or more of the following:
Central obesity (waist to hip ratio >0.90 in men, >0.85 in women) and/or body mass index >30 kg/m^2
Raised blood pressure (systolic blood pressure ≥140 mmHg and/or diastolic blood pressure ≥90 mmHg)
Raised triglycerides (≥1.7 mmol/l) and/or low HDL-cholesterol (<0.9 mmol/l in men, <1.0 mmol/l in women)
Microalbuminuria (urinary albumin excretion rate ≥20 ug/min or albumin/creatinine ratio ≥30 mg/g)
European Group for the Study of Insulin Resistance (EGIR) Definition [28], for non-diabetic individuals
Hyperinsulinemia (above the highest quartile of the non-diabetic background population) and 2 or more of the following:
Central obesity (waist circumference ≥94 cm in men, ≥80 cm in women)
Raised blood pressure (systolic blood pressure ≥140 mmHg and/or diastolic blood pressure ≥90 mmHg or current use of antihypertensive drugs)
Raised triglycerides (>2.0 mmol/l) and/or low HDL-cholesterol (<1.0 mmol/l) or current use of hypolipidemic drugs
Hyperglycemia (FPG 6.1-6.9 mmol/l)
National Cholesterol Education Program (NCEP) Definition [29,30]
3 or more of the following:
Central obesity (waist circumference >102 cm in men, >88 cm in women)
Raised blood pressure (systolic blood pressure ≥130 mmHg and/or diastolic blood pressure ≥85 mmHg or current use of antihypertensive drugs)
High triglycerides (≥1.7 mmol/l) or drug treatment for elevated triglycerides
Low HDL-cholesterol (<1.03 mmol/l in men, <1.29 mmol/l in women) or drug treatment for reduced HDL-cholesterol
High fasting plasma glucose (≥5.6 mmol/l) or drug treatment for elevated glucose
International Diabetes Federation (IDF) Definition [31]
Central obesity (defined as waist circumference ≥ 94 cm for Europid men and ≥ 80 for Europid women, with ethnicity specific values for other groups) plus any two of the four following factors:
Raised triglycerides (≥ 1.7 mmol/L), or specific treatment for this lipid abnormality
Reduced HDL-cholesterol: (< 1.03 mmol/L in men and < 1.29 mmol/L in women), or specific treatment for this lipid abnormality
Raised blood pressure: systolic blood pressure ≥ 130 mmHg or diastolic blood pressure ≥ 85 mmHg, or treatment of previously diagnosed hypertension
Raised fasting plasma glucose (≥ 5.6 mmol/L), or previously diagnosed type 2 diabetes
American Association of Clinical Endocrinologists (AACE) Definition [8,32], for non-diabetic individuals
2 or more of the following:
Raised blood pressure (systolic blood pressure ≥130 mmHg and/or diastolic blood pressure ≥85 mmHg or current use of antihypertensive drugs)
High triglycerides (≥1.7 mmol/l)
Low HDL-cholesterol (<1.03 mmol/l in men, <1.29 mmol/l in women)
Hyperglycemia (FPG 6.1-6.9 mmol/l and/or 2-hour post-load plasma glucose 7.8-11.0 mmol/l)

FPG, fasting plasma glucose; 2-hour PG, 2-hour plasma glucose; HDL-cholesterol, high-density lipoprotein cholesterol.

The Prevalence of the Metabolic Syndrome

The prevalence of the metabolic syndrome reported from different studies have varied widely, mainly because of differences in the definitions of the syndrome and in part because of differences in the characteristics of the populations studied [18,21,33-44]. Table 2 outlines the results of the prevalence of the metabolic syndrome among different studies. In the Finnish Botnia study, the prevalence of the metabolic syndrome using the original WHO definition was 15% in nondiabetic men and 10% in nondiabetic women, 84% in diabetic men and 78% in diabetic women [18]. The Botnia study, however, was not a truly population-based study, because it recruited people with type 2 diabetes and their relatives, and thus diabetes was present in over one third of the cohort. The EGIR assessed the prevalence of the metabolic syndrome using the WHO definition and its modification by the EGIR in eight European study cohorts including 8200 men and 9363 women [35]. In nondiabetic subjects the prevalence of the syndrome by the WHO definition in the age group 40-55 years varied between study cohorts from 7% to 36% in men and from 5% to 22% in women. When defined by the EGIR criteria, the syndrome was less frequent [35]. A recent data based on the NHANES-III survey that used the NCEP definition and did not exclude individuals with diabetes was conducted in the United States. It estimated that approximately 24% of the US adults have the metabolic syndrome, but found that there were marked differences in the prevalence between ethnic groups and noted that the prevalence was highest in Mexican Americans and lowest in blacks of both sexes [36]. Moreover, they compared the prevalence of the metabolic syndrome in the NHANES-III survey according to the WHO and NCEP definitions and found that the two definitions gave a similar prevalence in the entire sample, but in some population subgroups there was a substantial discordance between the two definitions in the classification of individuals as having or not having the syndrome [37]. The Strong Heart Study, using the NCEP definition, reported a high prevalence of the metabolic syndrome in American Indians aged 45-74 years; 55.2% in the whole study population and 35% in nondiabetic individuals [38].

Using the data of the DECODE (Diabetes Epidemiology: Collaborative analysis Of Diagnostic criteria in Europe) study, consisting of 11 European study cohorts with 4568 men and 5337 women aged 30-89 years, we assessed the prevalence of the metabolic syndrome using WHO and NCEP definitions (Table 3) (un-published data). A modification of the WHO definition of the metabolic syndrome was used. The subjects were considered to have the metabolic syndrome, if they had diabetes (known diabetes or fasting plasma glucose ≥7.0 mmol/l and/or 2-hour plasma glucose ≥11.1 mmol/l) or impaired glucose regulation (fasting plasma glucose of 6.1-6.9 mmol/l or 2-hour plasma glucose of 7.8-11.0 mmol) and/or insulin resistance (fasting plasma insulin above the highest sex- and cohort-specific quartile of the non-diabetic population) together with 2 or more of the following components: 1) central obesity, waist to hip ratio >0.90 in men, >0.85 in women and/or body mass index >30 kg/m^2; 2) hypertension, systolic blood pressure ≥140 mmHg and/or diastolic blood pressure ≥90 mmHg or using antihypertensive drugs; 3) dyslipidemia, raised plasma triglycerides (≥1.7 mmol/l) and/or low HDL-cholesterol (<0.9 mmol/l in men, <1.0 mmol/l in women). In the whole study population, the age-standardized prevalence of the metabolic syndrome were 28.2% in men and 21.3% in women using WHO definition, and 23.9% in men and 23.9% in women using NCEP definition. In non-diabetic people, the age-standardized prevalence of the metabolic syndrome were 24.7% in men and 17.9% in women using WHO definition, and 21.4% in men and 20.9% in women using NCEP definition.

Table 2. The prevalence of the metabolic syndrome

Study	Year of publication	Sample size	Age rang (years)	Using definition	Prevalence of the metabolic syndrome
The Botnia study [18]	2001	4483 with DM	35-70	WHO	Men: 15% in subjects with NGT, 64% in subjects with IFG/IGT, 84% in subjects with DM; Women, 10%, 42% and 78% respectively.
The Kuopio Ischemic Heart Disease Study [19]	2002	1209 men without DM	42-60	WHO	14.2%;
				NCEP	8.8%.
The EGIR [35]	2002	17563 with DM	20-81	WHO with DM	Men: <40 years, 14%; 40-55 years, 23%; >55 years, 41%; Women: <40 years, 4%; 40-55 years, 13%; >55 years, 26%;
				WHO without DM	Men: <40 years, 13%; 40-55 years, 20%; >55 years, 33%; Women: <40 years, 4%; 40-55 years, 11%; >55 years, 21%;
				EGIR without DM	Men: <40 years, 10%; 40-55 years, 9%; >55 years, 22%; Women: <40 years, 3%; 40-55 years, 7%; >55 years, 17%.
The NHANES-III survey [36]	2002	8814 with DM	≥20	NCEP with DM	Men: 24.0%; women, 23.4%.
The NHANES-III survey [37]	2003	8608 with DM	≥20	NCEP with DM	Men: 24.2%; women, 23.5%;
				WHO with DM	Men: 27.9%; women, 22.6%.
The Strong Heart Study [38]	2002	4549 with DM	45-74	NCEP with DM	55.2% in the whole study population;
				NCEP without DM	35% in non-diabetes individual.
The DECODE Study	Un-published	9905 with DM	30-89	WHO with DM	Men: 28.2%; women, 21.3%;
				NCEP with DM	Men: 23.9%; women, 23.9%;
				WHO without DM	Men: 24.7%; women, 17.9%;
				NCEP without DM	Men: 21.4%; women, 20.9%.
Chinese Study, Shanghai [39]	2004	2048 with DM	20-74	WHO with DM	17.1%
				NCEP with DM	10.95%
Korea National Health and Nutrition Survey [40]	2004	6147 with DM	≥25	Modified NCEP with DM*	Men: 22.1%; women, 27.8%;
				Modified NCEP with DM†	Men: 28.6%; women, 27.8%.
Korean metropolitan Study [41]	2004	40698	20-82	NCEP with DM	Men, 5.2%; women, 9.0%;
				Modified NCEP with DM*	Men, 9.8%; women, 12.4%;
				Modified NCEP with DM‡	Men, 13.2%; women, 13.1%.

Table 2. Continued

Study	Year of publication	Sample size	Age rang (years)	Using definition	Prevalence of the metabolic syndrome
Singapore National Health Survey [42]	2004	4723	18-69	NCEP with DM	Men, 13.1%; women, 11.0%;
				Modified NCEP with DM*	Men, 20.9%; women, 15.5%.
InterASIA [43]	2005	15 540	35-74	NCEP with DM	Men, 9.8%; women, 17.8%;
				Modified NCEP with DM*	Men, 13.6%; women, 16.6%.
Chinese Study in Beijing [44]	2006	2334	60-95	NCEP with DM	Men, 17.6%; women 39.2%;
				IDF with DM	Men, 34.8%; women, 54.1%.

Dm, diabetes; NGT, normal glucose tolerance; IFG, impaired fasting glucose; IGT, impaired glucose tolerance.

*using modified Asian criteria for abdominal obesity (waist circumference >90 cm in men and >80 cm in women).

†using modified Asian criteria for abdominal obesity (waist to hip ratio >0.9 in men and >0.85 in women).

‡using modified Asian criteria for body obesity (body mass index ≥25 kg/m^2)

Table 3. Prevalence (%) of the metabolic syndrome according to the WHO and NCEP definitions in the pooled data of DECODE study

	No. of subjects		The prevalence of the metabolic syndrome (including DM)				The prevalence of the metabolic syndrome (excluding DM)			
			Men		Women		Men		Women	
	Men	Women	WHO	NCEP	WHO	NCEP	WHO	NCEP	WHO	NCEP
30-39	372	435	15.3	13.5	8.3	9.4	15.1	13.5	7.0	8.1
40-49	1009	1243	24.1	22.5	12.8	17.0	21.7	21.0	11.2	15.2
50-59	1673	1885	33.1	28.3	22.3	26.8	28.5	25.5	18.8	24.3
60-69	1230	1436	37.6	30.1	34.7	36.0	32.0	26.9	28.8	30.8
≥70	284	338	40.8	31.3	45.9	45.9	33.2	23.3	38.0	38.8
Total	4568	5337	31.3	26.4	23.8	26.8	26.9	23.7	19.5	23.1
Total*			28.2	23.9	21.3	23.9	24.7	21.4	17.9	20.9

*Age-standardized prevalence was calculated using a standard European population.

Differences in cut-points of a single factor and in components of definitions of the metabolic syndrome lead to diversities in prevalences and in phenotypes of subjects identified as having the syndrome. For instance, the criteria of obesity in the WHO or NECP definitions of the metabolic syndrome does not apply to Asian populations because the criteria of obesity based on results obtained in Caucasian population. Two studies have compared the prevalence of the metabolic syndrome in Asian populations according to the original NCEP definition and modified NCEP definition using Asia-Pacific criteria for obesity [45]. In Singapore National Health Survey involving 4723 subjects aged 18-69 years, the prevalence of the metabolic syndrome using the original NCEP definition were 13.1% in men and 11.0% in women, but increased to 20.9% in men and 15.5% in women with modified Asian criteria for abdominal obesity (waist circumference >90 cm in men and >80 cm in women) [42]. In another study including 40 698 Korean metropolitan subjects aged 20-82 years, the age-adjusted prevalence of the metabolic syndrome using the original NCEP definition were 5.2% in men and 9.0% in women, and increased to 9.8% in men and 12.4% in women using modified Asian criteria for abdominal obesity (waist circumference >90 cm in men and >80 cm in women), and to 13.2% in men and 13.1% in women using modified Asian criteria for body obesity (body mass index $\geq$25 kg/m^2) [41].

In China, Gu and colleagues analyzed the data of the International Collaborative Study of Cardiovascular Disease in ASIA (InterASIA). Among the nationally representative sample of 15540 men and women aged 35-74 years, the prevalence of the metabolic syndrome was 9.8% in men and 17.8 in women by using NCEP definition [43]. A Chinese study with 2048 subjects aged 20-74 years compared the prevalence of the metabolic syndrome according to the WHO and NCEP definitions and indicated that the age-adjusted prevalence of the metabolic syndrome was higher by using WHO definition (17.1%) than by using NCEP definition (11.0%) [39]. He and associates [44] reported the prevalence of the metabolic syndrome among 2334 elderly Chinese aged 60-95 years. The prevalent metabolic syndrome was 17.6% in men and 39.2% in women by NCEP definition and increased to 34.8% in men and 54.1% in women, respectively, using IDF definition. The result from 1998 Korea National Health and Nutrition Survey reported that the prevalence of the metabolic syndrome was 22.1% in Korean men and 27.8% in women by using modified Asian criteria for abdominal obesity with waist circumference >90 cm in men and >80 cm in women, and 28.6% in men and 27.8% in women by using modified Asian criteria for abdominal obesity with waist to hip ratio >0.9 in men and >0.85 in women [40].

The prevalence of the metabolic syndrome was high in high-risk nondiabetic individuals (impaired glucose tolerance or impaired fasting glucose, also called "prediabetes") and diabetic patients. In the Finnish Botnia study, the prevalence of the metabolic syndrome using the original WHO definition was 64% in men and 42% in women with impaired glucose tolerance or impaired fasting glucose, 84% in diabetic men and 78% in diabetic women [18]. In the Finnish Diabetes Prevention Study, the prevalence of the metabolic syndrome was present in 78.4% of the men and 72.2% of the women with impaired glucose tolerance [46].

Overall, the prevalence of the metabolic syndrome varied widely among different studies due to the differences in the definitions of the syndrome and differences in the characteristics of the populations studied. Men had a higher prevalence of the metabolic syndrome than women in many, but not all studied populations (Tables 2 and 3).

The Metabolic Syndrome and Risk of Cardiovascular Disease

To investigate the contribution of the metabolic syndrome to cardiovascular morbidity and mortality, the relationship between the metabolic syndrome and CVD risk has been evaluated. Some prospective studies had, already before the publication of the WHO, EGIR, NCEP, IDF, and AACE definitions of the metabolic syndrome, examined the association of the clustering of the components of the metabolic syndrome with the risk of CVD using their own cut-offs for the components. Based on a large population-based Italian study of 22 256 men and 18 495 women, Trevisan et al. reported that the risk of total and CVD mortality increased with the increased numbers of metabolic abnormalities (high blood glucose, high blood pressure, low HDL cholesterol, and high triglycerides) in both men and women [33]. Age-adjusted risk for CVD mortality associated with none, any one, two, three, or full of the metabolic abnormalities were 1.00, 1.44 (95% CI, 0.99-2.07), 1.62 (95% CI, 1.11-2.35), 2.42 (95% CI, 1.63-3.59), 2.49 (95% CI, 1.46-4.23) in men, and 1.00, 2.68 (95% CI, 0.57-12.58), 5.55 (95% CI, 1.22-25.2), 11.2 (95% CI, 2.45-51.0), 15.9 (95% CI, 3.01-83.8) in women, respectively [33]. The Framingham Offspring Study, including 2406 men and 2569 women aged 19-74 years, examined the clustering of metabolic factors in relation to coronary heart disease (CHD) risk [34]. The 6 metabolic abnormalities considered were HDL cholesterol (the lowest sex-specific quintile), body mass index, systolic blood pressure, triglycerides, glucose, and total cholesterol (the highest quintiles). A cluster of 3 or more risk factors was associated with a 2.39 (95% CI, 1.56-3.66) and 5.90 (95% CI, 2.54-13.73) times greater risk of CHD in men and women, respectively, as compared with the absence of the clustering [34].

In the Botnia Study including diabetic subjects and combining data for men and women, the presence of the metabolic syndrome was associated with a 6-fold increase in CVD mortality (12.0% vs. 2.2%, $p<0.001$) during the 6.9-year follow-up [18]. Another Finnish study, the Kuopio Ischemic Heart Disease Study, has recently reported the results of a 11.4-year follow-up study of middle-aged men, examining the predictive value of both the WHO and NCEP definitions of the metabolic syndrome and their modifications with regard to CVD and all-cause mortality [19]. The prevalence of the metabolic syndrome ranged from 8.8% to 14.3% depending on the definition. The metabolic syndrome as defined by the WHO was associated with 1.9 times higher all-cause mortality and with 2.6 times higher CVD mortality, whereas the NCEP definition less consistently predicted all-cause and CVD mortality [19]. Several studies from the United States have assessed the association between the metabolic syndrome by the NCEP or WHO definitions and CVD risk [17,20,22,23,38]. One study based on the NHANES-II survey, including 2431 US adults aged 30-75 years, indicated that the presence of the metabolic syndrome had an increased risk of death from CVD, but no associations with the risk of death from CHD, stroke, diseases of the circulatory system, and all causes [20]. Moreover, the new analysis based on the same NHANES-II survey, including 6255 US adults aged 30-75 years, found that CHD, CVD, and total mortality were significantly higher in US adults with than in those without the metabolic syndrome [22]. In US adults with the metabolic syndrome but without diabetes, increased risk of CHD and CVD mortality also remained [22]. The San Antonio Heart study also examined the relation between the metabolic syndrome using both NCEP and WHO definitions and all-cause and

CVD mortality. In the general population, the metabolic syndrome based on NCEP definition predicted all-cause and CVD mortality, whereas the metabolic syndrome based on WHO definition predicted only CVD mortality [23]. In the Strong Heart Study of 2283 non-diabetic American Indian men and women, the presence of the metabolic syndrome was not a risk predictor for the incident CVD events [38]. Wilson et al. [17] analyzed the data from 3323 middle-aged adults who participated in the Framingham Offspring Study and were followed for over eight years. Among participants without CVD, men with the metabolic syndrome defined by NCEP criteria had age-adjusted relative risks of 2.88 (95% CI, 1.99-4.16) for CVD and 2.54 (95% CI, 1.62-3.98) for CHD compared with those without the metabolic syndrome. For women the corresponding relative risks were 2.25 (95% CI, 1.31-3.88) and 1.54 (95% CI, 0.68-3.53), respectively.

Using the data of the DECODE Study, consisting of 11 European study cohorts with 6156 nondiabetic men and 5356 women aged 30-89 years, we assessed by meta-analyses the predictive value of the metabolic syndrome with regard to all-cause and CVD mortality. In the DECODE study population, the presence of the metabolic syndrome by the modified WHO definition was a statistically significant predictor of total and CVD mortality in both non-diabetic men and women, after adjustment for age, cholesterol and smoking (Table 4) [21]. In men, with different definitions of the metabolic syndrome, multivariate-adjusted overall hazard ratios associated with the presence of the metabolic syndrome ranged from 1.39 to 1.47 for all-cause mortality and from 1.74 to 2.26 for CVD mortality, relative to men without the metabolic syndrome. In women, the corresponding hazard ratios ranged from 1.23 to 1.49 and from 1.56 to 2.78, respectively [21]. Moreover, DECODE Study also estimated CVD mortality in individuals with the metabolic syndrome on the basis of different definitions [26]. All definitions of the metabolic syndrome were associated with increased CVD mortality in men, but the association was weak in women. The corresponding hazard ratios for CVD mortality based on WHO, NCEP and IDF definitions were 2.09 (95% CI, 1.59–2.76), 1.74 (95% CI, 1.31–2.30), and 1.51 (95% CI, 1.15–1.99) in men, and 1.60 (95% CI, 1.01–2.51), 1.39 (95% CI, 0.89–2.18), and 1.53 (95% CI, 0.99–2.36) in women.

In the Hoorn Study [24], 615 men and 749 women aged 50-75 years without diabetes or a history of CVD at baseline survey were followed for 10 years in Holland. The prevalence of the metabolic syndrome at baseline ranged from 17% to 32% according to the NCEP, WHO, EGIR or AACE definitions. The NCEP definition was associated with a 2-fold of age-adjusted risk of fatal CVD in men and nonfatal CVD in women. For the WHO, EGIR and AACE definitions, the relative risks were slightly lower. Moreover, the risk increased with the number of metabolic syndrome components. In the British Regional Heart Study, 5128 men aged 40-59 years with no history of CVD or type 2 diabetes were observed for 20 years [16]. Those with the metabolic syndrome as defined by the NCEP had relative risks of 1.64 (95% CI, 1.41-1.90) for CHD and 1.61 (95% CI, 1.26-2.06) for stroke. In a Swedish cohort, 2322 men were followed for a maximum of 32.7 years [25]. The metabolic syndrome as defined by NCEP was a significant predictor of death from all cause (hazard ratio, 1.36; 95% CI, 1.17-1.58) and CVD (hazard ratio, 1.59; 95% CI, 1.29-1.95) independent of smoking, diabetes, hypertension and serum cholesterol.

Table 4. Meta-analyses of the association of the metabolic syndrome with the risk of all-cause and cardiovascular mortality in 7 DECODE study cohorts by sex [21]*

Definition of the metabolic syndrome	Number of subjects		All-cause mortality		Cardiovascular disease mortality	
	Men N = 4339	Women N = 5183	Men N = 418	Women N = 255	Men N = 161	Women N = 63
Any ≥2 of the components†	1525‡	1488	1.39 (1.15-1.68)	1.23 (0.96-1.57)	1.75 (1.28-2.39)	1.56 (0.93-2.60)
Any ≥3 of the components	543	534	1.47 (1.15-1.89)	1.41 (1.03-1.92)	1.74 (1.19-2.55)	2.17 (1.13-4.19)
Hyperinsulinemia plus any ≥2 of the other components	677	727	1.44 (1.17-1.84)	1.38 (1.02-1.87)	2.26 (1.61-3.17)	2.78 (1.57-4.94)
Hyperinsulinemia plus any ≥3 of the other components	331	330	1.43 (1.06-1.94)	1.49 (1.02-2.31)	1.98 (1.27-3.10)	2.74 (1.21-6.20)

*Data are given as hazard ratios (95% confidence intervals), adjusted for age, cholesterol and smoking. The modified WHO definition of the metabolic syndrome indicated by bolding.

†These components of the metabolic syndrome include: obesity, dyslipidemia, impaired glucose regulation, hypertension

‡Number of individuals who fulfilled the definition.

Prevention and Treatment of the Metabolic Syndrome

While CVD mortality has shown a significant downward trend in developed countries during the last decades, CVD is on the increase in the developing world [47,48]. It is clear that the presence of the metabolic syndrome is associated with a significantly increased risk of CVD morbidity and mortality regardless of the differences in the definitions. The results from clinical trials conducted have demonstrated that lifestyle-intervention (reduction of obesity, increase of physical activity and dietary changes) and drug treatment reduce the risk of progression from impaired glucose tolerance to type 2 diabetes and also improve several CVD risk factors [49-53]. Lifestyle-intervention would obviously be a relevant strategy also for the management of the metabolic syndrome, and may substantially reduce the risk of CVD associated with the syndrome. The effectiveness of lifestyle interventions needs, however, to be tested in large-scale trials. Before such trials can be adequately planned, further research is needed to validate and improve methods for the identification of individuals with the metabolic syndrome at high risk for CVD and premature mortality. Moreover, in order to understand the mechanism underlying the clustering of the metabolic abnormalities an international uniform definition of the syndrome is urgently needed.

Acknowledgements

This work has been supported by the Finnish Foundation for Cardiovascular Research.

References

[1] Kylin, E. (1923) Studien ueber das Hypertonie-Hyperglykämie-Hyperurikämiesyndrome. *Zentralblatt fuer Innere Medizin*. 44, 105-127

[2] Reaven, G. M. (1988) Banting lecture 1988. Role of insulin resistance in human disease. *Diabetes*. 37, 1595-1607.

[3] DeFronzo, R. & Ferrannini, E. (1991) Insulin resistance. A multifaceted syndrome responsible for NIDDM, obesity, hypertension, dyslipidemia, and atherosclerotic cardiovascular disease. *Diabetes Care*. 14, 173-194

[4] Kuusisto, J., Mykkanen, L., Pyorala, K. & Laakso, M. (1995) Hyperinsulinemic microalbuminuria. A new risk indicator for coronary heart disease. *Circulation*. 91, 831-837.

[5] Imperatore, G., Riccardi, G., Iovine, C., Rivellese, A. A. & Vaccaro, O. (1998) Plasma fibrinogen: a new factor of the metabolic syndrome. A population-based study. *Diabetes Care*. 21, 649-654.

[6] Meigs, J. B. (2000) Invited commentary: insulin resistance syndrome? Syndrome X? Multiple metabolic syndrome? A syndrome at all? Factor analysis reveals patterns in the fabric of correlated metabolic risk factors. *Am J Epidemiol*. 152, 908-911; discussion 912.

[7] Liese, A. D., Mayer-Davis, E. J. & Haffner, S. M. (1998) Development of the multiple metabolic syndrome: an epidemiologic perspective. *Epidemiol Rev.* 20, 157-172.

[8] Einhorn, D., Reaven, G. M., Cobin, R. H., Ford, E., Ganda, O. P., Handelsman, Y., Hellman, R., Jellinger, P. S., Kendall, D., Krauss, R. M., Neufeld, N. D., Petak, S. M., Rodbard, H. W., Seibel, J. A., Smith, D. A. & Wilson, P. W. (2003) American College of Endocrinology position statement on the insulin resistance syndrome. *Endocr Pract.* 9, 237-252

[9] Laws, A. & Reaven, G. M. (1993) Insulin resistance and risk factors for coronary heart disease. *Baillieres Clin Endocrinol Metab.* 7, 1063-1078.

[10] Haffner, S. M., Valdez, R. A., Hazuda, H. P., Mitchell, B. D., Morales, P. A. & Stern, M. P. (1992) Prospective analysis of the insulin-resistance syndrome (syndrome X). *Diabetes.* 41, 715-722

[11] Hanson, R. L., Imperatore, G., Bennett, P. H. & Knowler, W. C. (2002) Components of the "metabolic syndrome" and incidence of type 2 diabetes. *Diabetes.* 51, 3120-3127

[12] Laaksonen, D. E., Lakka, H. M., Niskanen, L. K., Kaplan, G. A., Salonen, J. T. & Lakka, T. A. (2002) Metabolic syndrome and development of diabetes mellitus: application and validation of recently suggested definitions of the metabolic syndrome in a prospective cohort study. *Am J Epidemiol.* 156, 1070-1077

[13] Lorenzo, C., Okoloise, M., Williams, K., Stern, M. P. & Haffner, S. M. (2003) The metabolic syndrome as predictor of type 2 diabetes: the San Antonio Heart Study. *Diabetes Care.* 26, 3153-3159

[14] Wang, J. J., Hu, G., Miettinen, M. E. & Tuomilehto, J. (2004) The Metabolic Syndrome and Incident Diabetes: Assessment of Four Suggested Definitions of the Metabolic Syndrome in a Chinese Population with High Post-prandial Glucose. *Horm Metab Res.* 36, 708-715

[15] Wang, J. J., Qiao, Q., Miettinen, M. E., Lappalainen, J., Hu, G. & Tuomilehto, J. (2004) The metabolic syndrome defined by factor analysis and incident type 2 diabetes in a chinese population with high postprandial glucose. *Diabetes Care.* 27, 2429-2437

[16] Wannamethee, S. G., Shaper, A. G., Lennon, L. & Morris, R. W. (2005) Metabolic syndrome vs Framingham Risk Score for prediction of coronary heart disease, stroke, and type 2 diabetes mellitus. *Arch Intern Med.* 165, 2644-2650

[17] Wilson, P. W., D'Agostino, R. B., Parise, H., Sullivan, L. & Meigs, J. B. (2005) Metabolic syndrome as a precursor of cardiovascular disease and type 2 diabetes mellitus. *Circulation.* 112, 3066-3072

[18] Isomaa, B., Almgren, P., Tuomi, T., Forsen, B., Lahti, K., Nissen, M., Taskinen, M. R. & Groop, L. (2001) Cardiovascular morbidity and mortality associated with the metabolic syndrome. *Diabetes Care.* 24, 683-689.

[19] Lakka, H. M., Laaksonen, D. E., Lakka, T. A., Niskanen, L. K., Kumpusalo, E., Tuomilehto, J. & Salonen, J. T. (2002) The metabolic syndrome and total and cardiovascular disease mortality in middle-aged men. *Jama.* 288, 2709-2716

[20] Ford, E. S. (2004) The metabolic syndrome and mortality from cardiovascular disease and all-causes: findings from the National Health and Nutrition Examination Survey II Mortality Study. *Atherosclerosis.* 173, 309-314

[21] Hu, G., Qiao, Q., Tuomilehto, J., Balkau, B., Borch-Johnsen, K., Pyorala, K. & The DECODE Study Group. (2004) Prevalence of the metabolic syndrome and its relation to all-cause and cardiovascular mortality in nondiabetic European men and women. *Arch Intern Med.* 164, 1066-1076

[22] Malik, S., Wong, N. D., Franklin, S. S., Kamath, T. V., L'Italien, G. J., Pio, J. R. & Williams, G. R. (2004) Impact of the metabolic syndrome on mortality from coronary heart disease, cardiovascular disease, and all causes in United States adults. *Circulation.* 110, 1245-1250

[23] Hunt, K. J., Resendez, R. G., Williams, K., Haffner, S. M. & Stern, M. P. (2004) National Cholesterol Education Program versus World Health Organization metabolic syndrome in relation to all-cause and cardiovascular mortality in the San Antonio Heart Study. *Circulation.* 110, 1251-1257

[24] Dekker, J. M., Girman, C., Rhodes, T., Nijpels, G., Stehouwer, C. D., Bouter, L. M. & Heine, R. J. (2005) Metabolic syndrome and 10-year cardiovascular disease risk in the Hoorn Study. *Circulation.* 112, 666-673

[25] Sundstrom, J., Riserus, U., Byberg, L., Zethelius, B., Lithell, H. & Lind, L. (2006) Clinical value of the metabolic syndrome for long term prediction of total and cardiovascular mortality: prospective, population based cohort study. *Bmj.* 332, 878-882

[26] Qiao, Q. (2006) Comparison of different definitions of the metabolic syndrome in relation to cardiovascular mortality in European men and women. *Diabetologia.* 49, 2837-2846

[27] WHO Consultation: Definition, diagnosis and classification of diabetes mellitus and its complications. Part 1: diagnosis and classification of diabetes mellitus. Geneva, World Health Organisation, 1999.

[28] Balkau, B. & Charles, M. A. (1999) Comment on the provisional report from the WHO consultation. European Group for the Study of Insulin Resistance (EGIR). *Diabet Med.* 16, 442-443

[29] National Institute of Health. (2001) Executive Summary of The Third Report of The National Cholesterol Education Program (NCEP) Expert Panel on Detection, Evaluation, And Treatment of High Blood Cholesterol In Adults (Adult Treatment Panel III). *Jama.* 285, 2486-2497.

[30] Grundy, S. M., Cleeman, J. I., Daniels, S. R., Donato, K. A., Eckel, R. H., Franklin, B. A., Gordon, D. J., Krauss, R. M., Savage, P. J., Smith, S. C., Jr., Spertus, J. A. & Costa, F. (2005) Diagnosis and management of the metabolic syndrome: an American Heart Association/National Heart, Lung, and Blood Institute Scientific Statement. *Circulation.* 112, 2735-2752

[31] Alberti, K. G., Zimmet, P. & Shaw, J. (2005) The metabolic syndrome--a new worldwide definition. *Lancet.* 366, 1059-1062

[32] Bloomgarden, Z. T. (2003) American Association of Clinical Endocrinologists (AACE) Consensus Conference on the Insulin Resistance Syndrome: 25-26 August 2002, Washington, DC. *Diabetes Care.* 26, 933-939

[33] Trevisan, M., Liu, J., Bahsas, F. B. & Menotti, A. (1998) Syndrome X and mortality: a population-based study. Risk Factor and Life Expectancy Research Group. *Am J Epidemiol.* 148, 958-966

[34] Wilson, P. W., Kannel, W. B., Silbershatz, H. & D'Agostino, R. B. (1999) Clustering of metabolic factors and coronary heart disease. *Arch Intern Med.* 159, 1104-1109.

[35] Balkau, B., Charles, M. A., Drivsholm, T., Borch-Johnsen, K., Wareham, N., Yudkin, J. S., Morris, R., Zavaroni, I., van Dam, R., Feskins, E., Gabriel, R., Diet, M., Nilsson, P. & Hedblad, B. (2002) Frequency of the WHO metabolic syndrome in European cohorts, and an alternative definition of an insulin resistance syndrome. *Diabetes Metab.* 28, 364-376

[36] Ford, E. S., Giles, W. H. & Dietz, W. H. (2002) Prevalence of the metabolic syndrome among US adults: findings from the third National Health and Nutrition Examination Survey. *Jama.* 287, 356-359.

[37] Ford, E. S. & Giles, W. H. (2003) A comparison of the prevalence of the metabolic syndrome using two proposed definitions. *Diabetes Care.* 26, 575-581

[38] Resnick, H. E., Jones, K., Ruotolo, G., Jain, A. K., Henderson, J., Lu, W. & Howard, B. V. (2003) Insulin resistance, the metabolic syndrome, and risk of incident cardiovascular disease in nondiabetic american indians: the strong heart study. *Diabetes Care.* 26, 861-867

[39] Jia, W. P., Xiang, K. S., Chen, L., Lu, J. X., Bao, Y. Q., Wu, Y. M. & Jiang, S. Y. (2004) A comparison of the application of two working definitions of metabolic syndrome in Chinese population. *Zhonghua Yi Xue Za Zhi.* 84, 534-538

[40] Kim, M. H., Kim, M. K., Choi, B. Y. & Shin, Y. J. (2004) Prevalence of the metabolic syndrome and its association with cardiovascular diseases in Korea. *J Korean Med Sci.* 19, 195-201

[41] Lee, W. Y., Park, J. S., Noh, S. Y., Rhee, E. J., Kim, S. W. & Zimmet, P. Z. (2004) Prevalence of the metabolic syndrome among 40,698 Korean metropolitan subjects. *Diabetes Res Clin Pract.* 65, 143-149

[42] Tan, C. E., Ma, S., Wai, D., Chew, S. K. & Tai, E. S. (2004) Can we apply the National Cholesterol Education Program Adult Treatment Panel definition of the metabolic syndrome to Asians? *Diabetes Care.* 27, 1182-1186

[43] Gu, D., Reynolds, K., Wu, X., Chen, J., Duan, X., Reynolds, R. F., Whelton, P. K. & He, J. (2005) Prevalence of the metabolic syndrome and overweight among adults in China. *Lancet.* 365, 1398-1405

[44] He, Y., Jiang, B., Wang, J., Feng, K., Chang, Q., Fan, L., Li, X. & Hu, F. B. (2006) Prevalence of the metabolic syndrome and its relation to cardiovascular disease in an elderly chinese population. *J Am Coll Cardiol.* 47, 1588-1594

[45] Steering Committee of the Western Pacific Region of the World Health Organization & the International Association for the Study of Obesity and the International Obesity Task Force. (2000) The Asia-Pacific perspective: redefining obesity and its treatment. Melbourne, Australia: Health Communications Australia Pty Limited, 2000. World Wide Web: http://www.obesityasiapacific.com/default.htm.

[46] Ilanne-Parikka, P., Eriksson, J. G., Lindstrom, J., Hamalainen, H., Keinanen-Kiukaanniemi, S., Laakso, M., Louheranta, A., Mannelin, M., Rastas, M., Salminen, V., Aunola, S., Sundvall, J., Valle, T., Lahtela, J., Uusitupa, M. & Tuomilehto, J. (2004) Prevalence of the Metabolic Syndrome and Its Components: Findings from a Finnish general population sample and the Diabetes Prevention Study cohort. *Diabetes Care*. 27, 2135-2140

[47] Murray, C. J. & Lopez, A. D. (1997) Mortality by cause for eight regions of the world: Global Burden of Disease Study. *Lancet*. 349, 1269-1276

[48] Reddy, K. S. & Yusuf, S. (1998) Emerging epidemic of cardiovascular disease in developing countries. *Circulation*. 97, 596-601

[49] Eriksson, K. F. & Lindgarde, F. (1991) Prevention of type 2 (non-insulin-dependent) diabetes mellitus by diet and physical exercise. The 6-year Malmo feasibility study. *Diabetologia*. 34, 891-898

[50] Pan, X., Li, G., Hu, Y., Wang, J., Yang, W., An, Z., Hu, Z., Lin, J., Xiao, J., Cao, H., Liu, P., Jiang, X., Jiang, Y., Wang, J., Zheng, H., Zhang, H., Bennett, P. & Howard, B. (1997) Effects of diet and exercise in preventing NIDDM in people with impaired glucose tolerance. The Da Qing IGT and Diabetes Study. *Diabetes Care*. 20, 537-544

[51] Tuomilehto, J., Lindstrom, J., Eriksson, J. G., Valle, T. T., Hamalainen, H., Ilanne-Parikka, P., Keinanen-Kiukaanniemi, S., Laakso, M., Louheranta, A., Rastas, M., Salminen, V. & Uusitupa, M. (2001) Prevention of type 2 diabetes mellitus by changes in lifestyle among subjects with impaired glucose tolerance. *N Engl J Med*. 344, 1343-1350

[52] Knowler, W. C., Barrett-Connor, E., Fowler, S. E., Hamman, R. F., Lachin, J. M., Walker, E. A. & Nathan, D. M. (2002) Reduction in the incidence of type 2 diabetes with lifestyle intervention or metformin. *N Engl J Med*. 346, 393-403

[53] Chiasson, J. L., Josse, R. G., Gomis, R., Hanefeld, M., Karasik, A. & Laakso, M. (2002) Acarbose for prevention of type 2 diabetes mellitus: the STOP-NIDDM randomised trial. *Lancet*. 359, 2072-2077

In: Metabolic Syndrome Research Trends
Editor: Thomas E. Batone, pp. 105-119
ISBN: 978-1-60456-224-8

Chapter IV

Associations Between Carbohydrate Intake and Risk for Coronary Heart Disease, Insulin Resistance and the Metabolic Syndrome

Maria Luz Fernandez[1,*] *and Marcela Vergara-Jimenez*[2]
[1]Department of Nutritional Sciences, University of Connecticut, Storrs, CT;
[2]Facultad de Ciencias Quimico-Biologicas, Universidad Autónoma de Sinaloa, Culiacán, Sinaloa, México

Abstract

Because the incidence of obesity has increased dramatically over the past 20 years, finding the most appropriate diets for losing weight has become a major issue. It is also well established that overweight individuals have a higher risk of developing insulin resistance, coronary heart disease (CHD) and diabetes type II. The amount of carbohydrate in the diet may play a significant role in the maintenance of body weight and in reducing the risk factors for chronic disease.

Dietary carbohydrates are indeed at the core of the debate regarding healthy diets that promote weight loss and decrease biomarkers for heart disease and the metabolic syndrome. Very low, moderate or high carbohydrate diets have been studied in their effects on body weight, dyslipidemias, insulin sensitivity, plasma glucose, leptin levels, inflammatory cytokines and adhesive molecules. Very low carbohydrate diets have been reported to effectively reduce body weight and improve plasma lipids and insulin sensitivity in studies of short duration between 4 to 24 weeks. Moderate and high carbohydrate diets have also been shown to have beneficial effects on anthropometrics and other cardiovascular risk factors depending on the duration of the study and the investigated population. Overall the controversies of the findings depend on the type of

* Corresponding author: Maria Luz Fernandez, Ph.D. University of Connecticut, Department of Nutritional Sciences, 3624 Horsebarn Rd. Ext. Storrs, CT 06269; Phone: 860-486-5547; Fax: 860-486-3674; Email: maria-luz.fernandez@uconn.edu

study (parallel versus randomized crossover) the duration of the intervention, the assessed subjects (normal versus diabetic or hyperlipidemic) and the retention of subjects, which appeared to be poor in the majority of the cases. All these factors still continue to make it difficult to interpret the available data and to reach conclusive statements regarding the relationship between dietary carbohydrate and chronic disease.

It is the purpose of the following review to evaluate a variety of clinical interventions conducted in the past 5 years in which dietary carbohydrate was one of the main variables under investigation. The effects of different dietary interventions varying in the amount of dietary carbohydrate on symptoms associated with the metabolic syndrome, insulin resistance and increased risk for CHD are discussed.

Keywords: Very low carbohydrate diets, High carbohydrate diets, coronary heart disease, metabolic syndrome, insulin resistance, plasma triglycerides, LDL-C, HDL-C, waist circumference.

Abbreviations

Apo,	apolipoprotein;
BBB,	blood-brain barrier;
BMI,	body mass index;
CAM-1,	cell adhesion molecule-1;
CHD,	coronary heart disease;
CNS,	central nervous system;
CRP,	C-reactive protein;
GI,	glycemic index;
HDL-C,	high density lipoprotein cholesterol;
IL-6,	Interleukin-6;
LDL-C,	low density lipoprotein cholesterol;
MetSyn,	metabolic syndrome;
TC,	total cholesterol;
TG,	triglycerides;
VAT,	visceral adipose tissue;
SCAT,	subcutaneous adipose tissue;
(TNF)α,	tumor necrosis factor;
WC,	waist circumference

Introduction

Current research does not support the theory that one weight loss program is successful for all populations [1,2]. The best approach on macronutrient composition, caloric restriction and levels of exercise is still disputed. Obesity is a public health challenge that claims approximately 300,000 lives a year [3] and depletes an estimated 9.4% of the health care budget [4]. Approximately 65% of the US population has a body mass index (BMI) of ≥ 25 kg/m^2 [5], which classifies them as overweight. Clinically, overweight and obese (BMI ≥ 30 kg/m^2) persons are at increased risk for coronary heart disease (CHD) and diabetes mellitus

Type 2 [6,7]. Adequate diets for the management and prevention of obesity, CHD, and diabetes are needed. However, experts disagree on what is the best "heart healthy" diet [8]. There still is controversy regarding dietary modifications that will result in weight loss, while maintaining a healthy plasma lipid and lipoprotein profile [9]. The maintenance of a healthy weight has been shown to be the best option to reduce the prevalence of biomarkers associated with chronic disease. Therefore, it is not surprising that food choices and selection of specific macronutrients aimed at reducing weight do play a major role in our health.

Recently, an increased interest on food choices varying in the concentration and type of macronutrients has emerged. It is mainly due to the higher prevalence of obesity, that the consumer has become more aware of the various food choices that are advertised to promote weight loss. Dietary carbohydrates appear to be the focal point of the surrounding confusion concerning a healthy weight loss. The American Public's main concern is with diets aimed at weight loss while the scientific community provides controversial or at the very least confusing information regarding the appropriate amount of carbohydrate to achieve the best results. It is well known for example that an excess intake of carbohydrate may have detrimental effects on the regulation of insulin [10] and on plasma triglyceride concentrations [11] while at the same time high carbohydrate diets are promoted for high-intensity resistance exercise [12]. Cohort studies have also shown an inverse association between complex carbohydrates and CHD [13]. However, other studies have demonstrated that carbohydrate intake is positively related to plasma TG, reduced insulin sensitivity and obesity [14]. Therefore it is vital to understand the interplay between insulin, dietary carbohydrates and potential abnormalities in metabolism, including biomarkers for CHD and diabetes type II.

It is particularly important to mention that per capita fructose consumption has increased during the past three decades within the same time frame as a marked increase in the prevalence of obesity [15,16]. Gross et al. [17] have shown that since 1963 carbohydrate intake has increased by 126 g/d with high fructose syrup providing 10% of total energy intake. In addition, the incidence of diabetes has increased by 47% suggesting that there could be a correlation between increased carbohydrate intake and higher prevalence of diabetes. Although refined carbohydrates have been linked to a wide array of chronic disease including diabetes, clear data are not readily available and controversy still remains [18]. In the past, fructose was considered to be beneficial in the dietary management of diabetes mellitus and insulin resistance because fructose ingestion resulted in smaller postprandial glycemic and insulin releases than do glucose and complex carbohydrates [19]. While high fructose corn syrup has a low GI and has been proposed as beneficial for diabetes type II [20], the concern about the effects of increasing plasma TG and decreasing HDL-C still remains [21]. Dietary fructose has been also associated with weight gain and induces insulin resistance, hyperlipidemia and hypertension in experimental animals. It is therefore possible that increased consumption of fructose could contribute to weight gain and its accompanying metabolic disturbances in humans.

Coronary Heart Disease and Dietary Carbohydrates

Numerous short-term studies have indicated that diets high in carbohydrates, particularly simple sugars (fructose and glucose) increase plasma TG concentrations and decrease HDL-C thus increasing the risk for CHD [22]. However, available epidemiological data indicate that high plasma TG could be more associated with the rate of absorption of dietary carbohydrate or glycemic index (GI) [23]. GI is defined as the increment area under the blood glucose response curve (IAUC) expressed as a percentage after the intake of a food containing 50 g carbohydrate by the same individual [24]. A randomized, parallel 10-wk study involving a high carbohydrate diet, reported a 10% decrease in LDL cholesterol (LDL-C) in subjects taking low compared to high GI foods [25]. Authors concluded that although there were no changes in body weight or appetite, the low GI diets may have a favorable effect in decreasing CHD risk. In contrast, a meta analysis of fifteen randomized clinical trials conducted by Kelly et al. [26] reported that the existing evidence regarding low GI and decrease risk for CHD is weak and that better controlled studies with longer duration are needed to reach any significant conclusions.

Dietary sucrose may increase hepatic TG synthesis and VLDL assembly and secretion and decrease the catabolism of TG-rich lipoproteins [27]. In addition, the presence of abdominal obesity appears to influence the effects of diets high in carbohydrates. This latter situation may be related to the increases in basal lipolysis observed in subjects with visceral obesity due to the higher fat depots, which results in a higher rate of fatty acids going to the liver. Reesterification of fatty acids in the liver provides a consistent substrate for increased VLDL production. In addition, the resistance of viscerally obese people to the action of insulin, may also contribute to the elevated concentrations of circulating TG [28]. In summary, dietary carbohydrate is highly associated with TG metabolism and the more pronounced response is observed in individuals with visceral obesity.

The optimal diet to reduce weight and cardiovascular risk factors cannot be generalized for all individuals. Both low carbohydrate and high carbohydrate (low fat) diets have been shown to cause beneficial effects on body weight and obesity-associated comorbidities with the low carbohydrate diet apparently having a greater beneficial effect at short term [28]. The use of low carbohydrate diets appears to have multiple beneficial effects on several risk factors associated with increased risk for CHD including regulation of dyslipidemias [29], lowering of blood pressure [30] and reduction in the production of inflammation markers such as cytokines and adhesive molecules [31]. Moderate carbohydrate diets (40% of energy) have also been proven successful in decreasing biomarkers for coronary heart disease [32]. Finally, a low caloric diet high in carbohydrate has been proven to successfully reduce LDL-C and overall improve plasma lipid levels [33].

Some dietary recommendations call for a low-fat (< 30% of energy), low saturated fat (< 7% of total energy) low cholesterol (< 300 mg/d) diet [34]. However high carbohydrate diets are controversial because they raise plasma TG and may negatively affect the composition and size of LDL, creating small dense LDL particles, and reduce HDL-C [35]. Sharman et al [36] conducted a study to analyze how healthy normolipidemic, normal weight men respond to a ketogenic diet in term of CHD biomarkers. Twelve men switched from their habitual diet (17% protein, 47% carbohydrate and 32% fat) to a ketogenic diet (30% protein, 8%

carbohydrate and 61% fat). Fasting serum TG and insulin concentrations significantly decreased, small increases in total and LDL-C, moderate increase in HDL-C and significant weigh loss (-2.2 kg) were found. The latter might be the cause of HDL and TG decreases in this study [36]. The same research team compared the effects of a very low-carbohydrates and a low-fat diet on fasting blood lipids and postprandial lipemia in overweight men [39]. Serum LDL-C concentrations from the low-fat diet group was the only reduced biomarker. The very low-carbohydrates diet significantly reduced TG, the TG/HDL-C ratio and glucose. Both diets reduced postprandial lipemia, but the reduction was greater with the very low-carbohydrates diet and also LDL-C particle size was larger with the very low-carbohydrate diet. This study therefore suggested that low-fat diets are good to reduce LDL-C.

Very low carbohydrate ketogenic diets appear to be valuable in the treatment of obesity and hyperlipidemia [30]. In addition, very low carbohydrate diets have been shown to be useful as an adjuct therapy for improving the plasma lipid profile in overweight subjects undergoing a stable statin therapy [37]. Several studies have been conducted comparing the effects of low- and high-carbohydrate diet on improving lipid profile and decreasing the risk for CHD. Stern et al. [38] compared overweight, hyperlipidemic volunteers randomly assigned to either a low-carbohydrate (< 20 g of carbohydrate per day) or a low-fat diet (< 30% energy from fat) during 24 weeks. Higher reductions in plasma TG and elevations in HDL-C were observed in those individuals taking the low carbohydrate diet [38]. However, the authors do mention that one limitation to the study was the intake of nutritional supplements by the low carbohydrate group that might have interfered with some of the observed results. Longer term studies have also shown that low carbohydrate diet have more favorable outcomes on dyslipidemias compared to calorie restricted diets with < 30% energy from fat in obese adults [38]. Participants were advised to either restrict carbohydrate intake or to restrict caloric intake by 500 calories per day. The reduction in weight after one year was 5.1 kg for the low carbohydrate and 3.1 kg for the low calorie diet. In addition, after one year, there was a 28% decrease in plasma TG following the low fat diet while no significant changes in plasma TG were observed in subjects following the low calorie diet. Further, after adjustment for covariates, hemoglobin A_{1c} levels improved in the low carbohydrate group only.

Because it has been postulated that several energy-consuming pathways are up-regulated with a very low intake of carbohydrates, a study was conducted in obese postmenopausal women in which protein and energy were maintained constant and only carbohydrate and fat varied significantly [39]. After 6 months, no differences in plasma lipids, glucose or insulin were observed between dietary groups. However, the group assigned to the very low carbohydrate diet presented a trend for TG reduction and lower plasma insulin levels, a trend that could become significant after more subjects are evaluated since this preliminary report only presents the results of 4 subjects [39].

In contrast Jacobs et al. [33] reported that a low fat diet (29% energy) was more effective in reducing plasma TG in hypertriglyceridemic patients than a high fat (40% energy) diet when the baseline concentrations of plasma TG were higher than 396 mg/dL. After analyzing the results for the 17 subjects who participated in this cross over design, the authors concluded that those individuals who were slightly hypertriglyceridemic had a very significant lowering of plasma TG following the high carbohydrate diet. However, 5 of the 9 subjects who had baseline plasma TG > 396 mg/dL benefited more by the low-fat intervention period [33].

In another randomized trial conducted for one year, 63 obese men and women were assigned to either a low- or a high-carbohydrate diet [40]. Subjects following the low carbohydrate diet lost more weight at 3 and 6 months, however, no significant differences between groups were observed after 1 year. At the end of the intervention changes in total cholesterol and LDL-C did not differ among participants. In contrast reductions in plasma TG and increases in HDL-C were more prominent in subjects following the low carbohydrate diet [40]. A significant observation reported by the authors was that LDL-C tended to increase after 3 months in subjects on the low carbohydrate compared to those in the high carbohydrate group ($P < 0.05$). Nevertheless, on the long term there were no significant differences in plasma LDL-C concentrations between groups suggesting that the weight loss compensated the adverse effects associated with high saturated fat consumption. The authors also raised the concern of the interpretation of the clinical significance of decreased TG and increased HDL-C in the context of high saturated fat and low fiber intake and pointed out the need for more studies to clarify the overall relationship of type of diet, weight loss and risk for CHD.

Results from a recent study in which the effects of different diets were evaluated on cardiovascular risk factors did not find significant associations between carbohydrate intake and body weight or improved plasma lipid profiles [41]. In this single center trial, 160 participants were randomly assigned to a very low carbohydrate or Atkins diet (< 20 g/d), a diet with 40% of calories derived from carbohydrate (Zone diet), a Weight Watchers diet where the participants limited their caloric intake and a very low fat diet (< 10% energy from fat) [41]. After 1 year all participants experienced a decrease in the LDL/HDL ratio and moderate decreases in weight. The percentage of subjects who completed the study ranged from 50% for the weight watchers to 65% for the group assigned to the Zone diet. Overall adherence was low and the observed improvement in cardiovascular risk factors was not different among dietary groups. Results from this study suggest that weigh loss was the most significant parameter associated with overall health benefits [41].

Lofgren et al. [32] recruited 70 overweight/obese pre-menopausal women to participate in a weight loss study consisting on a dietary modification including caloric restriction (85% of total energy expenditure) and a moderately low carbohydrate diet (40% of energy). All participants presented a significant decrease in plasma TG, apolipoprotein (apo) B and E concentrations and significant reductions in the smaller LDL subfractions. In addition there was a significant decrease in LDL susceptibility to oxidation as assessed by an increased lag time and a decrease in conjugated diene formation. All these beneficial effects were obtained in plasma lipids only with slight reduction in dietary carbohydrates. When step wise regression analysis was conducted, the changes in dietary carbohydrate had a significant contribution in the reduction of plasma TG after controlling for weight loss. Lower plasma TG are associated with a lower distribution of LDL into the smaller subfractions [14], therefore and because the smaller LDL are known to substantially increase the risk for coronary heart disease [42] overall the beneficial effect of this moderately low carbohydrate diet translates into lower risk for CHD.

A comparative parallel randomized study tested the standard American diet, a low-fat, high carbohydrate diet and the same diet in conjunction with olestra on risk factors for CHD in obese subjects [43]. The low-fat diet containing olestra had the most significant effects on weight loss with a decrease of 6.27 kg compared to 4 and 1.79 for the American diet and the low-fat diet, respectively. In addition, the olestra group had more beneficial effects on CHD risk due to significant decreases in plasma LDL-C and TG, which were not observed in the other two groups. HDL-C was not lowered after 9 months for any of the dietary groups. Authors concluded that the beneficial effects in the olestra group were mostly explained by the weight loss [43].

A summary of the results of very low, moderate and high carbohydrate intake and the effects on distinct biomarkers for chronic disease is presented in Table 1.

Table 1. Effects of low, moderate and high carbohydrate (CHO) intake on Biomarkers for CHD, Insulin Resistance and the Metabolic Syndrome

Study	CHO Amount	Duration	TG	LDL-C	HDL-C	LDL Size	LDL oxidation	Insulin	Glucose
Jacobs et al. [33][1]	42%	3-week	↓	↔	↔	ND	↓	ND	ND
Crossover design	52%	3 week	↓	↓	↔	ND	↓	ND	ND
Stern et al. [38]	33%	1 year	↓	↔	↓	ND	ND	↔	↓[2]
Parallel design	50%	1 year	↔	↔	↓	ND	ND	↔	↓
Yancy et al. [30]	10%	24-week	↓	↔	↑	ND	ND	ND	ND
Parallel design	~55%	24-week	↓	↔	↔	ND	ND	ND	ND
Sharman et al.	47%	6-week	↔	↓	↔	↔	↔	↓	↓
[29] Crossover design	8%	6-week	↓	↓	↔	↑	↔	↓	↔
Rodriguez-Villar	50%	6-week	↔	↔	↔	↑	↔	↔	↓
[54] Crossover design	40%	6-week	↓[3]	↔	↔	ND	↔	↔	↔
Zern et al.[4]	40%	10-week	↓	↓	↔	↑	↓	↓	↔
Foster et al. [40][5]	10%	1 year	↓	↔	↔	ND	ND	↔	↔
Parallel design	60 %	1 year	↔	↔	↑	ND	ND	↓	↔

Arrows indicate increases (↑), decreases (↓) or no changes (↔). ND = not determined.

[1] More favorable for patients with TG levels > 4.5 mmol/L, [2] Only in diabetic individuals, [3] TG in VLDL, [4] Compared to baseline (average 53%), [5] Significant decrease in LDL-C after 3 months in 60% CHO group.

The Metabolic Syndrome, Type II Diabetes and Dietary Carbohydrates

The term "metabolic syndrome (MetSyn)" is now preferable to "insulin resistance syndrome". Findings from the third National Health and Nutrition Survey demonstrated a prevalence of 25% in US individuals aged > 20 years, rising to 40% by age >60 [44]. The MetSyn is postulated to be resistance to insulin-mediated glucose disposal by muscle [45], 30% of adult males and 10-15% of postmenopausal women have this particular syndrome which is associated with an increased risk for heart disease.

The National Cholesterol Education Program (ATP III) [46] has classified individuals as having the MetSyn if three of the following characteristics are present: Plasma TG higher than 150 mg/dL, Plasma HDL-C lower than 45 mg/dL in men and 50 mg/dL in women, systolic/diastolic blood pressure > 125/80 mm of Hg, waist circumference (WC) > 88 cm in women and > 102 cm in men and fasting plasma glucose > 110 mg/dL. The prevalence of the MetSyn is high among Hispanics. In the III National Health and Nutrition Examination Survey, (NHANES III), Hispanics had the highest age-adjusted prevalence of the MetSyn, which was probably linked to the higher prevalence of obesity [47]. The presence of three or more features associated with the MetSyn, have been identified in the young Hispanic population (8-13 y old) with insulin resistance playing a major role in the observed dyslipidemias [48].

As described before, waist circumference seems to play an important role in the development of the MetSyn. While abdominal obesity is determined by the accumulation of both subcutaneous adipose tissue (SCAT) and visceral adipose tissue (VAT), some studies described that VAT appears to play a major role in the MetSyn [49]. VAT is located in the body cavity beneath the abdominal muscles, whereas SCAT is located beneath the skin and on top of the abdominal musculature, femoral and gluteal regions [50]. The "Portal Theory" suggests that insulin resistance and many of its related features could arise from VAT delivering free fatty acids in a high rate to the liver via the portal vein into which VAT directly drains. This in turn, would increase hepatic glucose production, reduce hepatic insulin clearance and finally lead to insulin resistance, hyperinsulinemia, hyperglycemia as well as non-alcoholic fatty liver disease [51].

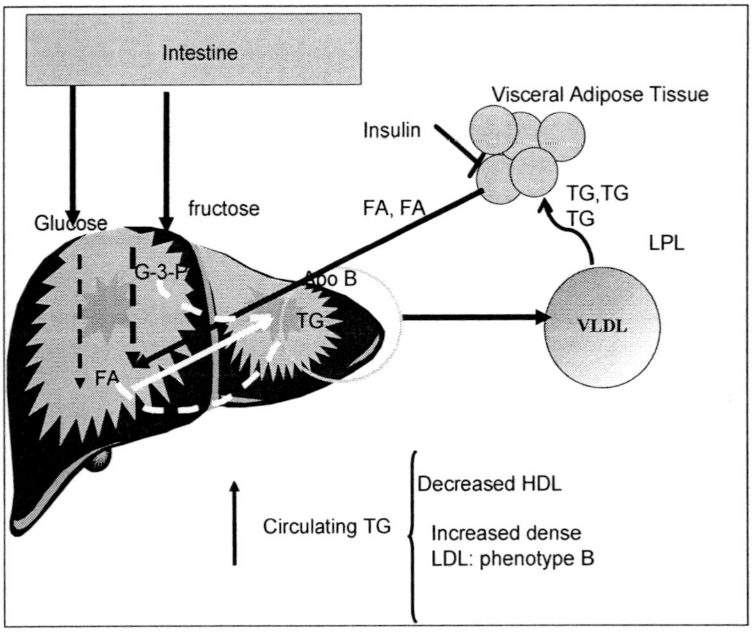

Figure 1. Increases in plasma triglycerides in subjects with the MetSyn and the consequences of a high carbohydrate diet. High carbohydrate diets promote the formation of free fatty acids. Glucose is converted to glucose 6-phospate as it enters the hepatocyte and through a series of reaction in which phsphofuctokinase, a highly regulated enzymes, the pathway progresses to lactate and then to fatty acids. In contrast, fructose bypasses this enzyme and thus it is more readily converted to fatty acids. Fatty acids are then used to form TG, which packaged with apo B result in increased secretion of VLDL. Subjects with the MetSyn because of the accumulation of visceral obesity, they develop insulin resistance and thus there is an unregulated secretion of fatty acids, which go back to the liver and are utilized for TG formation and packaging into VLDL promoting the increase of circulating TG.

Figure 1 illustrates the effects of a high carbohydrate diet in individuals with the MetSyn characterized for VAT accumulation. When carbohydrate is increased in the diet, higher concentrations of both glucose and fructose enter to the liver through portal circulation. Excess sugars can be readily converted into fatty acids, with fructose having a higher conversion rate due to the bypassing of phosphofructokinase, a highly regulated enzyme. In addition the quick formation of glyceraldehyde - 3 phosphate from fructose favors the esterification of fatty acids for TG synthesis. This pathway has a minor contribution to increasing the synthesis of VLDL. In addition, the increased flux of fatty acids from VAT to the liver due to insulin resistance make a significant contribution to VLDL assembly and secretion resulting in higher levels of circulating TG.

Very low-carbohydrate diets seem to improve all the biomarkers associated with the MetSyn [29]. Recent studies by Volek et al [2] showed that a short-term isoenergetic very low carbohydrate diet significantly decreased fasting and postpandrial TG, increased HDL-C, decreased the total cholesterol/HDL-C ratio and did not affect CRP or TNF-α. The large increase in HDL-C could have been due to increased production by hepatocytes and the intestinal mucosa and/or increased lipoprotein-lipase (LPL), which results in disassociation of surface components that are acquired by HDL-C. Studies conducted in mice fed with a high fat diet observed a very strong correlation between increases in postheparin LPL activity and increasing HDL-C [52]. In humans, moderate to high fat diets (46 – 65% of total energy) significantly increased postheparin plasma LPL activity and skeletal muscle LPL activity [53].

The macronutrient content of the diet has been linked to the insulin resistance syndrome, for example, the effects of a high monounsaturated fat diet and a high carbohydrate diet were tested on the resistance of LDL to oxidation in Type 2 diabetic patients in an intervention, which followed a randomized crossover design [54]. In addition, high-fat, particularly high saturated fat diets, induce weight gain, insulin resistance and hyperlipidemia in humans and animals. When the acceptability of the two diets was compared at the end of 6 weeks, the high fat diet was preferred by the patients. Although no significant effects on plasma cholesterol, TG, HDL-C, parameters of LDL oxidation, body weight or glycemic control were observed between the two dietary periods, significant reductions were observed in both VLDL cholesterol and TG during the high fat period. Authors concluded that a high fat diet rich in monounsaturated fat is a good alternative for patients with type II diabetes since the diet was found to be palatable and highly accepted by the patients plus there were some additional beneficial effects on the plasma lipid profiles of these individuals [54].

Optimizing macronutrients and food preparation can have beneficial effects in individuals with visceral fat. There are some reviews that support the metabolic benefits of controlling the GI and the glycemic load (GL). In a 12-month pilot study in teens, a conventional diet was compared to the lower GI diet, which resulted in a greater total weight and fat loss without regain from months 6-12. While insulin resistance increased in the conventional diet group, the lower GI group showed no change [55]. Data from cross-sectional studies have shown that by reducing energy intake and weight loss in obese type 2 diabetic subjects, an improvement in insulin sensitivity, blood glucose levels, lipid profile and blood pressure in the short-term is observed [56]. Recently, Silvestre et al [57] showed that compared to an energy restricted low-fat diet, a short term very low-carbohydrate diet was associated with greater weight and fat loss with an apparent preferential loss of central fat. McAuley et al. [58] conducted a study in which 96 insulin resistant women were assigned either to a very low carbohydrate diet, a moderate carbohydrate diet (40% energy) or a high carbohydrate diet during 16 weeks (8 weeks of weight loss and 8 weeks of weight maintenance). When compared to the high carbohydrate diet, women on the very low and moderate carbohydrate groups had a greater reduction in waist circumference ($P < 0.01$), plasma triglycerides (P

<0.01) and a better effect in reducing insulin resistance. Authors concluded that the very low and the moderate carbohydrate diets are more appropriate for reducing the risk for cardiovascular disease in type 2 diabetes patients and that the high carbohydrate diet needs to include a higher amount of fiber and possible reduce saturated fat to achieve the similar effects as the lower carbohydrate groups [58].

C-reactive protein (CRP) is considered an important marker of inflammation and a risk factor for the MetSyn [59]. CRP seems to be a powerful predictor for CHD and diabetes and is positively associated with both insulin resistance and the prevalence of the MetSyn. A very low carbohydrate diet was compared to a low fat diet in a weight loss intervention to assess the effects of macronutrient intake on the inflammatory response [29]. In a crossover design, 15 overweight subjects were given either a diet with < 10% energy derived from carbohydrates or a diet with <30% energy from fat. Both diets were equally successful in decreasing tumor necrosis factor (TNF)α, Interleukin-6(IL-6), CRP and cell adhesion molecule-1 (CAM-1) indicating that weight loss is the primary driving force to reduce inflammation biomarkers. A number of studies have demonstrated the association between glycemic load and levels of CRP. O'Brien et al demonstrated a significant reduction in CRP in women after 3 months of consuming a hypocaloric-very low carbohydrate diet than after consuming a energy-matched low fat diet [60]. Weight loss could be also implicated in the reduction of CRP concentrations, thus Tchernof et al [61] suggested that a hypoenergetic very low carbohydrate or low fat diet, if used for weight loss, may lower CRP as was observed by the O'Brien study and therefore reduce the CHD and the MetSyn risk.

Dietary carbohydrates may also have influence on leptin action. Studies by Havel et al demonstrated that consumption of high-fat meals, produced smaller postprandrial glucose and insulin responses than equicaloric high-carbohydrates meals, and reduced 24-h circulating leptin concentrations in humans [62]. Later on, Mueller et al associated the reductions of leptin concentrations to a decreased insulin-mediated glucose metabolism in adipose tissue [63]. Insulin and leptin function as key signals conveying information on energy intake and body fat stores to the Central Nervous System (CNS) for the long-term regulation of food intake and energy homeostasis [64]. It is possible that reduced insulin and leptin production contributes to increase energy intake, weight gain, and obesity in animals and humans consuming high-fat diets. Because fructose, unlike glucose, does not stimulate insulin secretion, Teff et al conducted a study where they hypothesized that rich fructose meals would result in lower leptin concentrations than meals containig the same amount of glucose. They fed 12 normal-weight women on 2 randomized days during which the subjects consumed three meals containing 55, 30 and 15% of total kilocalories from carbohydrates, fat, and proteins respectively, with 30% of kilocalories as either a fructose-sweetened (HFr) or glucose-sweetened (HGl) beverage. Meals were isocaloric in the two treatments. Consuming HFr beverages with meals resulted in lower circulating insulin and leptin concentrations and higer TG concentrations compared with consumption of HGl beverages [65]. Because insulin and leptin function as key signals to the CNS in the long-term regulation of energy balance, prolonged consumption of diets high in energy from fructose could lead to increased caloric intake and contribute to weigh gain and obesity. In addition, the elevation of TG concentrations after fructose consumption suggests that chronic fructose consumption, as in the case of diabetic patients, could contibute to atherogenesis, cardiovascular disease and the MetSyn. The relation between cerebrospinal fluid and serum levels of leptin in obese humans suggests that defective blood brain barrier (BBB) transport accounts for a great deal of leptin resistance in the CNS. Banks et al [66] conducted a study, where high-fat milk (98% of TG) and fat-free milk were used in vitro, in vivo and in situ in mice. They demonstrated that a high-fat diet significantly increased serum TG concentrations and that high TG levels directly inhibited the transport of leptin across the BBB and could be a major cause of leptin resistance across the CNS. Thus, authors suggested that serum TG are one of the major cause of the leptin resistance seen in both obesity and starvation [66]. This study demonstrates that just by lowering TG, it is possible to appreciate the effects of leptin on weight loss.

Conclusion

The review from these studies has demonstrated the importance of diet modifications in the maintenance of ideal body weight and on the reduction of biomarkers of chronic disease. It is evident that the amount of dietary carbohydrate plays a major role in determining plasma TG concentrations and other metabolic alterations associated with these plasma lipids. Elevated plasma TG are both a marker for the MetSyn and for increased risk for CHD. It is also evident from these studies that diets aimed at reducing obesity, a modifiable risk factor are beneficial independent of the amount of carbohydrates in the diet.

Although the high carbohydrate diet reduces LDL-C and with lifestyle modifications may slow the progression of atherosclerosis, evidence from the various clinical studies indicate that this diet may not be appropriate for patients who are obese (especially those with visceral obesity) or for subjects who are classified with the MetSyn. In contrast, the very low carbohydrate diet appears to be more effective for weight loss at short term and for reducing plasma TG, increasing HDL, increasing the concentration of large buoyant LDL and in some cases, reduce blood pressure and increase insulin sensitivity. However, the long-term benefits of this diet remain unconfirmed. The intake of reasonably low amounts of carbohydrate (~ 40% of total energy) could be a dietary intervention easier to follow for longer time periods and potentially become a useful alternative, specifically for those patients with hypertriglyceridemia, insulin resistance and the MetSyn.

References

[1] Mensink RP, Zock PL, Kester ADM, Katan MB. Effects of dietary fatty acids and carbohydrates on the ration of serum total to HDL cholesterol and on serum lipids and apolipoproteins: a meta-analysis of 60 controlled trials. *Am. J. Clin. Nutr.* 2003; 77: 146-1155.

[2] Volek JS, Sharman MJ, Gomez AL, Scheett TP, Kraemer WJ. An isoenergenic very low carbohydrate diet improves serum HDL cholesterol and triacylglycerol concentrations, the total cholesterol to HDL cholesterol ratio and postprandial lipemic responses compared with a low fat diet in normal weight, normolipidemic women. *J. Nutr.* 2003; 133:2756-2761.

[3] Must A, Spadano J, Coakley EH, Field AE, Colditz G, Dietz WH. The disease burden associated with overweight and obesity. *J. Am. Med. Assoc.* 1999; 282:1523-1529.

[4] Colditz G, Economic costs of obesity and inactivity. *Med Sci. Sports Exerc.* 1999; 31: S663-S667.

[5] Virgin SES, JA. Metabolic syndrome. J. *Am. Assoc. Oc. Health Nurs*. 2003; 51:38-37.

[6] Liu S, Willett WC, Manson JE, Hu FB, Rosner B, Colditz G. Relation between changes in intakes of dietary fiber and grain products and changes in weight and development of obesity among middle-aged women. *Am J. Clin. Nutr.* 2003; 78:920-927.

[7] Lofgren IE, Herron KL, Zern TL, West KL, Patalay M, Shachter NS, Koo SI, Fernandez, ML. Waist circumference is a better predictor than body mass index of coronary heart disease risk in overweight premenopausal women. *J. Nutr.* 2004; 134:1071-1076.

[8] Chahoud G, Aude YW & Methta JL. Dietary recommendations in the prevention and treatment of coronary heard disease: do we have the ideal diet yet? *Am. J. Cardiol.* 2004; 94:1260-1267.

[9] Hu FB, Manson JE, Willett WC. Types of dietary fat and risk of coronary heart disease: A critical review. *J. Am. Coll. Nutr.* 2001; 20:5-19.

[10] Velasquez-Mieyer PA, Cowan PA, Arheart KL, et al. Suppression of insulin secretion is associated with weight loss and altered macronutrient intake and preference in a subset of obese adults. *Int. J. Obes.* 2003; 27:219-226.

[11] Grundy SM. Dietary influences on serum lipids and lipoproteins. *J. Lipid Res.* 1990; 31:1149-1172.

[12] Thyfault JP, Carper MJ, Richmond SR, Hulver MW, Potteiger JA. Effect of liquid carbohydrate ingestion on markers of anabolism following high-intensity resistance exercise. *J. Strenght Con. Res.* 2004; 18:174-179.

[13] Rajala, M. and P.E. Scherer, Minireview: The adipocyte - at the crossroads of energy homeostasis, inflammation and atherosclerosis. *Endocrinology*, 2003; 144:3765-3773.

[14] Dreon DM, Fernstrom HA, Williams PT, Krauss RM. LDL subclass patterns and lipoprotein response to a low-fat, high-carbohydrate diet in women. *Arterioscler. Thromb. Vasc. Biol.* 1997; 17:707-714.

[15] Kuczmarski RJ, Flegal KM, Campbell SM and Johnson CL. Increasing prevalence of overweight among US adults. The National Health and Nutrition Examination Surveys, 1960 to 1991. *JAMA.* 1994; 272:205-211.

[16] Putnam JJ and Allshouse JE. Food consumption, prices and expeditures, 1970-1997. Washington, DC: U.S. Deparment of Agriculture, Economic research Service.

[17] Gross LS, Li L, Ford ES and Liu S. Increased consumption of refined carbohydrates and the epidemic of type 2 diabetes in the United States: an ecological assessment. *Am J. Clin. Nutr.* 2004:79:774-779.

[18] Jenkins DJA, Kendalll CWC, Marchie A, Augustin LSA. Too much sugar, too much carbohydrate or just too much? *Am. J. Clin. Nutr.* 2004; 79:711-712.

[19] Glinsmann WH and Bowman BA. The publica health significance of dietary fructose. *Am. J. Clin Nutr.* 1993; 58(suppl):820S-823S.

[20] Osei K and Bossetti B. Dietary fructose as a natural sweetener in poorly controlled type 2 diabetes: a 12-month crossover study of effects on glucose, lipoprotein and apolipoprotein metabolism. *Diabet. Med.* 1989; 6:506-511.

[21] Crapo PA, Koltermann OG and Henry RR. Metabolic consequence of two-week fructose feeding in diabetic subjects. *Diabetes Care* 1986; 9:111-119.

[22] Parks EJ & Hellerstein MK. Carbohydrate-induced hypertriacylglycerolemia : historical perspective and review of biological mechanisms. *Am. J. Clin. Nutr.* 2000; 71:412-413.

[23] Fried SK & Rao SP. Sugars, hyperriglyceridemia and cardiovascular disease. *Am. J. Clin. Nutr.* 2003: 78(suppl):873S-880S.

[24] Rizkalla SW, Bellisle F, Slama G. Health benefits of low glycaemic index foods, such as pulses, in diabetic patients and healthy individuals. *Br J Nutr.* 2002; 88(suppl 3):S255-S262.

[25] Sloth B, Krog-Mikkelsen I, flint A, Tetens I, Bjorck I, Vinoy S, Elmstahl H, Arstrup A, Lang V & Rabben A. No difference in body weight decrease between a low-glycemic index and high-glycemic index diet but reduced LFL cholesterol after 10-week ad libitum intake of the low-glycemic-index diet. *Am. J. Clin. Nutr.* 2004; 80:337-347.

[26] Kelly S, Frost G, Whitaker V & Summerbell C. Low glycemic index diets for coronary heart disease. *Cochrane Database Syst Rev.* 2004; 18:CD004467.

[27] Hellerstein MK. Carbohydrate-induced hypertriglyceridemia: modifying factors and implications for cardiovascular risk. *Curr. Op. Lipidol* 2002; 13:33-40.

[28] Klein S. Clinical trial experience with fat-restricted vs carbohydrate-restricted weight-loss diets. *Obes. Res.* 2004; 12:141S-144S.

[29] Sharman MJ, Gomez AL, Kraemer WJ & Volek JS. Very low-carbohydrate and low-fat diets affect fasting lipids and postrandial lipemia differently in overweight men. *J. Nutr.* 2004; 134:880-885.

[30] Yancy WS Jr, Olsen MK, Guyton JR, Bakst RP & Westman EC. A low – carbohydrate, ketogenic diet versus a low-fat diet to treat obesity and hyperlipidemia. *Annal. Int. Med.* 2004; 140:769-777.

[31] Sharman MJ & Volek JS. Weight loss leads to reductions in inflammatory biomarkers after a very-low-carbohydrate diet and low-fat diet in overweight men. *Clin. Sci.* 2004;107:365-369.

[32] Lofgren IE, Zern TL, Herron KL, West KL, Sharman M, Volek JS, Shachter NS, Koo SI and Fernandez ML. Weight loss reduces the atherogenicity of LDL in premenopausal women. *Metabolism Clin. Ext.* 2005; 54:133-1141.

[33] Jacobs B, De Angelis-Schierbaum G, Egert S, Assmann G & Kratz M. Individual serum triglyceride responses to high-fat and low-fat diets differ in men with modest and severe hypertriglyceridemia. *J Nutr.* 2004; 134:1400-1405.

[34] National Cholesterol Education Program Expert Panel on Detection, Evaluation and Tratment of High blood cholesterol in adults (adult treatment panel III). National Heart, lung and blood institute and national Institutes of Health, Bethesda, MD (NHI publication No. 01-3670) May 2001.

[35] Schneeman BO. Carbohydrate: friend or foe? Summary of research needs. *J. Nutr.* 2001; 131:2764S-2765S.

[36] Sharman MJ, Kraemer WJ, Love DM, Avery NG, Gómez AL, Scheett TP and Volek JF. A ketogenic diet favorable affects seru biomarkers for cardiovascular disease in normal weight men. *J.Nutr.* 2002; 132:1879-1885.

[37] Gann D. A low carbohydrate diet in overweight patients undergoing stable statin therapy raises high-density lipoprotein and lowers triglycerides substantially. *Clin. Cardiol.* 2004; 27:563-564.

[38] Stern L, Iqbal N, Seshadri P, Chicano KL, Daily DA, McGrory J, Williams M, Gracely EJ & Samaha FF. The effects of low-carbohydrate versus conventional weight loss diets in severely obese adults: One year follow-up of a randomized trial. *Ann Intern Med* 2004; 140:778-785.

[39] Segal-Isaacson CJ, Johnson S, Tomuta V, Crowell B & Stein DT. A randomized trial comparing low-fat and low carbohydrate diets matched for energy and protein. Obes. Res. 2004; 12:130S-140S.

[40] Foster GD, Wyatt HR, Hill JO, McGuckin BG, Brill C, Mohammed S, Szapary PO, Rader DJ, Edman JS & Klein S. A randomized trial of low-carbohydrate diet for obesity. *New. Eng. J. Med.* 2003; 328:2082-2090.

[41] Dansinger ML, Gleason JA, Griffith JL, Selker HP & Schaefer EJ. Comparison of the Atkins, Ornish,weight watchers, and zone diets for weight loss and heart disease risk reduction. A ramdomized trial. *Am. Med. Assoc.* 2005; 293: 43-53.

[42] Krauss RM. Atherogenic lipoprotein phenotype and diet-gene interactions. *J. Nutr.* 131:340S-343S.

[43] Lovejoy JC, Bray GA, Lefevre M, Smith SR, Most MM, Denkins YM, Volaufova J, Rood JC, Eldrige AL & Peters JC. Consumption of a controlled low-fat diet containing olestra for 9 months improves health risk factors in conjuction with weight loss in obese men: the Olé study. *Int. J. Obes.* 2003; 27:1242-1249.

[44] Ford ES, Giles WH, Dietz WH. Prevalence of metabolic syndrome among US adults-Finding from the Third National Health and Nutrition Examination Survey. *JAMA-J Am Med Assoc.* 2002; 287:356-359.

[45] Reaven GM. Diet and syndrome X. *Curr Atheroscler. Rep.* 2000;2:503-507.

[46] Expert Panel on Detection EaToHBCiA. Executive summary of the third report of the National Cholesterol Education Program (NCEP) Expert Panel on detection, evaluation and treatment of high blood cholesterol in adults (Adult Treatment Panel III). *J. Am. Med. Assoc.* 2001; 285:2486-2497.

[47] Flegal KM, Carroll MD, Ogden CL, Johnson CL. Prevalence and trends in obesity among US adults, 1999-2000. *J. Am. Med. Assoc.* 2002; 288:1723-1727.

[48] Cruz ML, Weigensberg MJ, Hunag TTK, \Ball G, Shaibi GQ & Goran MI. The metabolic syndrome in overweight Hispanic youth and the role of insulin sensitivity. *J. Clin Endocrinol. Met.* 2004; 89:108-113.

[49] Lamarche B. Abdominal obesity and its metabolic complications: implications for the risk of ischaemic heart disease. *Corno Artery Dis.* 1998; 9:473-481.

[50] Wajchenberg BL. Subcutaneous and visceral adipose tissue: their relation to the metabolic syndrome. *Endocr Rev.* 2000; 21:697-738.

[51] Bjorntorp P. "Portal" adipose tissue as a generator of risk factors for cardiovascular disease and diabetes. *Atherosclerosis.* 1990; 10:493-496.

[52] Clee SM, Zhang H, Bissada N, Miao L, Ehrenborg E, Benlian P, Shen GX, Angel A, LeBoeuf, Rc and Hayden MR. Relatioship between lipoprotein lipase and high density lipoprotein cholesterol in mice: modulation by cholesteryl ester transfer protein and dietary status. *J. Lipid Res.* 1997; 38:2079-2089.

[53] Campos H, Dreon DM and Krauss RM. Association of hepatic and lipoprotein lipase activities with changes in dietary composition and low density lipoprotein subclasses. *J. Lipid Res.* 1995; 36:462-472.

[54] Rodrigues-Villar C, Perez-Heras A, Mercade I, Casals E & Ros E. Comparison of a high-carbohydrate and ahihg-monounsaturated fat, olive-oil rich diet on the susceptibility of LDL to oxidative modification in subjects with Type 2 diabetes mellitus. *Diabet. UK. Diabet. Med.* 2003; 21:142-149.

[55] Ebbeling CB and Ludwig DS. Treating obesity in youth: should dietary glycemic load be a consideration?. *Adv Pediatr.* 2001; 48:179-217.

[56] Heilbonn LK, Noakes M and Clifton PM. Effect of energy restriction, weight loss, and diet composition on plasma lipids and glucose in patients with type 2 diabetes. *Diabetes Care.* 1999; 22:889-895.

[57] Silvestre R, Sharman MJ, Gómez AL, Judelson DA, Watson G, RuffinK, Kraemer WJ and Volek JS. A very low-carbohydrate diet results in greater reductions in body weight, whole body fat, and trunk fat than a low-fat diet in overweight subjects. *In Kings-brook conference on nutritional and metabolic aspects of low carbohydrate diets. Brooklyn, University of Connecticut (Storrs).* 2004.

[58] McAuley KA, Hopkins CM, Smith KJ, McLay RT, Williams SM, Taylor RW and Mann JI. Comparison of high-fat and high-protein diets with a high carbohydrate diet in insulin-resistant obese women. Diabetologia 2004(pub med, ahead of print).

[59] Libby P, Ridker PM and MASERI a. Inflammatory bio-markers and cardiovascular risk prediction. *Circulation.* 2002; 105:1135-1143.

[60] O'Brien KD, Brehm BJ, Seely RJ, Tener M, Daniels S and D Alessio D.A. Greater reduction of inflammatory markers with a low carbohydrate diet than with a carolically matched, low fat diet. *Presented at the American Heart Association,s Scientific Sessions.* 2002. November 19, Chicago IL (abs.# 117597).

[61] Tchernof A, Nolan A, Sites CK, Ades PA and Poehlman ET. Weight loss reduces C-reactive protein levels in obese postmenopausal women. *Circulation.* 2002;105:564-569.

[62] Havel PJ, Townsend r, Chaump L and teff K. High-fat meals reduce 24-h circulating leptin concentrations in women. *Diabetes.* 1999; 48:334-3341.

[63] Mueller WM, Gregoire FM, stanhope KL, Mobbs CV, Mizuno TM, Warden CH, stern JS and Havel PJ. Evidence that glucose metabolism regulates leptin secretion from cultured rat adipocytes. *Endocrinology.* 1998; 139:551-558.

[64] Havel PJ. Control of energy homeostasis and insulin action by adipocyte hormones: leptin, acylation stimulating protein, and adiponectin. *Curr Opin Lipidol.* 2002; 13:51-59.

[65] Teff KL, Elliott SS, Tschop M, Kieffer TJ, Rader D, Heiman M, Townsend RR, Keim NL, D'alessio D and Havel PJ. Dietary fructose reduces circulating insulin and leptin, attenuates postprandial suppression of ghrelin and increases triglycerides in women.*J Clin Endocrinol Metab.* 2004; 89:2963-2972.

[66] Banks WA, Coon AB, Robinson SM, Moinuddin A, Shultz JM, Nakaoke R, and Morley JE. Triglycerides induce leptin resistance at the blood-brain barrier. *Diabetes.* 2004; 53:1253-1260.

In: Metabolic Syndrome Research Trends
Editor: Thomas E. Batone, pp. 121-151
ISBN: 978-1-60456-224-8

Chapter V

Diets for Weight Reduction: The Recommended Diets and the Popular Diets

Annie Ferland and Paul Poirier[1]
Institut universitaire de cardiologie et de pneumologie,
Hôpital Laval, Université Laval, Sainte-Foy, Québec, Canada

Introduction

It is well recognized that the prevalence of metabolic abnormalities found in the presence of obesity is increasing within our sedentary population. In fact, obesity is a growing epidemic that is primarily due to environmental influences. There has been a rapid increase in obesity over the past 30 years in North America, whereas the recent prevalence estimations from self-reported data in Canada indicated that 15 % of the adult population is obese and 33 % is classified in the overweight category, while in the US nearly 1/3 of adults are obese, corresponding to almost 20 % of the US population [1-3]. This highlights the importance of environmental factors and lifestyle choices since obesity cannot be totally explained by genetic factors alone [4]. Unfortunately, sedentary lifestyle and increased energy intake predispose to high fat and high calorie food choices, and refined diet seems to be adopted by an increasing proportion of our population. This is leading to weight gain, positive energy balance, obesity and health-related complications. Thus, "at risk" obesity (abdominal obesity) is an important cause of metabolic complications, such as cardiovascular disease (CVD), type 2 diabetes and hypertension[5-7]. Indeed, the American Heart Association (AHA) has classified obesity as a modifiable risk factor for coronary heart disease (CHD) [8]. A variety of therapies may help to reduce the incidence of obesity, including diet, physical exercise, and pharmacological treatments. Weight loss is an essential component in the management of the metabolic complications of obesity. Low-fat diets have been advocated for weight loss for

[1] Corresponding author:Paul Poirier MD, PhD, FRCPC, FACC,Institut universitaire de cardiologie et de pneumologie ,Hôpital Laval,2725 Chemin Sainte-Foy ,Sainte-Foy, Québec, Canada,G1V 4G5,Telephone: 418-656-4767,Fax: 418-656-4562,E-mail:Paul.Poirier@crhl.ulaval.ca

many years. However, some popular diets such as the very low-carbohydrate (ketogenic) diets have challenged the effectiveness of conventional low-fat diets, partly because of there rapid efficiency in contrast to the continuing increased prevalence of obesity despite reductions of fat intake. Thus, several authors have compared the effectiveness of various weight loss approaches, such as those proposed by the official guidelines, to the "popular" diets (as Atkins, Ornish, The Zone, South Beach diet, Weight Watchers) in the management of obesity and its related complications. Although, there is a need to perform well designed clinical trials showing long-term safety and efficacy of low-carbohydrate diets, several studies have showed effective short-term weight loss and improved metabolic disturbances compared to low-fat diets. The major targets of intervention for proper treatment of the epidemic of obesity remain weight loss and active lifestyle. Even if different types of diet or diet/exercise combinations can produce weight loss; if this treatment is stopped, weight is regained. The current review underlines the clinical and the experimental evidence of the different dietary approaches for weight loss regarding obesity treatment and related metabolic complications. Despite numerous researches, there is still controversy regarding the optimal macronutrient content, and we also overview the issue of carbohydrate restriction versus fat restriction on weight loss and weight control in order to achieve effective weight loss and better health. Indeed, modest weight reduction (5 % to 10 % of body weight) can decrease total cholesterol, improve glucose tolerance and decrease blood pressure in overweight and obese patients [6;9-12]. We also briefly discuss the role of several dietary interventions, which can lower CHD risk and improve lipid profile.

Multiple Risk Factors Related to Obesity

1. Abdominal Obesity

It is now well known that abdominal fat distribution is strongly correlated with an increase in morbidity [5]. In fact, central distribution of fat is clearly related to metabolic complications of obesity such as insulin resistance, diabetes, hypertension or CAD in addition to the overall level of obesity by itself [21;22]. Indeed, it is clearly demonstrated that a high level of visceral fat is associated to a high level of small LDL-cholesterol particles and development of impaired glucose tolerance in obese subjects [21;23;24]. Since not all obese people should be considered at high risk of CAD, it is important for the clinician to use simple and effective tools to identify the obese "at risk" [25;26]. Clinicians may use simple non-invasive measurements to assess body fat and estimate easily abdominal obesity.

The AHA and the National Institute of Health (NIH) have adopted the Quetelet-Kaup index, or body mass index (BMI), as an indicator to measure adiposity and classify people as normal, overweight or obese [9]. The Canadian definition to classify people as overweight or obese is also defined by BMI, in accordance to the World Health Organization (WHO) guidelines and Health Canada [27;28]. BMI is defined as weight in kilograms divided by height in meters squared (kg/m^2). Obesity is defined by a BMI >30.0 kg/m^2 and overweight by a BMI between 25.0 and 29.9 kg/m^2 [9;27;28]. Waist circumference is probably a more useful tool that all clinician should use to evaluate abdominal fat during weight loss treatment. Although BMI and waist circumference are interrelated, increased waist circumference can be a better predictor of disease risk in adults who are categorized as normal or overweight in terms of BMI [9;26]. In accordance to the BMI and waist circumference definition, adults aged 18 years or more with a BMI between 25.0 and 34.9 kg/m^2 and a waist circumference of $\geq$ 102 cm for men and $\geq$ 88 cm for women have an increased risk for cardiovascular co-morbidity [9]. Considering that waist circumference is closely correlated to visceral adipose tissue and metabolic complications, simultaneous measurement of simple variables such as waist circumference and fasting plasma TG levels have also been suggested to be used as an inexpensive screening tool to identify men and women with high CAD risk [22;29]. Recently, the INTERHEART study has reported that classification of obesity measured by BMI is weaker than the waist-to-hip ratio in order to evaluate the risk of myocardial infarction worldwide [5]. This ratio, strongly related to visceral fat, was the best anthropometric predictor of myocardial infarction in both sexes, regardless of the presence of diabetes, dyslipidemia or hypertension, and in smokers and non-smokers [5]. Moreover, Yusuf et al have suggested that the use of waist-to-hip ratio as an obesity index instead of BMI may increase threefold the risk for myocardial infarction [5]. Abdominal obesity can also worsen the prognosis of patients with CAD. These patients have a 23 % increase risk of myocardial infarction and a 38 % increase risk of heart failure [26]. The factors related to obesity are complex and multifactorial, and lifestyle intervention should play a predominant role [7;9;26;30]. Table 1 presents the classification of normal weight, overweight and obesity according to the BMI and waist circumference.

Table 1. Classification of normal weight, overweight and obesity according to the body mass index (BMI) and waist circumference

	BMI (kg/m^2)	Obesity class	Disease Risk (Relative to Normal Weight and Waist circumference	
			Men $\leq$ 102 cm Women $\leq$ 88 cm	Men > 102 cm Women > 88 cm
Underweight	< 18.5		--	--
Normal	18.5-24.9		--	--
Overweight	25.0-29.9		Increased	High
Obesity	30.0-34.9	I	High	Very High
	35.0-39.9	II	Very High	Very High
Morbid obesity	< 40.0	III	Extremely High	Extremely High

Adapted from The Practical Guide: Identification, Evaluation, and Treatment of Overweight and Obesity in Adults. National Institutes of Health, National Heart, Lung, and Blood Institute, North American Association for the Study of Obesity

2. Blood Cholesterol and Lipoprotein Profile

Elevated LDL-cholesterol is one of the leading cause of CAD and is closely related to obesity. The AHA and the National Cholesterol Education Program (NCEP-ATP III) emphasizes dietary measures to achieve LDL-cholesterol goals, since reduction in LDL-cholesterol levels are associated with reduced CAD risk [7;20]. The food components, which have a major negative impact on LDL-cholesterol, are dietary saturated fatty acids, *trans*-unsaturated fatty acids and cholesterol. Dietary recommendations have emphasized the consumption of monounsaturated and polyusaturated fatty acids, and, to a lesser extent, soluble fibre and soy protein [20]. The NCEP-ATP III report has updated the recommendations for clinical management of high blood cholesterol, considering LDL-cholesterol as the primary target of cholesterol-lowering intervention [7]. Moreover, the recent AHA/NHLBI statement has proposed minor modifications to the NCEP-ATP III criteria by lowering the actual fasting blood glucose target [6]. The NCEP-ATP III and the AHA/NHLBI recommendations about the optimal cholesterol target is maintaining total cholesterol below 5.2 mmol/L and raising HDL-cholesterol to the highest extent possible [6;7]. It is generally advised to modifie cholesterol target in function of the presence of one or more risk factors such as cigarette smoking, high blood pressure (≥140/90 mm Hg), low HDL-cholesterol (<1,03 mmol/L), familial history of early CAD (aged ≤ 45 years for men and ≤ 55 years for women) [6;7]. In the absence of risk factors or the presence of only one risk factor, one is permitted to target a LDL-cholesterol below 4.14 mmol/L. The presence of two or more risk factors suggests targeting a LDL-cholesterol level below 3.36 mmol/L. The ultimate categorie considered very high risk is the one associated with the presence of CVD or diabetes. These patients should attain the lowest range of LDL-cholesterol (<2,59 mmol/L). Of note, sustained weight loss is an important issue regarding LDL-cholesterol management in some individuals [20].

3. Hypertension

The preponderance of high blood pressure is an important problem, while being a modifiable risk factor of CVD. About 43 millions individuals in United States have high blood pressure and only 47 % maintain optimal blood pressure [31]. Reducing weight by lifestyle modifications is a non-pharmacological recommended approach to reduce hypertension. Daily consumption of alcohol and sodium must be reduced since they can impact negatively on optimal blood pressure [32]. The 2005 Canadian Hypertension Education Program have recommended blood pressure target below 140/90 mm Hg in the presence of non-complicated hypertension or systolic hypertension, <130/80 mm Hg in the presence of diabetes and renal dysfunction and <125/75 mm Hg when hypertension is associated to proteinuria (>1g /24h) [33].

Reducing Obesity and Cardiovascular Disease by Dietary Practices: The Conventional Nutritional Approaches

Changes in deleterious lifestyle habits are considered the most efficient and the less expensive way to reduce obesity and its related cardiovascular risk. Caloric restriction is a common approach to create energy imbalance and weight reduction. A diet high in total fat is sometimes associated with excess body weight and high-density food choices [43]. Caloric restriction around 500 to 1000 kcal/day is recommended to achieve weight reduction [9;19;20]. Of importance, the optimal weight loss diet must have adequate nutritional composition to reduce risk factors. Guidelines for weight maintenance and weight reduction from AHA (previously designed Step 1 diet), NCEP-ATP III and the North American Association for the Study of Obesity /National Institute of Health (NAASO/NIH) recommended that total calories should be limited to <30 % as fat to induce a weight loss of 0.5 to 1 kg per week. The general element of the majority of existing recommendations is the use of a moderate caloric deficit to achieve a slow and progressive weight loss [6;7;9;20]. Dietary components, which influence directly LDL-cholesterol and promote thrombogenesis are saturated fat, cholesterol and *trans*-fatty acids. To achieve reduction in LDL-cholesterol, saturated fat intake should be limited to <7 % of the total energy intake, cholesterol level to less than 200 mg/day and 2 % to 3 % of total energy from *trans*-fatty acids (AHA nutrition therapy for specific subgroups, previously designed Step 2 diet for higher-risk individuals) [20]. These goals can be achieved by limiting intake of foods high in saturated fat, cholesterol and/or *trans*-fatty acids, such as tropical oils, fatty meats, egg yolks, shellfish, high-fat dairy products and prepared foods containing partially hydrogenated vegetable oils. Saturated fat should be substituted for higher proportion of monounsaturated fat, polyunsaturated fat and carbohydrate (e.g., more than 10% of total calories from polyunsaturated fat, more than 15 % of total from monounsaturated fat and 55% or more of total calories from complexes carbohydrates) [9;20]. Protein should be derived from lean sources of animal protein or plant sources and should provide approximately 15 % of total calories. Multiple evidences have shown that salt intake is directly related to high blood pressure and that lowering salt intake lowers blood pressure [32;44;45]. In fact, reducing sodium intake by 1800 mg per day (which correspond to 2/3 teaspoon of table salt) or achieving an average daily consumption of 2400 mg (1 teaspoon of table salt) is associated with systolic and diastolic blood pressure reductions [32;44;45]. Of note, the average intake of sodium in the United States is approximately 3500 mg per day (1½ teaspoon of table salt) [45]. Reducing sodium intake by choosing foods low in salt and limiting the amount of salt added to food is also an important target. Moreover, alcohol consumption should not exceed more than 2 drinks per day for men and 1 drink per day for women.

The practical guideline for identification, evaluation and treatment of overweight and obesity in adults from the NIH and NAASO recommends low calorie diet (which corresponds to the Step 1 diet from AHA) to induce weight loss in overweight and obese patients [9;20]. In general, diets containing 1000 to 1200 kcal per day should be recommended to most women. More so, diets between 1200 to 1600 kcal per day should be selected for men and for women who weigh 75 kg or more [9].

A more drastic approach for obese individuals presenting numerous risk factors is a very low calorie diet, providing approximately 800 kcal per day [19]. This diet requires special monitoring and supplementation, should be used in very limited circumstances, and under intensive medical supervision [9]. The common use of these diets decreased considerably during the last decades, corresponding to 50 % in the 1960s to 7,7 % in the 1990s (46). Weight reduction is generally more important under very low calorie diets vs. low calorie diets but several clinical trials reported that low calorie diets are as effective as very low calorie diet in producing weight loss after 1 year. On the other hand, significant weight regain is common regarding these diets [47;48]. The use of a very low calorie diet has been associated with significant long-term advantages. Wadden et al have compared weight loss of 49 obese women over one-year, randomly assigned to a low calorie diet (1200 kcal per day) and a very low calorie diet (420 kcal per day, for 16 weeks followed with 1200 kcal per day for 36 weeks) [48]. Women under the very low calorie diet lost significantly more weight through the first 26 weeks. However, they regained more easily their weight through the 26 weeks of the weight maintenance phase. Total weight losses after one year were comparable between the 2 groups, with a mean decrease of 11kg for the very low calorie diet and 12kg for the low calorie diet [48]. More so, the very low calorie diet, as liquid-protein-diet, has been associated with a prolonged QT interval and with sudden death [49]. These complications may be related to vitamin and mineral deficiencies, to a poor quality and/or inadequate quantity of protein consumed per day, to various concomitant drug regimen used by patients or to a prolonged adhesion to this kind of diet [50]. However, under appropriate medical control, no significant change of QT interval was reported [51;52].

The INTERHEART study have identified nine modifiable risk factors; lipoprotein profile, smoking, hypertension, diabetes, abdominal obesity, psychosocial factors, consumption of fruits and vegetables, alcohol intake, and regular physical activity, which predicts 90% of myocardial infarction worldwide in both sexes [34]. Since numerous patients with hypertension or CVD are overweight or obese and present high-risk waist circumference [35-37], weight loss should be the first line therapy prescribed by health professionals [8;20] This approach may improve insulin sensitivity and influence positively each metabolic abnormality (i.e. hypertension, diabetes, lipid disorder or preexisting CVD). Improved insulin sensibility (30-60 %) associated with substantial weight loss will be of benefit until there is weight regain [38]. Several methods and strategies are available, and it is important to target the right approach in order to achieve and maintain a healthy body weight. The awareness of foods and overall eating pattern must be emphasized

The AHA has established guidelines for reducing the risk of CVD by dietary and other lifestyle practices [20;39]. The energy balance should be maintained by matching the intake of energy to overall energy expenditure to achieve a healthy body weight. Patients must include a variety of fruits, vegetables, whole grains and cereal products, low-fat dairy products, low saturated fat and lean meats while eating adequate amounts of essential nutrients [20]. This eating pattern is essential to prevent or delay the development of obesity, hypertension, CVD, or other health related complications. Portion number and size should be monitored, and consumption of foods with low nutritional quality, high caloric density and refined sugars should be limited [20]. In general, a relative caloric restriction from 5% to 10% through 6 months is sufficient to reduce several risk factors of heart disease and stroke in people who are overweight or obese with comorbidities, even if optimal weight is not attained [9;19;40]. Increasing level of physical activity is also essential to achieve cardiovascular fitness and energy imbalance to induce weight reduction. Moreover, physical activity reduces the risk of high blood pressure, heart disease and diabetes [33;41]. Sedentary individuals are encouraged to practice 30 to 45 minutes of moderate level of physical activities and subsequently increase these activities to 60 minutes on most if not all days of the week [6;20;33;41;42].

Reducing Blood Pressure: The DASH Diet

It is well known that obesity, high sodium intake and alcohol consumption influence arterial blood pressure (BP). Recent evidences have shown that approximately 60 % of American adults have prehypertension or hypertension (53). The Dietary Approaches to Stop Hypertension (DASH)-diet is a carbohydrate-rich diet, currently advocated in several scientific dietary reports and guidelines such as the AHA and the NCEP-ATP III, for the prevention and treatment of BP in individuals with and without hypertension [9;20;32;45;54-56]. Table 2 presents the number of serving for each food group between the DASH diet and the Canada's food guide to healthy eating. The DASH trial demonstrated that a diet that emphasized vegetables, fruits and low-fat dairy products, whole grains, poultry, fish and nuts, and a limited amount of red meat, sweets and sugar-containing beverages, a decrease amounts of total fat, saturated fat and cholesterol can substantially lower mean systolic BP from 7.1 mm Hg in people without hypertension to 11.5 mm Hg in people with hypertension [32;44]. The Seventh Report of the Joint National Committee on Prevention, Detection, Evaluation, and Treatment of High Blood Pressure (JNC7) recommends several lifestyle modifications in order to manage hypertension. The major lifestyle modifications which have shown to lower BP include weight reduction which may reduce systolic BP by 5 mm Hg to 20 mm Hg per 10-kg weight loss, adoption of the DASH eating pattern and reducing the daily dietary sodium intake to no more than 100 mmol or 2.4 g sodium or 6 g sodium chloride (one teaspoon of sodium chloride = 2.4 g of sodium) [57]. More so, the alcohol consumption should be limited to no more than 2 drinks in most men and no more than one drink per day in women and lighter-weight individuals (1 drink is equivalent to a 341 mL beer, 150 mL glass of wine and 45 mL of spirituous) [57]. The effects of three different levels of dietary sodium intake in conjunction with the DASH diet or a control diet on 412 participants for 30 consecutive days was studied [45]. The subjects were randomly assigned to eat foods with high levels of sodium (150 mmol/day or 1½ teaspoon of table salt per day with an energy intake of 2100 kcal, reflecting the typical consumption in the United States), intermediate intake (100 mmol/day or 1 teaspoon of table salt per day, reflecting the upper limit of the current JNC7 national recommendations) and low intake (50 mmol/day or ½ teaspoon of table salt per day, below the current recommendation of 100 mmol/day from the DASH diet) [45]. A significant decrease in BP (-11.4 mm Hg and –5.5 mm Hg for the systolic BP and the diastolic BP respectively) were observed in the combined 50 mmol sodium intake/DASH diet intervention group [45].

Table 2. Number of serving for each food group between the DASH diet and Canada's food guide to healthy eating.

	Number of serving Canada's food guide for adults of 19-50 years	Number of serving DASH diet
Fruit	7-10 per day	4-5 per day
Vegetables		4-5 per day
Milk products	2 per day	2-4 per day
Grain products	6-8 per day	7-8 per day

Adapted from Eating Well with Canada's Food Guide & Appel LJ et coll. *N Engl J Med* 336:1117-1124, 1997

The Canadian Hypertension Education Program for the management of Hypertension has proposed recent recommendations [33]. These recommendations include lifestyle and nutritional modifications to prevent and/or treat hypertension such as: 30 to 60 minutes of aerobic exercise per day, achieving and maintaining an ideal body weight and waist circumference, limiting alcohol intake, reducing total fat and cholesterol intake and limiting salt consumption [33]. The European Society of Hypertension and the European Society of

Cardiology have also proposed guidelines, which are similar to the DASH, the JNC7 and the Canadian Hypertension Education Program recommendations [58]. Table 3 presents the lifestyle modifications to manage hypertension proposed by the DASH diet, the JNC7, the Canadian Hypertension Education Program and the European Society of Hypertension.

Table 3. Lifestyle modifications to manage hypertension proposed by the Dietary Approaches to Stop Hypertension (DASH)-diet, The Seventh Report of the Joint National Committee on Prevention, Detection, Evaluation, and Treatment of High Blood Pressure (JNC7), The Canadian Hypertension Education Program for the management of Hypertension and the European Society of Hypertension/European Society of Cardiology.

	DASH	**JNC7**	**Canadian Hypertension Education Program**	**European Society of Hypertension**
Weight reduction	Maintain ideal body weight	Maintain body weight: 18.5 kg/m^2 to 24.9 kg/m^2 *↓5-20 mm Hg systolic BP per 10-kg weight loss*	Maintain body weight: (18.5 kg/m^2 to 24.9 kg/m^2) Waist circumference: < 102 cm for men < 88 cm for women	Weight reduction to maintain ideal body weight
Maximal alcohol intake	2 drinks per day for most men 1 drink per day for women	2 drinks per day for most men 1 drink per day for women	14 drinks per week (2 drinks/day) for most men 9 drinks per week (1.3 drinks/day) for women	20-30 ml alcohol/day for men (30 ml = 2 drinks) 10-20 ml alcohol/day for women (15 ml = 1 drink)
Physical exercise	--	≥ 30 minutes of aerobic exercise most days of the week	30-60 minutes of aerobic exercise 4-7 days per week	30-45 minutes of aerobic exercise 3-4 days per week
Sodium intake	100 mmol or 2.4 g sodium per day (1 teaspoon of table salt)	100 mmol or 2.4 g sodium per day (1 teaspoon of table salt) *↓2-8 mm Hg systolic BP*	100 mmol or 2.4 g sodium per day (1 teaspoon of table salt)	80-100 mmol/day or 1.9-2.4 g per day (2/3 – 1 teaspoon of table salt) *↓BP 4-6 mm Hg*
Total fat	Decrease total fat, saturated fat and cholesterol Consume low-fat dairy products *↓7.1-11.5 mm Hg*	Decrease total fat and saturated fat Consume low-fat dairy products *↓8-14 mm Hg systolic BP*	Decrease total fat and cholesterol	Decrease total fat and saturated fat
Fruits and vegetables	Emphasized fruits an vegetables	Consume a diet rich in fruits and vegetables	Increase fruits and vegetables	Increase fruist and vegetables

Adapted from references 33, 56, 57 and 58

Lowering saturated fat intake is also an important target in the presence of hypertension and high serum lipids. The Lyon Diet Heart Study proposes a Mediterranean-type diet characterized by a low intake of total and saturated fats, increase intake of ω-3 fatty acids, high intake of fresh fruits, vegetables, whole grain cereals, antioxidants, vitamins, minerals and vegetable proteins [59]. An increase of 1 mm Hg of systolic BP is associated with an increase risk of 1 % to 2% of cardiovascular complications after myocardial infarction [59]. The optimal macronutrient substitutions for saturated fat (carbohydrate, protein or unsaturated fat) were recently evaluated in the OMNIHEART trial [60]. Three different diet interventions were assessed, such as a high-carbohydrate diet (similar to the DASH diet), a diet rich in protein (10 % higher in protein than the 2 other diets) and an unsaturated fat diet (10% higher in unsaturated fat sources such as olive oil, canola and safflower oil). Interestingly, partial substitution of carbohydrate with either protein or monounsaturated fat can further lower BP, improve lipid levels and reduce CVD risk [60].

The Non Conventional Nutritional Approach (Popular Diets)

Considering the alarming increase in the incidence and the prevalence of obesity, a large proportion of people experiment popular diets, which promote spectacular weight loss without efforts advocating important changes in carbohydrate and lipid consumption. Many of these diets restrain consumption of carbohydrate and have increased lipid consumption in order to restrict daily caloric consumption and increase satiety. Diets that may influence the postprandial insulin secretion are: glycemic index (GI), the Zone diet, the South Beach diet and the very low carbohydrate diets which induce satiety by increasing ketosis and decreasing gastro-intestinal motility (Atkins) [40]. Three different popular diets will be discussed further;

1. "Average" diet, such as the Mediterranean diet and the Weight Watchers program
2. Low-carbohydrate-diet or GI diet, very-high-protein diet (e.g. GI index, the Montignac diet, and the Zone diet)
3. Very low carbohydrate diet/very-high-protein/fat diet (e.g. Atkins and the South Beach diet);
4. Very-low-fat/Very-high-carbohydrate diet (e.g. Ornish).

"Average" Diet

The Mediterranean Diet

For many years, Mediterranean diet has been associated with beneficial effects related to cardiovascular health, cancer and increased life expectancy [59;66-68]. The increasing interest of this diet resulted from the Seven Countries Study from Keys et al., which demonstrated that traditional Mediterranean diet conferred a decrease mortality rate from CHD principally because of a low saturated fat content [67]. Many definitions characteristic of the Mediterranean diet have been suggested. In fact, the broad geographical region including the 16 countries that border the Mediterranean Sea and the different cultural, ethnic and agricultural production include different dietary practice. The Mediterranean-style diet related to a specific dietary pattern, has been presented in a pyramid by Willett WC et al [69]. The diet is characterized by abundant intakes of fresh fruits and vegetables, whole grain products, monounsaturated fat from olive oil and low-fat dairy product (principally from cheese and yogurt). Traditional Mediterranean diet also incorporates the following components: 1) high monounsaturated-to-saturated fat ratio, 2) moderate alcohol consumption and, 3) low consumption of meat and meat products. Some studies defined differently the daily consumption of meat, suggesting abundant intake of fish and poultry, and a restricted-to-moderated consumption of eggs (zero to 4 eggs per week) [69;70]. There is also a definition in terms of the macronutrients pattern, which supplied 25 % to 30 % of total energy intake from fat, with restricted consumption of saturated fat (<7 % to 8 % from total energy intake). Monounsaturated fats, antioxidants-rich foods (such as cranberries, blueberries or blackberries), high-fiber, and selenium rich foods (such as Brazil nuts, seafood or poultry) are also suggested [69]. A prevention trial performed by De Lorgeril et al has shown the cardioprotective effects of a Mediterranean type diet [68]. They report a 70 % reduction in the recurrence of myocardial infarction and cardiac death following a diet of <35 % of the energy as fat (from rapeseed oil), <10 % of energy as saturated fat, <4 % of the energy as ω-6 fatty acids and >0.6 % of energy as ω-3 fatty acids. The Lyon Diet Heart 4-year follow-up study has compared the traditional Mediterranean diet (increased fruits, vegetables, green legumes, fish, poultry and decreased red meat, pork, and butter) to the conventional diet for weight maintenance and weight reduction as suggested by the AHA (previously designed Step 1 diet) on the reduction of the rate of recurrence after a first myocardial infarction [59]. After 46 months of follow-up, the group following the Mediterranean diet presented a 72 % reduction in cardiac death and non-fatal myocardial infarction. Moreover, the risk of recurrent heart disease was lowered by 56 % [59]. The Mediterranean diet is also associated with beneficial modifications in total cholesterol, apoB concentration and LDL size particle [71-73]. Recently, Esposito K. et al have shown that a 2-year adherence to a Mediterranean-style diet is effective in reducing the prevalence of the metabolic syndrome and its associated cardiovascular risk [66]. Endothelial function and vascular inflammatory markers were assessed in 180 patients with metabolic syndrome. Patients in the intervention group have increased total daily consumption of fruits, vegetables, whole grains, nuts, and olive oil in accordance to the Mediterranean style diet. A significant weight loss was observed in the intervention group (-4.0 kg vs. –1.2 kg for the control group), reduced serum hs-CRP levels and inflammatory markers as well as decreased insulin resistance and improved endothelial function were also observed [66]

The Weight Watchers Program

The Weight Watchers program is a low-calorie diet designed to produce a weight loss of up to 0.9 kg per week. This program includes a food plan based on an exchange system list provided by the Weight Watchers corporation which determine point values of common food. The patient's total daily «points» allowance is determined by the current weight. Each "point" is equivalent to approximately 50 calories. The food plan is nutritionally balanced and the activity plan follows the current guidelines. The Weight Watchers program has also a behaviour modification plan for weight control focusing primarily on cognitive restructuring. Participants generally attend a 1-hour weekly group meeting to promote social support, provide written educational material and to weigh oneself weekly. Weight Watchers has sponsored 4 randomized, controlled trialson its program. Heshka et al. have compared the effect of a self-sufficient intervention to the commercial Weight Watchers program on weight loss in 423 overweight/obese men and women (average starting weight of 94.2 kg) [74]. Participant in the Weight Watchers group lost 4.8 kg of their initial weight during the 26 weeks treatment (-1.4 kg for the self-sufficient intervention group). Another study was performed in a cohort of 48 women with a history of breast cancer to prevent adverse prognosis related to obesity [75].

.They were randomly assigned to receive usual care, attend a weekly Weight Watchers group meeting, undergo individual counselling with a dietician, or receive both of the latter 2 interventions. At 1-year, the Weight Watchers group had lost 2.6 kg, those who had individual counselling lost 8.0 kg, those who underwent both interventions lost 9.4 kg and participants who received usual care gained 0.9 kg [75]. Higher weight loss is often achieved in the Weight Watchers groups compared to the standard diet or the control diet, because of the high rate of adherence in these groups, which was partly proportional to the frequency of the counselling approach and the individualized contact [74-76] Lowe et al have evaluated the weight loss maintenance among 1002 participants who had reached their goal weight 1 to 5 years previously. These results suggest a weight regain range between 31.5 % and 76.5 % from the initial weight [77]. Table 4 presents a summary of the main changes in the macronutrient composition of the conventional and the various average diets.

Low-Carbohydrate-Diet (and GI Index Diet)/Very-High-Protein Diet

Low Carbohydrate Diet or Glycemic Index of Food

Although controversial, the GI of foods is still a popular approach for weight loss and has been shown to improve insulin sensitivity [78]. Some international associations have adopted the GI as nutritional therapy for weight management as well as for type 2 diabetes. However, it is not the case of the American Diabetes Association and several other associations in the United States [79]. The WHO and the Food and Agriculture Organisation (FAO) have endorsed, since 1998, the use of the GI of food as an indicator of the impact of a carbohydrate-rich food on blood glucose response and have supported it as an interventional strategy in the treatment of diabetes, in conjunction with information about food composition to guide food choices [80;81]. This committee emphasizes the importance of carbohydrates in human nutrition for the promotion of good health and recommends the consumption of a high-carbohydrate diet (>55 % of total energy). Moreover, emphasis in carbohydrate-containing foods rich in non-starch polysaccharides with low GI are suggested. Actually, many official and/or suggested dietary guidelines and carbohydrate exchanges lists of food currently used for diabetes management are based on the GI of food in Australia, Canada and South Africa [82;83]. The GI concept is now more commonly used due to its potential for disease prevention related to lifestyle habits. In Australia, certain foods are incorporated in a GI trademark certification program labelling. A symbol is affixed on food labels to help consumers select low-GI foods. The nutritional composition meets the criteria established for a category of particular food. Moreover, the Australian dietary guidelines specifically recommend the consumption of low-GI cereal foods in order to achieve good health.

Table 4. Changes in the macronutrient composition of the conventional and the various average diets

	Moderate fat diets				Average diet	
	AHA Step I Diet (11)	AHA Step II Diet (11)	NCEP-ATPIII Diet (5)	DASH diet (45)	Mediterranean-Style (Lyon Heart study) (55)	Weight Watchers program (124)
Total fat (% kcal)	≤ 30	≤ 30	25 - 30	27	31	27
Saturated fat	8-10	< 7	< 7	6	8	10
Polyunsaturated	> 10	> 10	> 10	8	5	--
ω-6 linoleic acid	--	--	--	--	4	--
ω-9 oleic acid	--	--	--	--	1	--
Monounsaturated	> 15	> 15	> 20	13	13	--
Cholesterol (mg)	300	200	200	150	200	184
Carbohydrate (% kcal)	≥ 55	≥ 55	50-60	55	53	53
Protein (% kcal)	15	15	15	18	16	20
Fiber (g)	20-30	20-30	20-30	> 30	19	15
Sodium (mmol)	100	100	100	< 100	< 100	--
Alcohol (% kcal)	--	--	--	--	6	--

Adapted from references 7, 20, 56, 59, 137

David J. A. Jenkins has proposed the first table of GI of foods in 1981, and has published a list of 51 foods with their respective GI [84]. He has suggested that the proposed GI list may reflect the physiological effect of foods, since different carbohydrate foods with the same macronutrient composition can induce a different glycemic response. Per gram of carbohydrate, foods with a high GI produce a higher peak in postprandial blood glucose and a greater overall blood glucose response during the first 2 hours following the consumption of the carbohydrate-rich food than do foods with a low GI. According to Jenkins, the GI of food calculation is calculated using the area under the positive blood glucose response curve in response to the consumption of 50 g of carbohydrate provided by the proposed food divided by the area under the blood glucose response curve following the consumption of 50 g of carbohydrate provided by the control foods, generally white bread or sucrose [85;86]. Many food factors may influence the measure and the reproducibility of GI: 1) the type and the amount of protein and fat (decreases the blood glucose response), 2) the type and the amount of carbohydrate (ratio of amylose and amylopectin in the selected food) and fibres (fibres reduce the rate of absorption of glucose from the gut), 3) food processing and cooking (rise in blood glucose and insulin following the consumption of cooked as opposed to raw foods, and increase time of cooking is associated with an increase of glycemic response), 4) the ripeness of the food (changes in composition of the fruits as they are ripen can increase the glycemic response) and, 5) food processing (grinding, extruding and flaking can increase glycemic response) [87-89].

It is well documented that the low-GI index can achieve better metabolic and glycemic control in type 2 diabetic individuals [90-95], increase HDL-cholesterol concentration, decrease LDL-cholesterol and triglycerides concentrations [96-98], increase satiety [99-104] and improve insulin sensitivity [78]. Moreover, observational studies have shown that the chronic consumption of a diet with a high glycemic load (GI x dietary carbohydrate content) is independently associated with an increase risk of developing type 2 diabetes and CVD [105-107]. Some studies assume that the quantity and the quality of dietary carbohydrate can play a critical role in the pathogenesis of obesity[108-110]. Kopp et al have hypothesized that the current North-American high-glycemic index intake can induce a progressive dysregulation of the pancreatic beta cells, an adaptive hypertrophy of the pancreas resulting in postprandial hyperinsulinemia and insulin resistance, secondary to the chronic high-insulin stimulus in genetically predisposed subjects [110]. Moreover, some studies suggest that postprandial hyperinsulinemia decreases satiety and promotes glucose oxidation to the detriment of free fatty acids through lipolysis inhibition, inducing fat storage [110-112]. Consuming low-GI foods can be an efficient method to reduce daily energy intake and achieve weight control, through the decrease in appetite and the increase of satiety [100;103;113], as well as promoting free fatty acids oxidation [101]. Until now, more than 750 foods have been tested to assess their GI [114]. The low-GI foods include the majority of fruits and vegetables, leguminous and whole wheat bread, whereas high-GI foods include refined cereals products such as white bread, potatoes and rice. In general, when glucose is used as the standard for the GI measure, it is recommended to privilege most of the time food having a low-GI, equal or lower than 55, to consume periodically foods having a GI between 56 and 69 and avoid those which are higher than 70 [114]. However, it is generally agreed that there is a need for long-term clinical trials to establish the clinical relevance and the use of GI in relation to weight regulation, obesity, type 2 diabetes and CVD [115-118].

The Montignac Method

The Montignac Method is a low-GI index/low-fat/high-protein diet, which has been popular in Canada and Europe and was one of the first diets using the GI of foods in daily life. This diet is characterized by a low-GI index (GI < 50), low-fat-high-protein content and emphasis on the quality of food and the physiologic effects on blood glucose response [119]. The Montignac Method also recommends avoiding the combination of high-carbohydrate and high-fat foods in the same meal, unless the GI of carbohydrate foods are below 20 [119;120]. Combining high-carbohydrate/low-GI to high-protein foods and high-protein to high-fat foods in the same meal is also recommended. Food consumption is *ad libidum* until satiety [119;120]. Monounsaturated fat and polyunsaturated fat should be privileged over saturated fat in order ot achieved cardiovascular prevention [120]. Moreover, foods choices should be high in fibres to promote satiety [119]. The short term impact of the Montignac diet compared to the AHA diet for weight maintenance and reduction (Step 1 diet) on the metabolic profile of 12 overweight men has been reported [121]. The Montignac diet has shown to induce a spontaneous 25 % and 35 % decrease of daily energetic intake and plasma TG levels respectively. Moreover, a significant increase in LDL-cholesterol particle diameter and marked decreases in plasma insulin levels were also observed [121].

The South Beach Diet

The South Beach diet has been elaborated by Arthur Agatston, a cardiologist from Miami, who wanted to recommend a way for his heart disease patients to lose weight in a healthy, sustainable way. The South Beach diet emphasizes the "good carbohydrates" (low-GI) and "good fat" (17 % of total caloric intake from monounsaturated fat and 32 % to 14 % from polyunsaturated, varying through the 3 phases of the diet) and lean protein and uses the GI in order to choose the right foods to consume during this weight loss program [122]. It is speculated that the important glycemic response following the consumption of high-GI foods is directly related to weight gain and should be avoided during any kind of weight loss diet. However, most of the nutritional principles and theories regarding this diet are sparsely referenced in the book [122].

Three phases have to be followed through the South Beach diet. The initial phases of the diet consist of 2 phases of 2 weeks duration each and a third phase of 8 weeks for weight maintenance. The first 2 weeks is characterized by higher intake of fat (62 %) and protein (28 %), with a very low intake of carbohydrates (10 %). Not surprisingly, normal size portions should be consumed, and lean meat, fish, eggs, reduced-fat cheese, non-fat yogurt, nuts, and vegetables should be chosen. Bread, rice, potatoes, fruits, alcohol, sweets or every carbohydrate foods should be avoided during this period (2 weeks) to diminish sweetened foods craving. In the second phase, fat intake is decreased to 43 % whereas protein intake is increased to 30 % and carbohydrate intake to 27 %. Finally, during the phase 3, percentages of calories are 39 % from fat, 33 % from protein and 28 % from carbohydrate [122]. The conventional NCEP-ATPIII diet was compared to a isocaloric modified low-carbohydrate/high protein and monounsaturated fat diet (South Beach diet). The investigators found a greater weight loss over 3 months (6.1 kg vs. 3.4 kg for the South Beach compared to the NCEP-ATPIII diet respectively) with no significant amelioration in regard to blood lipid levels between groups [123].

The Zone Diet

The Zone diet is a low-carbohydrate/high protein diet. Percentages of daily total calories are approximately 36 % from carbohydrates, 34 % from protein and 29 % from fat (with 9 % from saturated fat) [124]. The "philosophy" behind the diet from the author Dr Barry Sears asserts that eating the right combination of foods (carbohydrates to protein and fat ratio) leads to decreased hunger, enhanced weight loss and increased energy [125]. The proponent of the Zone Diet suggest enhanced lipolysis through the regulation of glucose and insulin levels which optimize the body's metabolic function [125]. This diet does not prohibit particular foods or food groups. An emphasis is made on carbohydrates from fruits and vegetables sources and monounsaturated fat (such as olive oil, avocado, or almonds). However, high fat (or saturated fat) and high carbohydrates foods such as starches, bread, pasta and some types of fruit should be avoided [124;125]. Moreover, it seems imperative to eat in exact proportion (40/30/30) carbohydrate, protein and fat at each meal to attain the nutritional balance of the diet. A calculation system has been establish, as a equivalent system: it is recommended for a men to consume 4 blocks of carbohydrate, 4 blocks of protein and 4 blocks of fat at each meal and 1 block each of carbohydrate, protein and fat during snacks. The equivalents for women are 3 blocks during the meals and 1 during snacks. One block of protein is equivalent to 7 g (for example, 30 g of low-fat cheese), one block of carbohydrate is equivalent to 9 g (for example, considering the density, 1 block of carbohydrate is equivalent to ¼ cup of black eye peas or 10 cups of lettuce) and 1 block of fat is equivalent to 1.5 g (for example, 1/3 teaspoon of olive oil). Recently, Miyashita et al. have compared the impact of a low calories/low-carbohydrate diet (1000 kcal; 40 % carbohydrate, 25 % protein, and 35 % of fat) to a low calories/high carbohydrate diet (1000 kcal; 65 % carbohydrate, 25 % protein, and 10 % fat) on glucose, lipid metabolism, and on visceral fat accumulation. Twenty-two obese subjects with type 2 diabetes were randomly assigned to take one of these 2 diets for 1 month [126]. Considering that the 2 diets were equivalent in terms of total calories, a similar decrease in body weight and serum glucose levels was observed in both groups. However, an increase in serum HDL-cholesterol and a important decrease of visceral fat was observed in the low-carbohydrate diet group [126].

Actually, the Zone Diet, as all high-protein diets, is not recommended by the AHA in order to achieve weight loss [124]. Increasing protein proportion in the diet usually leads to increase intakes of total fat, saturated fat and cholesterol since the protein content is mainly from animal sources. Moreover, these types of diets can compromise intake of foods that provide essential vitamins and minerals, as well as potentially inducing cardiac, renal, bone and liver abnormalities [124]. The current premise of high-protein diets is interesting since it is related with low insulin levels associated with carbohydrates restrictions, which can play a role in weight regulation by enhancing lipolysis. Although insulin may play a role in weight regulation, protein intake can also stimulate postprandial insulin secretion and can result in either no change or a modest decrease in postprandial glucose levels [127-129]. Insulin may be regulated by several interacting factors, such as a 4-fold greater increase in glucagon secretion in response to a high-protein diet, resulting in a stimulation of gluconeogenesis, glycogenolysis and subsequent increase in circulating glucose concentrations [129]. Visceral obesity is associated with an increase in circulating insulin levels, which is known to acutely inhibit fat mobilization and oxidation. Moreover, these kinds of diets are often rigid and difficult to maintain long term.

Very-Low-Carbohydrate/Very-High-Protein/Fat Diet

The increasing popularity of diets with emphasis on carbohydrates restriction and high-protein intake are a concern in the United States and in Canada because of the lack of scientific evidence to support their claims associated with potential short and long-term adverse impacts on overall health. The popular version of this kind of diet recommends a severe restriction of daily carbohydrate intake to 20 g per day (the Atkins diet or the first phase of the South Beach diet), or approximately 5 % of total energy [130]. This carbohydrate restriction associated with a high-protein and high-fat diet content induces metabolic ketosis and subsequently a rapid weight loss. However, this initial weight loss may be attributed to loss of appetite associated with ketosis and to the diuretic effect of low-carbohydrates intake [131]. Some studies have reported the weight loss efficacy of low-carbohydrates diets regarding lipid profile. The effects of these diets were evaluated in the presence of obesity and/or dyslipidemia and diabetes [132-136]. Yancy et al have observed in 120 dyslipidemic obese subjects with a mean body weight of 96.8 kg, a two-fold weight loss decrease in the low-carbohydrates diet group (<20 g/day; -12.0 kg) compared to the caloric restricted diet (-6.5) [137]. Moreover, the low-carbohydrates diet group experienced a decrease in TG (-0,84 mmol/L *vs.* –0,31 mmol/L) and an increase in HDL-cholesterol levels (0,14 mmol/L *vs.* –0,04 mmol/L) compared to the low caloric diet. Recently, Foster et al have compared the efficacy of a carbohydrates restricted diet such as the Atkins diet versus a caloric restriction (1200-1500 kcal per day) in 63 obese subjects (mean body weight of 98 kg and BMI of 34 kg/m^2) [132]. The weight loss was more important in the "Atkins" group than the caloric restricted group after 6 months (7,6 *vs.* 2,7 kg respectively), but this weight loss was not different at 1 year (4,3 *vs.* 2,5 kg respectively) [132]. These two diets have a comparable impact after 12 months on blood pressure reduction and insulin response, and the "Atkins" diet was associated with a beneficial impact on triglycerides (a decrease of approximately 17 % from baseline after 1 year) and HDL-cholesterol (an increase of 11 % from baseline) [132]. The effects of a low-carbohydrates diet (<30 g per day, which was equivalent to a 250 ml orange juice in terms of grams of glucose) compared to the conventional low-fat diet (with a caloric deficit of 500 kcal/day) were also investigated in obese, type 2 diabetic and/or insulin-resistant subjects [134]. The intervention group had a greater loss of total body weight than the control group after 6 months of intervention (5,8 *vs.* 1,9 kg) [134]. A similar study was performed in 132 obese subjects randomly assigned to a low-carbohydrates diet or a caloric restriction of 500 kcal per day. These diet regimen did not induce a significant weight loss following 1-year of treatment [133]. Nevertheless, the lipid profile and glycemic control were improved in the low-carbohydrate group [133]. Some side effects were reported following the low-carbohydrate diet compared to the conventional low-fat diet such as constipation (68 % vs. 35 %), headaches (60 % vs. 40 %), muscular cramp (35 % vs. 7 %), diarrhea (23 % vs. 7 %) and general tiredness (25 % vs. 8 %) (137).

The Atkins Nutritional Approach

This weight loss regimen consists in a four step nutritional approach, including a 2-week introduction phase (Phase 1), an ongoing weight loss phase (Phase 2), a pre-maintenance phase (Phase 3) and, a lifetime maintenance phase (Phase 4) [130]. The diet "philosophy" of phase 1 is to induce a significant weight loss by reducing drastically carbohydrates consumption to stimulate fat metabolism via enhanced lipolysis while glycolysis will maintain adequate circulating blood glucose concentration [130]. The energetic intake from carbohydrates consists of a maximum of 20 g per day, primarily from salad and other non-starchy vegetables. This carbohydrate intake is clearly inferior to the dietary reference intakes from the NIH, the NAASO, the AHA and the NCEP-ATPIII, which correspond approximately to 180 g to 225 g per day for a daily energetic consumption of 1500 kcal [7;9;20;130]. Meat consumption (beef, fish, veal, eggs, poultry) is unlimited until satiety, cheese is limited to 90 g (which is equivalent to 3 slices of process cheese product), lettuce (salad, spinach or celery) to 500 ml/day, and vegetables low in carbohydrates (as broccoli and cauliflower) to 250 ml/day. Fruits, bread, pasta, rice, nuts and starchy vegetables such as potatoes must be avoided [130]. The utilisation of the GI of foods is also recommended in order to choose food with less influence on blood glucose level. During the second phase, the carbohydrate consumption is increased up to 25 g/day. Gradually, the net carbohydrate consumption is increased (5g-carbohydrates increment), until weight loss slows with less than 2.5 kg to 5 kg to be lost. The third phase begins when the participant approaches within 2.5 kg to 5 kg of the goal. Carbohydrates are increased weekly (5 g increment) as long as the subject continues to lose these last few kilos. Carbohydrates are increased until participants lose less than 0.5 kg per week [130]. The last phase (phase 4) recommends the steady daily consumption of carbohydrates, which was determined during the phase 3, in order to maintain weight loss.

Very-Low-Fat/Very-High-Carbohydrate Diet

A very low fat diet can be defined as one in which ≤15 % of total calories are derived from fat (equally distributed among saturated, monounsaturated and polyunsaturated fat). Approximately ≥70 % of total daily calories should be derived from carbohydrates and 15 % from protein. Even if very-low-fat diet may lead to important weight loss and improve lipid profile, they are not recommended for the general population since many studies have shown that weight loss is not sustained long term [138-141]. Moreover, in individuals with low HDL-cholesterol, high triglyceride and high insulin levels, it was reported that this kind of diet can amplify these abnormalities [141;142].

The Ornish Lifestyle Program

In contrast to the low-carbohydrates or the very-low-carbohydrates diets, the Ornish lifestyle program is rather a very low in fat and a very high carbohydrates diet [143]. Less than 10 % of total calories are from fat, 15 % from proteins and 75 % from complex carbohydrates, including a classification based on their starchy molecule, their chemical composition and their slower rate of carbohydrate absorption, as the GI of foods. A vegetarian diet, which includes eggs and low-fat dairy products, is suggested. It is also recommended to restrict cholesterol consumption to 100 mg daily and alcohol to less than 30 ml per day. Caffeine consumption is avoided and sodium is limited in the presence of hypertension, cardiovascular and renal disease. Physical activity, relaxation and meditation is strongly recommended. An observational study from Franklin et al has evaluated the adherence to the diet and nutrition component of a Ornish-type program on 10 subjects with CAD [144]. These patients followed a total vegetarian, very-low fat diet (10 % of total energy from fat) during 28 weeks.

Table 5. Changes in the macronutrient composition of most popular diets

	Very-low-fat/very-high-carbohydrate diet	**Low-carbohydrate/ very-high-protein diets**		**Very-low-carbohydrate/very-high-protein/fat diets**			
	The Ornish program (128)	The Montignac Method (107)		The Zone diet (111)	The South Beach Diet (109)	Atkins (111)	The Ornish program (128)
				Phase 1	Phase 2	Phase 3	
Total fat (% kcal)	**10**	32	29	62	43	39	68
Saturated fat	--	14	9	--	--	--	26
Carbohydrate (% kcal)	75	37	36	10	27	28	5
Protein (% kcal)	**15**	31	34	28	30	33	27
Alcohol (% kcal)	< 30 mL/day	--	1	A	A	A	--

Adapted from references 119, 122, 125, 130 and 143

Weight loss ranged from 0.1 kg to 11.7 kg without beneficial impact on lipid values [144]. Moreover, only one subject had 100 % adherence to the dietary principles [144]. Aldana et al have compared the effects of the Ornish program to the traditional cardiac rehabilitation program or no rehabilitation at all on 84 subjects treated for CAD [145]. The nutritional programs and the follow-up were more extensive than the previous study, including approximately 5 hours of nutritional consultation per week. A significant reduction of anginal frequency, body weight, BMI, systolic blood pressure, total cholesterol, LDL cholesterol, glucose and dietary fat were observed on the Ornish group compared to the traditional rehabilitation program [145]. Table 5 presents a summary of the main differences in the macronutrient composition of most popular diets.

Conclusion

Lifestyle and dietary modifications are important strategies in the management of obesity, hypertensionand CVD. Achieving normal lipoprotein profile, body weight and BP is primordial in the prevention and treatment of obesity and CVD. Conventional dietary guidelines provide nutritional recommendations; together with other healthy practices such as regular physical exercise and smoking cessation, to reduce health complications. Since some popular diets such as the very-low-fat diet or the high protein diet have challenged the effectiveness of conventional low-fat diet, further studies will be needed to establish the ideal macronutrient intake to achieve long-term weight reduction and health benefit. In conjunction with a suitable energy intake for maintaining a normal body weight, optimal carbohydrate, protein and fat dietary ratio should be determined to improve insulin sensitivity and lipids profile. These different diets seem to have variable short-term positive effects on weight reduction and lipids profile. Recently, Dansinger et al have assessed the adherence rates and the effectiveness of four popular diets (Atkins, Zone, Weight Watchers, and Ornish) for weight loss and cardiac risk factor reduction on 160 individuals [139]. Even if there was a significant reduction of total daily calories intake and body weight in all groups, each popular diet modestly reduced body weight and cardiac risk factors at 1 year. More importantly, this study demonstrated that long-term overall dietary adherence and maintenance were low using extreme macronutrient intake, since 42 % of the participants dropped out during this 1-year study [139]. Actually, these types of diets do not seem to have advantages over the conventional diets at one year, and the observance to these nutritional modifications is often difficult. The ideal treatment for long-term abdominal obesity, hypertension and CVD should be individualized, intensive and under the supervision of qualified health care professionals. There is no bad diet; the only good one is the one that will permit to achieve long-term weight balance and can contribute to reduce hypertension and CVD without nutrient deficit as well as all other risks.

References

[1] Belanger-Ducharme F, Tremblay A. Prevalence of obesity in Canada. *Obes Rev* 2005; 6(3):183-186.

[2] Mokdad AH, Bowman BA, Ford ES, Vinicor F, Marks JS, Koplan JP. The continuing epidemics of obesity and diabetes in the United States. *JAMA* 2001; 286(10):1195-1200.

[3] Baskin ML, Ard J, Franklin F, Allison DB. Prevalence of obesity in the United States. *Obes Rev* 2005; 6(1):5-7.

[4] Pérusse L, Bouchard C. Gene-diet interactions in obesity. *Am J Clin Nutr* 2000; 72(5 Suppl):1285S-1290S.

[5] Yusuf S, Hawken S, Ounpuu S, Bautista L, Franzosi MG, Commerford P et al. Obesity and the risk of myocardial infarction in 27,000 participants from 52 countries: a case-control study. *Lancet* 2005; 366(9497):1640-1649.

[6] Grundy SM, Cleeman JI, Daniels SR, Donato KA, Eckel RH, Franklin BA et al. Diagnosis and management of the metabolic syndrome: an American Heart Association/National Heart, Lung, and Blood Institute Scientific Statement. *Circulation* 2005; 112(17):2735-2752.

[7] The National Cholesterol Education Program - Adult Treatment Panel III. Executive Summary of The Third Report of The National Cholesterol Education Program (NCEP) Expert Panel on Detection, Evaluation, And Treatment of High Blood Cholesterol In Adults (Adult Treatment Panel III). *JAMA* 2001; 285(19):2486-2497.

[8] Eckel RH, Krauss RM. American Heart Association call to action: obesity as a major risk factor for coronary heart disease. AHA Nutrition Committee. *Circulation* 1998; 97(21):2099-2100.

[9] National Institutes of Health. The Pratical Guide Indentification, Evaluation and Treatment of Overweight and Obesity in Adults. *National Health, lung and blood institute North American Association for the Study of Obesity* 2002;1-80.

[10] Wing RR, Koeske R, Epstein LH, Nowalk MP, Gooding W, Becker D. Long-term effects of modest weight loss in type II diabetic patients. *Arch Intern Med* 1987; 147(10):1749-1753.

[11] Mertens IL, Van Gaal LF. Overweight, obesity, and blood pressure: the effects of modest weight reduction. *Obes Res* 2000; 8(3):270-278.

[12] Blackburn G. Effect of degree of weight loss on health benefits. *Obes Res* 1995; 3 Suppl 2:211s-216s.

[13] Alberti KG, Zimmet PZ. Definition, diagnosis and classification of diabetes mellitus and its complications. Part 1: diagnosis and classification of diabetes mellitus provisional report of a WHO consultation. *Diabet Med* 1998; 15(7):539-553.

[14] Isomaa B, Almgren P, Tuomi T, Forsen B, Lahti K, Nissen M et al. Cardiovascular morbidity and mortality associated with the metabolic syndrome. *Diabetes Care* 2001; 24(4):683-689.

[15] Eckel RH, Barouch WW, Ershow AG. Report of the National Heart, Lung, and Blood Institute-National Institute of Diabetes and Digestive and Kidney Diseases Working Group on the pathophysiology of obesity-associated cardiovascular disease. *Circulation* 2002; 105(24):2923-2928.

[16] Report of a WHO consultation. Definition of metabolic syndrome in definition, diagnosis, and classification of diabetes mellitus and its complications. Part I: Diagnosis and classification of diabetes mellitus. Alwan A, King H, 1996. World Health Organisation, pp 1-59.

[17] International Diabetes Federation. The IDF Consensus Worldwide Definition of the Metabolic Syndrome. International Diabetes Federation, editor. 2005. Brussels, Belgium, International Diabetes Federation, pp 1-7.

[18] Ford ES, Giles WH, Dietz WH. Prevalence of the metabolic syndrome among US adults: findings from the third National Health and Nutrition Examination Survey. *JAMA* 2002; 287(3):356-359.

[19] Wilson PW, Grundy SM. The metabolic syndrome: practical guide to origins and treatment: Part I. *Circulation* 2003; 108(12):1422-1424.

[20] Krauss RM, Eckel RH, Howard B, Appel LJ, Daniels SR, Deckelbaum RJ et al. AHA Dietary Guidelines: revision 2000: A statement for healthcare professionals from the Nutrition Committee of the American Heart Association. *Circulation* 2000; 102(18):2284-2299.

[21] Després JP. Abdominal obesity and the risk of coronary artery disease. *Can J Cardiol* 1992; 8(6):561-562.

[22] Pouliot MC, Després JP, Nadeau A, Moorjani S, Prud'homme D, Lupien PJ et al. Visceral obesity in men. Associations with glucose tolerance, plasma insulin, and lipoprotein levels. *Diabetes* 1992; 41(7):826-834.

[23] Després JP, Moorjani S, Lupien PJ, Tremblay A, Nadeau A, Bouchard C. Regional distribution of body fat, plasma lipoproteins, and cardiovascular disease. *Arteriosclerosis* 1990; 10(4):497-511.

[24] Poirier P, Després JP. Waist circumference, visceral obesity, and cardiovascular risk. *J Cardiopulm Rehabil* 2003; 23(3):161-169.

[25] Poirier P, Eckel RH. Obesity and cardiovascular disease. *Curr Atheroscler Rep* 2002; 4(6):448-453.

[26] Dagenais GR, Yi Q, Mann JF, Bosch J, Pogue J, Yusuf S. Prognostic impact of body weight and abdominal obesity in women and men with cardiovascular disease. *Am Heart J* 2005; 149(1):54-60.

[27] World Health Organization. Obesity: Preventing and Managing the Global Epidemic. WHO technical report series no. 894. 2000. Geneva, World Health Organisation.

[28] Health Canada. Canadian guidelines for body weight classification in adults. 2003. Ottawa.

[29] Lemieux I, Pascot A, Couillard C, Lamarche B, Tchernof A, Almeras N et al. Hypertriglyceridemic waist: A marker of the atherogenic metabolic triad (hyperinsulinemia; hyperapolipoprotein B; small, dense LDL) in men? *Circulation* 2000; 102(2):179-184.

[30] Janssen I, Katzmarzyk PT, Ross R. Body mass index, waist circumference, and health risk: evidence in support of current National Institutes of Health guidelines. *Arch Intern Med* 2002; 162(18):2074-2079.

[31] Burt VL, Whelton P, Roccella EJ, Brown C, Cutler JA, Higgins M et al. Prevalence of hypertension in the US adult population. Results from the Third National Health and Nutrition Examination Survey, 1988-1991. *Hypertension* 1995; 25(3):305-313.

[32] Appel LJ, Moore TJ, Obarzanek E, Vollmer WM, Svetkey LP, Sacks FM et al. A clinical trial of the effects of dietary patterns on blood pressure. DASH Collaborative Research Group. *N Engl J Med* 1997; 336(16):1117-1124.

[33] Khan NA, McAlister FA, Lewanczuk RZ, Touyz RM, Padwal R, Rabkin SW et al. The 2005 Canadian Hypertension Education Program recommendations for the management of hypertension: part II - therapy. *Can J Cardiol* 2005; 21(8):657-672.

[34] Yusuf S, Hawken S, Ounpuu S, Dans T, Avezum A, Lanas F et al. Effect of potentially modifiable risk factors associated with myocardial infarction in 52 countries (the INTERHEART study): case-control study. *Lancet* 2004; 364:937-952.

[35] Poirier P, Lemieux I, Mauriège P, Dewailly E, Blanchet C, Bergeron J et al. Impact of Waist Circumference on the Relationship Between Blood Pressure and Insulin. The Quebec Health Survey. *Hypertension* 2005.

[36] Macdonald SM, Reeder BA, Chen Y, Despres JP. Obesity in Canada: a descriptive analysis. Canadian Heart Health Surveys Research Group. *CMAJ* 1997; 157 Suppl 1:S3-S9.

[37] Johnson D, Prud'homme D, Després JP, Nadeau A, Tremblay A, Bouchard C. Relation of abdominal obesity to hyperinsulinemia and high blood pressure in men. *Int J Obes Relat Metab Disord* 1992; 16(11):881-890.

[38] Riccardi G, Giacco R, Rivellese AA. Dietary fat, insulin sensitivity and the metabolic syndrome. *Clin Nutr* 2004; 23(4):447-456.

[39] Klein S, Burke LE, Bray GA, Blair S, Allison DB, Pi-Sunyer X et al. Clinical implications of obesity with specific focus on cardiovascular disease: a statement for professionals from the American Heart Association Council on Nutrition, Physical Activity, and Metabolism: endorsed by the American College of Cardiology Foundation. *Circulation* 2004; 110(18):2952-2967.

[40] Riccardi G, Rivellese AA. Dietary treatment of the metabolic syndrome--the optimal diet. *Br J Nutr* 2000; 83 Suppl 1:S143-S148.

[41] US Department of Health and Human Services. Physical Activity and Health: A Report of the Surgeon General Executive Summary. Center for Disease Control and Prevention, 1996, pp 1-18.

[42] Pate RR, Pratt M, Blair SN, Haskell WL, Macera CA, Bouchard C et al. Physical activity and public health. A recommendation from the Centers for Disease Control and Prevention and the American College of Sports Medicine. *JAMA* 1995; 273(5).402-407.

[43] Tremblay A, Lavallée N, Almeras N, Allard L, Després JP, Bouchard C. Nutritional determinants of the increase in energy intake associated with a high-fat diet. *Am J Clin Nutr* 1991; 53(5):1134-1137.

[44] Vollmer WM, Sacks FM, Ard J, Appel LJ, Bray GA, Simons-Morton DG et al. Effects of diet and sodium intake on blood pressure: subgroup analysis of the DASH-sodium trial. *Ann Intern Med* 2001; 135(12):1019-1028.

[45] Sacks FM, Svetkey LP, Vollmer WM, Appel LJ, Bray GA, Harsha D et al. Effects on blood pressure of reduced dietary sodium and the Dietary Approaches to Stop Hypertension (DASH) diet. DASH-Sodium Collaborative Research Group. *N Engl J Med* 2001; 344(1):3-10.

[46] Poston WS, Haddock CK, Dill PL, Thayer B, Foreyt JP. Lifestyle treatments in randomized clinical trials of pharmacotherapies for obesity. *Obes Res* 2001; 9(9):552-563.

[47] Wadden TA. Treatment of obesity by moderate and severe caloric restriction. Results of clinical research trials. *Ann Intern Med* 1993; 119(7 Pt 2):688-693.

[48] Wadden TA, Foster GD, Letizia KA. One-year behavioral treatment of obesity: comparison of moderate and severe caloric restriction and the effects of weight maintenance therapy. *J Consult Clin Psychol* 1994; 62(1):165-171.

[49] Isner JM, Sours HE, Paris AL, Ferrans VJ, Roberts WC. Sudden, unexpected death in avid dieters using the liquid-protein-modified-fast diet. Observations in 17 patients and the role of the prolonged QT interval. *Circulation* 1979; 60(6):1401-1412.

[50] Frank S, Colliver JA, Frank A. Low-energy diets and prolonged QT intervals. *JAMA* 1987; 257(12):1601-1602.

[51] Doherty JU, Wadden TA, Zuk L, Letizia KA, Foster GD, Day SC. Long-term evaluation of cardiac function in obese patients treated with a very-low-calorie diet: a controlled clinical study of patients without underlying cardiac disease. *Am J Clin Nutr* 1991; 53(4):854-858.

[52] Moyer C.L., Holly R.H., Amsterdam E.A., Atkinson R.L. Effects of cardiac stress during a very-low-calorie diet and exercise program in obese women. *American Journal of Clinical Nutrition* 1989; 50:1324-1327.

[53] Wang Y, Wang QJ. The prevalence of prehypertension and hypertension among US adults according to the new joint national committee guidelines: new challenges of the old problem. *Arch Intern Med* 2004; 164(19):2126-2134.

[54] Lauber RP, Sheard NF. The American Heart Association Dietary Guidelines for 2000: a summary report. *Nutr Rev* 2001; 59(9):298-306.

[55] Svetkey LP, Sacks FM, Obarzanek E, Vollmer WM, Appel LJ, Lin PH et al. The DASH Diet, Sodium Intake and Blood Pressure Trial (DASH-sodium): rationale and design. DASH-Sodium Collaborative Research Group. *J Am Diet Assoc* 1999; 99(8 Suppl):S96-104.

[56] Zemel MB. Dietary pattern and hypertension: the DASH study. Dietary Approaches to Stop Hypertension. *Nutr Rev* 1997; 55(8):303-305.

[57] Chobanian AV, Bakris GL, Black HR, Cushman WC, Green LA, Izzo JL, Jr. et al. The Seventh Report of the Joint National Committee on Prevention, Detection, Evaluation, and Treatment of High Blood Pressure: the JNC 7 report. *JAMA* 2003; 289(19):2560-2572.

[58] European Society of Hypertension-European Society of Cardiology. 2003 European Society of Hypertension-European Society of Cardiology guidelines for the management of arterial hypertension. *J Hypertens* 2003; 21(6):1011-1053.

[59] De Lorgeril M, Salen P, Martin JL, Monjaud I, Delaye J, Mamelle N. Mediterranean diet, traditional risk factors, and the rate of cardiovascular complications after myocardial infarction: final report of the Lyon Diet Heart Study. *Circulation* 1999; 99(6):779-785.

[60] Appel LJ, Sacks FM, Carey VJ, Obarzanek E, Swain JF, Miller ER, III et al. Effects of Protein, Monounsaturated Fat, and Carbohydrate Intake on Blood Pressure and Serum Lipids: Results of the OmniHeart Randomized Trial. *JAMA* 2005; 294(19):2455-2464.

[61] Kelley DE, Goodpaster BH. Effects of exercise on glucose homeostasis in Type 2 diabetes mellitus. *Med Sci Sports Exerc* 2001; 33(6 Suppl):S495-S501.

[62] Moore LL, Visioni AJ, Wilson PW, D'Agostino RB, Finkle WD, Ellison RC. Can sustained weight loss in overweight individuals reduce the risk of diabetes mellitus? *Epidemiology* 2000; 11(3):269-273.

[63] Hollenbeck CB. Dietary fructose effects on lipoprotein metabolism and risk for coronary artery disease. *Am J Clin Nutr* 1993; 58(5 Suppl):800S-809S.

[64] Marshall JA, Hoag S, Shetterly S, Hamman RF. Dietary fat predicts conversion from impaired glucose tolerance to NIDDM. The San Luis Valley Diabetes Study. *Diabetes Care* 1994; 17(1):50-56.

[65] Matsuda M, Defronzo RA, Glass L, Consoli A, Giordano M, Bressler P et al. Glucagon dose-response curve for hepatic glucose production and glucose disposal in type 2 diabetic patients and normal individuals. *Metabolism* 2002; 51(9):1111-1119.

[66] Esposito K, Marfella R, Ciotola M, Di Palo C, Giugliano F, Giugliano G et al. Effect of a mediterranean-style diet on endothelial dysfunction and markers of vascular inflammation in the metabolic syndrome: a randomized trial. *JAMA* 2004; 292(12):1440-1446.

[67] Keys A, Menotti A, Karvonen MJ, Aravanis C, Blackburn H, Buzina R et al. The diet and 15-year death rate in the seven countries study. *Am J Epidemiol* 1986; 124(6):903-915.

[68] De Lorgeril M, Renaud S, Mamelle N, Salen P, Martin JL, Monjaud I et al. Mediterranean alpha-linolenic acid-rich diet in secondary prevention of coronary heart disease. *Lancet* 1994; 343(8911):1454-1459.

[69] Willett WC, Sacks F, Trichopoulou A, Drescher G, Ferro-Luzzi A, Helsing E et al. Mediterranean diet pyramid: a cultural model for healthy eating. *Am J Clin Nutr* 1995; 61(6 Suppl):1402S-1406S.

[70] Kris-Etherton P, Eckel RH, Howard BV, St Jeor S, Bazzarre TL. AHA Science Advisory: Lyon Diet Heart Study. Benefits of a Mediterranean-style, National Cholesterol Education Program/American Heart Association Step I Dietary Pattern on Cardiovascular Disease. *Circulation* 2001; 103(13):1823-1825.

[71] Goulet J, Lamarche B, Charest A, Nadeau G, Lapointe A, Desroches S et al. Effect of a nutritional intervention promoting the Mediterranean food pattern on electrophoretic characteristics of low-density lipoprotein particles in healthy women from the Quebec City metropolitan area. *Br J Nutr* 2004; 92(2):285-293.

[72] Lapointe A, Goulet J, Couillard C, Lamarche B, Lemieux S. A nutritional intervention promoting the Mediterranean food pattern is associated with a decrease in circulating oxidized LDL particles in healthy women from the Quebec City metropolitan area. *J Nutr* 2005; 135(3):410-415.

[73] Goulet J, Lamarche B, Nadeau G, Lemieux S. Effect of a nutritional intervention promoting the Mediterranean food pattern on plasma lipids, lipoproteins and body weight in healthy French-Canadian women. *Atherosclerosis* 2003; 170(1):115-124.

[74] Heshka S, Greenway F, Anderson JW, Atkinson RL, Hill JO, Phinney SD et al. Self-help weight loss versus a structured commercial program after 26 weeks: a randomized controlled study. *Am J Med* 2000; 109(4):282-287.

[75] Djuric Z, DiLaura NM, Jenkins I, Darga L, Jen CK, Mood D et al. Combining weight-loss counseling with the weight watchers plan for obese breast cancer survivors. *Obes Res* 2002; 10(7):657-665.

[76] Rippe JM, Price JM, Hess SA, Kline G, DeMers KA, Damitz S et al. Improved psychological well-being, quality of life, and health practices in moderately overweight women participating in a 12-week structured weight loss program. *Obes Res* 1998; 6(3):208-218.

[77] Lowe MR, Miller-Kovach K, Phelan S. Weight-loss maintenance in overweight individuals one to five years following successful completion of a commercial weight loss program. *Int J Obes Relat Metab Disord* 2001; 25(3):325-331.

[78] Frost G, Keogh B, Smith D, Akinsanya K, Leeds A. The effect of low-glycemic carbohydrate on insulin and glucose response in vivo and in vitro in patients with coronary heart disease. *Metabolism* 1996; 45(6):669-672.

[79] Schulze MB, Hu FB. Dietary approaches to prevent the metabolic syndrome: quality versus quantity of carbohydrates. *Diabetes Care* 2004; 27(2):613-614.

[80] FAO, WHO. Carbohydrates in humain nutrition. *FAO Food and nutrition paper* 1998; 66 (Rome):FAO.

[81] Nantel G. Glycemic carbohydrate: an international perspective. *Nutr Rev* 2003; 61(5 Pt 2):S34-S39.

[82] Canadian Diabetes Association. Clinical Practice Guidelines for the Prevcntion and Management of Diabetes in Canada. Canadian Journal of Diabetes 27[Supplement 2], 1-163. 2003.

[83] Franz MJ, Bantle JP, Beebe CA, Brunzell JD, Chiasson JL, Garg A et al. Nutrition principles and recommendations in diabetes. *Diabetes Care* 2004; 27 Suppl 1:S36-S46.

[84] Jenkins DJ, Wolever TM, Taylor RH, Barker H, Fielden H, Baldwin JM et al. Glycemic index of foods: a physiological basis for carbohydrate exchange. *Am J Clin Nutr* 1981; 34(3):362-366.

[85] Wolever TM, Jenkins DJ, Jenkins AL, Josse RG. The glycemic index: methodology and clinical implications. *Am J Clin Nutr* 1991; 54(5):846-854.

[86] Wolever TM, Vorster HH, Bjorck I, Brand-Miller J, Brighenti F, Mann JI et al. Determination of the glycaemic index of foods: interlaboratory study. *Eur J Clin Nutr* 2003; 57(3):475-482.

[87] Brand JC, Nicholson PL, Thorburn AW, Truswell AS. Food processing and the glycemic index. *Am J Clin Nutr* 1985; 42(6):1192-1196.

[88] Augustin LS, Franceschi S, Jenkins DJ, Kendall CW, La Vecchia C. Glycemic index in chronic disease: a review. *Eur J Clin Nutr* 2002; 56(11):1049-1071.

[89] Pi-Sunyer FX. Glycemic index and disease. *Am J Clin Nutr* 2002; 76(1):290S-298S.

[90] Jenkins AL, Jenkins DJ, Zdravkovic U, Wursch P, Vuksan V. Depression of the glycemic index by high levels of beta-glucan fiber in two functional foods tested in type 2 diabetes. *Eur J Clin Nutr* 2002; 56(7):622-628.

[91] Rizkalla SW, Bellisle F, Slama G. Health benefits of low glycaemic index foods, such as pulses, in diabetic patients and healthy individuals. *Br J Nutr* 2002; 88 Suppl 3:S255-S262.

[92] Kelley DE. Sugars and starch in the nutritional management of diabetes mellitus. *Am J Clin Nutr* 2003; 78(4):858S-864S.

[93] Heilbronn LK, Noakes M, Clifton PM. The effect of high- and low-glycemic index energy restricted diets on plasma lipid and glucose profiles in type 2 diabetic subjects with varying glycemic control. *J Am Coll Nutr* 2002; 21(2):120-127.

[94] Brand-Miller J, Hayne S, Petocz P, Colagiuri S. Low-glycemic index diets in the management of diabetes: a meta-analysis of randomized controlled trials. *Diabetes Care* 2003; 26(8):2261-2267.

[95] Willett W, Manson J, Liu S. Glycemic index, glycemic load, and risk of type 2 diabetes. *Am J Clin Nutr* 2002; 76(1):274S-280S.

[96] Ford ES, Liu S. Glycemic index and serum high-density lipoprotein cholesterol concentration among us adults. *Arch Intern Med* 2001; 161(4):572-576.

[97] Jenkins DJ, Wolever TM, Kalmusky J, Giudici S, Giordano C, Wong GS et al. Low glycemic index carbohydrate foods in the management of hyperlipidemia. *Am J Clin Nutr* 1985; 42(4):604-617.

[98] Jenkins DJ, Jenkins AL. The glycemic index, fiber, and the dietary treatment of hypertriglyceridemia and diabetes. *J Am Coll Nutr* 1987; 6(1):11-17.

[99] Ball SD, Keller KR, Moyer-Mileur LJ, Ding YW, Donaldson D, Jackson WD. Prolongation of satiety after low versus moderately high glycemic index meals in obese adolescents. *Pediatrics* 2003; 111(3):488-494.

[100] Roberts SB. Glycemic index and satiety. *Nutr Clin Care* 2003; 6(1):20-26.

[101] Brand-Miller JC, Holt SH, Pawlak DB, McMillan J. Glycemic index and obesity. *Am J Clin Nutr* 2002; 76(1):281S-285S.

[102] Ludwig DS, Majzoub JA, Al Zahrani A, Dallal GE, Blanco I, Roberts SB. High glycemic index foods, overeating, and obesity. Pediatrics 103[3], E26. 1999.

[103] Anderson GH, Woodend D. Effect of glycemic carbohydrates on short-term satiety and food intake. *Nutr Rev* 2003; 61(5 Pt 2):S17-S26.

[104] Warren JM, Henry CJ, Simonite V. Low glycemic index breakfasts and reduced food intake in preadolescent children. *Pediatrics* 2003; 112(5):e414-e419.

[105] Liu S, Willett WC, Stampfer MJ, Hu FB, Franz M, Sampson L et al. A prospective study of dietary glycemic load, carbohydrate intake, and risk of coronary heart disease in US women. *Am J Clin Nutr* 2000; 71(6):1455-1461.

[106] Salmeron J, Ascherio A, Rimm EB, Colditz GA, Spiegelman D, Jenkins DJ et al. Dietary fiber, glycemic load, and risk of NIDDM in men. *Diabetes Care* 1997; 20(4):545-550.

[107] Salmeron J, Manson JE, Stampfer MJ, Colditz GA, Wing AL, Willett WC. Dietary fiber, glycemic load, and risk of non-insulin-dependent diabetes mellitus in women. *JAMA* 1997; 277(6):472-477.

[108] Ludwig DS. Dietary glycemic index and the regulation of body weight. *Lipids* 2003; 38(2):117-121.

[109] Schulze MB, Hu FB. Dietary approaches to prevent the metabolic syndrome: quality versus quantity of carbohydrates. *Diabetes Care* 2004; 27(2):613-614.

[110] Kopp W. High-insulinogenic nutrition--an etiologic factor for obesity and the metabolic syndrome? *Metabolism* 2003; 52(7):840-844.

[111] Arner P. Control of lipolysis and its relevance to development of obesity in man. *Diabetes Metab Rev* 1988; 4(5):507-515.

[112] Saris WH. Sugars, energy metabolism, and body weight control. *Am J Clin Nutr* 2003; 78(4):850S-857S.

[113] Ball SD, Keller KR, Moyer-Mileur LJ, Ding YW, Donaldson D, Jackson WD. Prolongation of satiety after low versus moderately high glycemic index meals in obese adolescents. *Pediatrics* 2003; 111(3):488-494.

[114] Foster-Powell K, Holt SH, Brand-Miller JC. International table of glycemic index and glycemic load values: 2002. *Am J Clin Nutr* 2002; 76(1):5-56.

[115] Augustin LS, Franceschi S, Jenkins DJ, Kendall CW, La Vecchia C. Glycemic index in chronic disease: a review. *Eur J Clin Nutr* 2002; 56(11):1049-1071.

[116] Ludwig DS, Eckel RH. The glycemic index at 20 y. *Am J Clin Nutr* 2002; 76(1):264S-265S.

[117] Pawlak DB, Ebbeling CB, Ludwig DS. Spirited critique of glycaemic index (GI) and its role in the treatment of obesity. *Obes Rev* 2003; 4(1):73-74.

[118] Raben A. Should obese patients be counselled to follow a low-glycaemic index diet? No. *Obes Rev* 2002; 3(4):245-256.

[119] Montignac M. Je mange, je maigris et je reste mince! Flammarion (eds). *La méthode Montignac* 1999. Paris: J'ai Lu Publisher, pp9-318.

[120] Dumesnil JG, Montignac M. *Bon poids bon coeur avec la méthode Montignac* 2002. Flammarion (eds). Québec,.pp 15-269.

[121] Dumesnil JG, Turgeon J, Tremblay A, Poirier P, Gilbert M, Gagnon L et al. Effect of a low-glycaemic index--low-fat--high protein diet on the atherogenic metabolic risk profile of abdominally obese men. *Br J Nutr* 2001; 86(5):557-568.

[122] Agaststòn A. The delicious, doctor-designed, foolproof plan for fast and healthy weight lost. *The South Beach Diet* 2003. St-Martin's Griffin (eds); New York: St-Martin Press, pp 3-297.

[123] Aude YW, Agatston AS, Lopez-Jimenez F, Lieberman EH, Marie A, Hansen M et al. The national cholesterol education program diet vs a diet lower in carbohydrates and higher in protein and monounsaturated fat: a randomized trial. *Arch Intern Med* 2004; 164(19):2141-2146.

[124] St Jeor ST, Howard BV, Prewitt TE, Bovee V, Bazzarre T, Eckel RH. Dietary protein and weight reduction: a statement for healthcare professionals from the Nutrition Committee of the Council on Nutrition, Physical Activity, and Metabolism of the American Heart Association. *Circulation* 2001; 104(15):1869-1874.

[125] Sears B, Lawren B. Zone: Revolutionary life plan. *Enter the Zone* 1995. Canada: Harper Collins Publisher, pp 1-288.

[126] Miyashita Y, Koide N, Ohtsuka M, Ozaki H, Itoh Y, Oyama T et al. Beneficial effect of low carbohydrate in low calorie diets on visceral fat reduction in type 2 diabetic patients with obesity. *Diabetes Res Clin Pract* 2004; 65(3):235-241.

[127] Gulliford MC, Bicknell EJ, Scarpello JH. Differential effect of protein and fat ingestion on blood glucose responses to high- and low-glycemic-index carbohydrates in noninsulin-dependent diabetic subjects. *Am J Clin Nutr* 1989; 50(4):773-777.

[128] Tremblay A. Nutritional determinants of the insulin resistance syndrome. *Int J Obes Relat Metab Disord* 1995; 19 Suppl 1:S60-S68.

[129] Gannon MC, Nuttall FQ, Saeed A, Jordan K, Hoover H. An increase in dietary protein improves the blood glucose response in persons with type 2 diabetes. *Am J Clin Nutr* 2003; 78(4):734-741.

[130] Atkins RC. Dr Atkins' new diet revolution. *The Atkins Diet* 1998. New York: Harper Collins Publisher, pp3-560.

[131] A critique of low-carbohydrate ketogenic weight reduction regimens. A review of Dr. Atkins' diet revolution. *JAMA* 1973; 224(10):1415-1419.

[132] Foster GD, Wyatt HR, Hill JO, McGuckin BG, Brill C, Mohammed BS et al. A randomized trial of a low-carbohydrate diet for obesity. *N Engl J Med* 2003; 348(21):2082-2090.

[133] Stern L, Iqbal N, Seshadri P, Chicano KL, Daily DA, McGrory J et al. The effects of low-carbohydrate versus conventional weight loss diets in severely obese adults: one-year follow-up of a randomized trial. *Ann Intern Med* 2004; 140(10):778-785.

[134] Samaha FF, Iqbal N, Seshadri P, Chicano KL, Daily DA, McGrory J et al. A low-carbohydrate as compared with a low-fat diet in severe obesity. *N Engl J Med* 2003; 348(21):2074-2081.

[135] Westman EC, Yancy WS, Edman JS, Tomlin KF, Perkins CE. Effect of 6-month adherence to a very low carbohydrate diet program. *Am J Med* 2002; 113(1):30-36.

[136] Lara-Castro C, Garvey WT. Diet, insulin resistance, and obesity: zoning in on data for Atkins dieters living in South Beach. *J Clin Endocrinol Metab* 2004; 89(9):4197-4205.

[137] Yancy WS, Jr., Olsen MK, Guyton JR, Bakst RP, Westman EC. A low-carbohydrate, ketogenic diet versus a low-fat diet to treat obesity and hyperlipidemia: a randomized, controlled trial. *Ann Intern Med* 2004; 140(10):769-777.

[138] Lichtenstein AH, Van Horn L. Very low fat diets. *Circulation* 1998; 98(9):935-939.

[139] Dansinger ML, Gleason JA, Griffith JL, Selker HP, Schaefer EJ. Comparison of the Atkins, Ornish, Weight Watchers, and Zone diets for weight loss and heart disease risk reduction: a randomized trial. *JAMA* 2005; 293(1):43-53.

[140] Sheppard L, Kristal AR, Kushi LH. Weight loss in women participating in a randomized trial of low-fat diets. *Am J Clin Nutr* 1991; 54(5):821-828.

[141] Kasim-Karakas SE, Almario RU, Mueller WM, Peerson J. Changes in plasma lipoproteins during low-fat, high-carbohydrate diets: effects of energy intake. *Am J Clin Nutr* 2000; 71(6):1439-1447.

[142] Chen YD, Coulston AM, Zhou MY, Hollenbeck CB, Reaven GM. Why do low-fat high-carbohydrate diets accentuate postprandial lipemia in patients with NIDDM? *Diabetes Care* 1995; 18(1):10-16.

[143] Ornish D. *Dr Dean Ornish's Program for Reversion Heart Disease* 1992. New York: Ivy Publisher, pp 3-672.

[144] Franklin TL, Kolasa KM, Griffin K, Mayo C, Badenhop DT. Adherence to very-low-fat diet by a group of cardiac rehabilitation patients in the rural southeastern United States. *Arch Fam Med* 1995; 4(6):551-554.

[145] Aldana SG, Whitmer WR, Greenlaw R, Avins AL, Salberg A, Barnhurst M et al. Cardiovascular risk reductions associated with aggressive lifestyle modification and cardiac rehabilitation. *Heart Lung* 2003; 32(6):374-382.

[146] Gaziano JM, Manson JE, Branch LG, Colditz GA, Willett WC, Buring JE. A prospective study of consumption of carotenoids in fruits and vegetables and decreased cardiovascular mortality in the elderly. *Ann Epidemiol* 1995; 5(4):255-260.

[147] Manson JE, Gaziano JM, Spelsberg A, Ridker PM, Cook NR, Buring JE et al. A secondary prevention trial of antioxidant vitamins and cardiovascular disease in women. Rationale, design, and methods. The WACS Research Group. *Ann Epidemiol* 1995; 5(4):261-269.

[148] Rissanen T, Voutilainen S, Nyyssonen K, Salonen JT. Lycopene, atherosclerosis, and coronary heart disease. *Exp Biol Med (Maywood)* 2002; 227(10):900-907.

[149] Mosca L, Rubenfire M, Mandel C, Rock C, Tarshis T, Tsai A et al. Antioxidant nutrient supplementation reduces the susceptibility of low density lipoprotein to oxidation in patients with coronary artery disease. *J Am Coll Cardiol* 1997; 30(2):392-399.

[150] Lonn E, Bosch J, Yusuf S, Sheridan P, Pogue J, Arnold JM et al. Effects of long-term vitamin E supplementation on cardiovascular events and cancer: a randomized controlled trial. *JAMA* 2005; 293(11):1338-1347.

[151] Lonn E, Yusuf S, Hoogwerf B, Pogue J, Yi Q, Zinman B et al. Effects of vitamin E on cardiovascular and microvascular outcomes in high-risk patients with diabetes: results of the HOPE study and MICRO-HOPE substudy. *Diabetes Care* 2002; 25(11):1919-1927.

[152] Kritchevsky SB, Tell GS, Shimakawa T, Dennis B, Li R, Kohlmeier L et al. Provitamin A carotenoid intake and carotid artery plaques: the Atherosclerosis Risk in Communities Study. *Am J Clin Nutr* 1998; 68(3):726-733.

[153] Kushi LH, Folsom AR, Prineas RJ, Mink PJ, Wu Y, Bostick RM. Dietary antioxidant vitamins and death from coronary heart disease in postmenopausal women. *N Engl J Med* 1996; 334(18):1156-1162.

[154] Rimm EB, Stampfer MJ, Ascherio A, Giovannucci E, Colditz GA, Willett WC. Vitamin E consumption and the risk of coronary heart disease in men. *N Engl J Med* 1993; 328(20):1450-1456.

[155] Stampfer MJ, Hennekens CH, Manson JE, Colditz GA, Rosner B, Willett WC. Vitamin E consumption and the risk of coronary disease in women. *N Engl J Med* 1993; 328(20):1444-1449.

[156] Yusuf S, Dagenais G, Pogue J, Bosch J, Sleight P. Vitamin E supplementation and cardiovascular events in high-risk patients. The Heart Outcomes Prevention Evaluation Study Investigators. *N Engl J Med* 2000; 342(3):154-160.

[157] Sesso HD, Buring JE, Norkus EP, Gaziano JM. Plasma lycopene, other carotenoids, and retinol and the risk of cardiovascular disease in men. *Am J Clin Nutr* 2005; 81(5):990-997.

[158] Sesso HD, Buring JE, Norkus EP, Gaziano JM. Plasma lycopene, other carotenoids, and retinol and the risk of cardiovascular disease in women. *Am J Clin Nutr* 2004; 79(1):47-53.

[159] Sesso HD, Liu S, Gaziano JM, Buring JE. Dietary lycopene, tomato-based food products and cardiovascular disease in women. *J Nutr* 2003; 133(7):2336-2341.

[160] Boushey CJ, Beresford SA, Omenn GS, Motulsky AG. A quantitative assessment of plasma homocysteine as a risk factor for vascular disease. Probable benefits of increasing folic acid intakes. *JAMA* 1995; 274(13):1049-1057.

[161] Folsom AR, Nieto FJ, McGovern PG, Tsai MY, Malinow MR, Eckfeldt JH et al. Prospective study of coronary heart disease incidence in relation to fasting total homocysteine, related genetic polymorphisms, and B vitamins: the Atherosclerosis Risk in Communities (ARIC) study. *Circulation* 1998; 98(3):204-210.

[162] Danesh J, Lewington S. Plasma homocysteine and coronary heart disease: systematic review of published epidemiological studies. *J Cardiovasc Risk* 1998; 5(4):229-232.

[163] Ubbink JB, Vermaak WJ, van der MA, Becker PJ. Vitamin B-12, vitamin B-6, and folate nutritional status in men with hyperhomocysteinemia. *Am J Clin Nutr* 1993; 57(1):47-53.

[164] Spoelstra-DE Man AM, Smulders YM, Dekker JM, Heine RJ, Bouter LM, Nijpels G et al. Homocysteine levels are not associated with cardiovascular autonomic function in elderly Caucasian subjects without or with type 2 diabetes mellitus: the Hoorn Study. *J Intern Med* 2005; 258(6):536-543.

[165] Sagara M, Kanda T, NJelekera M, Teramoto T, Armitage L, Birt N et al. Effects of dietary intake of soy protein and isoflavones on cardiovascular disease risk factors in high risk, middle-aged men in Scotland. *J Am Coll Nutr* 2004; 23(1):85-91.

[166] Anderson JW, Johnstone BM, Cook-Newell ME. Meta-analysis of the effects of soy protein intake on serum lipids. *N Engl J Med* 1995; 333(5):276-282.

[167] Wong WW, Smith EO, Stuff JE, Hachey DL, Heird WC, Pownell HJ. Cholesterol-lowering effect of soy protein in normocholesterolemic and hypercholesterolemic men. *Am J Clin Nutr* 1998; 68(6 Suppl):1385S-1389S.

[168] Crouse JR, III, Morgan T, Terry JG, Ellis J, Vitolins M, Burke GL. A randomized trial comparing the effect of casein with that of soy protein containing varying amounts of isoflavones on plasma concentrations of lipids and lipoproteins. *Arch Intern Med* 1999; 159(17):2070-2076.

[169] Teixeira SR, Potter SM, Weigel R, Hannum S, Erdman JW, Jr., Hasler CM. Effects of feeding 4 levels of soy protein for 3 and 6 wk on blood lipids and apolipoproteins in moderately hypercholesterolemic men. *Am J Clin Nutr* 2000; 71(5):1077-1084.

[170] Jenkins DJ, Kendall CW, Mehling CC, Parker T, Rao AV, Agarwal S et al. Combined effect of vegetable protein (soy) and soluble fiber added to a standard cholesterol-lowering diet. *Metabolism* 1999; 48(6):809-816.

[171] Duane WC. Effects of soybean protein and very low dietary cholesterol on serum lipids, biliary lipids, and fecal sterols in humans. *Metabolism* 1999; 48(4):489-494.

[172] Ashton EL, Dalais FS, Ball MJ. Effect of meat replacement by tofu on CHD risk factors including copper induced LDL oxidation. *J Am Coll Nutr* 2000; 19(6):761-767.

[173] Sacks FM, Lichtenstein A, Van Horn L, Harris W, Kris-Etherton P, Winston M. Soy Protein, Isoflavones, and Cardiovascular Health. An American Heart Association Science Advisory for Professionals From the Nutrition Committee. *Circulation* 2006.

[174] Jenkins DJ, Kendall CW, Vuksan V, Vidgen E, Parker T, Faulkner D et al. Soluble fiber intake at a dose approved by the US Food and Drug Administration for a claim of health benefits: serum lipid risk factors for cardiovascular disease assessed in a randomized controlled crossover trial. *Am J Clin Nutr* 2002; 75(5):834-839.

[175] Ziai SA, Larijani B, Akhoondzadeh S, Fakhrzadeh H, Dastpak A, Bandarian F et al. Psyllium decreased serum glucose and glycosylated hemoglobin significantly in diabetic outpatients. *J Ethnopharmacol* 2005; 102(2):202-207.

[176] Jenkins DJ, Wolever TM, Rao AV, Hegele RA, Mitchell SJ, Ransom TP et al. Effect on blood lipids of very high intakes of fiber in diets low in saturated fat and cholesterol. *N Engl J Med* 1993; 329(1):21-26.

[177] Sierra M, Garcia JJ, Fernandez N, Diez MJ, Calle AP. Therapeutic effects of psyllium in type 2 diabetic patients. *Eur J Clin Nutr* 2002; 56(9):830-842.

[178] Heinemann T, Kullak-Ublick GA, Pietruck B, von Bergmann K. Mechanisms of action of plant sterols on inhibition of cholesterol absorption. Comparison of sitosterol and sitostanol. *Eur J Clin Pharmacol* 1991; 40 Suppl 1:S59-S63.

[179] Plat J, Mensink RP. Plant stanol and sterol esters in the control of blood cholesterol levels: mechanism and safety aspects. *Am J Cardiol* 2005; 96(1A):15D-22D.

[180] Grundy SM. Stanol esters as a component of maximal dietary therapy in the National Cholesterol Education Program Adult Treatment Panel III report. *Am J Cardiol* 2005; 96(1A):47D-50D.

[181] Katan MB, Grundy SM, Jones P, Law M, Miettinen T, Paoletti R. Efficacy and safety of plant stanols and sterols in the management of blood cholesterol levels. *Mayo Clin Proc* 2003; 78(8):965-978.

[182] Miettinen TA, Puska P, Gylling H, Vanhanen H, Vartiainen E. Reduction of serum cholesterol with sitostanol-ester margarine in a mildly hypercholesterolemic population. *N Engl J Med* 1995; 333(20):1308-1312.

[183] Gylling H, Miettinen TA. Serum cholesterol and cholesterol and lipoprotein metabolism in hypercholesterolaemic NIDDM patients before and during sitostanol ester-margarine treatment. *Diabetologia* 1994; 37(8):773-780.

[184] Patch CS, Tapsell LC, Williams PG. Plant sterol/stanol prescription is an effective treatment strategy for managing hypercholesterolemia in outpatient clinical practice. *J Am Diet Assoc* 2005; 105(1):46-52.

[185] Cater NB, Garcia-Garcia AB, Vega GL, Grundy SM. Responsiveness of plasma lipids and lipoproteins to plant stanol esters. *Am J Cardiol* 2005; 96(1A):23D-28D.

[186] Jenkins DJ, Kendall CW, Marchie A, Faulkner DA, Wong JM, de Souza R et al. Direct comparison of a dietary portfolio of cholesterol-lowering foods with a statin in hypercholesterolemic participants. *Am J Clin Nutr* 2005; 81(2):380-387.

[187] Salen P, de Lorgeril M. GISSI-Prevenzione trial. *Lancet* 1999; 354(9189):1555-1557.

[188] Matthan NR, Jordan H, Chung M, Lichtenstein AH, Lathrop DA, Lau J. A systematic review and meta-analysis of the impact of omega-3 fatty acids on selected arrhythmia outcomes in animal models. *Metabolism* 2005; 54(12):1557-1565.

[189] Marchioli R, Barzi F, Bomba E, Chieffo C, Di Gregorio D, Di Mascio R et al. Early protection against sudden death by n-3 polyunsaturated fatty acids after myocardial infarction: time-course analysis of the results of the Gruppo Italiano per lo Studio della Sopravvivenza nell'Infarto Miocardico (GISSI)-Prevenzione. *Circulation* 2002; 105(16):1897-1903.

[190] Kris-Etherton PM, Harris WS, Appel LJ. Fish consumption, fish oil, omega-3 fatty acids, and cardiovascular disease. *Circulation* 2002; 106(21):2747-2757.

[191] Burr ML, Fehily AM, Gilbert JF, Rogers S, Holliday RM, Sweetnam PM et al. Effects of changes in fat, fish, and fibre intakes on death and myocardial reinfarction: diet and reinfarction trial (DART). *Lancet* 1989; 2(8666):757-761.

[192] Raitt MH, Connor WE, Morris C, Kron J, Halperin B, Chugh SS et al. Fish oil supplementation and risk of ventricular tachycardia and ventricular fibrillation in patients with implantable defibrillators: a randomized controlled trial. *JAMA* 2005; 293(23):2884-2891.

[193] Brouwer IA, Zock PL, Wever EF, Hauer RN, Camm AJ, Bocker D et al. Rationale and design of a randomised controlled clinical trial on supplemental intake of n-3 fatty

acids and incidence of cardiac arrhythmia: SOFA. *Eur J Clin Nutr* 2003; 57(10):1323-1330.

[194] Christensen JH, Riahi S, Schmidt EB, Molgaard H, Kirstein PA, Heath F et al. n-3 Fatty acids and ventricular arrhythmias in patients with ischaemic heart disease and implantable cardioverter defibrillators. *Europace* 2005; 7(4):338-344.

[195] Connor WE. Importance of n-3 fatty acids in health and disease. *Am J Clin Nutr* 2000; 71(1 Suppl):171S-175S.

[196] Harris WS. n-3 fatty acids and serum lipoproteins: human studies. *Am J Clin Nutr* 1997; 65(5 Suppl):1645S-1654S.

In: Metabolic Syndrome Research Trends
Editor: Thomas E. Batone, pp. 153-170
ISBN: 978-1-60456-224-8

Chapter VI

Metabolic Syndrome Treatment: Therapeutic Lifestyle Change

***David Alexander Leaf*[*],**
Departments of Medicine, Greater Los Angeles V.A. Healthcare System
U.C.L.A. School of Medicine, Los Angeles, California, USA
***Ronald W. Deitrick*,**
Department of Exercise Science
University of Scranton, Scranton, Pennsylvania 18510, USA
Nancy D. Harada
UCLA Schools of Medicine and Public Health
Geriatric Research, Education & Clinical Center
VA Greater Los Angeles Healthcare System,
11301 Wilshire Blvd., Los Angeles, California 90073, USA

Abstract

Background

During the past two decades, Metabolic Syndrome (MetS) in the U.S. has increased to the point of being ‘epidemic’, primarily due to the increased prevalence of obesity. MetS is associated with increased coronary artery disease (CAD) risk. Although dietary interventions are a fundamental component of therapeutic lifestyle change (TLC) programs aimed at weight reduction, physical activity and exercise play a pivotal in reinforcing and sustaining long-term weight loss.

[*] Address correspondence to: David Alexander Leaf M.D., M.P.H.; Division of General Internal Medicine, 111G, Greater Los Angeles V.A. Healthcare System, 11301 Wilshire Blvd., Los Angeles, California, 90073; Tel (310) 268-3254; FAX (310) 268-4933; E-mail: David.Leaf@med.va.gov

Methods

This article reviews and describes MetS including approaches for implementing physical activity in the context of TLC interventions. These include center- and phone-based programs as well as provider-based intervention settings.

Results and Conclusions

While TLC interventions aimed at reducing MetS are a public imperative, the most effective intervention remains to be elucidated. The various approaches used can be described as effective and having common characteristics. Further research is needed to determine the best method for reducing the risk of MetS.

Keywords: Physical activity, obesity, lifestyle, cardiovascular disease risk, insulin resistance

Over the past two decades, the prevalence of the Metabolic Syndrome (MetS) in the US has progressively increased to the point that it is now regarded as 'epidemic'. [1] This trend is primarily due to the increasing prevalence of obesity, which is up 74% since 1991. According to the latest National Health and Nutrition Examination Survey (NHANES), an estimated 131 million American adults are overweight or obese. [2] The prevalence of MetS increases among aging and sedentary individuals. [3,4,5]

Table 1. NCEPT MetS Criteria*

1.	Abdominal obesity (waist circumference > 102 cm [40 inches] in men, > 88 cm [35 inches] in women).
2.	Triglycerides $\geq$ 150 mg/dL
3.	Plasma high-density lipoprotein (HDL)-cholesterol < 40 mg/dL in men, < 50 mg/dL in women.
4.	Blood pressure elevation ($\geq$130/$\geq$85 mm Hg [or receiving anti-hypertensive therapy]).
5.	Fasting plasma glucose > 110 mg/dL.

* Three or more of the above conditions must be present.

According to National Cholesterol Education Program criteria MetS is defined as having 3 or more of the following conditions: 1. Abdominal obesity (waist circumference > 102 cm [40 inches] in men, > 88 cm [35 inches] in women); 2. Triglycerides $\geq$ 150 mg/dL; 3. Plasma high-density lipoprotein (HDL)-cholesterol < 40 mg/dL in men, < 50 mg/dL in women; 4. Blood pressure elevation ($\geq$130/$\geq$85 mm Hg [or receiving anti-hypertensive therapy]); 5. Fasting plasma glucose > 110 mg/dL. [6] This definition has recently been validated [7] and is summarized in Table 1.

MetS is associated with increased CAD risk. [8-14] A recent analysis of 6,447 men with CAD enrolled in the West of Scotland Coronary Prevention Study (WSCOP) showed the presence of MetS at baseline predicted CAD events (Hazard Ratio = 1.30 [1.00 to 1.67]) in a multivariate model incorporating conventional CAD risk factors. [8] Men with 4 or 5 features of MetS had a 3.7-fold increased risk for CAD events than those with none. In another study, Wong et al. [14] have shown that controlling blood pressure and lipid-related CAD risk factors prevents cardiac deaths in 90.5% of men and 82.1% of women. Similar findings have recently been reported in an analysis of lower risk populations, [9] underscoring that MetS is associated with CAD risk that is not entirely accounted for by traditional CAD risk scoring paradigms. These findings indicate that MetS treatment can greatly impact clinical outcomes.

MetS-associated increases in adiposity may be an important component of this syndrome. The NHANES III has shown increased visceral adipose tissue, i.e. central obesity measured by waist circumference, exacerbates the risk for MetS. [15] In that study of 14,924 men and women high waist circumference values were associated with virtually a two-fold increased prevalence of MetS irrespective if a person was normal weight, overweight, or obese. Yet, the risk of MetS increases as a function of body adiposity. [16] Increased body adiposity increases visceral adipose tissue and MetS risk [17] while exercise-induced weight loss reduces central obesity. [18] Hence, interventions aimed at body weight reduction can reduce the risk of MetS.

Reaven [19] is recognized for his seminal work showing that a number of metabolic disturbances reflecting increased coronary artery disease (CAD) risk are associated with insulin resistance. These metabolic disturbances are clinically manifested as overlapping conditions that include insulin resistance, MetS, and Type II diabetes mellitus. Current evidence suggests that a high accumulation of visceral adipose tissue (i.e., central obesity measured by waist circumference) is a main cause of insulin resistance that can be causally involved in the etiology of many MetS components. [20-22] Although the molecular basis of this condition is complicated and remains to be clarified, a current unifying hypothesis is that this condition arises from increased intracellular fatty acids that may interfere with pathways involved with glucose transport. [23] Recent findings indicate that impaired mitochondrial ATP production constitutes an underlying predisposition to this condition. [24] Ultimately insulin resistance develops in obesity and MetS because of alterations in partitioning of fat between adipocytes and the muscle and liver. Intracellular accumulation of fatty acid metabolites in insulin-responsive tissues (i.e., hepatic and skeletal muscle) rather than in adipocytes causes insulin signaling defects and insulin resistance. These alterations in glucose transport activity are likely the result of dysregulation of intramyocellular fatty acid metabolism, whereby fatty acids cause insulin resistance by activation of a serine kinase cascade, leading to decreased insulin-stimulated insulin receptor substrate (IRS)-1 tyrosine phosphoinositol 3-kinase (P13K) activity, a required step in insulin stimulated glucose transport into muscle via GLUT4, a glucose transporter. [23,25]

These findings support the current National Cholesterol Educational Program Adult Treatment Panel (NCEPATP) guidelines recommending long-term participation in total lifestyle change (TLC) weight loss programs of diet and physical exercise intervention for preventing and treating MetS. [6] Most components of MetS are related separately to lifestyle factors such as weight control, [26] diet, [27-31] and physical activity. [32-34] Although dietary interventions are a fundamental component of TLC programs aimed at weight reduction, physical activity and exercise play a pivotal in reinforcing and sustaining long-term weight loss. A recent call to action for clinicians emphasizes the importance of physical activity for reducing the global obesity epidemic. [1,5] The purpose of this article is to review and describe MetS including approaches for implementing physical activity in the context of TLC interventions. These include center- and phone-based programs as well as provider-based interventions.

Background

In this section, we first review the rationale for the role of physical exercise training in reducing MetS. Then we review the current guidelines that recommend physical activity interventions aimed at weight reduction and the basis for these recommendations. Next we briefly discuss the current recommendations regarding TLC programs for reducing MetS. Finally we review the barriers to implementing physical exercise and TLC programs, describe programs that have been successfully implemented, and the elements of these programs that serve as the theoretical underpinnings of provider-based exercise interventions.

The Role of Physical Exercise Training in Reducing MetS

Physical exercise is a potent intervention for the prevention and treatment of MetS and its clinical sequelae. The term 'physical exercise training' is often misused as being synonymous with 'leisure time physical activity'. Physical exercise training can be defined as repeated bouts of exercise aimed at increasing physical performance (i.e., maximal aerobic capacity {VO_{2max}}) for the purpose of athleticism and competition rather than for health promotion and disease prevention, while leisure time physical activity includes all of the non-occupational physical pursuits that are encompassed in daily living, including physical exercise training. [35] While the term 'leisure time physical activity' is often semantically used in this context for the purposes of our discussion we will use the term physical activity in this connotation to indicate *moderate intensity physical activity* exemplified by walking.

Exercise-induced improved insulin sensitivity and reduction in the risk for diabetes mellitus and MetS result largely from modest (5 to 10 percent) reductions in adiposity. Recently Watkins et al. [36] evaluated the effects of a 6 month low fat, hypocaloric dietary program in conjunction with a walking-jogging program of approximately 35 minutes 3 to 4 times weekly on insulin sensitivity (a surrogate of MetS). Among the 53 men and women randomized to receive i.) Exercise only (n = 21), ii.) Exercise plus diet (n = 21), or iii.) Control (n = 11) those with exercise plus diet showed the greatest amount of reduction in body adiposity and largest amount of improvements in insulin response. In a randomized trial of patients with type 2 diabetes mellitus, patients who performed high intensity aerobic physical exercise training 3 times per week for 2 months increased aerobic capacity by 41% and insulin sensitivity by 46%. [37] Physical exercise causes increased insulin sensitivity in those who exercise on a regular basis. [38,39] Exercise training does not correct but compensates for the defects in muscle insulin resistance by increasing the expression of GLUT4 (cellular glucose receptors). [40] Heightened insulin sensitivity appears to be mediated by post-receptor insulin signaling, specifically at the distal steps of the insulin/P13K-signaling cascade, that leads to GLUT4 translocation and increased cellular uptake of serum glucose. [41-43] Physical exercise training-induced weight loss preferentially reduces visceral adipose tissue. [18,44] Randomized, controlled trials have shown that physical exercise training reduces intra-abdominal adiposity by approximately 28% in obese men [45] and over 20% in older and 17% in younger normal weight men [46] in a dose-response manner. [47] Physical exercise training has been shown to reduce prevalence of MetS. The HERITAGE Study showed that 105 subjects with MetS reduced the prevalence of MetS by 30.5% following a 20-week aerobic physical exercise training program. [48]

Current Guidelines Recommend Participation in Moderate Intensity Physical Activity (PA) not PET

Although physical exercise training can effectively reduce MetS risk, pragmatically it has not been shown to be effective because people are unwilling to participate in long-term physical exercise training. This problem has been recognized in the current guidelines of the Centers for Disease Control and the American College of Sports Medicine [49] and Healthy People 2010 [50] who recommend participation in moderate intensity physical activity 150 minutes /week (i.e., 30 minutes 5 days per week). Walking exemplifies a common form of moderate intensity physical activity. Leaf et al. [51] evaluated the feasibility of a calorie expenditure program for prescribing physical activity among community-dwelling elderly individuals using a 20 week center-based walking intervention. Center-based interventions provided at entry, 2, 6, and 10 weeks gradually advanced weekly calorie expenditure in a home-based walking program from 300 calories at entry to 1,200 calories at week 10. Walking was prescribed in terms of minutes needed to be walked each day to achieve the weekly calorie expenditure goal that was individualized based upon each person's customary walking speed and body weight. Nineteen of the initial 20 men and women (mean age $\pm$ SD = 71.2 $\pm$ 5 years) who entered the study were successfully participating in the program at the 20-week conclusion.

Moderate intensity physical activity is also associated with reduced total- and CAD-related mortality. [52,53] Ongoing participation in regular physical activity is critical for reducing CAD: Paffenbarger et al. [54] have shown that current participation in regular physical activity rather than a remote personal history of athleticism confers CAD risk reduction. The effect of physical activity on CAD risk reduction is likely multi-factorial and may not specifically affect atherogenesis: Physical activity reduces oxidative stress, [55] and thrombogenesis. [56] Yet, a major mechanism by which physical activity lowers CAD risk involves exercise-mediated reductions in the components that comprise the constellation of MetS-defining criteria: Body adiposity, [57,58] insulin resistance, [59] blood pressure, [60] and plasma lipids and lipoproteins (physical activity lowers triglycerides and raises plasma HDL-cholesterol levels). [58,61-63] Physical activity is an important modality for promoting long-term weight loss. [64,65] Women randomized to participate in regular physical activity, especially walking, a frequently used form of physical activity, had significant reductions in total body fat and intra-abdominal fat during a 12-month period compared with non-exercising women. [66,67] Long-term weight loss is more effectively sustained by higher volumes of regular physical activity as compared to modest amounts. [68]

Sedentary behavior has recently been associated with increased MetS risk. [4] Epidemiological studies indicate that physical activity exerts a protective effect from insulin resistance and type 2 diabetes mellitus. [69-71] A recent Finnish cohort study of 2,017 men and 2,352 women followed for a 9.4 year period found that sedentary behavior was associated with increased risk for new-onset diabetes mellitus with i.) both obesity and insulin resistance, ii.) either obesity or insulin resistance, and iii.) a normal BMI without insulin resistance. [70] Similarly a study of 1,069 men without diabetes mellitus or CAD who participated in the Kuopio Ischemic Heart Disease Risk Factor Study found those who engaged in at least moderate intensity physical activity for $<$ 1 hour per week were 60 percent more likely to have MetS than those engaging in $>$ 3 hours per week even after adjusting for confounders. [71] These findings underscore the importance of moderate intensity physical activity for reducing the progression of insulin-resistance and its associated CAD-related sequelae.

Program-Based Interventions for Reducing MetS

The key to addressing MetS is a lifestyle intervention program. TLC intervention programs combining dietary counseling with moderate intensity physical activity have been successful for weight reduction. [72,73] Typically this involves weight loss resulting from a combination of dietary counseling and increased physical activity and has been shown to reduce the prevalence of insulin resistance/diabetes mellitus [72] and its MetS-related components. [43]

Maintaining changes in both dietary and exercise behaviors are important for improving long-term weight loss. [69,70] Men and women randomized to receive either conventional aerobic-based PET or a physical activity program had a similar magnitude in reductions of body fat after two years. [60] A recent study by Jakicic et al. [73] supports the current guideline recommendations [49,50] regarding the degree of exercise intensity required to promote and sustain weight loss. Among 201 sedentary women randomized to receive i.) vigorous intensity/high duration, ii.) moderate intensity/high duration, iii.) moderate intensity/moderate duration, or iv.) vigorous intensity/moderate duration accompanied by a low fat, hypocaloric diet showed no significant differences in the amount of weight reduction after 12 months (i.] 8.9 $\pm$ 7.3 kg, ii.] 8.2 $\pm$ 7.6 kg, iii.] 6.3 $\pm$ 5.6 kg, and iv.] 7.0 $\pm$ 6.4 kg). Moreover a TLC program of moderate intensity PA in conjunction with a hypocaloric, low-fat diet can reduce insulin resistance and the risk for diabetes mellitus as has been demonstrated by the prototype model implemented by The Diabetes Prevention Program Research Group [72] that is described later.

Barriers to PA and Programs Aimed at Reducing these Barriers

Although participation in a 20-week exercise program is adequate to substantially reduce the prevalence of MetS and MetS-associated risk factors in a primary prevention setting, [48] long-term participation in PA is essential to sustain body weight and MetS-risk reduction. Despite the recommended Centers for Disease Control/American College of Sports Medicine and Exercise [49] and Healthy People 2010 [50] guidelines for increasing physical activity to control body weight, the majority of adults remain inactive. [5] Patients like many other individuals, are unlikely to participate in long-term exercise programs due to such factors as inconvenience and the expense of frequent travel to their exercise sessions. [74]

The Health Belief Model [75] posits that people are more likely to action if they believe that they are vulnerable or susceptible to the consequences of a behavior. Furthermore, people need to believe they are capable of changing their lifestyles and that these changes will lead to positive outcomes. Table 2. Summarizes the four basic conditions for behavioral change.

Table 2. Four Basic Conditions for Behavioral Change

a)	Awareness and understanding of information
b)	Awareness of potential benefit of change
c)	Individual feels able to perform activity or habit
d)	Accessible mode of change and supportive social environment.

The major barriers to physical exercise include:

i) Willingness to exercise,
ii) Ability to exercise, and
iii) Adherence to exercise.

i) Willingness to Exercise

Change in physical activity participation can be conceptualized in health-behavior theoretical models as a dynamic process with individuals moving through a series of stages as they adopt and maintain a new behavior, recognizing that recidivism is part of this process. [76,78,79] Although this model was initially developed to explain the stages and processes involved in smoking cessation [77], it has since been employed in exercise behavior. [78,81] Individuals can be categorized into stages of motivational readiness for exercise participation. [80,82-84] Young et al. [85] recently demonstrated that the stage of motivational readiness predicts adherence to a 9 month exercise intervention in 342 men and women randomized to receive; i.) diet intervention only, ii.) exercise intervention only, iii.) diet plus exercise interventions, or iv.) delayed intervention (i.e., control). The questionnaire identified exercise activities including brisk walking, jogging, swimming, and aerobic dancing and classifies individuals into 5 stages of readiness to exercise categories based on their responses to a series of statements. These stages include; a.) pre-contemplation, b.) contemplation, c.) preparation, d.) action, and e.) maintenance. The study used self-reported activity logs to define exercise adherence (i.e., the monthly volume summary score). Because of the small numbers of participants reported being in the pre-contemplation phase at baseline, this stage was not evaluated, and the action and maintenance stages were combined for the analysis. For men exercise intervention goals were reached by 54% who were in the contemplation stage, 69% in the preparation stage, and 68% in the action/maintenance stage. For women exercise intervention goals were reached by 35% who were in the contemplation stage, 67% in the preparation stage, and 24% in the action/maintenance stage. These findings indicate that the motivational readiness to exercise questionnaire can be used to identify individuals who are most likely to participate in long-term physical exercise.

ii) Ability to Exercise

Physical limitations such as spinal cord injury and limb amputation can limit the ability to exercise as can debilitating medical vascular conditions such as CAD, cerebrovascular accidents and peripheral arterial disease. For these conditions rehabilitative rather than 'wellness' programs are the preferred setting for exercise.

iii) Adherence to Exercise

Long-term adherence to exercise is historically low and approaches 60 percent after one year. [86,87] Adherence issues can be grossly dichotomized as a) program logistics, and b) sustained behavioral motivation.

a) Program Logistics

The low adherence to participation in long-term on-site exercise programs has been an impetus to explore other program logistics that may increase exercise accessibility including home- and community-based venues. *Home-based* exercise programs have been evaluated by King et al. [87] in a trial randomizing 160 women and 197 men to either 52-week programs of; i.) higher-intensity group-based exercise training, ii.) higher-intensity home-based exercise training, and iii.) lower-intensity home-based exercise training. Participants in the group-based programs attended 3 sessions each week for once year while the participants in the home-based programs received phone contact once per week for the first 4 weeks, biweekly for the following 4 weeks, then one monthly for 12 months. This study found one-year adherence greater in higher intensity (80%) and lower-intensity (76%) home-based programs than in the higher-intensity group-based program (44%). Moreover when those in each group who had completed at least 75% of the prescribed exercise sessions were compared the higher-intensity home–based program increased VO_{2max} to a greater extent than did its group-based counterpart. *Community-based* exercise interventions have been evaluated in the Community Healthy Activities Model Program for Seniors (CHAMPS) showing that referral to a community-based program that provides exercise resources as part of a comprehensive plan to increase physical activity levels among seniors contributed to a greater percentage of subjects in the intervention group (68%) compared with a non-intervention group (35%) who were physically active after 6 months. [88] More recently CHAMPS II, based on the earlier CHAMPS, evaluated the effect of a lifestyle program that promoted increased physical activity levels for older adults based upon a personal choice model. [89] Subjects recruited from a large multi-specialty group practice were randomized to receive a 1-year physical activity promotion program or to a wait-list control group. The program provided individualized client-centered motivational, behavioral, and cognitive techniques to encourage participants to join classes and programs in the community and/or develop an exercise program of their own. The results of this program showed those randomized to receive the exercise intervention significantly increased their physical activity levels compared with the control group. These findings indicate that programs utilizing self-directed community-based physical exercise resources can greatly improve long-term exercise success.

b) Sustained Behavioral Motivation

Behavioral theories such as social cognitive theory [90] underscore the importance of ongoing monitoring, follow-up, and feedback in helping to facilitate sustained adherence to physical activity and other health promotion interventions. [90] The ‘case management’ approach [91,92] relying heavily on telephone contacts has been found to be consistently effective in community-based exercise promotion trials. [87,88,93,94] A recent study with elderly VA primary care patients demonstrated increased home-based walking and fitness over one year using case management nurse counseling with telephone and mail follow-up. [95]

Successful TLC Programs

The most successful programs for TLC that will be discussed later, such as the Diabetes Prevention Program, [72] involve both weight loss and physical activity initiating with more intensive weekly center-based sessions that then fade to lower intensity as the program progresses. [72,73] However, the application of these programs may be limited because patients may have difficulty in attending program sessions. Phone-based programs, although less likely to be as effective in causing weight loss, may be more effectively implemented because of their convenience and provide fewer barriers to access to a larger group of patients.

Although home- and community-based programs have *both* generally been regarded to achieve good physical activity adherence they have minimal impact in affecting and sustaining clinically significant weight loss necessary to reduce MetS risk. Successful programs for TLC involving both weight loss through diet and physical activity have used center-based reinforcement sessions with dietary counseling initially administered on a weekly basis which then fade to lower intensity as the program progresses. [72,93,94] The Trial of Nonpharmacologic Interventions in the elderly (TONE) a randomized study in men and women aged 60 to 80 years aimed at achieving and maintaining a 4.5 kg. weight loss combined with dietary sodium restriction exemplifies this approach. [57] Subjects receiving the lifestyle intervention met with nutrition and exercise counselors in individual and small group sessions on a regular basis and had a 4.7 kg weight reduction after 30 weeks compared with the 0.9 kg weight reduction in those receiving usual care.

Recently the Diabetes Prevention Program Research Group employed a 16-lesson center-based TLC program that administered a curriculum covering diet, exercise, and behavior in conjunction with a dietary and physical activity programs to help participants achieve and maintain their goal of a 7 percent weight loss [72] in a group of 3,234 non-diabetics who were at high-risk for diabetes mellitus. The two major goals of the Diabetes Prevention Program lifestyle intervention were; i.) a minimum of 7% weight loss/weight maintenance and ii.) a minimum of 150 min/week of physical activity similar in intensity to brisk walking. Both goals were hypothesized to be feasible, safe, and effective based on previous clinical trials in other countries. [89-93] The methods used to achieve these lifestyle goals include the following key features: 1) individual case managers or "lifestyle coaches;" 2) frequent contact with participants; 3) a structured, state-of-the-art, 16-session core-curriculum that taught behavioral self-management strategies for weight loss and physical activity; 4) supervised physical activity sessions; 5) a more flexible maintenance intervention, combining group and individual approaches, motivational campaigns, and "restarts;" 6) individualization through a "toolbox" of adherence strategies; 7) tailoring of materials and strategies to address ethnic diversity; and finally 8) an extensive network of training, feedback, and clinical support. [96-100] The curriculum, taught by case managers in a face-to-face center-based venue was administered on a weekly basis for the first 8 weeks, biweekly for the next 16 weeks, then monthly for the remainder of the long-term intervention. Those receiving this center-based LTC intervention were more successful in sustaining weight loss and reduced their incidence of diabetes by 58% after a 3-year follow-up period compared with the non-intervention group.

Phone-based interventions have been used successfully in medical case-management [91] and for promoting physical activity. [87,88,95] This intervention modality is attractive because it represents a potentially inexpensive and convenient form of intervention. In many areas of health promotion, minimal treatment interventions are being evaluated to address the issue of treatment practicality. Minimal intensity treatment approaches such as correspondence programs are often rated as more preferable than face-to-face formats [103] but there are mixed results when applying minimal interventions weight loss. [104-108] One type of minimal intervention, phone calls and mailings, have been used successfully as a maintenance strategy for weight loss [109] and to assist in managing weight over the holiday season. [110] However, phone calls and mailings were less effective in other studies. [111] Recently Boutelle et al. [112] employed an 8–week minimal intervention dietary-based weight loss program that involved weekly educational mailings and phone calls (5 minutes) in a group of 26 obese (BMI = 34.7 $\pm$ 4.9) Veteran men. Those randomized to receive this intervention showed a tendency for increased weight reduction (3.9 $\pm$ 6.1 lbs) compared with the control patients (1.6 $\pm$ 3.3 lbs) after 8 weeks. The findings from this study suggest that a similar program of longer duration and involving more intensive telephone intervention sessions in a larger group of patients. Phone-based programs are regarded to be as effective as center-based programs for increasing participation in physical activity. However, as discussed, center-based TLC interventions have a more substantial impact on weight reduction than currently studied phone-based interventions. Phone-based interventions providing TLC interventions that are more intensive both in content and duration than those previously described are potentially an alternative for patients who cannot or will not attend center-based TLC sessions. Hence, phone-based interventions, although less effective on an individual basis, potentially can involve a larger population of patients than home-based interventions. Such a phone-based TLC intervention merits comparison with conventionally established face-to-face center-based interventions such as the one administered by the Diabetes Prevention Program.

Practitioner-Based Interventions for Reducing MetS

Although exercise guidelines indicate that practitioners should have an active role in promoting physical activity, health practitioners do not routinely counsel patients about physical activity in the usual care-wellness setting [113] and focus primarily on patients who are at high risk for disease. [114] The Activity Counseling Trial (ACT) was a multi-center trial that randomized 395 women and 479 men to receive i.) physician advice with educational materials, ii.) physician advice plus interactive mail and behavioral counseling assistance at physician visits, or iii.) physician advice and assistance plus regular investigator-initiated phone counseling and behavioral classes. [115] After 24 months among women VO_{2max} was greater in the assistance (group ii.) and the counseling (group iii.) groups than in the advice group (group i.) although no group differences in levels of self-reported physical activity were noted. No differences were noted among the groups of men for either VO_{2max} or self-reported physical activity. These findings indicate that exercise promotion when provided in the usual primary care setting may not be adequate to substantially affect long-term physical activity behaviors. However, although program-based TLC interventions can play an important role in reducing MetS, the role of the clinician to successfully impact TLC success has been emphasized. [5]

The 33rd Bethesda Conference on Preventive Cardiology identified a need to understand better the barriers to professional adherence to prevention guidelines a the community, provider, and patient levels. [116] The conference urges placing special focus groups on vulnerable groups, including the economically disadvantaged, elderly individuals, and ethnic minorities. A recent survey of medical residents and attending physicians in a large, urban public hospital identified 2 main barriers to effective prevention counseling: lack of training in prevention, and our system's emphasis on acute care rather than preventive care. [117]

In order to be successful the clinician must believe that the patient is capable of change, and must understand the ABCs, i.e. attitude, beliefs, and core values of the patient. Prior to TLC counseling it is important for a clinician to obtain information regarding the patient's lifestyle in order to tailor TLC counseling to the individual. Moreover a medical history and physical examination can identify patients with medical conditions that require rehabilitative exercise interventions. Suggesting one change at a time, i.e. single concept learning is more effective than trying to persuade patients to change their entire behavior pattern. According to Bandura's Social Learning Theory, behavior is learned and can be unlearned. [90] People learn most effectively when they are actively involved in the decision-making process and believe that they can change. The provider and patient should collaborate in developing a plan and setting goals for behavior change. Although individuals need adequate information on which to base a decision to change they must also believe in their own ability to make changes and must be encouraged to strive for positive outcomes. Individuals need the skills, support, and resources tailored to them. The goal for physical activity should be specific. Although current recommendations suggest 30 minutes of moderate intensity a day on at least 5 days a week, this recommendation may not seem meaningful to most patients. In this context a specific goal would be to 'take an evening stroll with the family'.

Conclusion

While TLC interventions to reduce MetS are a public health imperative, the most effective interventions remain to be defined. Successful center-, phone-, and provider-based interventions need to adhere to similar theoretical underpinnings. Current findings suggest that there may be an overlap in the effectiveness in the use of these various approaches, and, as is apparent for lifestyle change programs, these different forms of intervention may be complementary to each other. Indeed further studies are important to delineate how these different approaches can best be employed to reduce the risk for MetS.

References

[1] Mokdad AH, Bowman BA, Ford ES, Vinicor F, Marks JS, Koplan JP. The continuing epidemics of obesity and diabetes in the United States. *JAMA*. 2001; 286:1195-2000.

[2] Flegal KM, Carroll MD, Ogden CL, Johnson CL. Prevalence and trends in obesity among US adults. *JAMA*. 2003; 289:76-79.

[3] Ford ES, Giles WH, Dietz WH. Prevalence of the metabolic syndrome among US adults. Findings from the Third National Health and Nutrition Examination Survey. *JAMA*. 2002; 287:356-359.

[4] Park Y-W, Zhu S, Palaniappan L, Heshka S, Carnethon MR, Heymsfield SB. The metabolic syndrome. Prevalence and associated risk factor findings in the US population from the Third National Health and Nutrition Examination Survey, 1988-1994. *Arch Intern Med*. 2003; 163:427-436.

[5] Manson JE, Skerret PJ, Greenland, Van Itallie TB. The escalating pandemics of obesity and sedentary lifestyle. A call to action for clinicians. *Arch Intern Med*. 2004; 164:249-258.

[6] Expert Panel on Detection, Evaluation, and Treatment of High blood Cholesterol In Adults. Executive summary of the third report of the National Cholesterol Education Program Expert Panel on Detection, Evaluation, and Treatment of High Blood Cholesterol in Adults. *JAMA*. 2001; 285:2486-2497.

[7] Laaksonen DE, Lakka HM, Niskanen LK, Kaplan GA, Salonen JT, Lakka TA. Metabolic syndrome and development of diabetes mellitus: application and validation of recently suggested definition of the metabolic syndrome. *Am J Epidemiol*. 2002; 156:1070-1077.

[8] Sattar N, Gaw A, Scherbakova O, et al. Metabolic syndrome with and without C-reactive protein as a predictor of coronary heart disease and diabetes in the West of Scotland Coronary Prevention Study. *Circulation*. 2003; 108:414-419.

[9] Girman CJ, Rhodes T, Mercuri M, et al. The metabolic syndrome and risk of major events in the Scandanavian Simvastatin Survival Study (4S) and the Air Force/Texas Coronary Atherosclerosis Prevention Study (AFCAPS/TexCAPS). *Am J Cardiol*. 2004; 93:136-141.

[10] HuG, Quiao Q, Tuomilehto J, Balkau B, Borch-Johnsen K, and Pyorala K. Prevalence of the metabolic syndrome and its relation to all-cause and cardiovascular mortality in nondiabetic European men and women. *Arch Intern Med*. 2004; 164:1066-1076.

[11] Solymoss BC, Bourassa MG, Campeua L, Sniderman A, Marcil M, Lesperance J, Levesque S, and Varga S. Effect of increasing metabolic syndrome score on atherosclerotic risk profile and coronary artery disease angiographic severity. *Am J Cardiol*. 2004; 93:159-164.

[12] Pyorala M, Miettinen H, Halonen P, Laakso M, Pyorala K. Insulin resistance syndrome predicts the risk of coronary heart disease and stroke in healthy middle-aged men: the 22-year follow-up results of the Helsinki Policemen Study. *Circulation*. 1998; 98:398-404.

[13] Arad Y, Newstein D, Cadet F, Roth M, Guerci AD. Association of multiple risk factors and insulin resistance with increased prevalence of asymptomatic coronary artery disease by electron-beam computed tomographic study. *Arterioscler Thromb Vasc Biol*. 2001; 21:2051-2058.

[14] Wong ND, Pio JR, Franklin SS, L'Italien GJ, Kamath TV, Williams GR. Preventing coronary events by optimal control of blood pressure and lipids in patients with the metabolic syndrome. *Am J Cardiol*. 2003; 91:1421-1426.

[15] Janssen I, Katzmarzyk PT, Ross R. Body mass index, waist circumference, and health risk. Evidence in support of current National Institute of Health guidelines. *Arch Intern Med*. 2002; 162:2074-2079.

[16] Ashton WD, Nanchahal K, Wood DA. Body mass index and metabolic risk factors for coronary heart disease in women. *Eur Heart J.* 2001; 22:46-55.

[17] Haffner SM, Mykkanen L, Festa A, Burke J, Stern M. Insulin resistant pre-diabetic subjects have more atherogenic risk factors than insulin sensitive pre-diabetic subjects: implications for preventing coronary heart disease during the pre-diabetic state. *Circulation.* 2000; 101:975-980.

[18] Slenz CA, Duscha BD, Johnson JL, et al. Effects of the amount of exercise on body weight, body composition, and measures of central obesity. STRRIDE- a randomized controlled study. *Arch Intern Med.* 2004; 164:31-39.

[19] Reaven GN. Role of insulin resistance in human disease. *Diabetes.* 1988; 37:1596-1607.

[20] Lemieus S, Despres JP. Metabolic complications of visceral obesity: contribution to the aetiology of type 2 diabetes and implications for prevention and treatment. *Diabetes Metab.* 1994; 20:375-393.

[21] Despres JP. Visceral obesity: A component of the insulin resistance dyslipidemic syndrome. *Can J Cardiol.* 1994; 10:17B-22B.

[22] Haffner SM. The insulin resistance syndrome revisited. *Diabetes Care.* 1996; 19:275-277.

[23] Shulman GI. Cellular mechanisms of insulin resistance. *J Clin Invest.* 2000; 206:171-176.

[24] Petersen KF, Dufour S, Befroy D, Garcia R, Shulman GI. Impaired mitochondrial activity in the insulin-resistant offspring of patients with type 2 diabetes. *N Engl J Med.* 2004; 350:664-671.

[25] Shuldine AR, McLenithan. Genes and the pathophysiology of type 2 diabetes: more than just the Randle cycle all over again. *J Clin Invest.* 2004; 114:1414-1417.

[26] Reaven GM. Diet and syndrome X. *Curr Atherosler Rep.* 2000; 2:503-507.

[27] Abbassi F, McLaughlin T, Lamendola C, et al. High carbohydrate diets, triglyceride-rich lipoproteins, and coronary heart risk. *Am J Cardiol.* 2000; 85:45-48.

[28] Wirtalt E, Hedblad B, Guilberg B, et al. Food patterns and components of the metabolic syndrome in men and women: a cross-sectional study within the Malmo Diet and Cancer cohort. *Am J Epidemiol.* 2001; 154:1150-1159.

[29] Ludwig DS, Periera MA, Kroenke CH, et al. Dietary fiber, weight gain, and cardiovascular disease risk factors in young adults. *JAMA.* 1999; 282:1539-1546.

[30] Periera MA, Jacobs DRJ, Van Horn L, Stattery ML, Kartashov AI, Ludwig DS. Dietary consumption, obesity, and the insulin resistance syndrome in young adults in the CARDIA Study. *JAMA.* 2002; 287:2081-2089.

[31] Fung TT, Rimm EB, Spiegelman D, et al. Association between dietary patterns and plasma biomarkers of obesity and cardiovascular disease risk. *Am J Clin Nutr.* 2001; 73:61-67.

[32] Miyatake N, Nishikawa H, Morishita A, et al. Daily walking reduces visceral adipose tissue areas and improves insulin resistance in Japanese obese subjects. *Diabetes Res Clin Pract.* 2002; 58:101-107.

[33] Meigs JB, D'Agostino RBSr, Wilson PWF, Cupples LA, Nathan DM, Singer DE. Risk variable clustering in the insulin resistance syndrome. The Framingham Offspring Study. *Diabetes.* 1997; 46:1494-1600.

[34] McAuley KA, Williams SM, Mann JI, et al. Intensive lifestyle changes are necessary to improve insulin sensitivity: a randomized controlled trial. *Diabetes Care*. 2002; 25:445-452.

[35] Caspersen CJ, CJ, Powell KE, Christensen GM. Physical activity, exercise, and physical fitness. *Public Health Rep*. 1985; 100:125-131.

[36] Watkins LL, Sherwood A, Feinglos M, Hinderliter A, Babyak M, Gullette E, Waugh R, Blumenthal JA. Effects of exercise and weight loss on cardiac risk factors associated with Syndrome X. *Arch Intern Med*. 2003; 163:1889-1895.

[37] Mourier A, Gautier JF, De Kerviler E. Mobilization of visceral adipose tissue related to the improvement in insulin sensitivity in response to physical exercise training in NIDDM: effects of branched-chain amino acid supplements. *Diabetes Care*. 1997; 20:385-391.

[38] Kirwan JP, del Aguila LF, Hernandez JM, Williamson DL, O' Gorman DJ, Lewis R, Krishman RK. Regular exercise enhances insulin activation of IRS-associated PI3-kinase in human skeletal muscle. *J Appl Physiol*. 2000; 88:797-803.

[39] Kirwan JP, Jing M. Modulation of insulin signaling in human skeletal muscle in response to exercise. *Exerc Sport Sci Rev*. 2002; 30:85-90.

[40] Ivy JL. Muscle insulin resistance amended with exercise training: Role of GLUT4 Expression. *Med Sci Sports Exerc*. 2004; 36:1207-1211.

[41] Hawley JA, Houmard JA. Preventing insulin resistance through exercise: a cellular approach. *Med Sci Sports Exerc*. 2004; 36:1187-1190.

[42] Berggren JR, Hulver MW, Dohm GL, Houmard JA. Weight loss and exercise: implications for muscle lipid metabolism and insulin action. *Med Sci Sports Exerc*. 2004; 136:1191-1195.

[43] Bruce CR, Hawley JA. Improvements in insulin resistance with aerobic exercise training: A lipocentric approach. *Med Sci Sports Exerc*. 2004; 136:1196-1201.

[44] Mayo MJ, Grantham JR, Balasekaran G. Exercise-induced weight loss preferentially reduces abdominal fat. *Med Sci Sports Exerc*. 2003; 35:207-213.

[45] Ross R, Dagone D, Jones PJH, Smith H, Paddags A, Hudson R, Janssen. Reduction in obesity and related comorbid conditions after diet-induced weight loss or exercise-induced weight loss in men. *Ann Intern Med*. 2000; 133:92-103.

[46] Schwartz RS, Shuman WP, Larson V, Cain KC, Fellingham GW, Beard JC, Kahn SE, Stratton JR, Cerqueira MD, Abass IB. The effect of intensive endurance exercise training on body fat distribution in young and older men. *Metabolism*. 1991; 40:545-551.

[47] Ross R, Janssen I. Physical activity, total and regional obesity: dose response considerations. *Med Sci Sports Exerc*. 2001; 33:S521-527.

[48] Katzmarzyk PT, Leon AS, Wilmore JH, skinner JS, Rao DC, Rankinen T, Bouchard C. Targeting the metabolic syndrome with exercise: Evidence from the HERITAGE Family Study. *Med Sci Sports Exerc*. 2003; 35:1703-1709.

[49] Pate RR, Pratt M, Blair SN. Physical Activity and Public Health. A recommendation from the Centers for Disease Control and Prevention and the American College of Sports Medicine. *JAMA*. 995; 273:402-407.

[50] Healthy People 2010: Volume II. Conference Edition. Washington DC: USD Dept of Health and Human Services: 2000.

[51] Leaf DA, Reuben DB. "Lifestyle" interventions for promoting physical activity: A kilocalorie expenditure-based home feasibility study. *Am J Med Sci.* 1996; 312:68-75.

[52] Lee I-M, Skerrett PJ. Physical activity and all-cause mortality: what is the dose-response relation? *Med Sci Sports Exerc.* 2001; 33:S459-S471.

[53] Leon AS, Connett J, Jacobs DR, Rauramaa R. Leisure –time physical activity nd risk of coronary heart disease and death: the Multiple Risk Factor Intervention Trial. *JAMA.* 1987; 258:2386-2396.

[54] Paffenbarger RS, Hyde RT, Wing AL, Hsieh C.-C. Physical activity, all-cause mortality and longevity of college alumni. *N Engl J Med.* 1986; 314:605-614.

[55] Leaf DA, Kleinman MT, Hamilton M, Deitrick RW. The exercise-induced oxidative stress paradox: the effects of physical exercise training. *Am J Med Sci.* 1999; 317:295-300.

[56] Wannamethee SG, Lowe GDO, Whincup PH, Rumley A, Walker M, Lennon L. Physical activity and hemostatic and inflammatory variables in men. *Circulation.* 2002; 105:1785-1790.

[57] Whelton PK, Appel LJ, Espeland MA, et al. Sodium reduction and weight loss in the treatment of hypertension in older persons. A randomized controlled trial of Nonpharmacologic Interventions in the Elderly (TONE). *JAMA.* 1998; 279:839-846.

[58] Leaf DA, Parker DL, McAfee JR. The relationship of physical activity to CAD risk factors: Lipids, lipoproteins, percent body fat, and blood pressure. *J Cardiopulm Rehab.* 1989; 9(12): 497-505.

[59] Rankinen T, Suomela-Markkanene T, Vaisanene S, Helminen A, Penttila I, Berg A, Bouchard C, Rauramaa R. Relationship between changes in physical activity and plasma insulin during a 2.5-year follow-up study. *Metabolism.* 1997; 46:1418-1423.

[60] Dunn AL, Marcus BH, Kampert JB, Garcia ME, Kohl HL, Blair SN. Comparison of lifestyle and structured interventions to increase physical activity and cardiorespiratory fitness: a randomized trial. *JAMA.* 1999; 281:327-334.

[61] Bouchard C, Rankinen T. Individual differences in response to regular physical activity. *Med Sci Sports Exerc.* 2001; 33:S446-S451.

[62] Leaf DA, Parker DL, Schaad D. Changes in VO_{2max}, physical activity, and body fat with chronic exercise: effects of plasma lipids. *Med Sci Sports and Exerc.* 1997; 29:1152-1159.

[63] Duncan JJ, Gordon NF, Scott CB. Women walking for health and fitness. How much is enough? *JAMA.* 1991; 266:3291-3297.

[64] Jakicic JM, Gallagher KI. Exercise considerations for the sedentary, overweight adult. *Exerc Sport Sci Rev.* 2003; 31:91-95.

[65] Klem ML, Wing RR, McGuire MT, Seagle HM, Hill JO. A descriptive study of individuals successful at long-term maintenance of substantial weight loss. *Am J Clin Nutr.* 1997; 66:239-246.

[66] Jakicic JM, Winters C, Lang W, Wing RR. Effects of intermittent exercise and use of home exercise equipment on adherence, weight loss, and fitness in overweight women: a randomized trial. *JAMA.* 1999; 282:1554-1560.

[67] Irwin ML, Yasui Y, Ulrich CM, Bowen D, Rudolph RE, Schwartz RS, Yukawa M, Aiello E, Potter JD, McTiernan A. Effect of exercise on total and intra-abdominal body fat in post menopausal women, a randomized controlled trial. *JAMA.* 2003; 289:323-330.

[68] Jakicic JM, Wing RR, Butler BA, Robertson RJ. Prescribing exercise in multiple short bouts versus one continuous bout: effects of adherence, cardiorespiratory fitness, and weight loss in overweight women. *Int J Obes*. 1995; 19:893-901.

[69] Kelly DE, Goodpaster BH. The effects of exercise on glucose homeostasis in Type 2 diabetes mellitus. *Med Sci Sports Exerc*. 2001; 33:S495-S501.

[70] Hu G, Lindstrom J, Valle T, Eriksson JG, Jousilahti P, Silventoinen K, Qiao Q, Tuomilehto J. Physical activity, body mass index, and risk of Type 2 diabetes in patients with normal or impaired glucose regulation. *Arch Intern Med.* 2004; 164:892-896.

[71] Lakka TA, Laaksonen DE, Lakka H-M, Mannikko N, Niskanen LK, Rauramaa R, and Salonen JT. Sedentary lifestyle, poor cardiorespiratory fitness, and the metabolic syndrome. *Med Sci Sports Exerc*. 2003; 35:1279-1286.

[72] Diabetes Prevention Program Research Group. Reduction in the incidence of type 2 diabetes with lifestyle intervention or metformin. *N Eng J Med.* 2002; 346:393-403.

[73] Jakicic JM, Marcus BH, Gallagher KI, Napolitano M, Lang W. Effect of exercise duration and intensity on weight loss in overweight, sedentary women. *JAMA.* 2003; 290:1323-1330.

[74] Marcus BH, Dubbert PM, Forsyth LH, McKenzie TL, Stone EJ, Dunn AL, Blair SN. Physical activity behavior change: Issues in adoption and maintenance. *Health Psychology*. 2000; 19(1,S): 32-41.

[75] Rosenstock I. In Glanz K, et al., Eds. *Health Behavior and Education: Theory, Research and Practice*. San Francisco: Jossey-Bass, 1990.

[76] Prochaska JO, Velicer WF. The transtheoretical model of health behavior change. *Am J Health Promotion*. 1997; 12:38-48.

[77] Prochaska JO, DiClemente CC. Stages and processes of self-change of smoking: toward an integrative model of change. *J Consult Clin Psychol*. 1983,51:390-395.

[78] Dishman RK. Compliance/adherence in health-related exercise. *Health Psychol.* 1982; 1:237-267.

[79] Sallis JF, Haskell WL, Fortman S, et al. Predictors of adoption and maintenance of physical activity in a community sample. *Prev Med.* 1985; 15:331-341.

[80] Marcus BH, Owen N. motivational readiness, self-efficacy and decision-making for exercise. *J Appl Social Psychol*. 1992; 22:3-16.

[81] Marcus BH, Selby VS, Niaura RS, et al. Self-efficacy and the stages of exercise behavior change. *Res Q Exerc Sport*. 1992; 63:60-66.

[82] Marcus BH, Rossi JS, Selby VC, et al. The stages and processes of exercise adoption and maintenance in a worksite sample. *Health Psychol.* 1992; 11:386-395.

[83] Herrick AB, Stone WJ, Mettler MM. Stages of change, decisional balance, and self-efficacy across four health behaviors in a worksite environment. *Am J Health Promot*. 1997; 12:49-56.

[84] Marcus BH, Pinto BM, Simkin LR, et al. Application of theoretical models to exercise behavior among employed women. *Am J Health Promot*. 1994; 49:49-55.

[85] Young DR, King AC, Sheehan M, Stefaneik ML. Stage of motivational readiness: predictive ability for exercise behavior. *Am J Health Behav*. 2002; 26:331-341.

[86] Dishman RK, Sallis JF, Orenstein DR. The determinants of physical activity and exercise. *Pub Health Rep*. 1985; 100; 158-171.

[87] King AC, Haskell WL, Taylor B, Kraemer HC, DeBusk RF. Group-vs Home-based exercise training in healthy older men and women. A community-based clinical trial. *JAMA*. 1991; 266:1535-1542.

[88] Stewart AL, Mills KM, Sepsis PG, King AC, McLellan BY, Roltz K, Ritter P. Evaluation of CHAMPS, A physical activity promotion program for older adults. *Ann Behav Med*. 1997; 19:353-361.

[89] Stewart AL, Verboncoeur CJ, McLellan BY, et al. Physical activity outcomes of CHAMPS II: A physical activity promotion program for older adults. *J Gerontol*. 2000; 56A:M465-M470.

[90] Bandura A. *Social foundations of thought and action: a social cognitive theory*. Englewood Cliffs, NJ: Prentice-Hall, 1986.

[91] DeBusk RF, et al. A case-management system for coronary risk factor modification after acute myocardial infarction. *Ann Intern Med*. 1994:120; 721-729.

[92] Wasson J, et al. Telephone care as a substitute for routine clinic follow-up. *JAMA*. 1992; 267:1788-1793.

[93] Appel LJ, Champagne CM, Harsha DW, Cooper LS, Obarzenek E, Elmer PJ, Stevens VJ, Vollmer WM, Lin PH, Svetkey LP, Stedman SW, Young DR. Writing group of the PREMIER collaborative research group. *JAMA*. 2003; 289:2083-2093.

[94] Ard JD, Grambow SC, Liu D, Slentz CA, Kras WE, Svetkey PL. The effect of the PREMIER interventions on insulin sensitivity. *Diabetes Care*. 2004; 27:340-347.

[95] Dubbert PM, Cooper KM, Kirchner KK, Meydrech EM, and Bilbrew D. Effects of nurse counseling on walking for exercise in elderly primary care patients. *Journal of Gerontology: Medical Sciences*. 2002; 57A:M733-M740.

[96] Eriksson KF, Lindgarde F: Prevention of type 2 (non-insulin-dependent) diabetes mellitus by diet and physical exercise. *Diabetologia*. 1991:34:891–898.

[97] Page RCL, Harnden KE, Cook JTE, Turner RC: Can life-styles of subjects with impaired glucose tolerance be changed? A feasibility study. *Diabet Med*. 1992; 9:562–566.

[98] Bourn DM, Mann JI, McSkimming BJ, Waldron MA, Wishart JD: Impaired glucose tolerance and NIDDM. Does a lifestyle intervention program have an effect? *Diabetes Care*. 1994; 17:1311–1319.

[99] Pan X-R, Li G-W, Hu Y-H, Wang J-X, Yang W-Y, An Z-X, Hu Z-X, Lin J, Xiao J-Z, Cao H-B, Liu P-A, Jiang X-G, Jiang Y-Y, Wang J-P, Zheng H, Zhang H, Bennett PH, Howard BV: Effects of diet and exercise in preventing NIDDM in people with impaired glucose tolerance: the Da Qing IGT and Diabetes Study. *Diabetes Care*. 1997; 20:537–544.

[100] Tuomilehto JLJ, Eriksson JG, Valle TT, Hamalainin H, Ilanne-Parikka P, Keinanen-Kiukaanniemi S, Laakso M, Louheranta A, Rastas M, Salminen V, Uusitupa M: Prevention of type 2 diabetes mellitus by changes in lifestyle among subjects with impaired glucose tolerance. *N Engl J Med*. 2001; 344:1343–1392.

[101] The Diabetes Prevention Program Research Group. The Diabetes Prevention Program (DPP) Research group. *Diabetes Care*. 2002; 25:2165-2171.

[102] www.bsc.gwu.edu/dpp/manuals.htmlvdoc

[103] Sherwood NE, Morton N, Jeffery RW, et al. Consumer preferences in format and type of community-based weight control programs. *Am J Health Promot.* 1998; 13:12-18.

[104] Jeffery RW, Hellerstedt WE, Schmid TL. Correspondence programs for smoking cessation and weight control: a comparison of two strategies in the Minnesota Heart Health Program. *Health Psychol.* 1990; 9:585-598.

[105] Cameron R, MacDonald MA, Schlegel PR, et al. Toward the development of self-help health behavior change programs: weight loss by correspondence. *Can J Public Health.* 1990; 81:2175-279.

[106] Jeffery RW, Danaher BG, Killen J, et al. Self-administered programs for health behavior change: smoking cessation and weight reduction by mail. *Addict Behav.* 1982; 7:57-63.

[107] O'Loughlin J, Paradis G, Meshefedjian G, et al. Evaluation of an 8-week mailed healthy-weight intervention. *Prev Med.* 1998; 27:288-95.

[108] Saelens BE, Sallis JF, Wilfley DE, et al. Behavioral weight control for overweight adolescents initiated in primary care. *Obes Res.* 2002; 10:22-32.

[109] Perri MG, Nezu AM, Patti ET, et al. Effect of length of treatment on weight loss. *J Consult Clin Psychol.* 1989; 57:450-452.

[110] Boutelle KN, Kirshenbaum DS, Baker RC, et al. How can obese weigh controllers minimize weight gain during the high risk holiday season? By self-monitoring very consistently. *Health Psychol.* 1999; 18:364-368.

[111] Hellerstedt WL, Jeffery RW. The effects of a telephone-based intervention on weight loss. *Am J Health Promot.* 1997; 11:177-182.

[112] Boutelle K, Dubbert PM, Vander Weg. A pilot study evaluating a minimum contact telephone and mail weight management intervention for primary care patients. *Eating and Weight Disorders* (In Press).

[113] Wee McCarthy EP, David RB, Phillips RS. Physician counseling about exercise. *JAMA.* 1999; 282:1583-1588.

[114] Wells KB, et al. The practices of general and subspecialty internists in counseling about smoking and exercise. *Am J Pub Health.* 1986; 76:1009-1013.

[115] The Writing Group of the ACT Research Group. The effects of physical activity counseling in primary care. The ACTS: A randomized control trial. *JAMA.* 2001; 286:677-687.

[116] Aedes PA, Kottke TE, Miller NH, et al. Task Force #3 – Getting results: who where, how? *J Am Coll Cardiol.* 2002; 40:615-629.

[117] Tsui JI, Dodson K, Jacobson TA. Cardiovascular disease prevention counseling in residency: resident and attending physician attitudes and practices. *J Natl Med Assoc.* 2004; 96:1080-1091.

In: Metabolic Syndrome Research Trends
Editor: Thomas E. Batone, pp. 171-190
ISBN: 978-1-60456-224-8

Chapter VII

The Emerging Role of Inflammatory Markers in the Metabolic Syndrome

*Ali A. Rizvi**
Division of Endocrinology, Diabetes, and Metabolism,
University of South Carolina, School of Medicine,
Columbia, SC 29203 USA.

Abstract

The metabolic syndrome consists of a constellation of risk factors including obesity, glucose intolerance, hypertension, and dyslipidemia in the setting of insulin resistance that confers an increased risk of cardiovascular disease and type 2 diabetes. Although the major pathophysiologic mechanisms are still in the process of being elucidated, the possible role of inflammation, cytokines, and atherogenic markers has received attention lately. Recent studies suggest that inflammatory markers like C-reactive protein (CRP), Interleukin (IL)-6, and Tumor Necrosis Factor (TNF)-α mirror oxidative stress and may be instrumental in the final pathway of adverse vascular outcomes in the metabolic syndrome. Other adipocytokines produced by fatty tissue are also altered, with lower levels of adiponectin and increased leptin and resistin. Elevated Plasminogen Activator Inhibitor (PAI)-1 and fibrinogen levels, and derangement in clotting factors correlate with the degree of insulin resistance and may contribute to the prothrombotic tendency. Taken together, these abnormalities shift the balance of endothelial function towards an abnormal state that heightens the risk of atherothrombosis. Lifestyle factors and medications can have a profound effect in modifying these parameters. The phenomenal increase in the prevalence of obesity has accentuated the various clinical manifestations and pathopysiologic underpinnings of this epidemic. Continued research looking at the role of inflammation and cytokines in the genesis and propagation of the metabolic syndrome should provide a window into its pathogenesis at the cellular and humoral

* Correspondence concerning this article should be addressed to Ali A. Rizvi, MD, FACP, Associate Professor of Medicine, Division of Endocrinology, Diabetes, and Metabolism, University of South Carolina School of Medicine, Two Medical Park, Suite 502, Columbia, SC 29203, USA. Ph: 803-540-1000; Fax: 803-540-1050; Email: arizvi@gw.mp.sc.edu.

level, improve the understanding of disease mechanisms, and open up possibilities for effective therapeutic interventions in the future.

Keywords: metabolic syndrome, inflammation, C-reactive protein, adipocytokines, insulin resistance

Introduction: Vascular Inflammation, Metabolic Syndrome, Insulin Resistance, and Atherosclerosis

The prevalence of the metabolic syndrome or insulin resistance syndrome is increasing because of global changes in obesity, sedentary lifestyle, and the ageing of the population [1]. This syndrome consists of a clustering of cardiovascular risk factors in the setting of increased body weight (indicated mainly by increased waist circumference and body mass index or BMI). Insulin resistance is believed to play a major role in the underlying pathophysiology of the metabolic syndrome, contributing to atherosclerosis and increasing the risk of glucose intolerance and diabetes [2]. Thus a process of chronic and incremental damage to the arterial wall is begun that eventually leads to vascular complications. The resultant adverse cardiovascular events are usually clinically evident and well recognized. The various stages of the atherosclerotic process have been delineated [3], and have their origins in insults to the endothelium from a combination of factors. These predisposing conditions include the well-known risk factors, including hypertension, hyperlipidemia, hyperglycemia, and smoking [4]. Sustained noxious stimuli interact over time to damage the vascular integrity and shift the balance of the endothelial milieu towards one that promotes injury and progressive failure of repair mechanisms [5]. Chemotaxis of mononuclear cells ensues, leading to their adhesion, migration, and differentiation within the vessel wall. Deposition of lipids within the macrophages is favored by the availability of easily oxidizable lipoproteins. Meanwhile, migration and proliferation of smooth muscle cells into the intima forms a fibrous cap over this “fatty streak” and leads to the appearance of an atherosclerotic lesion [6]. At some point during its subsequent progression, the altered pathology predisposes to the formation of a thrombus, usually initiated by plaque rupture. Indeed, vulnerable plaques have been identified that seem to have distinctive morphological composition and are prone to rupture [7]. The end-result is a vascular event that can have catastrophic consequences.

It is generally agreed that a heightened, proinflammatory picture precedes and perpetuates the atherosclerotic process [8]. There may be an increased genetic susceptibility to oxidative stress that lays the groundwork for ongoing damage [9]. Insulin resistance has been implicated in not only accelerating the inflammation [10], but also being the ultimate catalyst for glucose intolerance, dyslipidemia, and hypertensive damage. The picture, however, is complicated and controversial. The “insulin resistance hypothesis” contends that an inability to satisfactorily maintain insulin-mediated glucose uptake into tissues has a broad array of deleterious ramifications, some of which can be directly linked to the resultant hyperinsulinemia [11]. However, both the NCEP ATP III and the IDF criteria for the diagnosis of the metabolic syndrome are based on clinical and laboratory measurements and are devoid of the need for direct computation of insulin resistance [12,13]. What is established is the unequivocal importance of these criteria as risk factors for cardiovascular disease and type 2 diabetes. Therefore, the central role of insulin resistance in a definition of the metabolic syndrome meant for use in clinical practice is unclear. In addition, weight gain and obesity will increase both inflammation and insulin resistance [14]. In fact, in some studies, the bulk of association between the two can be explained on the basis of increased body weight alone [15]. However, not all obese individuals are insulin-resistant or display a proinflammatory picture. In short, although the metabolic syndrome had its origins as the "insulin resistance syndrome" and is still preferred to be called by that name by some people, the part that insulin resistance itself plays in its causation and sequelae is yet to be fully defined. On the other hand, a wealth of evidence is accumulating regarding the connection between markers of inflammation and the clinically-defined 'metabolic syndrome' [16,17].

Inflammatory Markers as "Non-traditional" Risk Factors in the Metabolic Syndrome and Related Conditions

Inflammation is regarded as a contributor to morbidity in the closely related conditions of cardiovascular disease, obesity, the metabolic syndrome, and type 2 diabetes and has been the focus of extensive research recently [18,19]. Inflammatory markers like C-reactive protein (CRP), fibrinogen, the interleukins, tumor necrosis factor-alpha (TNF-α), tissue-type plasminogen activator, and serum amyloid A (SAA) have been included in the ever-expanding list of emerging or "non-traditional" risk factors for the atherosclerotic process [20] (figure 1). They mirror oxidative stress and generation of free radicals that can promote vascular damage, endothelial injury, plaque rupture, and athero-thrombosis [21]. Studies have established a significant inflammatory component in the background of clinically recognizable risk factors (for example, hypertension, hyperglycemia, dyslipidemia, obesity, and smoking) [22]. Inflammatory proteins like CRP have been shown to predict, and correlate independently with, major cardiovascular end-points like myocardial infarction and death [23,24].

Hypercoagulability states and hemostatic factors like fibrinogen have been postulated to play a pathologic role in the development of vascular complications, ostensibly through abnormal rheology and elevated blood viscosity [25,26]. Prospective studies show that low-grade systemic inflammation is associated with not only the development of diabetes, but also its large-vessel and microvascular complications [27,28,29]. Retinopathy and nephropathy are linked to increased levels of inflammatory markers in both type 1 and type 2 diabetes [30,31]. However, it is not clear if CRP measurement in diabetes and the metabolic syndrome provides added information beyond that obtained through the established risk factors. Increased body mass index (BMI) with or without the presence of the metabolic syndrome or diabetes, accounted for the bulk of the pro-inflammatory picture in some analyses [28]. The effect of race on variation in inflammatory markers has also been noted in Caucasians and African-Americans [32]. Therefore, more research is needed before screening can be advocated [32,33].

Since cardiovascular disease (CVD) and the metabolic syndrome are closely linked, any discussion of cardiac risk factors must necessarily overlap with the criteria designated for the metabolic syndrome. The traditional risk factors for CVD – positive family history, hypertension, diabetes, dyslipidemia, and smoking – explain a preponderant amount of morbidity and mortality, especially when combined with abdominal obesity, sedentary lifestyle, and diet composition. However, these traditional or established factors do not fully account for the CVD burden in certain populations (for example, those with diabetes) [34,35]. Attention has been focused recently on whether the "nontraditional" risk factors are independently associated with vascular risk, and if they provide clinically significant prognostic value beyond the established ones [35,36]. Interestingly, these emerging factors are almost exclusively circulating markers, and tend to cluster together among themselves and with the traditional factors [37]. Examples of these markers that have been studied in some detail include CRP, fibrinogen, the adipocytokines, and the proinflammatory cytokines. Several epidemiologic studies demonstrate that CRP is a reliable predictor of future cardiovascular events in individuals free of disease at baseline [23,24]. However, three important questions remain to be answered in the analysis of these new risk factors vis-à-vis coronary disease: firstly, since these parameters are acute-phase reactants that segregate with the traditional risk factors, do they confer some measure of independent risk or merely reflect what can already be gleaned from known information? Second, are they simply markers or do they represent true mediators of the underlying extent of inflammation? Some argue that they are simply epiphenomena with little direct pathogenetic role in disease causation. However, the inherent proinflammatory actions of some of these markers point to a possible etiologic and pathologic implication in the disease process. Finally, it is not yet clear if clinical management can be altered on the basis of screening for these emerging factors. The answer to this last question is predicated on whether a treatment is developed that directly targets the various inflammatory markers without altering the established risk factors and subsequently evaluating clinical outcomes.

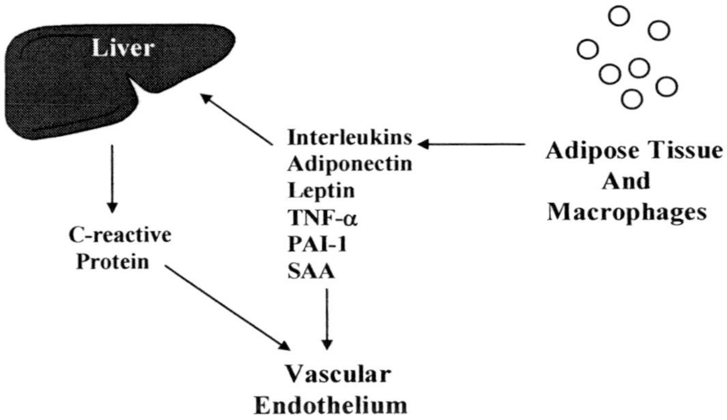

Figure 1. Interactions between adipose tissue, liver, and the vascular endothelium by way of the inflammatory markers and cytokines.

C-reactive Protein

CRP is the best-known marker of inflammation and has been touted as an independent risk factor for cardiovascular disease on the basis of recent studies. It is a member of the pentraxin family, which consists of five noncovalently associated peptides surrounding a central core. It is an acute-phase reactant that is synthesized in the liver and activates the classical pathway of complement through the immune system. Various proinflammatory cytokines such as tumor necrosis factor and interleukin-1 derived from vascular endothelium and adipose tissue stimulate its formation. The release of interleukin-6 from macrophages by increased oxidative stress and infection may be the original insult that initiates this process. CRP has been shown to tilt the balance of endovascular health towards a proatherogenic state by reducing the synthesis and biological activity of nitric oxide, upregulating endothelin-1, and activating cell adhesion molecules.

Numerous studies have revealed that persons that have the most or all features of the metabolic syndrome have increased levels of CRP [38,39,40]. It has been linked to insulin resistance, dyslipidemic states, blood pressure, and increased amounts of other proinflammatory cytokines [41]. The Insulin Resistance and Atherosclerosis Study showed that CRP values correlated with body mass index (BMI), waist circumference, and fasting hyperinsulinemia [42]. There is a linear correlation between CRP and the number of metabolic abnormalities present, namely upper-body obesity, dyslipidemia, hyperglycemic states, and hypertension [43]. For all levels of glucose, the presence of metabolic syndrome was associated with an increase in the prevalence of CVD [44]. The metabolic syndrome appears to be associated with inflammation in addition to being an important marker of CVD risk. CVD prevalence is greater in persons with metabolic syndrome without diabetes than in those with diabetes who do not have the metabolic syndrome [45]. CRP levels in nondiabetic persons increase with worsening glycemia and particularly with postload glycemia [46,47]. The Third National Health and Nutrition Examination Survey (NHANES III) data confirmed that subjects with the metabolic syndrome were more likely to have higher levels of CRP and other markers of inflammation [45]. Based on Framingham scores, CRP adds prognostic information to the predictive power of other CVD risk factors like cholesterol, hypertension, and cigarette use [20]. It confers a stronger predisposition to CVD than other known inflammatory markers such as homocysteine, IL-6, and SAA, circulating levels of which parallel CRP, intracellular adhesion molecule-1 (ICAM)-I [48,49], as well as low-density lipoprotein (LDL), the time-honored correlate of cardiovascular risk [50]. Obese persons have improvement in insulin sensitivity and in CRP with weight loss. On the other hand, obese persons with normal insulin sensitivity with low CRP levels do not show further decrease following weight loss. This suggests that improvement in insulin sensitivity rather than weight loss mediates the reduction in CRP [51].

The reasons for the discrepant results regarding the benefit of using CRP in evaluating risk are not known. Possible explanations include different sets of populations studied, and their retrospective versus prospective nature. CRP, as well as other inflammatory markers, is acutely elevated in stress, illnesses, infections, and vascular events like myocardial infarction and unstable angina. CRP appears to be of greatest use in risk assessment of persons who have intermediate CVD risk (10-20%/10 years) [22]. Insulin resistance is associated with increased CRP levels, and in some studies CRP has been found to be an independent CVD risk factor [52-56]and a marker of insulin resistance [57-60]. Three studies examined the relationship between CRP, the metabolic syndrome, and incident cardiovascular events [57,61,62]. In these large population studies, CRP was a strong independent predictor of events, and its predictive value was equal to that of the metabolic syndrome. In two studies [55,61] the age-adjusted relative risk of future events was the same in subjects with high CRP without the metabolic syndrome and in subjects with low CRP with the metabolic syndrome. Interestingly, in subjects with both elevated CRP levels and the presence of the metabolic syndrome, the relative risk of events was double than in the other subgroups. This indicates that CRP measurement might have extra predictive power when added to the clinical definition of the metabolic syndrome. Rutter et al. [62] also found that CRP and the metabolic syndrome were independent risk factors, but in contrast to the two other reports, combining CRP and metabolic syndrome did not improve the predictive value of either used alone. Reilly et al. [63] also found that CRP did not add significantly to the metabolic syndrome, but their study did not include CVD outcomes.

Adiponectin

Our understanding of the functions of the adipose tissue has changed significantly with research suggesting that it not merely an inert storage site for excess energy. Instead, fatty tissue appears to be hormonally active and gives rise to a number of biologically active substances that regulate, and correlate with, insulin sensitivity, vascular function, and atherosclerotic disease. Collectively known as "adipocytokines", these molecules include, but are not limited to, adiponectin, leptin, resistin, IL-6, TNF-α, and plasminogen activator inhibitor-1 (PAI-1). An emerging concept is that obesity leads to infiltration of adipose tissues by macrophages which produce most of the inflammatory cytokines that are commonly measured [19] and contribute to insulin resistance. In addition, both macrophages and adipose tissue cells are thought to produce factors like IL-6 that secondarily increase hepatic CRP synthesis. Overfeeding may lead to a state of chronic macrophage activation, increased cytokines, central obesity, insulin resistance, and overproduction of the hepatic products of cytokine activation.

Adiponectin is produced by fat cells, and has properties that inhibit inflammation and enhance insulin sensitivity. It increases glucose transport and fatty acid oxidation. In animal studies, a deficiency of this cytokine can permit changes in metabolism to take place that favor the development of a metabolic syndrome phenotype [64]. It has been shown to suppress endothelial dysfunction, lipid accumulation, smooth muscle proliferation, and inhibit atherosclerotic changes in vessel walls. Low levels of adiponectin are found in subjects with diabetes and obesity, and correlate with insulin resistance and the future development of glucose intolerance and the metabolic syndrome. It has anti-inflammatory and antiatherogenic properties at the molecular level, such as decreasing the expression of adhesion molecules, reducing monocyte adhesion to endothelial cells, and suppressing various proatherogeic steps, such as uptake of oxidized LDL, foam cell formation, and proliferation and migration of vascular smooth muscle cells [65]. Other effects include increased insulin sensitivity and free fatty-acid oxidation oxidation, and decreased hepatic glucose production, and intracellular triglycerides. Adiponectin levels are lower in obesity and in prediabetes, and persons with higher levels of adiponectin have greater insulin sensitivity regardless of weight [66].

The question of whether a better understanding of the relationship between adiponectin and inflammation will lead to new or improved ways of addressing the metabolic syndrome is still unresolved. The connection between adiponectin and the clinical correlates of the metabolic syndrome is complex. It is interesting that obesity by itself in not necessarily associated with hypoleptinemia. Visceral obesity is predominantly associated with reduced levels of adiponectin. Obese women who have normal amounts of upper-body adipose tissue have normal adiponectin levels [67]. Low adiponectin was predictive of an increased future risk of coronary thrombosis in the Health Professionals Follow-up Study (HPFS), even after controlling for age, body weight, blood pressure, glucose control, physical activity, and tobacco use [68]. There seems to be a close relationship between adiponectin and HDL cholesterol [67,68] and the predictive power of adiponectin can partly be explained on their co-segregation.

In summary, adiponectin is inversely associated with insulin resistance, inflammation, blood pressure, LDL cholesterol, HDL cholesterol, and triglyceride levels. Multiple studies have established a correlation between adiponectin and CVD [69-72] and low levels of this adipocytokine found in subjects with the clinical characteristics of the metabolic syndrome.

Other Adipocytokines and Inflammatory Markers

Other markers of inflammation, described in some detail below, correlate with both insulin resistance and hyperinsulinemia. Since they are also elevated in obesity and in the presence of cardiovascular risk factors [42], they provide further evidence towards the idea that inflammation is an integral part of the components of the metabolic syndrome. CRP, the most extensively studied inflammatory marker, is strongly associated with adipose-derived cytokines including interleukin-6 and TNF-α [73]. These are likely to be elevated in obese insulin-resistant subjects, especially in those with upper-body fat deposition, but not generally in obese subjects who are insulin-sensitive [51]. Since these markers have been linked to dyslipidemia, hypertension, and insulin levels [42,74], they have been implicated in the genesis and progression of CVD [7,17].

Interleukin-6 is a cytokine that is produced in part in the adipose tissue, especially omental fat. It is released in response to stress and stimulation through the sympathetic nervous system. Several studies suggest that it is a central mediator of the inflammatory response, and tends to correlates closely with CRP [75,76]. IL-6 is increased with increasing insulin resistance and in the presence of multiple features of the metabolic syndrome [77]. It increases hepatic triglyceride secretion and may be a factor in central obesity and insulin resistance. It seems to exert its metabolic actions both through its actions in the central nervous system (CNS) and on peripheral organs. Levels of IL-6 are linked to insulin resistance and adiposity [78]. Its exact pathogenetic in glucose and lipid homeostasis in human is still a matter of debate.

Tumor Necrosis Factor-α is produced by largely by adipose tissue, but also by macrophages and endothelial cells. Its levels correlate with amount of adipose tissue, and it has a role in modulating insulin sensitivity [79]. It has been linked to the increase in insulin resistance seen with obesity [80], although a consistent correlation of TNF-α with BMI has not been conclusively demonstrated. Although it has been implicated in states of increased insulin resistance, passive immunization with antibodies to TNF-α does not improve insulin sensitivity.

The discovery of *leptin* generated great interest when it was found to have a role in obesity, energy balance, and appetite regulation. Hypoleptinemia has been linked to weight gain, fat deposition in organs such as the liver, muscle, and pancreatic islets, clinical features of the metabolic syndrome, and a general proinflammatory state [81]. Leptin could have the property of lowering insulin levels. Resistance to leptin may be connected to the hyperinsulinemia that is the earliest compensatory defect in the pathway towards the metabolic syndrome and glucose intolerance. Efforts at harnessing the known properties of this hormone to therapeutic purposes have so far been unsuccessful.

Leptin is secreted by adipocytes and binds to receptors in the CNS, where it suppresses appetite and decreases food intake. In the peripheral tissues, it enhances insulin sensitivity in muscle and fatty tissue, while preventing fat storage in organs such as the liver and pancreas [82]. It functions as a signaling factor that keeps the CNS informed of the status of energy availability in the body, especially as it pertains to the adipose tissue. Weight gain and overfeeding increase leptin expression and secretion, while reduced food intake suppresses them [83]. Leptin deficient mice (*ob/ob* mice) manifest extreme obesity. In humans, typical obesity is associated with increased leptin levels, signifying underlying leptin resistance. Whether leptin-resistant individuals are, therefore, prone to becoming overweight or if obesity aggravates resistance to leptin action is not entirely clear. The metabolic syndrome is also associated with increased levels of leptin [84]. However, most of this elevation can probably be explained on the basis of the extra weight alone. Does insulin resistance and the presence of other features of the metabolic syndrome modulate leptin release, or are more apt to be present if leptin resistance is present, is the subject of future debate and research.

Additional research has unveiled another adipocyte-derived cytokine, *resistin,* that is elevated in obesity and impaired glucose tolerance. Its role in the genesis and pathophysiology of the metabolic syndrome, however, remains to be fully elucidated.

Finally, insulin resistance is associated with a number of other inflammatory markers that have generated interest, such as secretory phospholipase A2, e-selectin, ICAM-1, and SAA [17]. Most of these are acute-phase reactants, whose production in the liver is induced by the interleukins and TNF-α. SAA appears to be a "scavenger" apolipoprotein that is closely linked with high-density lipoprotein (HDL). t is involved in lipid transport in the circulation, accelerating cholesterol uptake from damaged tissues, and may also play a role in immune regulation. Increased levels SAA that are seen after myocardial infarction are associated with an elevated risk of a recurrent coronary event [84]. In short, it may have an integrative role in such seemingly diverse areas as inflammation, atherosclerosis, and immunity. Further research is essential to unraveling its exact place in the inflammatory cascade and the obesity-metabolic syndrome spectrum. It is safe to say that, based on results of research done thus far, the inflammatory cytokines are critical in affecting the balance of endothelial health; obesity, insulin resistance, stress, presence of the metabolic syndrome components, and other acute or chronic insults tend to tilt the balance towards a more proinflammatory picture and lead an environment conducive to atherogenesis and thrombosis. Components of the metabolic syndrome as well as the syndrome itself are associated with various measures of inflammation. This inflammatory picture is low-grade but chronic, and is associated with an increased risk for cardiovascular disease and diabetes. It provides a putative pathogenetic mechanism for the increased risk of adverse vascular outcomes that are experienced by individuals with the metabolic syndrome.

Hypercoagulablity and Hemostasis in the Metabolic Syndrome

The metabolic syndrome has been found to be associated with increased levels of fibrinogen [85,86] enhanced platelet adhesion [87] and impaired fibrinolysis [88,89] and elevated PAI-1 [90]. The latter is probably the most consistent abnormality seen in persons with the metabolic syndrome. In addition, endothelial dysfunction is linked to increased levels of clotting factors like factor VIII and von Willibrand's factor [91]. These changes are closely associated with insulin resistance and cardiovascular risk factors. The overall effect is an increased tendency to clotting and thrombus formation, as well as a reduced capacity to mitigate the pro-thrombotic tendency from impaired fibrinolysis. An elevated risk of atherothrombosis and cardiovascular obstructive events ensues.

PAI-1 levels are strongly associated with dyslipidemia, hyperinsulinemia, and hypertension [92,93]. It is noteworthy that the effect of increased PAI-1 was mitigated to a nonsignificant level after adjusting for BMI and elevated triglycerides in one study [94] In the Cardiovascular Health Study [93] levels of procoagulant factors and vitamin K-dependent proteins were studied in association with the different components of the metabolic syndrome. PAI-1 stood out as having the most consistent correlation with body weight, hyperglycemia, and hyperinsulinemia. TNF-α and IL-6 have been shown to induce synthesis of fibrinogen in the liver. Additional evidence of the connection between insulin resistance and defective fibrinolysis is provided by the possible involvement of the renin-angiotensin system and abnormalities of platelet function. The former is activated in obese, insulin-resistant subjects, who have higher levels of angiotensinogen and increased PAI-1 formation and release. Increased platelet activation and aggregation is found in subjects with the metabolic syndrome and type 2 diabetes as well [87].

In summary, the metabolic syndrome is a hypercoagulable state that is a feature of the underlying insulin resistance. It predisposes to clot formation in the milieu of endothelial dysfunction, endovascular atheromatous change, and abnormal blood rheology. Studies to date have shown evidence for a pathophysiologic role of the inflammatory markers in promoting a prothrombotic tendency and impairing the ability of fibrinolytic repair and resumption of blood flow. However, many of the interconnections between the coagulation system, inflammation, and the individual risk factors of the metabolic syndrome have yet to be clearly delineated.

Metabolic Syndrome and Inflammation in the Pediatric Population

Although a wealth of information about the metabolic syndrome has accumulated in adults, research about the prevalence and manifestations of the syndrome among children and adolescents is limited. Preliminary studies reveal that, like their adult counterparts, children and adolescents with the metabolic syndrome are more likely than those without this syndrome to show evidence of low-grade inflammation and increased levels of proinflammatory cytokines.

The association between obesity and elevated concentrations of CRP in children and adolescents has been clearly established [95,96]. The percentage of children and adolescents with an elevated concentration of CRP (>3.0 mg/l) is manifold higher among those with the metabolic syndrome compared with those who did not have the syndrome. In these studies, visceral obesity was the component that was responsible for much of the difference in concentrations of CRP. Concentrations of CRP have also been significantly associated with the other four components of the metabolic syndrome [97,98]. However, after adjustment for an anthropometric measure, many of these associations were seriously weakened and often failed to achieve statistical significance. Although no studies have thus far shown that children and adolescents with evidence of low-grade inflammation are more likely to develop cardiovascular disease or diabetes than those without such evidence, obesity in childhood does increase the risk for diabetes in childhood and a variety of diseases in adulthood [99]. Results of a recent study suggest that the presence of the metabolic syndrome and abdominal obesity among children and adolescents may be lay the foundation for the emergence of cardiovascular disease and diabetes later in life through early low-grade inflammation [100]. To reduce the potential adverse effects of the inflammation that accompanies the metabolic syndrome, a concerted public health and behavioral approach is needed to reduce the burden of obesity and physical inactivity in children. This strategy will not only prevent the development of the syndrome and its attendant proinflammatory manifestations, but also ameliorate these features in those who already have the metabolic syndrome or its components

Effect of Various Interventions on Inflammatory Markers in the Metabolic Syndrome

The trio of the metabolic syndrome, cardiovascular disease, and increased inflammation has assumed enhanced priority because of their direct implication in fueling the epidemics of type 2 diabetes and vascular disease [17,101]. In the absence of any approved drug therapy, modulation of the inflammatory state by lifestyle factors in the metabolic syndrome assumes paramount importance [102]. This is even more significant in view of the fact that dietary factors and lack of physical activity in the modern-day world forms the basis for the enormous increase in the prevalence of the metabolic syndrome. It makes sense, therefore, to attack the very dynamics that contribute to the genesis of the syndrome. Attainment of an ideal body weight and normalization of BMI, preferably by a combination of physical activity and a calorie-restricted diet, form the cornerstone of therapeutic measures for the metabolic syndrome. Weight loss has been shown to reduce the inflammatory markers associated with insulin resistance. The composition of the diet is important as well – a Mediterranean-style diet rich in fruits, nuts, whole grains, and olive oil has been shown to have a beneficial effect on the metabolic syndrome and its clinical and inflammatory components [103]. Polyunsaturated, omega-3, and linoleic acid supplementation has also been shown to help [104]. Weight loss reduces the prevalence of steatohepatitis, an emerging facet of the metabolic syndrome that is closely associated with increased inflammatory markers [105]. Exercise has been shown to reduce the proinfammatory and prothrombotic picture in individuals who have the clinical criteria of the metabolic syndrome [106]. Sustained physical activity also has a salutary effect on chemokines and other mediators in insulin resistance [107]. The involvement of dieticians and other health care professionals is of vital importance in educating individuals of the need for dietary modifications in preventing the adverse sequelae of obesity and the metabolic syndrome [108]. Cigarette smoking has been shown to elevate proinflammatory markers as well as insulin resistance itself in a Japanese study [109].

There are no drugs that have been approved solely for the treatment of the metabolic syndrome or for targeting the heightened inflammatory state involved therein. At the time of writing, no guidelines recommend routine testing, targeting, or monitoring of CRP levels, the most extensively studies marker in states on insulin resistance. However, medication already in use for the treatment of metabolic conditions like diabetes, hypertension, and dyslipidemia have been shown to reduce inflammation in susceptible individuals through various mechanisms. A detailed description of the actions of these drugs on markers of inflammation is beyond the scope of this review. Perhaps the best known are the thiazolidinediaones, agents that directly ameliorate insulin resistance by acting on the peroxisome-proliferator activator receptor-gamma (PPAR-γ) nuclear receptors. Numerous studies have proven their efficacy in reducing markers of inflammation [110,111,112] and improving endothelial function and lipid profile and blood pressure. The two agents currently available on the market, rosiglitazone and pioglitazone, have both been studied in this respect. An unwanted side-effect, however, is the tendency to weight gain, fluid accumulation, and possible precipitation of overt congestive heart failure. Although this class of medications is widely used for the treatment of type 2 diabetes, it is not yet approved for use in prediabetes or the metabolic syndrome.

Several other medications have approved indications and target risk factors for cardiovascular disease as well as individual components of the metabolic syndrome. The HMG Co-A reductase inhibitors ("statins") are proven for their lipid-lowering properties and for reducing cardiac and all-cause mortality. Several large clinical trials showed that they decreased inflammatory markers, notably CRP levels, in high-risk individuals with dyslipidemia, diabetes, and the metabolic syndrome [55,113,114]. This action is part of their non-lipid-lowering, or pleotropic, efficacy on the vascular endothelium [115,116]. Fibric-acid derivatives have also been advocated as useful agents in counter-acting the elevated inflammatory milieu of the metabolic syndrome [117].

Two other therapeutic modalities appear to be beneficial in the metabolic syndrome by reducing the proinflammatory and thrombotic cascade: targeting the renin-angiotensin system through the use of angiotensin-converting enzyme inhibitors [118] and angiotensin-receptor blocking agents [119] and use of aspirin to decrease the primary as well as secondary incidence of coronary thrombosis in patients with existing cardiovascular disease or those with multiple risk factors [120]. Most individuals with the metabolic syndrome will satisfy the clinical requirement for use of these agents and it is plausible that a significant portion of their salutary mechanisms are mediated by means of their anti-inflammatory actions. Specifically targeting the inflammatory pathways and mediators in insulin resistance and the metabolic syndrome is still uncharted territory, though a promising next step, of future drug therapy [121,122].

The Inflammatory Markers as Screening Tools and Therapeutic Targets

There is currently no consensus in using the markers of inflammation as screening tools or as risk factors to be targeted. This area appears to be embroiled in controversy and confusion, although some recommendations have been put forth [8,9]. The argument for testing of individuals at moderate risk for cardiovascular disease is based on further stratifying their risk status and assist in clinical management. On the other hand, some contend that the role of these acute-phase reactants in disease causation is not established, and therefore screening would not be helpful in leading to a change in management strategy for the majority of patients tested. Additionally, the lack of specific and proven therapeutic interventions targeting these markers (beyond what is already being recommended) is also a factor against using them in routine clinical setting. Whether to include CRP or some other inflammatory marker in the clinical criteria used in the diagnosis of the metabolic syndrome is dependent upon elucidation of their exact role in the pathogenesis of the syndrome and their connection to underlying insulin resistance. In other words, the question of whether these markers are merely the mirror of a chronic vasculotoxic pattern or are causally involved in endothelial dysfunction and atherosclerosis is central from the viewpoint of using them for screening, assessment, and treatment in the metabolic syndrome and related conditions. Further research is needed to clarify the etiology of the metabolic syndrome at the molecular and inflammatory level and possibly to a definition that includes one or more of the inflammatory markers. Hopefully, a new model of the metabolic syndrome can be validated so that its predictive value is inclusive of clinical as well as laboratory criteria. Additional studies concerning the markers of inflammation, ideally performed in a prospective, randomized, and interventional manner, should help in translating the knowledge gained in the laboratory to the bedside.

References

[1] Cameron AJ, Shaw JE, Zimmet PZ. The metabolic syndrome: prevalence in worldwide populations. *Endocrinol. Metab. Clin. North. Am.* 2004;33:351-375.

[2] Reaven GM. Insulin resistance, cardiovascular disease, and the metabolic syndrome: how well do the emperor's clothes fit? *Diabetes Care* 2004;27:1011-1012.

[3] Ross R: Atherosclerosis: an inflammatory disease. *N. Engl. J. Med.* 1999;340:115–126.

[4] Wannamethee SG, Lowe GD, Shaper AG, Rumley A, Lennon L, Whiner PH, Insulin resistance, haemostatic and inflammatory markers and coronary heart disease risk factors in type 2 diabetic men with and without coronary heart disease. *Diabetologia.* 2004;47(9):1557-1565.

[5] Sjoholm A, Nystrom T. Endothelial inflammation in insulin resistance. *Lancet* 2005;365(9459):610-612.

[6] Ceriello A, Motz E. Is oxidative stress the pathogenic mechanism underlying insulin resistance, diabetes, and cardiovascular disease? The common soil hypothesis revisited. *Arterioscler. Thromb. Vasc. Biol.* 2004;24:816-823.

[7] Hansson JK. Inflammation, atherosclerosis, and coronary artery disease. *N. Engl. J. Med.* 2005;352:1685-1695.

[8] Black PH. The inflammatory response is an integral part of the stress response: Implications for atherosclerosis, insulin resistance, type II diabetes and metabolic syndrome X. *Brain. Behav. Immun.* 2003 Oct;17(5):350-64. Review.

[9] Shinozaki K, Kashiwagi A, Masada M, Okamura T. Molecular mechanisms of impaired endothelial function associated with insulin resistance. *Curr. Drug. Targets Cardiovasc. Haematol. Disord.* 2004;4:1-11.

[10] Fernandez-Real JM, Ricart W. Insulin resistance and chronic cardiovascular inflammatory syndrome. *Endocr. Rev.* 2003;24(3):278-301.

[11] Reaven GM, Laws A. Insulin resistance, compensatory hyperinsulinaemia, and coronary heart disease. *Diabetologia.* 1994;37(9):948-52.

[12] Expert Panel on Detection, Evaluation, and Treatment of High Blood Cholesterol in Adults: Executive Summary of the Third Report of the National Cholesterol Education Program (NCEP) Expert Panel on Detection, Evaluation, and Treatment of High Blood Cholesterol in Adults (Adult Treatment Panel III). *JAMA*, 2001;285:2486-2497.

[13] International Diabetes Federation: The IDF consensus worldwide definition of the metabolic syndrome. IDF Executive Office, Brussels, Belgium. *www.idf.org.*

[14] Clinical guidelines on the Identification, Evaluation, and Treatment of Overweight and Obesity in Adults – The Evidence Report, National Institutes of Health. *Obes. Res.* 1998;6(suppl 2):51S-209S.

[15] Sung RY, Tong PC, YU CW, et al. High prevalence of insulin reistance and metabolic syndrome in overweight/obese preadolescent Homg Kong Chinese children aged 9-12 years. *Diabetes Care* 2003;26:250-151.

[16] Chan JC, Cheung JC, Stehouwer CD, Emeis JJ, Tong PC, Ko GT, Yudkin JS. The central roles of obesity-associated dyslipidaemia, endothelial activation and cytokines in the Metabolic Syndrome--an analysis by structural equation modelling. *Int. J. Obes. Relat. Metab. Disord.* 2002;26(7):994-1008.

[17] Tracy RP. Inflammation, the metabolic syndrome and cardiovascular risk. *Int. J. Clin. Pract. Suppl.* 2003;134:10-17.

[18] Danesh J, Wheeler JG, Hirschfield GM, et al. C-reactive protein and other markers of inflammation in the prediction of coronary artery disease. *N. Engl. J. Med.* 2004;350:1387-1397.

[19] Wannamethee SG, Lowe GD, Shaper AG, Rumley A, Lennon L, Whiner PH, Insulin resistance, haemostatic and inflammatory markers and coronary heart disease risk factors in type 2 diabetic men with and without coronary heart disease. *Diabetalogia* 2004;47(9):1557-1565.

[20] Muntner P, He J, Chen J, Fonseca V, Whelton PK. Prevalence of non-traditional cardiovascular risk factors among persons with impaired fasting glucose, impaired glucose tolerance, diabetes, and the metabolic syndrome: analysis of the Third National Health and Nutrition Examination Survey (NHANES III). *Ann. Epidemiol.* 2004;14(9):686-695.

[21] Hsueh WA, Quinones MJ. Role of endothelial dysfunction in insulin resistance. *Am. J. Cardiol.* 2003:92:10J-17J.

[22] Pearson TA, Mensah GA, Alexander RW, et al. Markers of inflammation and cardiovascular disease: application to clinical and public health practice: a statement for healthcare professionals from the Centers for Disease Control and Prevention and the American Heart Association. *Circulation* 2003;107:499-511.

[23] Ridker PM, Cushman M, Stampfer MJ, Tracy RP, Hennekens CH. Inflammation, aspirin, and the risk of cardiovascular disease in apparently healthy men. *N. Engl. J. Med.* 1997;336:973-979. (*Erratum, N. Engl. J. Med.* 1997;337:356).

[24] Ridker PM, Rifai N, Rose L, Buring JE, Cook NR. Comparison of C-reactive protein and low-density lipoprotein cholesterol levels in the prediction of first cardiovascular events. *N. Engl. J. Med.* 2002;347-1557-1565.

[25] Bruno G, Cavallo-Perin P, Bargero G, et al. Hyperfibrinogenemia and metabolic syndrome in type 2 diabetes: a population-based study. *Diabetes. Metab. Res. Rev.* 2001;17(2): 124-130.

[26] Carr ME. Diabetes mellitus: a hypercoagulable state. *J. Diabetes. Complications.* 2001;15(1):44-54.

[27] Stehouwer CDA, Gall M, Twisk JWR, Knudsen E, Emeis JJ, Parving H. Increased urinary albumin excretion, endothelial dysfunction, and chronic low-grade inflammation in type 2 diabetes. Progressive, interrelated, and independently associated with risk of death. *Diabetes* 2002;51:1157-1165.

[28] Duncan BB, Schmidt MI, Pankow JI, et al. Low-grade systemic inflammation and the development of type 2 diabetes. The Atherosclerosis Risk in Communities study. *Diabetes* 2003;52:1799-1805.

[29] Freeman DJ, Norrie J, Caslake MJ, et al. C-reactive protein is an independent predictor of risk for the development of diabetes in the West of Scotland Coronary Prevention Study. *Diabetes* 2002;51:1596-1600.

[30] Asakawa H, Tokunaga K, Kawakami F. Elevation of fibrinogen and thrombin-antithrombin III complex levels of type 2 diabetes patients with retinopathy and nephropathy. *J. Diabetes. Complications.* 2000;14(3):121-126.

[31] Saraheimo M, Teppo AM, Forsblom C, Fagerudd J, Groop PH. Diabetic nephropathy is associated with low-grade inflammation in type 1 diabetic patients. *Diabetalogia* 2003;46(10):1402-1407.

[32] Tall AR. C-reactive protein reassessed. *N Engl J Med* 2004;350:1450-1452.

[33] Mosca L. C-reactive protein – to screen or not to screen? *N. Engl. J. Med.* 2002;347:1615-1617.

[34] Hackam DG, Anand SS. Emerging risk factors for atherosclerotic vascular disease: a critical review of the evidence. *JAMA* 2003;290(7):932-940.

[35] Streja D, Cressey P, Rabkin SW. Associations between inflammatory markers, traditional risk factors, and complications in patients with type 2 diabetes mellitus. *J. Diabetes Complications* 2003;17(3):120-127.

[36] Bhatt DL, Topol EJ. Need to test the inflammation hypothesis. *Circulation* 2002;106:136-140.

[37] Ceriello A, Motz E. Is oxidative stress the pathogenic mechanism underlying insulin resistance, diabetes, and cardiovascular disease? The common soil hypothesis revisited. *Arterioscler. Thromb. Vasc. Biol.* 2004;24:816-823.

[38] Ridker PM, Buring JE, Cook NR, Rifai N. C-reactive protein, the metabolic syndrome, and risk of incident cardiovascular events: an 8-year follow-up of 14,719 initially healthy American women. *Circulation* 2003;107:391–397.

[39] Pradhan AD, Cook NR, Buring JE, Manson JE, Ridker PM. C-reactive protein is independently associated with fasting insulin in nondiabetic women. *Arterioscler. Thromb. Vasc. Biol.* 2003;23:650–655.

[40] Rutter MK, Meigs JB, Sullivan LM, D'Agostino RB Sr, Wilson PW. C-reactive protein, the metabolic syndrome, and prediction of cardiovascular events in the Framingham Offspring Study. *Circulation* 2004;110:380–385.

[41] Yudkin JS, Stehouwer CD, Emeis JJ, Coppack SW. C-reactive protein in healthy subjects: associations with obesity, insulin resistance, and endothelial dysfunction: a potential role for cytokines originating from adipose tissue? *Arterioscler. Thromb. Vasc. Biol.* 1999;19:972–978.

[42] Festa A, D'Agostino R Jr, Howard G, Mykkanen L, Tracy RP, Haffner SM. Chronic subclinical inflammation as part of the insulin resistance syndrome: the Insulin Resistance Atherosclerosis Study (IRAS). *Circulation* 102:42–47, 2000

[43] Ridker PM, Wilson PW, Grundy SM. Should C-reactive protein be added to metabolic syndrome and to assessment of global cardiovascular risk? *Circulation* 2004;109:2818–2825.

[44] Isomaa B, Almgren P, Tuomi T, Forsen B, Lahti K, Nissen M, Taskinen MR, Groop L. Cardiovascular morbidity and mortality associated with the metabolic syndrome. *Diabetes Care* 2001;24:683-689.

[45] Alexander CM, Landsman PB, Teutsch SM, Haffner SM, Third National Health and Nutrition Examination Survey (NHANES III), National Cholesterol Education Program (NCEP): NCEP-defined metabolic syndrome, diabetes, and prevalence of coronary heart disease among NHANES III participants age 50 years and older. *Diabetes* 2003;52:1210-1214.

[46] Freeman DJ, Norrie J, Caslake MJ, et al. C-reactive protein is an independent predictor of risk for the development of diabetes in the West of Scotland Coronary Prevention Study. *Diabetes* 2002;51:1596-1600.

[47] Pradhan A, Manson J, Rifai N, Buring J, Ridker P. C-reactive protein, interleukin 6, and risk of developing type 2 diabetes mellitus. *JAMA* 2001;286:3327-334.

[48] Hackam DG, Anand SS. Emerging risk factors for atherosclerotic vascular disease: a critical review of the evidence. *JAMA* 2003;290(7):932-940.

[49] Danesh J, Wheeler JG, Hirschfield GM, Eda S, Eiriksdottir G, Rumley A, Lowe GD, Pepys MB, Gudnason V: C-reactive protein and other circulating markers of inflammation in the prediction of coronary heart disease. *N. Engl. J. Med.* 2004;350: 1387-1397.

[50] Ridker PM, Rifai N, Rose L, Buring JE, Cook NR: Comparison of C-reactive protein and low-density lipoprotein cholesterol levels in the prediction of first cardiovascular events. *N. Engl. J. Med.* 2002;347: 1557-1565.

[51] McLaughlin T, Abbasi F, Lamendola C, Liang L, Reaven G, Schaaf P, Reaven P: Differentiation between obesity and insulin resistance in the association with C-reactive protein. *Circulation* 2002;106:2908-2912.

[52] Danesh J, Collins R, Appleby P, Peto R. Association of fibrinogen, C-reactive protein, albumin, or leukocyte count with coronary heart disease: meta-analyses of prospective studies. *JAMA* 1998;279:1477–1482.

[53] Ridker PM, Hennekens CH, Buring JE, Rifai N. C-reactive protein and other markers of inflammation in the prediction of cardiovascular disease in women. *N. Engl. J. Med.* 2000;342:836–843.

[54] Ridker PM. Clinical applications of C-reactive protein for cardiovascular disease detection and prevention. *Circulation* 2003;107:363–369.

[55] Ridker PM, Cannon CP, Morrow D, Rifai N, Rose LM, McCabe CH, Pfeffer MA, Braunwald E. C-reactive protein levels and outcomes after statin therapy: Pravastatin or Atorvastatin Evaluation and Infection Therapy-Thrombolysis in Myocardial Infarction 22 (PROVE IT-TIMI 22). *N. Engl. J. Med.* 2005;352:20–28.

[56] Ridker PM, Buring JE, Cook NR, Rifai N. C-reactive protein, the metabolic syndrome, and risk of incident cardiovascular events: an 8-year follow-up of 14,719 initially healthy American women. *Circulation* 2003;107:391–397.

[57] Pradhan AD, Cook NR, Buring JE, Manson JE, Ridker PM. C-reactive protein is independently associated with fasting insulin in nondiabetic women. *Arterioscler. Thromb. Vasc. Biol.* 2003;23:650–655.

[58] Yudkin JS, Stehouwer CD, Emeis JJ, Coppack SW. C-reactive protein in healthy subjects: associations with obesity, insulin resistance, and endothelial dysfunction: a potential role for cytokines originating from adipose tissue? *Arterioscler. Thromb. Vasc Biol.* 1999;19:972–978.

[59] McLaughlin T, Abbasi F, Lamendola C, Liang L, Reaven G, Schaaf P, Reaven P. Differentiation between obesity and insulin resistance in the association with C-reactive protein. *Circulation* 2002;106:2908–2912.

[60] Festa A, D'Agostino R Jr, Howard G, Mykkanen L, Tracy RP, Haffner SM. Chronic subclinical inflammation as part of the insulin resistance syndrome: the Insulin Resistance Atherosclerosis Study (IRAS). *Circulation* 2000;102:42–47.

[61] Sattar N, Gaw A, Scherbakova O, Ford I, O'Reilly DS, Haffner SM, Isles C, Macfarlane PW, Packard CJ, Cobbe SM, Shepherd J. Metabolic syndrome with and without C-reactive protein as a predictor of coronary heart disease and diabetes in the West of Scotland Coronary Prevention Study. *Circulation* 2003;108:414–419.

[62] Rutter MK, Meigs JB, Sullivan LM, D'Agostino RB Sr, Wilson PW. C-reactive protein, the metabolic syndrome, and prediction of cardiovascular events in the Framingham Offspring Study. *Circulation* 2004;110:380–385.

[63] Reilly MP, Wolfe ML, Rhodes T, Girman C, Mehta N, Rader DJ. Measures of insulin resistance add incremental value to the clinical diagnosis of metabolic syndrome in association with coronary atherosclerosis. *Circulation* 2004;110:803–809.

[64] Trujillo ME, Scherer PE. Adiponectin – journey from an adipocyte secretory protein to biomarker of the metabolic syndrome. *J. Intern. Med* .2005;257(2):167-175.

[65] Chandran M, Phillips SA, Ciaraldi T, Henry RR. Adiponectin: more than just another fat cell hormone? *Diabetes Care* 2003;26:2442–2450.

[66] Weyer C, Funahashi T, Tanaka S, Hotta K, Matsuzawa Y, Pratley RE, Tataranni PA. Hypoadiponectinemia in obesity and type 2 diabetes: close association with insulin resistance and hyperinsulinemia. *J. Clin. Endocrinol. Metab* .2001;86:1930–1935.

[67] Matsubara M, Maruoka S, Katayose S. Decreased plasma adiponectin concentrations in women with dyslipidemia. *J. Clin. Endocrinol. Metab.* 2002;87:2764–2769.

[68] Kazumi T, Kawaguchi A, Sakai K, Hirano T, Yoshino G. Young men with high-normal blood pressure have lower serum adiponectin, smaller LDL size, and higher elevated heart rate than those with optimal blood pressure. *Diabetes Care* 2002;25:971–976.

[69] Kumada M, Kihara S, Sumitsuji S, Kawamoto T, Matsumoto S, Ouchi N, Arita Y, Okamoto Y, Shimomura I, Hiraoka H, Nakamura T, Funahashi T, Matsuzawa Y, Osaka CAD Study Group. Association of hypoadiponectinemia with coronary artery disease in men. *Arterioscler. Thromb. Vasc. Biol.* 2003;23:85–89.

[70] Kojima S, Funahashi T, Sakamoto T, Miyamoto S, Soejima H, Hokamaki J, Kajiwara I, Sugiyama S, Yoshimura M, Fujimoto K, Miyao Y, Suefuji H, Kitagawa A, Ouchi N, Kihara S, Matsuzawa Y, Ogawa H. The variation of plasma concentrations of a novel, adipocyte derived protein, adiponectin, in patients with acute myocardial infarction. *Heart* 2003;89:667–672.

[71] Zoccali C, Mallamaci F, Tripepi G, Benedetto FA, Cutrupi S, Parlongo S, Malatino LS, Bonanno G, Seminara G, Rapisarda F, Fatuzzo P, Buemi M, Nicocia G, Tanaka S, Ouchi N, Kihara S, Funahashi T, Matsuzawa Y. Adiponectin, metabolic risk factors, and cardiovascular events among patients with end-stage renal disease. *J. Am. Soc. Nephrol.* 2002;13:134–141.

[72] Pischon T, Girman CJ, Hotamisligil GS, Rifai N, Hu FB, Rimm EB. Plasma adiponectin levels and risk of myocardial infarction in men. *JAMA* 2004;291:1730–1737.

[73] Kershaw EE, Flier JS: Adipose tissue as an endocrine organ. *J. Clin. Endocrinol. Metab.* 2004;89:2548–2556.

[74] Yudkin JS, Stehouwer CD, Emeis JJ, Coppack SW. C-reactive protein in healthy subjects: associations with obesity, insulin resistance, and endothelial dysfunction: a potential role for cytokines originating from adipose tissue? *Arterioscler. Thromb. Vasc Biol* 1999;19:972–978.

[75] McCarty MF. Interleukin-6 as a central mediator of cardiovascular risk associated with chronic inflammation, smoking, diabetes, and visceral obesity: down-regulation with essential fatty acids, ethanol, and pentoxifylline. *Med. Hypotheses.* 1999;52(5):465-477.

[76] Fasshauer M, Paschke R. Regulation of adipocytokines and insulin resistance. *Diabetologia* 2003;46(12):1594-1603.

[77] Vozarova B, Weyer C, Hanson K, et al. Circulating interleukin-6in relation to adiposity, insulin action, and insulin secretion. *Obes. Res.* 2001:9:414-417.

[78] Bastard JP, Jardel C, Bruckert E, Blondy P, Capeau J, Laville M, Vidal H, Hainque B. Elevated levels of interleukin 6 are reduced in serum and subcutaneous adipose tissue of obese women after weight loss. *J. Clin. Endocrinol. Metab.* 2000;85:3338-3342.

[79] Hotamisligil GS. Adipose expression of tumor necrosis factor: direct role in obesity-linked insulin resistance. *Science* 1993:259:87-91.

[80] Kern PA, Saghizadeh M, Ong JM, Bosch RJ, Deem R, Simsolo RB. The expression of tumor necrosis factor in human adipose tissue: regulation by obesity, weight loss, and relationship to lipoprotein lipase. *J. Clin. Invest.* 1995:95:2111-2119.

[81] Otero M, Lego R, Lago F, el al. Leptin, from fat to inflammation: old questions and new insights. *FEBS Lett* 2005;579(2):295-301.

[82] Unger RH. Longevity, lipotoxicity, and leptin: the adipocyte defense against feasting and famine. *Biochimie* 2005;87(1):57-64.

[83] Franks PW, Brage S, Luan J, Ekelund U, Rahman M, Farooqi IS, et al. Leptin predicts a worsening of the features of the metabolic syndrome independently of obesity. *Obes. Res.* 2005;13(8):1476-1484.

[84] Ridker PM, Rifai N, Pfeifer MA, Sacks FM, Moye LA, Goldman S, et al. Inflammation, pravastatin, and the risk of coronary events after myocardial infarction in patients with average cholesterol levels. *Circulation* 1998;98(9)839-844.

[85] Ernst E, Resch KL: Fibrinogen as a cardiovascular risk factor: a meta-analysis and review of the literature. *Ann. Intern. Med.* 18:956–963, 1993

[86] Imperatore G, Riccardi G, Iovine C, Rivellese AA, Vaccaro O: Plasma fibrinogen: a new factor of the metabolic syndrome: a population-based study. *Diabetes Care* 21:649–654, 1998

[87] Schram MT, Stehouver CD. Endothelial dysfunction, cellular adhesion molecules and the metabolic syndrome. *Horm. Metab. Res.* 2005;37(suppl 1):49-55.

[88] Potter van Loon BJ, Kluft C, Radder JK, Blankenstein MA, Meinders AE: The cardiovascular risk factor plasminogen activator inhibitor type 1 is related to insulin resistance. *Metabolism* 42:945–949, 1993

[89] Festa A, D'Agostino R Jr, Mykkanen L, Tracy RP, Zaccaro DJ, Hales CN, Haffner SM: Relative contribution of insulin and its precursors to fibrinogen and PAI-1 in a large population with different states of glucose tolerance: the Insulin Resistance Atherosclerosis Study (IRAS). *Arterioscler. Thromb. Vasc. Biol.* 19:562–568, 1999

[90] Dandona P, Aljada A, Chaudhuri A, Mohanty P, Garg R. Metabolic syndrome: a comprehensive perspective based on interactions between obesity, diabetes, and inflammation. *Circulation* 2005;111(11):1448-1454.

[91] Conlan MG, Folsom AR, Finch A, Davis CE, Sorlie P, Marcucci G, et al. Associations of factor VIII and von Willibrand factor with age, race, sex, and risk factors for atherosclerosis: the atherosclerosis risk in communities (ARIC) study. *Thromb. Haemost.* 1993;70:380-385.

[92] Janand-Delenne B, Chagnaud C, Raccah D, Alessi MC, Juhan-Vague I, Vague P. Visceral fat as a main determinant of plasminogen activator inhibitor 1 level in women. *Int. J. Obes. Relat. Metab. Disord.* 1998;22:312-317.

[93] Sakkinen PA, Wahl P, Cushman M, Lweis MR, Tracy RP. Clustering of procoagulation, inflammation, and fibrinolysis variables with metabolic factors in insulin resistance syndrome. *Am. J. Epidemiol.* 2000;152:897-907.

[94] Juhan-Vague I, Pyke SD, Alessi MC, Jespersen J, Haverkate F, Thompson SG. Fibrinolytic factors and the risk of myocardial infarctionor sudden death in patients with angina pectoris: ECAT study group. European concerted action on thrombosis and disabilities. *Circulation* 1996;94:2057-2063.

[95] Cook DG, Mendall MA, Whincup PH, Carey IM, Ballam L, Morris JE, Miller GJ, Strachan DP: C-reactive protein concentration in children: relationship to adiposity and other cardiovascular risk factors. *Atherosclerosis* 2000;149:139–150.

[96] Visser M, Bouter LM, McQuillan GM, Wener MH, Harris TB: Low-grade systemic inflammation in overweight children. *Pediatrics* 200;107:E13.

[97] Wu DM, Chu NF, Shen MH, Chang JB: Plasma C-reactive protein levels and their relationship to anthropometric and lipid characteristics among children. *J. Clin. Epidemiol.* 2003;56:94–100.

[98] Vikram NK, Misra A, Dwivedi M, Sharma R, Pandey RM, Luthra K, Chatterjee A, Dhingra V, Jailkhani BL, Talwar KK, Guleria R: Correlations of C-reactive protein levels with anthropometric profile, percentage of body fat and lipids in healthy adolescents and young adults in urban North India. *Atherosclerosis* 2003;168:305–313.

[99] Must A, Jacques PF, Dallal GE, Bajema CJ, Dietz WH: Long-term morbidity and mortality of overweight adolescents: a follow-up of the Harvard Growth Study of 1922 to 1935. *N. Engl. J. Med.* 1992;327:1350–1355.

[100] Gungor N, Thompson T, Sutton-Tyrrell K, Janosky J, Arslanian S. Early signs of cardiovascular disease in youth with obesity and type 2 diabetes. *Diabetes Care* 2005;28:1219-1221.

[101] Sorrentino MJ. Implications of the metabolic syndrome: the new epidemic. *Am. J. Cardiol.* 2005;96(4A):3E-7E.

[102] Pritchett AM, Foreyt JP, Mann DL. Treatment of the metabolic syndrome: the impact of lifestyle modification. *Curr. Atheroscler. Rep.* 2005;7(2):95-102.

[103] Esposito K, Marfella R, Ciotola M, Di Palo C, Giugliano F, Giugliano G, D'Armiento M, D'Andrea F, Giugliano D. Effect of a mediterranean-style diet on endothelial dysfunction and markers of vascular inflammation in the metabolic syndrome: a randomized trial. *JAMA* 2004;292(12):1440.

[104] Riserus U, Basu S, Jovinge S, Fredrikson GN, Arnlov J, Vessby B. Supplementation with conjugated linoleic acid causes isomer-dependent oxidative stress and elevated C-reactive protein: a potential link to fatty acid-induced insulin resistance. *Circulation* 2002;106(15):1925-1929.

[105] Luyckx FH, Lefebvre PJ, Scheen AJ. Non-alcoholic steatohepatitis: association with obesity and insulin resistance, and influence of weight loss. *Diabetes Metab.* 2000;26(2):98-106.

[106] Pitsavos C, Panagiotakos DB, Chrysohoou C, Kavouras S, Stefanadis C. The associations between physical activity, inflammation, and coagulation markers, in people with metabolic syndrome: the ATTICA study. *Eur. J. Cardiovasc. Prev. Rehabil.* 2005;12(2):151-158.

[107] Troseid M, Lappegard KT, Claudi T, Damas JK, Morkrid L, Brendberg R, Mollnes TE. Exercise reduces plasma levels of the chemokines MCP-1 and IL-8 in subjects with the metabolic syndrome. *Eur. Heart. J.* 2004;25(4):349-355.

[108] Bray GA, Champagne CM. Obesity and the Metabolic Syndrome: implications for dietetics practitioners. *J. Am. Diet. Assoc.* 2004;104(1):86-89.

[109] Ishizaka N, Ishizaka Y, Toda E, Hashimoto H, Nagai R, Yamakado M. Association between cigarette smoking, metabolic syndrome, and carotid arteriosclerosis in Japanese individuals. *Atherosclerosis.* 2005;181(2):381-388.

[110] Chu JW, Abbasi F, Lamendola C, McLaughlin T, Reaven GM, Tsao PS. Effect of rosiglitazone treatment on circulating vascular and inflammatory markers in insulin-resistant subjects. *Diab. Vasc. Dis. Res.* 2005;2(1):37-41.

[111] Arner P. The adipocyte in insulin reistance: key molecules and the impact of the thiazolidinediones. *TRENDS in Endocrinol. Metab.* 2003;14(3):137-145.

[112] Iushibashi M, Egashira K, Hiasa K, Inoue S, Ni W, Zhao Q, et al. Antiinflammatory and antiarteriosclerotic effects of pioglitazone. *Hypertension* 2002;40:687-693.

[113] Scandinavian Simvastatin Survival Study Group. Randomised trial of cholesterol lowering in 4444 patients with coronary heart disease: the Scandinavian simvastatin survival study (4S). *Lancet* 1994;344:1383-9.

[114] Kinjo K, Sato H, Sakata Y, et al. Relation of C-reactive protein and one-year survival after acute myocardial infarction with versus without statin therapy. *Am J Cardiol* 2005;96(5):617-621.

[115] Elrod JW, Lefer DJ. The effects of statins on endothelium, inflammation, and cardioprotection. *Drugs News Perspect* 2005;18(4):229-236.

[116] Jialal I, Stein D, Balis D, Grundy SM, Adams-Huet B, Devaraj S: Effects of hydroxymethyl glutaryl coenzyme A reductase inhibitor therapy on high sensitive C-reactive protein levels. *Circulation* 2001;103:1933-1935.

[117] Maki KC. Fibrates for treatment of the metabolic syndrome. *Curr. Atheroscler. Rep.* 2004 J;6(1):45-51.

[118] Dagenais NJ, Jamali F. Protective effects of angiotensin II interruption: evidence for antiinflammatory actions. *Pharmacotherapy* 2005;25(9):1213-1229.

[119] Sierra C, de la Sierra A. Antihypertensive, cardiovascular, and pleiotropic effects of angiotensin-receptor blockers. *Curr. Opin. Nephrol. Hypertens.* 2005;14(5):435-441.

[120] American College of Endocrinology (ACE) Position Statement on the Insulin Resistance Syndrome. *Endocr. Pract.* 2003;9(No. 3):236-252.

[121] van Oostrom AJ, van Wijk J, Cabezas MC. Lipaemia, inflammation and atherosclerosis: novel opportunities in the understanding and treatment of atherosclerosis. *Drugs* 2004;64 Suppl 2:19-41.

[122] Garg R, Tripathy D, Dandona P. Insulin resistance as a proinflammatory state: mechanisms, mediators, and therapeutic interventions. *Curr. Drug. Targets.* 2003;4(6):487-492.

In: Metabolic Syndrome Research Trends
Editor: Thomas E. Batone, pp. 191-224

ISBN: 978-1-60456-224-8

Chapter VIII

Obesity, Metabolic Syndrome, and Weight Management

***Jian Huang*[1*] *and Donna Carden*[1,2*]**

Department of Medicine[1] and Emergency Medicine[2] Louisiana State University Health Sciences Center-Shreveport, Louisiana, USA

Abstract

The metabolic syndrome (MS) describes a cluster of cardiovascular risk factors, including central adiposity, insulin resistance or overt type 2 diabetes mellitus (DM2), atherogenic dyslipidemia, and elevated blood pressure or overt hypertension. Obesity, especially central adiposity, is associated with insulin resistance, the central feature of MS. Predictably, the incidence of MS increases with increasing body mass index (BMI) but also occurs with weight gain, even at normal weight. MS predisposes individuals to the development of DM2 and is responsible for increased all cause and coronary artery disease (CAD) mortality. MS, therefore, likely represents a latent disease process that may be viewed as preclinical diabetes or preclinical atherosclerosis. Because transitional conditions are more amenable to therapeutic intervention than late-stage disease, it is becoming increasingly recognized that early identification and treatment of MS is necessary to prevent CAD mortality. Recent clinical trials have demonstrated that weight loss through lifestyle modification with or without pharmacologic intervention can improve all components of MS. Although the exact mechanisms underlying MS remain undefined, physicians can contribute to improved long-tem clinical outcome by endorsing a healthy lifestyle that promotes weight loss or maintenance and physical activity. This may lead to the reduction in morbidity and mortality associated with obesity, DM2, and MS.

* Data for correspondence for Jian Huang, MD. Associate Professor of Medicine, Department of Medicine, Louisisana State University, Health Sciences Center. PO Box 33932 1501, Kings Highway, Shreveport, LA 71130-3932. Tel: (318)675-5621 Fax: (318)675-7176 E-mail: jhuang@lsuhsc.edu.

* Donna Carden, MD, Professor of Medicine and Emergency Medicine, Department of Emergency Medicine. Louisisana State University Health Sciences Center, 1501 Kings Highway, Shreveport, LA 71130-3932. Tel: (318)675-6659 E-mail: dcarde@lsuhsc.edu

Introduction

The metabolic syndrome (MS) refers to a cluster of cardiovascular risk factors, including abdominal obesity, insulin resistance with or without glucose intolerance, atherogenic dyslipidemia (DLP), elevated blood pressure and a proinflammatory as well as a prothrombotic state. [1, 2] Although various organizations differ on the components and emphasis placed on risk factors associated with MS, there is agreement that central to the pathogenesis of MS is its association with insulin resistance, type 2 diabetes mellitus (DM2) and premature atherosclerosis. The clustering of risk factors associated with DM2 and premature atherosclerosis was initially identified in the 1950's and continued to be refined throughout the 1980's. [3-10] However, Raven brought special attention to this group of risk factors with the suggestion that insulin resistance was an important link to DM2 and coronary artery disease (CAD) and termed the association, "Syndrome X".[11] Subsequently, insulin resistance or hyper-insulinemia was determined to be central to the development of MS. [1, 12-24] Other components of MS have been suggested and include microalbuminuria,[19] increased uric acid, [15] lipolytic enzymes, [25] free fatty acids, [26] TNF-alpha, [27] interleukin-6, [28] C-reactive protein (CRP), [29-31] von Willebrand factor (vWF), [31] fibrinogen, [31] and plasminogen activating inhibitor 1 (PAI-1). [31, 32] The terminology and major risk factors associated with MS are summarized in Table 1.

The exact prevalence of MS is not clearly defined. One of the reasons for the lack of clarity is that different emphasis has been placed on the various components of MS by a number of organizations. (Table 2) [1, 2, 19, 22, 23] However, it is clear that the prevalence of MS varies among different geographic, ethnic, age, and gender groups. [33-45] Furthermore, the relationship of MS to DM2 and CAD has also been well established by epidemiologic and clinical studies. [11, 16, 30, 46-52]

MS, CAD Risk, and Morbidity and Mortality

CAD is the leading cause of death in the United States and numerous factors enhance the risk of CAD mortality. [53] For example, excess body weight is associated with shortened life expectancy, [53-55] and increased CAD mortality.[56, 57] Moreover, both pre-hypertension and overt hypertension (HTN) contribute to increased CAD risk. [58] Insulin resistance, in the presence or absence of overt DM2, is associated with atherogenic DLP characterized by elevated triglycerides (TG) and diminished high-density-lipoprotein cholesterol (HDL-C), [59, 60] and is a predictor of CAD events. [61-66] However, the overall CAD risk among individuals with MS is far greater than the simple arithmetic sum of its individual components. [67-70] Not only does MS predispose to the development of DM2 [16, 46, 47] and CAD, [30, 46, 48-50] it is also responsible for increased all-cause [49, 51, 52] as well as CAD mortality. [46, 49, 51, 68, 71, 72]

Table 1. Terminology and Components Associated with the Metabolic Syndrome

Author/Year/ (Reference)	Nomenclature	Components							
		OB	DLP	↑BP/ HTN	IR/DM	↑UA/ Gout	↑UAlb	Pro-Thromb	Sed
Vague 1956/1980 (3,9)	Android Obesity/ Diabetogenic Obesity	X			X	X			
Avogaro 1965 (4)	Three Metabolic Disorders	X	X		X				
Camus 1966 (10)	Trisyndrome		X		X	X			
Reaven 1988 (11)	Syndrome X		X	X	X				
Kaplan 1989 (13)	Deadly Quartet	X	X	X	X				
DeFronzo 1991 (14)	Insulin Resistance Syndrome	X	X	X	X				
Zimmet 1991 (15)	Syndrome X Plus	X	X	X	X	X			X
Haffner 1992 (16)	Insulin Resistance Syndrome		X	X	X				
Kesaniemi 1992 (17)	Multiple Metabolic Syndrome	X	X	X	X				
Hjermann 1992 (12)	Metabolic Cardiovascular Syndrome	X	X	X	X			X	
Despres 1993 (18)	Insulin Resistance Dyslipidemia Syndrome	X	X		X				
WHO 1998 (19)	Metabolic Syndrome	X	X	X	X			X	
Hansen 1999 (20)	Metabolic Syndrome X	X	X	X	X				
Groop 2001 (21)	Dysmetabolic Syndrome	X	X	X	X			X	
NCEP 2001 (1)	Metabolic Syndrome	X	X	X	X				
EGIR 2002 (22)	Insulin Resistance Syndrome	X	X	X	X				
AACE 2003 (23)	Insulin Resistance Syndrome	X	X	X	X				X

NCEP = National Cholesterol Education Program; WHO = World Health Organization; AACE = American Association of Clinical Endocrinologists; EGIR = European Group for the Study of Insulin Resistance; OB: Obesity, or increased waist circumference, or increased waist to hip ratio; DLP: Dyslipidemia; BP: Blood pressure; HTN: Hypertension; IR: Insulin resistance; DM: Diabetes mellitus; UA: Uric acid; UAlb: Urine albumin; Pro-Thromb: Prothrombotic state; Sed: Sedentary lifestyle.

The Role of Obesity in the Development of MS

Obesity may be the most important risk factor in the development of MS. Obesity is a chronic disease associated with a number of serious health consequences. [73-75] While some causes of preventable death are declining, the death rate attributable to overweight or obesity as a result of poor diet and physical inactivity has risen markedly over the last decade and may soon exceed tobacco use as the leading cause of preventable death. [53] Obesity, particularly abdominal obesity, is a major contributor to the development of insulin resistance, DM2, HTN, and atherogenic DLP, all of which are major components of MS. [74, 76-80] Thus, abdominal obesity is critical to the development of insulin resistance which in turn, is the central feature of MS. [79-82]

The prevalence of obesity has reached epidemic proportions. [75, 83, 84] Currently, more than 65% of American adults are overweight (body mass index defined as weight in kg/ height in m^2 (BMI)>/= 25) or obese (BMI>/=30). [84] The prevalence of DM2 and MS is also near epidemic in the United States and continues to increase. [33, 34, 75, 83, 85] Seventeen million American adults have been diagnosed with DM2 and another 16 million have pre-diabetes and are thus at high risk of developing overt DM2. [86] The lifetime risk for DM2 among individuals born in 2000 in the United States is estimated at 32.8% for males and

38.5% for females. [87] It is also estimated that 27% of the adult population has MS based on recent data analysis of the Third National Health and Nutrition Examination Survey (NHANES III) (1999-2000), [33] an increase from 24% in NHANES III (1988-1994). [34] In parallel, the prevalence of MS among US adolescents also increased from 4.2% to 6.4% during the same time period. [35, 88] MS is also more prevalent in obese teens. [89] Health risks associated with MS continue from adolescence into adulthood, [90, 91] making adolescent MS a major risk factor for adult cardiovascular disease.

Table 2. Definitions of the Metabolic Syndrome

NCEP (1)	WHO (19)	AACE* (23)	EGIR* (22)
At least 3 of the following: 1. FPG>/=110mg/dl 2. Abdominal obesit: WC>40 inches or 102 cm (M); >35 inches or 88cm (F) 3. TG>/=150mg/dl 4. HDL <40mg/dl (M); <50mg/dl (F) 5. BP: >/=130/85 mmHg	IR defined as one of the following: 1. IFG 2. IGT 3. DM2 4. glucose uptake below the lowest quartile for background population under investigation under hyperinsulinemic euglycemic conditions Plus any 2 of the following: 1. BP>/=160/90mmHg or Rx for HTN 2. TG>/= 150mg/dl 3. HDL<35mg/dl (M) <39mg/dl (F) 4. BMI>30 kg/m2 and or WHR>0.9 (M) >0.85 (F) Urinary Alb excretion rate >/=20ug/min or Alb/Cr >/=20mg/g	Diagnosis depends on clinical judgment based on the following risk factors: 1. BMI>/=25 kg/m2 2. TG>/=150mg/dl 3. HDL<40mg/dl (M); <50mg/dl (F) 4. BP>/=130/85mmHg 5. FPG 110 -125mg/dl 6. 2-hour post-glucose challenge 140-200mg/dl 7. Others: personal history of CVD, HTN, GDM or IGT PCOS, NAFLD, or AN; family history of DM2, HTN or CVD; sedentary lifestyle; age>40; non-Caucasian ethnicity	Hyperinsulinemia defined as fasting insulin concentration above the upper quartile for the non-diabetic subjects Plus at least 2 of the following: 1. FPG>/=110mg/dl 2. BP>/=140/90mmHg or Rx for HTN 3. TG>180mg/dl and/or HDL<40mg/dl and/or Rx for DLP 4. WC>/=94 cm (M); >/=80 cm (F)

* Defined only for non-diabetic subjects.

NCEP = National Cholesterol Education Program; WHO = World Health Organization; AACE = American Association of Clinical Endocrinologists; EGIR = European Group for the Study of Insulin Resistance; FPG = fasting plasma glucose; WC = waist circumference; TG = triglycerides; HDL = high-density lipoprotein cholesterol; BP = blood pressure; IR = insulin resistance; IFG = impaired fasting glucose; IGT = impaired glucose tolerance; DM2 = type 2 diabetes mellitus; HTN = hypertension; M = male; F = female; BMI = body mass index; Alb = albumin; Cr = creatinine; CVD = cardiovascular disease; PCOS = polycystic ovary syndrome; GDM: gestational diabetes; NAFLD: non-alcoholic fatty liver disease; AN: acanthosis nigricans.

The total health care costs attributable to obesity are estimated at hundreds of billions of US dollars per year with at least $90 billion in direct health care costs annually in the US alone. [92] Most of the costs are associated with DM2, CAD, and HTN. [74, 93, 94] As obesity, DM2, and MS become more prevalent, these trends can be expected to translate into excess cardiovascular morbidity and mortality and higher health-care expenditures. [49, 50, 52, 56, 74, 92-96]

Subclinical Atherosclerosis and MS

As outlined above, the term MS has been used to describe a state of insulin resistance and associated metabolic derangements. Because it would take years to assess effects of risk factors on symptomatic cardiovascular events, surrogate markers have been used to investigate the effect of insulin resistance and MS on atherosclerosis. For example, the degree of subclinical atherosclerosis, as measured by carotid artery intima-media thickness, was found to be significantly greater in patients with MS. [97] Further, increased coronary artery calcium scores as determined by electron beam tomography, a marker of subclinical coronary atherosclerosis, was reported in the majority of asymptomatic MS patients, independent of their 10-year, Framingham risk score for CAD. [98] Compared to control subjects, patients with MS with angiographically proven normal coronary arteries also have evidence of impaired coronary blood flow suggestive of coronary microvascular endothelial dysfunction. [99] Finally, an inverse relationship between insulin sensitivity and carotid atherosclerosis was reported in the Insulin Resistance Atherosclerosis Study (IRAS). [100] After adjustment for established risk factors, the presence of MS was found to be associated with a two fold increased risk of CAD in the Atherosclerosis Risk in Community Study (ARIC) [97] Therefore, insulin resistance and MS represent important risk factors for the development and progression of atherosclerosis, even before gross pathology is recognizable using standard methods. Widespread recognition of the significant association of insulin resistance and MS with accelerated atherosclerosis and CAD progression may prompt earlier and more aggressive therapeutic intervention in insulin resistance states. Recognition of MS as a unique disease state with high CAD risk is gaining acceptance as the interventional target for primary and secondary CAD prevention. [1, 2]

Obesity and MS

Population-based cohort studies provide support for the hypothesis that the different components of MS are linked through obesity. [101] A key feature of MS is abdominal obesity, the deposition of excess adipose tissue in visceral compartments, which gives rise to insulin resistance. There is a progressive loss of insulin sensitivity with increased BMI [79] that is directly related to the degree of visceral adiposity. [80, 81] Waist circumference (WC) has been widely accepted as a surrogate for abdominal obesity in clinical practice. [1, 73] NHANES III data showed that, with few exceptions, within the normal weight (BMI: 18.5-24.9), overweight (BMI: 25-29.9), and class I obesity (BMI: 30-34.9) categories, those with high WC values are increasingly likely to have HTN, DM2, DLP, and MS compared with those with normal WC values. [102]

Weight Gain and MS

Recently, the Coronary Artery Risk Development in Young Adults (CARDIA) study reported that not only a higher BMI in young adulthood but also weight gain over 15 years predicts development of MS. [103] A study of 30 nondiabetic, premenopausal women followed for 7 years showed that weight gain, especially in the form of increased visceral adipose tissue, was associated with deterioration in glucose-insulin homeostasis. [104] Just as a higher BMI is associated with an increased incidence of DM2, weight gain predicts the development of DM2, independent of baseline adiposity. [105, 106] Higher BMI and weight gain are also linked to increased disease mortality. In the Cancer Prevention Study II, a prospective study of mortality among men and women in the US, the risk of death from all causes, cardiovascular disease, as well as cancer increased with elevated BMI for both genders and all age groups. [56] In the Nurses' Health Study, a weight gain of 10 kg after age 18 in women was associated with increased mortality in middle adulthood. [107] Thus, weight gain, visceral adiposity and obesity are all associated with excess cardiovascular risk and mortality.

Weight gain and obesity result from excess dietary intake and insufficient energy expenditure. [76] Availability of calorie-dense foods and decreased activity requirements of modern society have been linked with the obesity epidemic. [76] Aside from tobacco use, poor diet and physical inactivity are recognized as the principle contributors to morbidity and mortality, being responsible for 400,000 deaths in 2000. [53]

Dietary Habits, Physical Activity and MS

Dietary habits and physical activity are modifiable risk factors for obesity and the development of multiple components associated with MS. [73, 108] Several nutrients appear to influence insulin sensitivity, although their effects appear to be modest. Total fat correlates inversely with insulin sensitivity, but only in obese individuals. [109] Increased energy intake from saturated and trans-fat is associated with insulin resistance and risk of MS or DM2, [109-115] whereas polyunsaturated fat intake decreases the incidence of DM2. [115] Low intake of dietary fiber, fruits and vegetables is also associated with increased risk of DM2 or MS. [116-118] Moreover, the type of carbohydrate in food products can be categorized by its glycemic index, defined as the ratio of 2-hour post-prandial plasma glucose to the 2-hour level following ingestion of a similar amount of glucose. For a given amount of carbohydrate, diets rich in high glycemic index foods are associated with an increased risk of DM2. [115, 116, 118] Data from NHANES III (1988-1994) indicate that a diet relatively low in carbohydrate is associated with a significantly lower risk of MS. [119]

Physical inactivity is also a risk factor for MS. [103, 119] The relationship between MS risk and lifestyle-related factors was studied using data from a representative US sample in NHANES III. According to this cross-sectional logistic model, MS risk is substantially lower in individuals who are physically active and maintain a BMI in the non-obese range. [119] In the Canada Fitness Survey observational cohort study, anthropometric and physical fitness measures were obtained in 3719 men and 3854 women 20-59 years of age. High cardiorespiratory fitness was associated with lower levels of total and abdominal obesity for any given BMI compared to those with low cardiorespiratory fitness, independent of gender. [120] In the European Youth Heart Study of 589 children, an inverse relationship was found between physical activity and MS risk even after adjusting for other potential confounders. [121] In a nondiabetic, Caucasian population from the UK, a strong inverse association between physical activity and MS was documented, especially in unfit individuals. [122] Similarly in the Aerobics Center Longitudinal Study, an inverse relationship between MS prevalence and muscle strength and cardiorespiratory fitness in men across normal, overweight, and obese BMI categories was reported. [123] Likewise, MS prevalence was markedly lower across progressively higher levels of cardiorespiratory fitness in women of different ages. [124] Thus, there is substantial evidence that physical activity and enhanced cardiorespiratory fitness dramatically reduce the risk of MS.

Although physical activity and cardiorespiratory fitness are recognized deterrents of MS, CDC data from 2004 indicate that only 30.5% of US adults aged 18 or over engage in regular leisure-time physical activity. This estimate is down from 33.2% for the same period in 2003. [125] Decline in physical activity was also reported in US adolescent females in the National Heart, Lung, and Blood Institute Growth and Health Study. [126] Given the high and increasing prevalence of MS, poor dietary habits [53] and decline in physical activity in US adults and adolescents, [33-35, 125, 126] it is apparent that promotion of a healthy diet and regular exercise as part of a therapeutic intervention in the treatment of obesity and MS is necessary.

Metabolically Obese Normal-Weight, Metabolic Fitness and MS

Not all insulin resistant individuals are overweight or obese, nor are all overweight or obese individuals insulin resistant. BMI can underestimate or overestimate the degree of fatness depending on the individual's muscularity. [73, 74] The concept of the metabolically obese, normal-weight (MONW) individual was originally suggested over 20 years ago for those with normal or near normal BMI but with one of three conditions that improves with caloric restriction: DM2, HTN, and elevated TG. [127] Examination of phenotypic differences between MONW women and women with normal weight and metabolic profile revealed greater total as well as visceral fat and lower physical activity and energy expenditure in MONW women despite similar age, BMI and fat-free mass. [128] Recent analysis of data from 7602 adults from NHANES III confirms that MS is not limited to obese patients and, in fact, it is relatively common among normal weight or slightly overweight individuals. [129] While it is clear that MS increases with BMI, weight gain itself, even in normal weight individuals, is also associated with increased prevalence of MS. [104, 129] Thus, it has been proposed that those with MS, but a BMI of 18.5-26.9 kg/m^2, be classified as MONW. [129] Accordingly, rather than focusing primarily on body weight, many health professionals emphasize lifestyle modifications through diet and exercise to achieve the "metabolic fitness", defined as the absence of biochemical risk factors for MS, such as DLP, insulin resistance, preclinical DM2 and HTN. [130]

Abdominal Adiposity, Waist Circumference and MS

The fact that MS is common, even in normal weight individuals, lead to identification of abdominal adiposity as an independent risk factor for MS. [1] Results from NHANES III documented that abdominal adiposity and WC are more closely linked to cardiovascular disease risk factors than BMI. [131] Although WC and BMI are interrelated, WC provides an independent prediction of disease risk. [73] In fact, the Nurses' Health Study documented that WC is strongly associated with increased CAD risk in normal weight women and those with a WC > 76.2 cm (30 inches). [132] Predictably, it has been suggested that WC be included as part of the routine physical exam. [133] Given the increasing prevalence of obesity, DM2, and MS, [33, 34, 75, 83] and the increasing prevalence of abdominal obesity as measured by WC, [134, 135] preventing weight gain and overweight among persons with healthy weights and avoiding further weight gain among those already overweight are important public health goals. Appropriate attention should also be given to increase in WC even if overall weight remains stable or within the normal range. [136]

Weight Loss and MS

Since all components of MS are closely associated with obesity or the metabolically obese state, weight reduction or maintenance and physical activity are the corner stone of treatment of MS. However, treatment of obesity is challenging because body weight is determined by the integration of many biological and environmental factors. Non-pharmacological methods of weight loss are effective in the short-term but there is an unsatisfactory overall success rate with dietary treatment of obesity [137]. There is also a relative paucity of long-term studies using pharmalogic approaches to weight loss. [138] Moreover, one-third to two-thirds of weight lost, regardless of approach outside of surgery, is regained within one year and almost all is regained within five years. [139, 140]

Because of the difficulties in achieving permanent weight control, many experts emphasize adoption of life-long habits conducive to weight control and overall health rather than temporary measures for drastic weight loss. A program that encompasses regular physical activity with energy expenditure of more than 1,500 kcal/week and modest energy intake from a variety of nutritionally balanced food has the potential to meet such a treatment goal. There is mounting evidence that modest (5-10%) weight reduction through dietary modification and physical activity improves blood pressure, glucose tolerance, and lipid levels among obese patients. [73, 141-150] Many professionals recommend modest weight reduction or weight maintenance with emphasis on "metabolic fitness". For those whose health is impacted by excess body weight, the goal of weight management should be to achieve better health and well being over the long term, and not simply to lose weight.

Treatment of MS

The primary treatment goal of MS is prevention of DM2 and cardiovascular events. Currently, there are no firm guidelines on the optimal management of blood pressure, DLP, impaired glucose tolerance and insulin resistance in patients with MS because of limited data examining the efficacy of risk-modification of these MS components. Nevertheless, MS and DM2 share the common feature of insulin resistance and can be viewed as a disease continuum with DM2 representing the severe end of the metabolic derangement.

National Cholesterol Education Program (NCEP) recognizes MS as a secondary target for risk reduction therapy with specific recommendations for weight loss through lifestyle modification that affect components of MS. [1] Weight loss or prevention of weight gain improves glucose tolerance and insulin sensitivity and can delay or prevent the onset of DM2 and is therefore essential in the treatment of MS. [147, 148, 150, 151] Blood pressure control remains an important component of treatment strategies for MS, since low HDL and elevated blood pressure were identified in NHANES III as the most significant CAD predictors in MS patients. [36] Lipid modification plays a vital role in the prevention and treatment of atherosclerosis and reduction of CAD events. [1, 152] Although recent data suggest a beneficial effect of bariatric surgery for obese patients with DM2, HTN, and DLP, [153] surgical treatment for weight loss should be reserved for those in whom other treatment modalities have failed and who have clinically severe obesity and co-morbidities.

Lifestyle Intervention, Weight Loss and MS

Weight loss improves all components of MS and is central to cardiovascular risk reduction. Even modest weight loss (5-10 %) has beneficial effects on lipids, blood pressure, and blood glucose. [73, 154] A combination of diet modification and increased physical activity is recommended for long-term weight management. [1, 73, 74] Weight loss is more directly associated with restriction of caloric intake and duration of dietary adherence and not type of diet. [155, 156] Physical activity is an integral part of weight loss therapy and weight maintenance. [73]

Dietary Modification

There are countless dietary weight loss programs available. While current dietary recommendations for weight loss suggest that a healthful adult diet derive 45-65% energy from carbohydrate, 20-35% from fat with restricted saturated fat, and 10-35% from protein, [1, 73, 157-162] (Table 3.), popular diets often advocate low carbohydrate (< 10% for very low carbohydrate diet; < 45% for low carbohydrate diet) with corresponding increases in fat intake. [163-165] However, an energy-rich, high fat diet contributes to weight gain and obesity. [166]

Evidence suggests that a diet high in carbohydrate may increase triglyceride (TG), lower HDL, [167, 168] and may increase postprandial glucose and insulin levels in patients with DM2. [169] Low-fat, calorie-restricted diets, such as those recommended by the American Heart Association (AHA), National Cholesterol Education Program (NCEP) and American Diabetes Association (ADA), are relatively high in carbohydrate. [1, 158, 161] For MS patients with high TG and low HDL-C, NCEP suggests that carbohydrate intake be limited to less than 60%, perhaps as low as 50%, of total calories. Additionally, most carbohydrates should be complex such as those found in whole grains, vegetables, fruits, and low fat dairy products. [1]

Emerging data suggests that saturated fat and trans-fat are two cholesterol-increasing fatty acids, while unsaturated fat, particularly monounsaturated fat, has favorable effects on lowering LDL-C. [1] NCEP suggests that the upper limit of total fat intake be 35% with saturated fat limited to less than 7%. Saturated fat should be substituted with unsaturated, especially monounsaturated fat. [1] Dietary Guidelines for Americans 2005 were recently released and suggest similar recommendations regarding dietary fat intake. [162]

Implementation of these recommendations may not only reduce LDL-C, but also lower TG and raise HDL-C in patients with MS.[1, 161]

Recently, several randomized clinical trials of low carbohydrate diets for weight loss among obese individuals have been reported. Compared to traditional caloric and fat restricted diets, low carbohydrate diets produced a significantly greater weight loss for 3 [170] to 6 months, [171-173] but not at 1-year. [172, 174] Participants on the low carbohydrate diet maintained most of their 6-month weight loss, whereas those on the caloric and fat restricted diet continued to lose weight throughout the year. [174] Significant metabolic benefits on serum TG and HDL-C were observed with low-carbohydrate diets in some, [172, 174] but not all participants and studies. [170, 171] Low carbohydrate diets were also associated with significant improvements in insulin sensitivity only at 6-months [173] and glycemic control only in a subgroup of patients with DM2 at 6-month and 12-month follow-up. [173, 174] Adherence to the low carbohydrate diet was poor [171-174] and voluntary restriction of food intake and gradual increase in carbohydrate intake was common among those on low carbohydrate diets. [171, 173]

Table 3. Dietary Guidelines for Weight Management

Recommending Agency (Reference)	Carbohydrate (%)	Fat (%)	Protein (%)	Recommendation for weight loss/maintenance
WHO (157)	55-60	20-30	15	Reduce energy intake by 500-600 kcal/d for weight loss
NIH/NAASO (73)	>/=55	</=30	15	Reduce energy intake by 500-1000 kcal/d for weight loss
ADA[1] (158)	60-70	<30	15-20	Reduce energy intake by 500-1000/d
ADA[2] (160)	Moderate fat, high carbohydrate	<30	Not specified	Reduce energy intake by 500-1000/d
AHA (161)	Not stated	</=30	15	Reduce energy intake by 500-1000/d
NCEP (1)	50-60	25-35	15	Balance energy intake and expenditure to maintain desirable weight or prevent weight gain
IOM (159)	45-65	20-35	10-35	Balance intake of essential macronutrients
USDA (162)	Not specified	20-35	Not specified	Maintain healthy weight by balancing intake of calories and exercise

WHO = World Health Organization; NIH = National Institutes of Health; NAASO = North American Association for the Study of Obesity; ADA[1] = American Diabetes Association; ADA[2] = American Dietetic Association; AHA = American Heart Association; NCEP = National Cholesterol Education Program; IOM = Institute of Medicine; USDA: United States Department of Agriculture.

Randomized clinical trials of low carbohydrate dietary interventions in obese subjects with multiple CAD risk factors or known MS have documented similar effects on weight and waist circumference reduction, decrease in TG, increase in HDL-C levels, and improvement in insulin sensitivity at 4 to 16-months follow-up. [156, 174-176] As seen in other reports, the overall adherence rates were low for all types of diets. [156] Another randomized study compared the effect of a Mediterranean-style diet with that of a control diet on CAD risk reduction among 180 overweight or obese patients with MS. The two diets were similar in total calories and percent calories from carbohydrate, fat, and protein. However, patients on the Mediterranean diet were instructed to increase intake of complex carbohydrates, fiber, mono- and polyunsaturated fat, and decrease intake of saturated fat and cholesterol. At the end of a two-year follow-up, those on the Mediterranean diet had significantly greater weight and WC reduction, decrease in blood pressure, insulin resistance, TG and increase in HDL-C. There was also a significant reduction in the number of patients who continued to meet the diagnostic criteria for MS after the two-year Mediterranean diet intervention. [177]

In a recent meta-analysis of 107 studies of low versus high carbohydrate diets, weight loss was found to be associated with reduced caloric intake and longer diet duration but not with reduced carbohydrate content. [155] Therefore, negative energy balance provides weight loss regardless of the macronutrient composition of the diet and caloric restriction is the essential component of weight loss treatment.[178] Low carbohydrate diets may facilitate short-term weight loss compared to traditional calorie and fat restricted diets. However, low carbohydrate intake appears to be unsustainable and long-term safety and efficacy results of low carbohydrate diets are lacking.

There is insufficient evidence to make recommendations for or against the use of low-carbohydrate diets, particularly for those older than age 50, for use longer than 90 days, or for diets of 20 grams of carbohydrates or less per day. [155] Although controversy exists regarding low fat versus low carbohydrate weight loss diets, [179] there is a significant body of evidence that suggests that successful weight loss can be achieved by creation of a sustained energy deficit through a combination of regular exercise and a nutritionally balanced and varied diet.

Dietary Intervention and Lipid Profile

Changes in lipid profile through weight loss diets have been reported in obese patients with insulin resistance with or without MS. A decrease in total cholesterol and TG levels was reported with a low carbohydrate, very low calorie diet among obese individuals and MS patients followed for an average of 4 months. [176] Reponses of TG and HDL-C to the low carbohydrate diet were more favorable than to the conventional low fat, calorie-restricted diet at 12-months in obese patients with DM2 and MS. [174] A study comparing Atkins, Ornish, Weight Watchers, and Zone diets for weight loss and CAD risk reduction in obese patients with known MS components documented a persistent increase in HDL in all these weight loss programs except Ornish, while decreases in TG were not significant at the end of 12-months. [156] Similar results with a low carbohydrate diet were reported in obese, hyperinsulinemic subjects at 16 months. [175] Both elevated HDL and reduced TG were observed with a low carbohydrate diet in obese, hyperlipidemic patients [180] and with the Mediterranean diet in MS patients. [177] On the other hand, a low fat, high carbohydrate diet with a simple to complex carbohydrate ratio of 1:2 and ad libitum energy intake resulted in moderate weight reduction and decrease in both total cholesterol and HDL-C after 6 months in patients with MS compared to a high fat, low carbohydrate diet. An increase in TG was observed when the ratio of simple to complex carbohydrate was reversed. [181]

Dietary Intervention and Insulin Sensitivity

In addition to weight loss, significant improvement of fasting insulin level or insulin sensitivity was observed with a low-carbohydrate or a low-fat, calorie-restricted diet in obese, hyperinsulinemic subjects or obese patients with MS components at one-year.[156, 175] However, the beneficial effects on insulin sensitivity from the low carbohydrate diet did not persist beyond 6-months in obese patients with DM2 and MS. [173, 174] On the other hand, the Mediterranean diet, rich in complex carbohydrates, fiber, and unsaturated fat, resulted in enhanced insulin sensitivity in MS patients for up to 2 years. [177] The importance of glycemic load in the development of DM2 among pre-diabetic subjects was recently demonstrated by the results of the Study to Prevent Non-Insulin-Dependent Diabetes Mellitus (STOP-NIDDM). In this large, randomized controlled trial, treatment with acarbose, an alpha-glucosidase inhibitor which slows the digestion of satrches, reduced new-onset DM2 by 25% compared to placebo after a 3-year follow-up. [182] More encouragingly, diabetes prevention studies employing therapeutic lifestyle changes (TLC) with an emphasis on low saturated fat, high-fiber diet and regular exercise have demonstrated significant improvement in glucose tolerance and up to a 58% reduction in the incidence of new DM2 along with modest weight loss. These studies were conducted in different geographic areas, among ethnically diverse populations, in the settings of intensive training program and community-based primary care and with relatively long-term follow-up. [141, 147, 148, 150, 151]

Dietary Intervention and Blood Pressure Control

Weight loss through dietary modification is associated with improved blood pressure in obese individuals.[73] Diets rich in fiber with low saturated and high unsaturated fat lower blood pressure, especially when combined with restricted sodium intake. [183] Interestingly, acarbose not only diminished the incidence of DM2, but also reduced new-onset HTN in pre-diabetic patients by 34%. [184] In one non-randomized cohort study, a very low carbohydrate, high protein diet also produced substantial reduction in weight and blood pressure in obese MS patients after 4 months. [176] However, other investigations have reported that dietary intervention did not lead to a persistent lowering of blood pressure in obese patients with manifestations of MS. [156, 174, 175] The Mediterranean diet, on the other hand, has been shown to significantly reduce blood pressure compared to a conventional, low fat diet, even after two years. [177]

Dietary Intervention and Inflammation

The effects of weight loss diets on serum inflammatory markers have also been reported in obese patients. C-reactive protein was significantly reduced in obese subjects with some or all components of MS by a low carbohydrate diet, conventional, low-fat, calorie-restricted diet, or a Mediterranean diet. [156, 175, 177] The Mediterranean diet also reduced the proinflammatory mediators interleukin-6 (IL-6), IL-7, and IL-18. [177]

Physical Activity

Exercise is an important component of weight loss therapy even though it is not associated with substantially greater weight loss than diet alone. [73] In fact, successful weight loss is best attained through combined diet and exercise to optimize energy deficit. [185] Sustained physical activity is beneficial for weight maintenance after initial weight loss is achieved through dietary modification and in the prevention of weight gain. [73, 186] Adequate physical activity is also beneficial for reducing CAD risk beyond weight loss itself. [73, 187] The effects of physical activity on cardiovascular outcomes evaluated in 2803 diabetic men in the Health Professionals' Follow-up Study demonstrated that volume and intensity of physical activity were both important determinants of reduced mortality. [188] Moderate exercise with expenditure of approximately 1000 calories on most, preferably all, days of the week is recommended for weight loss and maintenance. [73] In addition, resistance training plays an important role in achieving and maintaining healthy weight. Although studies of strength training have not documented significant changes in body weight, they have demonstrated increases in fat-free body mass and decreases in fat mass. [189, 190]

Most of the benefits of resistance training can be achieved with two 15-20-minute sessions per week. [191] Exercise should incorporate both upper ad lower body musculature and be performed in a slow and controlled manner in order to minimize injury. Current guidelines recommend a minimum of 30-minute, moderate-intensity physical activity on most, preferably all, days of the week. [73, 186, 187, 192-195] (Table 4)

Table. 4 Guidelines on Exercise for CAD Risk Reduction

Recommending Agency (Reference)	Type of Prevention	Volume of Exercise	Intensity of Exercise	Duration (continuous or accumulated) of Exercise	Frequency of Exercise
HLB/NAASO (73)	Primary	1000Kcal/week	Moderate	>/=30 minutes	Most/all days of the week
NIH (187)	Primary	Not specified	Moderate	>/=30 minutes	Most/all days of the week
CDC (186)	Primary	200kcal/day	Moderate	>/=30 minutes	Most/all days of the week
ACSM (193)	Primary	Not specified	40-85%VO_2R	20-60 minutes	3-5 days/week
AHA (194)	Primary	Not specified	Not specified	30-60 minutes	4-6 days/week
ACSM (195)	Secondary	Not specified	>/= 40%VO_2R	20-60 minutes	3-5 days/week
AHA (194)	Secondary	Not specified	50-80% VO_2R	20-30 minutes	3-4 days/week

HLB/NAASO: National Heart Lung and Blood Institute/North American Association for the study of Obesity; NIH: National Institutes of Health; CDC: Centers for Disease Control; ACSM: American College of Sports Medicine; AHA: American Heart Association. VO_2R: Maximum oxygen uptake reserve.

Physical Activity and Lipid Profile

Physically active individuals have higher HDL and lower TG than sedentary individuals. [196] Furthermore, atherogenic DLP respond favorably to exercise training. [196] For example, aerobic exercise and resistance training increases HDL-C and decreases TG, [197-199] changes that may persist for as much as 36 months in MS patients. [200] The Health, Risk Factors, Exercise Training and Genetics (HERITAGE) Family study compared the effects of a 20-week endurance exercise program on men with favorable and unfavorable lipid profiles. Individuals with atherogenic DPL had significantly greater reductions in apolipoprotein B and greater increases in HDL-C than the control group or those with isolated low HDL-C. [201]

Physical Activity and Insulin Sensitivity

Regular exercise increases insulin sensitivity in skeletal muscle [202] and exercise training even without weight loss increases insulin sensitivity in previously sedentary adults. [203] In the Finnish Diabetes Prevention Study (DPS) of 522 middle aged, pre-diabetic patients, those treated with combined diet and exercise showed significantly improved fasting glucose, 2-hour post- challenge glucose, and HbA1c at the end of one year. [141] However, the effect remained statistically significant only for HbA1c at 3 years. [148] Along with significant weight and WC reduction, DM2 incidence was reduced by 58% in the intervention group compared to the control group. [141] The US Diabetes Prevention Program (DPP) enrolled 3234 pre-diabetic patients and randomly assigned them to standard lifestyle recommendations with metformin or placebo or an intensive lifestyle modification group. Patients in the intensive lifestyle modification group also had 58% reduction in DM2 incidence, improved insulin sensitivity and significant weight loss. [150] In a randomized, controlled study of 79 normoglycemic, insulin resistant men and women, reductions in weight and WC occurred in parallel with changes in insulin sensitivity in the group treated with intensive diet and exercise after 4-months of intervention. [204]

Physical Activity and Blood Pressure Control

Physical activity is associated with reduction of blood pressure. [145] Ambulatory blood pressure measurements provide evidence that endurance training lowers blood pressure in sedentary men. [205] However, some studies have failed to show a clinically meaningful reduction in blood pressure with endurance training. [206] There are few reports on the effect of exercise on blood pressure in MS and most studies include both a diet and an exercise intervention. In the Finnish Diabetes Prevention Study, significant reductions in systolic and diastolic blood pressure in pre-diabetic patients were observed with diet plus exercise. [141] However, other investigators reported no change in blood pressure in insulin resistant patients participating in a 4-month combined diet and exercise program. [204]

Physical Activity and Inflammation

Prothrombotic and proinflammatory states are seen in individuals with MS. [2] The presence of serum inflammatory markers especially is associated with a significant risk of CAD in healthy individuals [207] and in MS patients [30] CRP in particular is related to the number of MS components present and is recognized as a risk factor for CAD. [30] Physical activity has been documented to be inversely related to levels of inflammatory markers including: fibrinogen, blood viscosity, platelet counts, coagulation factors VIII and IX, von Willebrand factor, fibrin D-dimer, tissue plasminogen activator antigen, CRP, even after adjusting for confounding factors. [208] A beneficial effect of frequent leisure-time physical activity on obesity-related inflammatory markers has also been described. [209] Finally, a significant reduction in monocyte chemoattractant protein-1 (MCP-1], IL-8 and visceral fat has bee reported in MS patients treated with exercise and pravastatin compared to those treated with pravastatin alone. [210] Thus, exercise may play a role in alleviating the prothrombotic and proinflammatory state in MS.

Pharmacological Intervention, Weight Loss and MS

Currently, there is little experimental or outcome data on cardiovascular mortality with pharmacologic weight loss agents. [138] Sibutramine, an appetite suppressant, and orlistat, a lipase inhibitor, are the only approved agents for long-term use in weight loss that have been extensively studied. Both medications have modest efficacy in promoting and maintaining weight loss, an effect that may benefit those with insulin resistance and pre-diabetes.

Sibutramine plus an AHA diet significantly increases weight loss and improves lipids when compared to placebo in obese patients with high TG and low HDL characteristic of MS. [211] Orlistat improves fasting blood glucose and fasting insulin levels in obese patients with and without DM2. [212, 213] For example, in a double-blind, prospective study, 3305 obese patients with or without IGT were randomized to TLC plus orlistat or placebo. Orlistat combined with TLC produced greater weight loss over 4 years and resulted in significant reductions in the incidence of DM2 in a subgroup with IGT. [214] In a post hoc analysis, weight loss induced by a 52-week, calorie-restricted diet plus orlistat was also associated with significant reductions in TG and increases in HDL-C in obese MS patients compared with obese subjects without MS. [215] Finally, orlistat plus a calorie-restricted diet has been reported to significantly reduce weight, WC and systolic blood pressure, and improve fasting glucose and insulin sensitivity compared to diet alone in MS patients with co-existing DM2. [216] Interestingly, orlistat-treated patients had a marked reduction in estimated 10-year risk of vascular events and were much less likely to continue to meet criteria for MS at the end of the study period. [216]

Metformin is a pharmacologic agent associated with improvement of insulin sensitivity and weight loss in obese patients without insulin resistance. [217-219] Metformin appears to decrease caloric intake by suppressing appetite, thereby potentiating weight loss. [220] Interestingly, metformin-induced weight loss appears to preferentially affect adipose tissue. [221]

The effects of metformin on weight loss and insulin sensitivity have also been documented in pre-diabetic and insulin resistant patients. For example, addition of metformin to TLC in the Diabetes Prevention Program resulted in moderate weight reduction, improved glucose tolerance, and a 31% reduction in new onset DM2. Although impressive, these effects were even less dramatic than those achieved with intensive TLC. [150] Polycystic ovary syndrome (PCOS) is a disorder strongly associated with insulin resistance. [23] Treatment of obese women with or without PCOS and obese, hyperinsulinemic adolescent girls with metformin plus a low-caloric diet resulted in weight loss comparable to sibutramine and orlistat [218] and improved insulin sensitivity. [217-219] Thus, metformin, although not an approved weight loss agent, does facilitate weight loss and improves insulin sensitivity.

Despite the positive effects of weight loss agents on insulin resistance, lipid profile and development of DM2 reported in some studies, reports examining the effect of these agents on long-term cardiovascular mortality are largely unavailable. However, in the UK Prospective Diabetes Study (UKPDS), 1704 overweight patients with newly diagnosed DM2 were randomized to treatment with diet, metformin, sulfonylurea, or insulin. Only metformin treatment, over a period of approximately 10 years, was associated with significant reductions in myocardial infarction. [222]

Other Pharmacologic Interventions

Hydroxymethylglutaryl-coenzyme A (HMG-CoA) reductase inhibitors (statin), fibrates, and thiazolidinediones (TZD), pharmacologic agents without direct weight loss effects, have been reported to improve some aspects of MS including atherogenic DLP, insulin resistance, and inflammation. Moreover, subgroup analysis of several large randomized clinical trials indicates that angiotensin converting enzyme inhibitors (ACE-I) and angiotensin receptor blockers (ARB) not only lower blood pressure but also improve insulin sensitivity [223] and reduce new-onset DM2. [224-227] Since both insulin resistance and elevated blood pressure are major components of MS, treatment of hypertensive MS patients with an ACE-I or ARB appears attractive. These reports provide direct evidence that agents not directly related to weight loss are effective in improving the metabolic profile in MS.

It appears that the beneficial effects of statins on CAD risk reduction in patients with DM2 or MS are at least partially related to lipid modification. [228-232] A recent post hoc analysis from the Scandinavian Simvastatin Survival Study (4S) documented that the absolute CAD risk reduction with simvastatin was most evident in a subgroup of patients with MS. [232] This is in contrast to the results obtained in the Anglo-Scandinavian Cardiac Outcomes Trial-Lipid Lowering Arm (ASCOT-LLA) in which atorvastatin reduced CAD events only in subjects without MS. [233] Differences in baseline LDL may account for outcome differences in these two studies with statins being less effective if basal LDL is not high. [232]

Although unproven, it is also possible that the differences in CAD risk reduction observed between statins, may represent differences in the effect of individual drugs on glucose metabolism. For example, in the West of Scotland Coronary Prevention Study (WOSCOPS), pravastatin resulted in a 30% reduction of new-onset DM2, [234] an effect not observed with simvastatin in the Heart Protection Study [229] or atorvastatin in ASCOT-LLA [233] If this hypothesis is correct, it might be predicted that statins that prevent or delay DM2 would more effectively lower overall CAD risk than those that have less effect on DM2 prevention. Although there is indirect evidence to support this hypothesis, it remains speculative.

In contrast to statins, fibrates produce greater reductions in TG and increases in HDL-C with less LDL-C lowering effects. In a post hoc analysis of the Helsinki Heart Study (HHS), gemfibrozil reduced CAD events most in individuals with higher BMI, high TG and low HDL-C levels. [235] Similar findings were reported in the Veterans Affairs HDL Intervention Trial (VA-HIT). [236] Thus, fibrates appear to have a beneficial effect on atherogenic lipid profile as well as cardiovascular mortality among patients with insulin resistance.

TZDs increase insulin sensitivity and have favorable effects on lipid profiles in patients with insulin resistance. In these patients, TZDs are associated with significant improvements in glucose tolerance and an 89% reduction in new-onset DM2 compared to subjects not treated with any anti-diabetic agent. [237] Similar results were reported in the Troglitazone in Prevention of Diabetes (TRIPOD) study in Hispanic women with history of gestational DM and insulin resistance. [238] Despite similar salutary effects on insulin sensitivity, the TZDs have discrepant effects on lipids. [239, 240] Furthermore, concerns exist regarding weight gain from fluid retention and worsening of heart failure with the use of these agents. Therefore, although TZDs may exert beneficial effects on lipids and insulin sensitivity, their role in preventing cardiovascular events remains unclear.

As described above, MS appears to be associated with a pro-inflammatory and pro-thrombotic state [2, 28-31, 241] Atorvastatin, [242] gemfibrozil, [243] rosiglitazone, [244] and irbesartan [245] have all been reported to significantly reduce inflammatory or pro-thrombotic markers in pre-diabetic, diabetic, or MS patients. Although these interventions appear to modulate pro-inflammatory and pro-thrombotic markers, controlled trials are needed to determine whether such intervention translates into improved clinical outcomes.

Surgical Intervention, Weight Loss and MS

Weight loss surgery is an option for weight reduction in patients with severe obesity, i.e. a BMI>/= 40, or a BMI>/= 35 and co-morbid conditions. [73] Weight loss surgery provides significant, sustained weight loss in most patients for over five years. [73] Two types of operations have proven to be effective: gastric volume restriction and gastric bypass surgeries. [73] Mortality rates associated with the surgeries vary depending on co-morbidities. A recent meta-analysis examined the impact of bariatric surgery on weight loss, operative mortality, and four obesity-associated co-morbidities, including DM2, DLP, HTN, and obstructive sleep apnea. [153] Surgery elicited substantial weight loss and operative mortality at 30 days or less was 0.1% for the restrictive procedures and 0.5% for gastric bypass procedures but increased to 1.1% for biliopancreatic diversion or duodenal switch procedures. [153] All bariatric surgeries were associated with significant improvements in glucose tolerance or even DM2 resolution with more pronounced effects observed with malabsorptive as compared to restrictive procedures. Interestingly, resolution of DM2 often occurred days following surgery, before significant weight loss was achieved. [153, 246] The temporal relationship between bariatric surgery and resolution or improvement in DM2 may therefore be related to changes in gut hormones regulating glucose metabolism rather than weight loss *per se*. [153]

Improvement in lipid profile was seen in the vast majority of patients undergoing bariatric surgery, although there are differences observed between surgical procedures. [153] Blood pressure reduction also occurred in the majority of patients undergoing bariatric surgery, but in contrast to surgical effects on DM2 and DPL, blood pressure reduction appeared to be independent of operative procedure. [153] Thus a majority of patients with DM2, HTN, and DLP, experience significant improvement or complete resolution of metabolic derangements in addition to the marked weight loss following bariatric surgery. The differences in results observed on DM2 and DLP with different forms of weight loss surgery provides indirect evidence that nutrient absorption and gut hormones play an integral role in the genesis of the metabolic abnormalities of obesity. [153]

Global Risk Reduction and MS

Recently, the INTERHEART study of 29,000 individuals from 52 countries revealed that modifiable risk factors account for more than 90% of the risk of myocardial infarction across all age, gender, and geographic groups. [247] According to a recent study using mathematical modeling, optimal control of blood pressure and lipids would result in prevention of more than 80% of CAD events in patients with MS. [248] Multifactorial intervention in patients with DM2 has been demonstrated to improve glycosylated hemoglobin values, blood pressure, and fasting lipid profile, and to produce significant reductions in complications from DM2 as well as cardiovascular events. [249] The concept of global risk reduction for health promotion and disease prevention was advocated in a recent joint scientific statement from the American Cancer Society, the American Diabetes Association, and the American Heart Association. [250] Multifactorial intervention in patients with MS may provide the mechanism for such global risk reduction.

Conclusion

Physicians face the challenge of an epidemic of obesity, DM2, and MS with severe public health consequences. Early recognition of MS and aggressive implementation of therapeutic strategies to halt the syndrome at its pre-clinical stages are keys to preventing DM2, CAD and CAD mortality. Adequate treatment requires targeting multiple risk factors and components of MS, including obesity, insulin resistance, pre-diabetes or overt DM2, pre-hypertension or overt HTN, and atherogenic DLP. TLC remains the mainstay of treatment of obesity and MS with emphasis on adoption of a healthy diet and regular physical activity. Pharmacological intervention also appears to play an important role in the treatment of obesity, glucose intolerance, atherogenic DLP, elevated blood pressure and MS. Surgery is reserved for those with severe obesity and co-morbid conditions and those who fail to response to TLC with or without pharmacologic intervention.

Although the exact mechanisms underlying MS remain to be determined, physicians can immediately contribute to improved long-term outcome by endorsing a healthy lifestyle that promotes weight loss or at least, weight maintenance and increased physical activity. This may lead to the reduction in morbidity and mortality associated with obesity, DM2, and MS.

References

[1] Executive Summary of The Third Report of The National Cholesterol Education Program (NCEP) Expert Panel on Detection, Evaluation, And Treatment of High Blood Cholesterol In Adults (Adult Treatment Panel III). *JAMA* 2001;285(19):2486-97.

[2] Grundy SM, Brewer HB, Jr., Cleeman JI, Smith SC, Jr., Lenfant C. Definition of metabolic syndrome: Report of the National Heart, Lung, and Blood Institute/American Heart Association conference on scientific issues related to definition. *Circulation* 2004;109(3):433-8.

[3] Vague J. The degree of masculine differentiation of obesities: a factor determining predisposition to diabetes, atherosclerosis, gout, and uric calculous disease. *Am J Clin Nutr* 1956;4(1):20-34.

[4] Avogaro P, Creapaldi G. Essential hyperlipidemia, obesity and diabetes. *Diabetologia* 1965;1:137.

[5] Welborn TA, Breckenridge A, Rubinstein AH, Dollery CT, Fraser TR. Serum-insulin in essential hypertension and in peripheral vascular disease. *Lancet* 1966;1(7451):1336-7.

[6] Welborn TA, Wearne K. Coronary heart disease incidence and cardiovascular mortality in Busselton with reference to glucose and insulin concentrations. *Diabetes Care 1979*;2(2):154-60.

[7] Pyorala K. Relationship of glucose tolerance and plasma insulin to the incidence of coronary heart disease: results from two population studies in Finland. *Diabetes Care* 1979;2(2):131-41.

[8] Modan M, Halkin H, Almog S, et al. Hyperinsulinemia. A link between hypertension obesity and glucose intolerance. *J Clin Invest* 1985;75(3):809-17.

[9] Vague J, Vague P, Tramoni M, Vialettes B, Mercier P. Obesity and diabetes. *Acta Diabetol Lat* 1980;17(2):87-99.

[10] Camus JP. [Gout, diabetes, hyperlipimia: a metabolic trisyndrome]. *Rev Rhum Mal Osteoartic* 1966;33(1):10-4.

[11] Reaven GM. Banting lecture 1988. *Role of insulin resistance in human disease. Diabetes* 1988;37(12):1595-607.

[12] Hjermann I. The metabolic cardiovascular syndrome: syndrome X, Reaven's syndrome, insulin resistance syndrome, atherothrombogenic syndrome. *J Cardiovasc Pharmacol* 1992;20 Suppl 8:S5-10.

[13] Kaplan NM. The deadly quartet. Upper-body obesity, glucose intolerance, hypertriglyceridemia, and hypertension. *Arch Intern Med* 1989;149(7):1514-20.

[14] DeFronzo RA, Ferrannini E. Insulin resistance. A multifaceted syndrome responsible for NIDDM, obesity, hypertension, dyslipidemia, and atherosclerotic cardiovascular disease. *Diabetes Care* 1991;14(3):173-94.

[15] Zimmet PZ. Kelly West Lecture 1991. Challenges in diabetes epidemiology--from West to the rest. *Diabetes Care* 1992;15(2):232-52.

[16] Haffner SM, Valdez RA, Hazuda HP, Mitchell BD, Morales PA, Stern MP. Prospective analysis of the insulin-resistance syndrome (syndrome X). *Diabetes* 1992;41(6):715-22.

[17] Kesaniemi YA, Lilja M, Kervinen K, Rantala A. Multiple metabolic syndrome: aspects of genetic epidemiology and molecular genetics. *Ann Med* 1992;24(6):461-4.

[18] Despres JP. The insulin resistance-dyslipidemia syndrome: the most prevalent cause of coronary artery disease? *Cmaj* 1993;148(8):1339-40.

[19] Alberti KG, Zimmet PZ. Definition, diagnosis and classification of diabetes mellitus and its complications. Part 1: diagnosis and classification of diabetes mellitus provisional report of a WHO consultation. *Diabet Med* 1998;15(7):539-53.

[20] Hansen BC. The metabolic syndrome X. Ann N Y Acad Sci 1999;892:1-24.

[21] Groop L, Orho-Melander M. The dysmetabolic syndrome. *J Intern Med* 2001;250(2):105-20.

[22] Balkau B, Charles MA, Drivsholm T, et al. Frequency of the WHO metabolic syndrome in European cohorts, and an alternative definition of an insulin resistance syndrome. *Diabetes Metab* 2002;28(5):364-76.

[23] Einhorn D, Reaven GM, Cobin RH, et al. American College of Endocrinology position statement on the insulin resistance syndrome. *Endocr Pract* 2003;9(3):237-52.

[24] Foster DW. Insulin resistance--a secret killer? *N Engl J Med* 1989;320(11):733-4.

[25] Knudsen P, Eriksson J, Lahdenpera S, Kahri J, Groop L, Taskinen MR. Changes of lipolytic enzymes cluster with insulin resistance syndrome. *Botnia Study Group. Diabetologia* 1995;38(3):344-50.

[26] Ferrannini E, Baldi S, Stern M. Circulating free fatty acids are an integral part of the insulin resistance syndrome. *Diabetes* 1995;44:182A.

[27] Hotamisligil GS, Arner P, Caro JF, Atkinson RL, Spiegelman BM. Increased adipose tissue expression of tumor necrosis factor-alpha in human obesity and insulin resistance. *J Clin Invest* 1995;95(5):2409-15.

[28] Pickup JC, Mattock MB, Chusney GD, Burt D. NIDDM as a disease of the innate immune system: association of acute-phase reactants and interleukin-6 with metabolic syndrome X. *Diabetologia* 1997;40(11):1286-92.

[29] Tamakoshi K, Yatsuya H, Kondo T, et al. The metabolic syndrome is associated with elevated circulating C-reactive protein in healthy reference range, a systemic low-grade inflammatory state. *Int J Obes Relat Metab Disord* 2003;27(4):443-9.

[30] Ridker PM, Buring JE, Cook NR, Rifai N. C-reactive protein, the metabolic syndrome, and risk of incident cardiovascular events: an 8-year follow-up of 14 719 initially healthy American women. *Circulation* 2003;107(3):391-7.

[31] Yudkin JS. Abnormalities of coagulation and fibrinolysis in insulin resistance. Evidence for a common antecedent? *Diabetes Care* 1999;22 Suppl 3:C25-30.

[32] Juhan-Vague I, Thompson SG, Jespersen J. Involvement of the hemostatic system in the insulin resistance syndrome. A study of 1500 patients with angina pectoris. The ECAT Angina Pectoris Study Group. *Arterioscler Thromb* 1993;13(12):1865-73.

[33] Ford ES, Giles WH, Mokdad AH. Increasing prevalence of the metabolic syndrome among u.s. Adults. *Diabetes Care* 2004;27(10):2444-9.

[34] Ford ES, Giles WH, Dietz WH. Prevalence of the metabolic syndrome among US adults: findings from the third National Health and Nutrition Examination Survey. *Jama* 2002;287(3):356-9.

[35] Duncan GE, Li SM, Zhou XH. Prevalence and trends of a metabolic syndrome phenotype among u.s. Adolescents, 1999-2000. *Diabetes Care* 2004;27(10):2438-43.

[36] Alexander CM, Landsman PB, Teutsch SM, Haffner SM. NCEP-defined metabolic syndrome, diabetes, and prevalence of coronary heart disease among NHANES III participants age 50 years and older. *Diabetes* 2003;52(5):1210-4.

[37] Bonora E, Kiechl S, Willeit J, et al. Prevalence of insulin resistance in metabolic disorders: the Bruneck Study. *Diabetes* 1998;47(10):1643-9.

[38] Schmidt MI, Duncan BB, Watson RL, Sharrett AR, Brancati FL, Heiss G. A metabolic syndrome in whites and African-Americans. The Atherosclerosis Risk in Communities baseline study. *Diabetes Care* 1996;19(5):414-8.

[39] Karter AJ, Mayer-Davis EJ, Selby JV, et al. Insulin sensitivity and abdominal obesity in African-American, Hispanic, and non-Hispanic white men and women. The Insulin Resistance and Atherosclerosis Study. *Diabetes* 1996;45(11):1547-55.

[40] Tan CE, Ma S, Wai D, Chew SK, Tai ES. Can we apply the National Cholesterol Education Program Adult Treatment Panel definition of the metabolic syndrome to Asians? *Diabetes Care* 2004;27(5):1182-6.

[41] Lee WY, Park JS, Noh SY, Rhee EJ, Kim SW, Zimmet PZ. Prevalence of the metabolic syndrome among 40,698 Korean metropolitan subjects. *Diabetes Res Clin* Pract 2004;65(2):143-9.

[42] Ilanne-Parikka P, Eriksson JG, Lindstrom J, et al. Prevalence of the metabolic syndrome and its components: findings from a Finnish general population sample and the Diabetes Prevention Study cohort. *Diabetes Care* 2004;27(9):2135-40.

[43] Enkhmaa B SK, Anuurad E, Nogi A, Keiko K, Yamasaki M, Oyunsuren T, Yamane Y. Prevalence of the metabolic syndrome using the third report of the National Cholesterol Education Program Expert Panel on detection, evaluation, and treatment of high blood cholesterol in adults (ATP III) and the modified ATP III definitions for Japanese and Mongolians. Clinica Chimica Acta. 2005;352(1-2):105-13.

[44] Balkau B, Vernay M, Mhamdi L, et al. The incidence and persistence of the NCEP (National Cholesterol Education Program) metabolic syndrome. The French D.E.S.I.R. study. *Diabetes Metab* 2003;29(5):526-32.

[45] Park YW, Zhu S, Palaniappan L, Heshka S, Carnethon MR, Heymsfield SB. The metabolic syndrome: prevalence and associated risk factor findings in the US population from the Third National Health and Nutrition Examination Survey, 1988-1994. *Arch Intern Med* 2003;163(4):427-36.

[46] Sattar N, Gaw A, Scherbakova O, et al. Metabolic syndrome with and without C-reactive protein as a predictor of coronary heart disease and diabetes in the West of Scotland Coronary Prevention Study. *Circulation* 2003;108(4):414-9.

[47] Lorenzo C, Okoloise M, Williams K, Stern MP, Haffner SM. The metabolic syndrome as predictor of type 2 diabetes: the San Antonio heart study. *Diabetes Care* 2003;26(11):3153-9.

[48] Isomaa B, Almgren P, Tuomi T, et al. Cardiovascular morbidity and mortality associated with the metabolic syndrome. *Diabetes Care* 2001;24(4):683-9.

[49] Lakka HM, Laaksonen DE, Lakka TA, et al. The metabolic syndrome and total and cardiovascular disease mortality in middle-aged men. *Jama* 2002;288(21):2709-16.

[50] Vega GL. Results of Expert Meetings: Obesity and Cardiovascular Disease. Obesity, the metabolic syndrome, and cardiovascular disease. *Am Heart J* 2001;142(6):1108-16.

[51] Marroquin OC, Kip KE, Kelley DE, et al. Metabolic syndrome modifies the cardiovascular risk associated with angiographic coronary artery disease in women: a report from the Women's Ischemia Syndrome Evaluation. *Circulation* 2004;109(6):714-21.

[52] Malik S, Wong ND, Franklin SS, et al. Impact of the metabolic syndrome on mortality from coronary heart disease, cardiovascular disease, and all causes in United States adults. *Circulation* 2004;110(10):1245-50.

[53] Mokdad AH, Marks JS, Stroup DF, Gerberding JL. Actual causes of death in the United States, 2000. *Jama* 2004;291(10):1238-45.

[54] Allison DB, Fontaine KR, Manson JE, Stevens J, VanItallie TB. Annual deaths attributable to obesity in the United States. *Jama* 1999;282(16):1530-8.

[55] Fontaine KR, Redden DT, Wang C, Westfall AO, Allison DB. Years of life lost due to obesity. *Jama* 2003;289(2):187-93.

[56] Calle EE, Thun MJ, Petrelli JM, Rodriguez C, Heath CW, Jr. Body-mass index and mortality in a prospective cohort of U.S. adults. *N Engl J Med* 1999;341(15):1097-105.

[57] Wilson PW, D'Agostino RB, Sullivan L, Parise H, Kannel WB. Overweight and obesity as determinants of cardiovascular risk: the Framingham experience. *Arch Intern Med* 2002;162(16):1867-72.

[58] Warnock DG, Textor SC. Hypertension. *Am J Kidney Dis* 2004;44(2):369-75.

[59] Brunzell JD, Hokanson JE. Dyslipidemia of central obesity and insulin resistance. *Diabetes Care* 1999;22 Suppl 3:C10-3.

[60] Ginsberg HN, Huang LS. The insulin resistance syndrome: impact on lipoprotein metabolism and atherothrombosis. *J Cardiovasc Risk* 2000;7(5):325-31.

[61] Kuusisto J, Lempiainen P, Mykkanen L, Laakso M. Insulin resistance syndrome predicts coronary heart disease events in elderly type 2 diabetic men. *Diabetes Care* 2001;24(9):1629-33.

[62] Kannel WB, McGee DL. Diabetes and cardiovascular disease. The Framingham study. *Jama* 1979;241(19):2035-8.

[63] Pyorala M, Miettinen H, Laakso M, Pyorala K. Hyperinsulinemia predicts coronary heart disease risk in healthy middle-aged men: the 22-year follow-up results of the Helsinki Policemen Study. *Circulation* 1998;98(5):398-404.

[64] Haffner SM, Lehto S, Ronnemaa T, Pyorala K, Laakso M. Mortality from coronary heart disease in subjects with type 2 diabetes and in nondiabetic subjects with and without prior myocardial infarction. *N Engl J Med* 1998;339(4):229-34.

[65] Lempiainen P, Mykkanen L, Pyorala K, Laakso M, Kuusisto J. Insulin resistance syndrome predicts coronary heart disease events in elderly nondiabetic men. *Circulation* 1999;100(2):123-8.

[66] Fontbonne A, Charles MA, Thibult N, et al. Hyperinsulinaemia as a predictor of coronary heart disease mortality in a healthy population: the Paris Prospective Study, 15-year follow-up. *Diabetologia* 1991;34(5):356-61.

[67] Maheux P, Jeppesen J, Sheu WH, et al. Additive effects of obesity, hypertension, and type 2 diabetes on insulin resistance. *Hypertension* 1994;24(6):695-8.

[68] Reilly MP, Rader DJ. The metabolic syndrome: more than the sum of its parts? *Circulation* 2003;108(13):1546-51.

[69] Haffner SM. Impaired glucose tolerance, insulin resistance and cardiovascular disease. *Diabet Med* 1997;14 Suppl 3:S12-8.

[70] Bonora E, Targher G, Formentini G, et al. The Metabolic Syndrome is an independent predictor of cardiovascular disease in Type 2 diabetic subjects. Prospective data from the Verona Diabetes Complications Study. *Diabet Med* 2004;21(1):52-8.

[71] Ninomiya JK, L'Italien G, Criqui MH, Whyte JL, Gamst A, Chen RS. Association of the metabolic syndrome with history of myocardial infarction and stroke in the Third National Health and Nutrition Examination Survey. *Circulation* 2004;109(1):42-6.

[72] Kip KE, Marroquin OC, Kelley DE, et al. Clinical importance of obesity versus the metabolic syndrome in cardiovascular risk in women: a report from the Women's Ischemia Syndrome Evaluation (WISE) study. *Circulation* 2004;109(6):706-13.

[73] *The practical guide to the identification, evaluation, and treatment of overweight and obesity in adults.* National Institutes of Health, United States Department of Health and Human Services. Rockville, MD. NIH Publication No. 00-4080. 2000.

[74] *The Surgen General's call to action to prevent and decrease overweight and obesity.* United States Department of Health and Human Servces. Office of the Surgeon General. Rockville, MD. 2001.

[75] Mokdad AH, Ford ES, Bowman BA, et al. Prevalence of obesity, diabetes, and obesity-related health risk factors, 2001. *Jama* 2003;289(1):76-9.

[76] Kopelman PG. Obesity as a medical problem. *Nature* 2000;404(6778):635-43.

[77] Sowers JR. Obesity as a cardiovascular risk factor. *Am J Med* 2003;115 Suppl 8A:37S-41S.

[78] Bray GA. Medical consequences of obesity. *J Clin Endocrinol Metab* 2004;89(6):2583-9.

[79] Ferrannini E, Natali A, Bell P, Cavallo-Perin P, Lalic N, Mingrone G. Insulin resistance and hypersecretion in obesity. European Group for the Study of Insulin Resistance (EGIR). *J Clin Invest* 1997;100(5):1166-73.

[80] Montague CT, O'Rahilly S. The perils of portliness: causes and consequences of visceral adiposity. *Diabetes* 2000;49(6):883-8.

[81] Kelley DE, Williams KV, Price JC, McKolanis TM, Goodpaster BH, Thaete FL. Plasma fatty acids, adiposity, and variance of skeletal muscle insulin resistance in type 2 diabetes mellitus. *J Clin Endocrinol Metab* 2001;86(11):5412-9.

[82] Ferrannini E, Haffner SM, Mitchell BD, Stern MP. Hyperinsulinaemia: the key feature of a cardiovascular and metabolic syndrome. *Diabetologia* 1991;34(6):416-22.

[83] Mokdad AH, Bowman BA, Ford ES, Vinicor F, Marks JS, Koplan JP. The continuing epidemics of obesity and diabetes in the United States. *Jama* 2001;286(10):1195-200.

[84] Hedley AA, Ogden CL, Johnson CL, Carroll MD, Curtin LR, Flegal KM. Prevalence of overweight and obesity among US children, adolescents, and adults, 1999-2002. *Jama* 2004;291(23):2847-50.

[85] Kereiakes DJ, Willerson JT. Metabolic syndrome epidemic. *Circulation* 2003;108(13):1552-3.

[86] HHS, ADA warn Americans of "pre-diabetes", encorage people to take healthy steps to reduce risks. United, States Department of Health and Human Services. Available at: http://www.hhs.gov/news/press/2002press/20020327.html. 2002.

[87] Narayan KM, Boyle JP, Thompson TJ, Sorensen SW, Williamson DF. Lifetime risk for diabetes mellitus in the United States. *Jama* 2003;290(14):1884-90.

[88] Weiss R, Dziura J, Burgert TS, et al. Obesity and the metabolic syndrome in children and adolescents. *N Engl J Med* 2004;350(23):2362-74.

[89] Goodman E, Daniels SR, Morrison JA, Huang B, Dolan LM. Contrasting prevalence of and demographic disparities in the World Health Organization and National Cholesterol Education Program Adult Treatment Panel III definitions of metabolic syndrome among adolescents. *J Pediatr* 2004;145(4):445-51.

[90] Bao W, Srinivasan SR, Wattigney WA, Berenson GS. Persistence of multiple cardiovascular risk clustering related to syndrome X from childhood to young adulthood. The Bogalusa Heart Study. *Arch Intern Med* 1994;154(16):1842-7.

[91] Eisenmann JC, Welk GJ, Wickel EE, Blair SN. Stability of variables associated with the metabolic syndrome from adolescence to adulthood: the Aerobics Center Longitudinal Study. *Am J Hum Biol* 2004;16(6):690-6.

[92] Manson JE, Skerrett PJ, Greenland P, VanItallie TB. The escalating pandemics of obesity and sedentary lifestyle. A call to action for clinicians. *Arch Intern Med* 2004;164(3):249-58.

[93] Thompson D, Wolf AM. The medical-care cost burden of obesity. *Obes Rev* 2001;2(3):189-97.

[94] Hogan P, Dall T, Nikolov P. Economic costs of diabetes in the US in 2002. *Diabetes Care* 2003;26(3):917-32.

[95] Rao SV, Donahue M, Pi-Sunyer FX, Fuster V. Results of Expert Meetings: Obesity and Cardiovascular Disease. Obesity as a risk factor in coronary artery disease. *Am Heart J* 2001;142(6):1102-7.

[96] Kleinman JC, Donahue RP, Harris MI, Finucane FF, Madans JH, Brock DB. Mortality among diabetics in a national sample. *Am J Epidemiol* 1988;128(2):389-401.

[97] McNeill AM, Rosamond WD, Girman CJ, et al. Prevalence of coronary heart disease and carotid arterial thickening in patients with the metabolic syndrome (The ARIC Study). *Am J Cardiol* 2004;94(10):1249-54.

[98] Kullo IJ, Cassidy AE, Peyser PA, Turner ST, Sheedy PF, 2nd, Bielak LF. Association between metabolic syndrome and subclinical coronary atherosclerosis in asymptomatic adults. *Am J Cardiol* 2004;94(12):1554-8.

[99] Turhan H, Erbay AR, Yasar AS, Bicer A, Sasmaz H, Yetkin E. Impaired coronary blood flow in patients with metabolic syndrome: documented by Thrombolysis in Myocardial Infarction (TIMI) frame count method. *Am Heart J* 2004;148(5):789-94.

[100] Howard G, O'Leary DH, Zaccaro D, et al. Insulin sensitivity and atherosclerosis. The Insulin Resistance Atherosclerosis Study (IRAS) Investigators. *Circulation* 1996;93(10):1809-17.

[101] Maison P, Byrne CD, Hales CN, Day NE, Wareham NJ. Do different dimensions of the metabolic syndrome change together over time? Evidence supporting obesity as the central feature. *Diabetes Care* 2001;24(10):1758-63.

[102] Janssen I, Katzmarzyk PT, Ross R. Body mass index, waist circumference, and health risk: evidence in support of current National Institutes of Health guidelines. *Arch Intern Med* 2002;162(18):2074-9.

[103] Carnethon MR, Loria CM, Hill JO, Sidney S, Savage PJ, Liu K. Risk factors for the metabolic syndrome: the Coronary Artery Risk Development in Young Adults (CARDIA) study, 1985-2001. *Diabetes Care* 2004;27(11):2707-15.

[104] Lemieux S, Prud'homme D, Nadeau A, Tremblay A, Bouchard C, Despres JP. Seven-year changes in body fat and visceral adipose tissue in women. Association with indexes of plasma glucose-insulin homeostasis. *Diabetes Care* 1996;19(9):983-91.

[105] Koh-Banerjee P, Wang Y, Hu FB, Spiegelman D, Willett WC, Rimm EB. Changes in body weight and body fat distribution as risk factors for clinical diabetes in US men. *Am J Epidemiol* 2004;159(12):1150-9.

[106] Colditz GA, Willett WC, Rotnitzky A, Manson JE. Weight gain as a risk factor for clinical diabetes mellitus in women. *Ann Intern Med* 1995;122(7):481-6.

[107] Manson JE, Willett WC, Stampfer MJ, et al. Body weight and mortality among women. *N Engl J Med* 1995;333(11):677-85.

[108] Kreuter MW, Scharff DP, Brennan LK, Lukwago SN. Physician recommendations for diet and physical activity: which patients get advised to change? *Prev Med* 1997;26(6):825-33.

[109] Mayer-Davis EJ, Monaco JH, Hoen HM, et al. Dietary fat and insulin sensitivity in a triethnic population: the role of obesity. The Insulin Resistance Atherosclerosis Study (IRAS). *Am J Clin Nutr* 1997;65(1):79-87.

[110] Maron DJ, Fair JM, Haskell WL. Saturated fat intake and insulin resistance in men with coronary artery disease. The Stanford Coronary Risk Intervention Project Investigators and Staff. *Circulation* 1991;84(5):2020-7.

[111] Vessby B. Dietary fat, fatty acid composition in plasma and the metabolic syndrome. *Curr Opin Lipidol* 2003;14(1):15-9.

[112] Laaksonen DE, Lakka TA, Lakka HM, et al. Serum fatty acid composition predicts development of impaired fasting glycaemia and diabetes in middle-aged men. *Diabet Med* 2002;19(6):456-64.

[113] Lovejoy JC, Champagne CM, Smith SR, et al. Relationship of dietary fat and serum cholesterol ester and phospholipid fatty acids to markers of insulin resistance in men and women with a range of glucose tolerance. *Metabolism* 2001;50(1):86-92.

[114] Hu FB, Manson JE, Stampfer MJ, et al. Diet, lifestyle, and the risk of type 2 diabetes mellitus in women. *N Engl J Med* 2001;345(11):790-7.

[115] Salmeron J, Hu FB, Manson JE, et al. Dietary fat intake and risk of type 2 diabetes in women. *Am J Clin Nutr* 2001;73(6):1019-26.

[116] Salmeron J, Manson JE, Stampfer MJ, Colditz GA, Wing AL, Willett WC. Dietary fiber, glycemic load, and risk of non-insulin-dependent diabetes mellitus in women. *Jama* 1997;277(6):472-7.

[117] Ford ES, Mokdad AH, Giles WH, Brown DW. The metabolic syndrome and antioxidant concentrations: findings from the Third National Health and Nutrition Examination Survey. *Diabetes* 2003;52(9):2346-52.

[118] Schulze MB, Liu S, Rimm EB, Manson JE, Willett WC, Hu FB. Glycemic index, glycemic load, and dietary fiber intake and incidence of type 2 diabetes in younger and middle-aged women. *Am J Clin Nutr* 2004;80(2):348-56.

[119] Zhu S, St-Onge MP, Heshka S, Heymsfield SB. Lifestyle behaviors associated with lower risk of having the metabolic syndrome. *Metabolism* 2004;53(11):1503-11.

[120] Ross R, Katzmarzyk PT. Cardiorespiratory fitness is associated with diminished total and abdominal obesity independent of body mass index. *Int J Obes Relat Metab Disord* 2003;27(2):204-10.

[121] Brage S, Wedderkopp N, Ekelund U, et al. Features of the metabolic syndrome are associated with objectively measured physical activity and fitness in Danish children: the European Youth Heart Study (EYHS). *Diabetes Care* 2004;27(9):2141-8.

[122] Franks PW, Ekelund U, Brage S, Wong MY, Wareham NJ. Does the association of habitual physical activity with the metabolic syndrome differ by level of cardiorespiratory fitness? *Diabetes Care* 2004;27(5):1187-93.

[123] Jurca R, Lamonte MJ, Church TS, et al. Associations of muscle strength and fitness with metabolic syndrome in men. *Med Sci Sports Exerc* 2004;36(8):1301-7.

[124] Farrell SW, Cheng YJ, Blair SN. Prevalence of the metabolic syndrome across cardiorespiratory fitness levels in women. *Obes Res* 2004;12(5):824-30.

[125] Leisure-time physical activity. National Health Interview Survey. Available at http://www.cdc.gov/nchs/about/major/nhis/released200412.htm. 2004.

[126] Kimm SY, Glynn NW, Kriska AM, et al. Decline in physical activity in black girls and white girls during adolescence. *N Engl J Med* 2002;347(10):709-15.

[127] Ruderman NB, Schneider SH, Berchtold P. The "metabolically-obese," normal-weight individual. *Am J Clin Nutr* 1981;34(8):1617-21.

[128] Dvorak RV, DeNino WF, Ades PA, Poehlman ET. Phenotypic characteristics associated with insulin resistance in metabolically obese but normal-weight young women. *Diabetes* 1999;48(11):2210-4.

[129] St-Onge MP, Janssen I, Heymsfield SB. Metabolic syndrome in normal-weight Americans: new definition of the metabolically obese, normal-weight individual. *Diabetes Care* 2004;27(9):2222-8.

[130] Nisoli E, Carruba MO. Emerging aspects of pharmacotherapy for obesity and metabolic syndrome. *Pharmacol Res* 2004;50(5):453-69.

[131] Zhu S, Wang Z, Heshka S, Heo M, Faith MS, Heymsfield SB. Waist circumference and obesity-associated risk factors among whites in the third National Health and Nutrition Examination Survey: clinical action thresholds. *Am J Clin Nutr* 2002;76(4):743-9.

[132] Rexrode KM, Carey VJ, Hennekens CH, et al. Abdominal adiposity and coronary heart disease in women. *Jama* 1998;280(21):1843-8.

[133] Wang J. Waist circumference: a simple, inexpensive, and reliable tool that should be included as part of physical examinations in the doctor's office. *Am J Clin Nutr* 2003;78(5):902-3.

[134] Ford ES, Mokdad AH, Giles WH. Trends in waist circumference among U.S. adults. *Obes Res* 2003;11(10):1223-31.

[135] Okosun IS, Choi ST, Boltri JM, et al. Trends of abdominal adiposity in white, black, and Mexican-American adults, 1988 to 2000. *Obes Res* 2003;11(8):1010-7.

[136] Willett WC, Dietz WH, Colditz GA. Guidelines for healthy weight. *N Engl J Med* 1999;341(6):427-34.

[137] Ayyad C, Andersen T. Long-term efficacy of dietary treatment of obesity: a systematic review of studies published between 1931 and 1999. *Obes Rev* 2000;1(2):113-9.

[138] Padwal R, Li SK, Lau DC. Long-term pharmacotherapy for overweight and obesity: a systematic review and meta-analysis of randomized controlled trials. *Int J Obes Relat Metab Disord* 2003;27(12):1437-46.

[139] Panel. NTAC. Methods for voluntary weight loss and control. *Ann Intern Med* 1993;119:764-70.

[140] Wadden TA. Treatment of obesity by moderate and severe caloric restriction. Results of clinical research trials. *Ann Intern Med* 1993;119(7 Pt 2):688-93.

[141] Tuomilehto J, Lindstrom J, Eriksson JG, et al. Prevention of type 2 diabetes mellitus by changes in lifestyle among subjects with impaired glucose tolerance. *N Engl J Med* 2001;344(18):1343-50.

[142] Wassertheil-Smoller S, Blaufox MD, Oberman AS, Langford HG, Davis BR, Wylie-Rosett J. The Trial of Antihypertensive Interventions and Management (TAIM) study. Adequate weight loss, alone and combined with drug therapy in the treatment of mild hypertension. *Arch Intern Med* 1992;152(1):131-6.

[143] Wing RR, Koeske R, Epstein LH, Nowalk MP, Gooding W, Becker D. Long-term effects of modest weight loss in type II diabetic patients. *Arch Intern Med* 1987;147(10):1749-53.

[144] Osterman J, Lin T, Nankin HR, Brown KA, Hornung CA. Serum cholesterol profiles during treatment of obese outpatients with a very low calorie diet. Effect of initial cholesterol levels. *Int J Obes Relat Metab Disord* 1992;16(1):49-58.

[145] Halbert JA, Silagy CA, Finucane P, Withers RT, Hamdorf PA, Andrews GR. The effectiveness of exercise training in lowering blood pressure: a meta-analysis of randomised controlled trials of 4 weeks or longer. *J Hum Hypertens* 1997;11(10):641-9.

[146] Hu FB, Sigal RJ, Rich-Edwards JW, et al. Walking compared with vigorous physical activity and risk of type 2 diabetes in women: a prospective study. *Jama* 1999;282(15):1433-9.

[147] Pan XR, Li GW, Hu YH, et al. Effects of diet and exercise in preventing NIDDM in people with impaired glucose tolerance. The Da Qing IGT and Diabetes Study. *Diabetes Care* 1997;20(4):537-44.

[148] Lindstrom J, Louheranta A, Mannelin M, et al. The Finnish Diabetes Prevention Study (DPS): Lifestyle intervention and 3-year results on diet and physical activity. *Diabetes Care* 2003;26(12):3230-6.

[149] Hardman AE. Interaction of physical activity and diet: implications for lipoprotein metabolism. *Public Health Nutr* 1999;2(3A):369-76.

[150] Knowler WC, Barrett-Connor E, Fowler SE, et al. Reduction in the incidence of type 2 diabetes with lifestyle intervention or metformin. *N Engl J Med* 2002;346(6):393-403.

[151] Eriksson KF, Lindgarde F. Prevention of type 2 (non-insulin-dependent) diabetes mellitus by diet and physical exercise. The 6-year Malmo feasibility study. *Diabetologia* 1991;34(12):891-8.

[152] Yusuf S. Two decades of progress in preventing vascular disease. *Lancet* 2002;360(9326):2-3.

[153] Buchwald H, Avidor Y, Braunwald E, et al. Bariatric surgery: a systematic review and meta-analysis. *Jama* 2004;292(14):1724-37.

[154] Van Gaal LF, Wauters MA, De Leeuw IH. The beneficial effects of modest weight loss on cardiovascular risk factors. *Int J Obes Relat Metab Disord* 1997;21 Suppl 1:S5-9.

[155] Bravata DM, Sanders L, Huang J, Krumholz HM, Olkin I, Gardner CD. Efficacy and safety of low-carbohydrate diets: a systematic review. *Jama* 2003;289(14):1837-50.

[156] Dansinger ML, Gleason JA, Griffith JL, Selker HP, Schaefer EJ. Comparison of the Atkins, Ornish, Weight Watchers, and Zone diets for weight loss and heart disease risk reduction: a randomized trial. *Jama* 2005;293(1):43-53.

[157] *Obesity: preventing and managing the global epidemic.* Report of a WHO Consultation Technical Report Series 894. World Health Organization. Geneva, Switzerland. 2000.

[158] Franz MJ, Bantle JP, Beebe CA, et al. Nutrition principles and recommendations in diabetes. *Diabetes Care* 2004;27 Suppl 1:S36-46.

[159] *Dietary reference intakes for energy, carbohydrate, fiber, fat, fatty acids, cholesterol, protein, and aminoacids (macronutrients).* Institute of Medicine. Washington, DC: National Academy Press;. 2002.

[160] Cummings S, Parham ES, Strain GW. Position of the American Dietetic Association: weight management. *J Am Diet Assoc* 2002;102(8):1145-55.

[161] Krauss RM, Eckel RH, Howard B, et al. AHA Dietary Guidelines: revision 2000: A statement for healthcare professionals from the Nutrition Committee of the American Heart Association. *Circulation* 2000;102(18):2284-99.

[162] Dietary Guidelines for Americans 2005. United States Department of Health and Human Services, Department of Agriculture. Available at *http://www.healthierus.gov/dietaryguidelines/*. 2005.

[163] Sears B LB. *The zone: a dietary road map.* New York, NY: Harper Collins. 1995.

[164] Atkins R. *Dr. Atkin's new diet revolution.* New York, NY: Avon Books. 1998.

[165] Agatston A. *The South Beach diet.* Emmaus, PA: Rodale Press. 2003.

[166] Astrup A. Healthy lifestyles in Europe: prevention of obesity and type II diabetes by diet and physical activity. *Public Health Nutr* 2001;4(2B):499-515.

[167] Knittle JL, Ahrens EH, Jr. Carbohydrate Metabolism in Two Forms of Hyperglyceridemia. *J Clin Invest* 1964;43:485-95.

[168] Katan MB. Effect of low-fat diets on plasma high-density lipoprotein concentrations. *Am J Clin Nutr* 1998;67(3 Suppl):573S-6S.

[169] Rasmussen OW, Thomsen C, Hansen KW, Vesterlund M, Winther E, Hermansen K. Effects on blood pressure, glucose, and lipid levels of a high-monounsaturated fat diet compared with a high-carbohydrate diet in NIDDM subjects. *Diabetes Care* 1993;16(12):1565-71.

[170] Aude YW, Agatston AS, Lopez-Jimenez F, et al. The national cholesterol education program diet vs a diet lower in carbohydrates and higher in protein and monounsaturated fat: a randomized trial. *Arch Intern Med* 2004;164(19):2141-6.

[171] Brehm BJ, Seeley RJ, Daniels SR, D'Alessio DA. A randomized trial comparing a very low carbohydrate diet and a calorie-restricted low fat diet on body weight and cardiovascular risk factors in healthy women. *J Clin Endocrinol Metab* 2003;88(4):1617-23.

[172] Foster GD, Wyatt HR, Hill JO, et al. A randomized trial of a low-carbohydrate diet for obesity. *N Engl J Med* 2003;348(21):2082-90.

[173] Samaha FF, Iqbal N, Seshadri P, et al. A low-carbohydrate as compared with a low-fat diet in severe obesity. *N Engl J Med* 2003;348(21):2074-81.

[174] Stern L, Iqbal N, Seshadri P, et al. The effects of low-carbohydrate versus conventional weight loss diets in severely obese adults: one-year follow-up of a randomized trial. *Ann Intern Med* 2004;140(10):778-85.

[175] Brinkworth GD, Noakes M, Keogh JB, Luscombe ND, Wittert GA, Clifton PM. Long-term effects of a high-protein, low-carbohydrate diet on weight control and cardiovascular risk markers in obese hyperinsulinemic subjects. *Int J Obes Relat Metab Disord* 2004;28(5):661-70.

[176] Case CC, Jones PH, Nelson K, O'Brian Smith E, Ballantyne CM. Impact of weight loss on the metabolic syndrome. *Diabetes Obes Metab* 2002;4(6):407-14.

[177] Esposito K, Marfella R, Ciotola M, et al. Effect of a mediterranean-style diet on endothelial dysfunction and markers of vascular inflammation in the metabolic syndrome: a randomized trial. *Jama* 2004;292(12):1440-6.

[178] Bray GA. Low-carbohydrate diets and realities of weight loss. *Jama* 2003;289(14):1853-5.

[179] Connor WE, Connor SL. Should a low-fat, high-carbohydrate diet be recommended for everyone? The case for a low-fat, high-carbohydrate diet. *N Engl J Med* 1997;337(8):562-3; discussion 6-7.

[180] Yancy WS, Jr., Olsen MK, Guyton JR, Bakst RP, Westman EC. A low-carbohydrate, ketogenic diet versus a low-fat diet to treat obesity and hyperlipidemia: a randomized, controlled trial. *Ann Intern Med* 2004;140(10):769-77.

[181] Poppitt SD, Keogh GF, Prentice AM, et al. Long-term effects of ad libitum low-fat, high-carbohydrate diets on body weight and serum lipids in overweight subjects with metabolic syndrome. *Am J Clin Nutr* 2002;75(1):11-20.

[182] Chiasson JL, Josse RG, Gomis R, Hanefeld M, Karasik A, Laakso M. Acarbose for prevention of type 2 diabetes mellitus: the STOP-NIDDM randomised trial. *Lancet* 2002;359(9323):2072-7.

[183] Sacks FM, Svetkey LP, Vollmer WM, et al. Effects on blood pressure of reduced dietary sodium and the Dietary Approaches to Stop Hypertension (DASH) diet. DASH-Sodium Collaborative Research Group. *N Engl J Med* 2001;344(1):3-10.

[184] Chiasson JL, Josse RG, Gomis R, Hanefeld M, Karasik A, Laakso M. Acarbose treatment and the risk of cardiovascular disease and hypertension in patients with impaired glucose tolerance: the STOP-NIDDM trial. *Jama* 2003;290(4):486-94.

[185] Wood PD, Stefanick ML, Williams PT, Haskell WL. The effects on plasma lipoproteins of a prudent weight-reducing diet, with or without exercise, in overweight men and women. *N Engl J Med* 1991;325(7):461-6.

[186] Pate RR, Pratt M, Blair SN, et al. Physical activity and public health. A recommendation from the Centers for Disease Control and Prevention and the American College of Sports Medicine. *Jama* 1995;273(5):402-7.

[187] Physical activity and cardiovascular health. NIH Consensus Development Panel on Physical Activity and Cardiovascular Health. *Jama* 1996;276(3):241-6.

[188] Tanasescu M, Leitzmann MF, Rimm EB, Hu FB. Physical activity in relation to cardiovascular disease and total mortality among men with type 2 diabetes. *Circulation* 2003;107(19):2435-9.

[189] Cullinen K, Caldwell M. Weight training increases fat-free mass and strength in untrained young women. *J Am Diet Assoc* 1998;98(4):414-8.

[190] Mazzetti SA, Kraemer WJ, Volek JS, et al. The influence of direct supervision of resistance training on strength performance. *Med Sci Sports Exerc* 2000;32(6):1175-84.

[191] Feigenbaum MS, Pollock ML. Prescription of resistance training for health and disease. *Med Sci Sports Exerc* 1999;31(1):38-45.

[192] Thompson PD, Buchner D, Pina IL, et al. Exercise and physical activity in the prevention and treatment of atherosclerotic cardiovascular disease: a statement from the Council on Clinical Cardiology (Subcommittee on Exercise, Rehabilitation, and Prevention) and the Council on Nutrition, Physical Activity, and Metabolism (Subcommittee on Physical Activity). *Circulation* 2003;107(24):3109-16.

[193] Pollock ML, Gaesser GA, Butcher JD, et al. ACSM position stand: the recommended quantity and quality of exercise for developing and maintaining cardiorespiratory and muscular fitness, and flexibility in healthy adults. *Med Sci Sports Exerc* 1998;30(6):975-91.

[194] Fletcher GF. How to implement physical activity in primary and secondary prevention. A statement for healthcare-professionals from the Task Force on Risk-reduction, American Heart Association. *Circulation* 1997;96(1):355-7.

[195] *American College of Sports Medicine. Guidelines for exercise testing and prescription, 6th ed.* Baltimore, MD: Lippincott Williams & Wilkins;. 2000.

[196] Durstine JL, Haskell WL. Effects of exercise training on plasma lipids and lipoproteins. *Exerc Sport Sci Rev* 1994;22:477-521.

[197] Durstine JL, Grandjean PW, Cox CA, Thompson PD. Lipids, lipoproteins, and exercise. *J Cardiopulm Rehabil* 2002;22(6):385-98.

[198] Halbert JA, Silagy CA, Finucane P, Withers RT, Hamdorf PA. Exercise training and blood lipids in hyperlipidemic and normolipidemic adults: a meta-analysis of randomized, controlled trials. *Eur J Clin Nutr* 1999;53(7):514-22.

[199] Tucker LA, Silvester LJ. Strength training and hypercholesterolemia: an epidemiologic study of 8499 employed men. *Am J Health Promot* 1996;11(1):35-41.

[200] Christ M, Iannello C, Iannello PG, Grimm W. Effects of a weight reduction program with and without aerobic exercise in the metabolic syndrome. *Int J Cardiol* 2004;97(1):115-22.

[201] Couillard C, Despres JP, Lamarche B, et al. Effects of endurance exercise training on plasma HDL cholesterol levels depend on levels of triglycerides: evidence from men of the Health, Risk Factors, Exercise Training and Genetics (HERITAGE) Family Study. *Arterioscler Thromb Vasc Biol* 2001;21(7):1226-32.

[202] Goodyear LJ, Kahn BB. Exercise, glucose transport, and insulin sensitivity. *Annu Rev Med* 1998;49:235-61.

[203] Duncan GE, Perri MG, Theriaque DW, Hutson AD, Eckel RH, Stacpoole PW. Exercise training, without weight loss, increases insulin sensitivity and postheparin plasma lipase activity in previously sedentary adults. *Diabetes Care* 2003;26(3):557-62.

[204] McAuley KA, Williams SM, Mann JI, et al. Intensive lifestyle changes are necessary to improve insulin sensitivity: a randomized controlled trial. *Diabetes Care* 2002;25(3):445-52.

[205] Van Hoof R, Hespel P, Fagard R, Lijnen P, Staessen J, Amery A. Effect of endurance training on blood pressure at rest, during exercise and during 24 hours in sedentary men. *Am J Cardiol* 1989;63(13):945-9.

[206] Gilders RM, Dudley GA. Endurance exercise training and treatment of hypertension. The controversy. *Sports Med* 1992;13(2):71-7.

[207] Pai JK, Pischon T, Ma J, et al. Inflammatory markers and the risk of coronary heart disease in men and women. *N Engl J Med* 2004;351(25):2599-610.

[208] Wannamethee SG, Lowe GD, Whincup PH, Rumley A, Walker M, Lennon L. Physical activity and hemostatic and inflammatory variables in elderly men. *Circulation* 2002;105(15):1785-90.

[209] Pischon T, Hankinson SE, Hotamisligil GS, Rifai N, Rimm EB. Leisure-time physical activity and reduced plasma levels of obesity-related inflammatory markers. *Obes Res* 2003;11(9):1055-64.

[210] Troseid M, Lappegard KT, Claudi T, et al. Exercise reduces plasma levels of the chemokines MCP-1 and IL-8 in subjects with the metabolic syndrome. *Eur Heart J* 2004;25(4):349-55.

[211] Dujovne CA, Zavoral JH, Rowe E, Mendel CM. Effects of sibutramine on body weight and serum lipids: a double-blind, randomized, placebo-controlled study in 322 overweight and obese patients with dyslipidemia. *Am Heart J* 2001;142(3):489-97.

[212] Hollander PA, Elbein SC, Hirsch IB, et al. Role of orlistat in the treatment of obese patients with type 2 diabetes. A 1-year randomized double-blind study. *Diabetes Care* 1998;21(8):1288-94.

[213] Ballinger A, Peikin SR. Orlistat: its current status as an anti-obesity drug. *Eur J Pharmacol* 2002;440(2-3):109-17.

[214] Torgerson JS, Hauptman J, Boldrin MN, Sjostrom L. XENical in the prevention of diabetes in obese subjects (XENDOS) study: a randomized study of orlistat as an adjunct to lifestyle changes for the prevention of type 2 diabetes in obese patients. *Diabetes Care* 2004;27(1):155-61.

[215] Reaven G, Segal K, Hauptman J, Boldrin M, Lucas C. Effect of orlistat-assisted weight loss in decreasing coronary heart disease risk in patients with syndrome X. *Am J Cardiol* 2001;87(7):827-31.

[216] Didangelos TP, Thanopoulou AK, Bousboulas SH, et al. The ORLIstat and CArdiovascular risk profile in patients with metabolic syndrome and type 2 DIAbetes (ORLICARDIA) Study. *Curr Med Res Opin* 2004;20(9):1393-401.

[217] Pasquali R, Gambineri A, Biscotti D, et al. Effect of long-term treatment with metformin added to hypocaloric diet on body composition, fat distribution, and androgen and insulin levels in abdominally obese women with and without the polycystic ovary syndrome. *J Clin Endocrinol Metab* 2000;85(8):2767-74.

[218] Gokcel A, Gumurdulu Y, Karakose H, et al. Evaluation of the safety and efficacy of sibutramine, orlistat and metformin in the treatment of obesity. *Diabetes Obes Metab* 2002;4(1):49-55.

[219] Freemark M, Bursey D. The effects of metformin on body mass index and glucose tolerance in obese adolescents with fasting hyperinsulinemia and a family history of type 2 diabetes. *Pediatrics* 2001;107(4):E55.

[220] Yki-Jarvinen H, Nikkila K, Makimattila S. Metformin prevents weight gain by reducing dietary intake during insulin therapy in patients with type 2 diabetes mellitus. *Drugs* 1999;58 Suppl 1:53-4; discussion 75-82.

[221] Stumvoll M, Nurjhan N, Perriello G, Dailey G, Gerich JE. Metabolic effects of metformin in non-insulin-dependent diabetes mellitus. *N Engl J Med* 1995;333(9):550-4.

[222] Effect of intensive blood-glucose control with metformin on complications in overweight patients with type 2 diabetes (UKPDS 34). UK Prospective Diabetes Study (UKPDS) Group. *Lancet* 1998;352(9131):854-65.

[223] Pollare T, Lithell H, Berne C. A comparison of the effects of hydrochlorothiazide and captopril on glucose and lipid metabolism in patients with hypertension. *N Engl J Med* 1989;321(13):868-73.

[224] Hansson L, Lindholm LH, Niskanen L, et al. Effect of angiotensin-converting-enzyme inhibition compared with conventional therapy on cardiovascular morbidity and mortality in hypertension: the Captopril Prevention Project (CAPPP) randomised trial. *Lancet* 1999;353(9153):611-6.

[225] Yusuf S, Sleight P, Pogue J, Bosch J, Davies R, Dagenais G. Effects of an angiotensin-converting-enzyme inhibitor, ramipril, on cardiovascular events in high-risk patients. The Heart Outcomes Prevention Evaluation Study Investigators. *N Engl J Med* 2000;342(3):145-53.

[226] Lindholm LH, Ibsen H, Dahlof B, et al. Cardiovascular morbidity and mortality in patients with diabetes in the Losartan Intervention For Endpoint reduction in hypertension study (LIFE): a randomised trial against atenolol. *Lancet* 2002;359(9311):1004-10.

[227] Julius S, Kjeldsen SE, Weber M, et al. Outcomes in hypertensive patients at high cardiovascular risk treated with regimens based on valsartan or amlodipine: the VALUE randomised trial. *Lancet* 2004;363(9426):2022-31.

[228] Wilhelmsen L, Pyorala K, Wedel H, Cook T, Pedersen T, Kjekshus J. Risk factors for a major coronary event after myocardial infarction in the Scandinavian Simvastatin Survival Study (4S). Impact of predicted risk on the benefit of cholesterol-lowering treatment. *Eur Heart* J 2001;22(13):1119-27.

[229] Collins R, Armitage J, Parish S, Sleigh P, Peto R. MRC/BHF Heart Protection Study of cholesterol-lowering with simvastatin in 5963 people with diabetes: a randomised placebo-controlled trial. *Lancet* 2003;361(9374):2005-16.

[230] Sacks FM, Tonkin AM, Craven T, et al. Coronary heart disease in patients with low LDL-cholesterol: benefit of pravastatin in diabetics and enhanced role for HDL-cholesterol and triglycerides as risk factors. *Circulation* 2002;105(12):1424-8.

[231] Colhoun HM, Betteridge DJ, Durrington PN, et al. Primary prevention of cardiovascular disease with atorvastatin in type 2 diabetes in the Collaborative Atorvastatin Diabetes Study (CARDS): multicentre randomised placebo-controlled trial. *Lancet* 2004;364(9435):685-96.

[232] Pyorala K, Ballantyne CM, Gumbiner B, et al. Reduction of cardiovascular events by simvastatin in nondiabetic coronary heart disease patients with and without the metabolic syndrome: subgroup analyses of the Scandinavian Simvastatin Survival Study (4S). *Diabetes Care* 2004;27(7):1735-40.

[233] Sever PS, Dahlof B, Poulter NR, et al. Prevention of coronary and stroke events with atorvastatin in hypertensive patients who have average or lower-than-average cholesterol concentrations, in the Anglo-Scandinavian Cardiac Outcomes Trial--Lipid Lowering Arm (ASCOT-LLA): a multicentre randomised controlled trial. *Lancet* 2003;361(9364):1149-58.

[234] Freeman DJ, Norrie J, Sattar N, et al. Pravastatin and the development of diabetes mellitus: evidence for a protective treatment effect in the West of Scotland Coronary Prevention Study. *Circulation* 2001;103(3):357-62.

[235] Tenkanen L, Manttari M, Manninen V. Some coronary risk factors related to the insulin resistance syndrome and treatment with gemfibrozil. Experience from the Helsinki Heart Study. *Circulation* 1995;92(7):1779-85.

[236] Robins SJ, Rubins HB, Faas FH, et al. Insulin resistance and cardiovascular events with low HDL cholesterol: the Veterans Affairs HDL Intervention Trial (VA-HIT). *Diabetes Care* 2003;26(5):1513-7.

[237] Durbin RJ. Thiazolidinedione therapy in the prevention/delay of type 2 diabetes in patients with impaired glucose tolerance and insulin resistance. *Diabetes Obes Metab* 2004;6(4):280-5.

[238] Buchanan TA, Xiang AH, Peters RK, et al. Preservation of pancreatic beta-cell function and prevention of type 2 diabetes by pharmacological treatment of insulin resistance in high-risk hispanic women. *Diabetes* 2002;51(9):2796-803.

[239] Chilcott J, Tappenden P, Jones ML, Wight JP. A systematic review of the clinical effectiveness of pioglitazone in the treatment of type 2 diabetes mellitus. *Clin Ther* 2001;23(11):1792-823; discussion 1.

[240] Freed MI, Ratner R, Marcovina SM, et al. Effects of rosiglitazone alone and in combination with atorvastatin on the metabolic abnormalities in type 2 diabetes mellitus. *Am J Cardiol* 2002;90(9):947-52.

[241] Rutter MK, Meigs JB, Sullivan LM, D'Agostino RB, Sr., Wilson PW. C-reactive protein, the metabolic syndrome, and prediction of cardiovascular events in the Framingham Offspring Study. *Circulation* 2004;110(4):380-5.

[242] Costa A, Casamitjana R, Casals E, et al. Effects of atorvastatin on glucose homeostasis, postprandial triglyceride response and C-reactive protein in subjects with impaired fasting glucose. *Diabet Med* 2003;20(9):743-5.

[243] Despres JP, Lemieux I, Pascot A, et al. Gemfibrozil reduces plasma C-reactive protein levels in abdominally obese men with the atherogenic dyslipidemia of the metabolic syndrome. *Arterioscler Thromb Vasc Biol* 2003;23(4):702-3.

[244] Haffner SM, Greenberg AS, Weston WM, Chen H, Williams K, Freed MI. Effect of rosiglitazone treatment on nontraditional markers of cardiovascular disease in patients with type 2 diabetes mellitus. *Circulation* 2002;106(6):679-84.

[245] Sola S, Mir MQ, Cheema FA, et al. Irbesartan and lipoic acid improve endothelial function and reduce markers of inflammation in the metabolic syndrome: results of the Irbesartan and Lipoic Acid in Endothelial Dysfunction (ISLAND) study. *Circulation* 2005;111(3):343-8.

[246] Pories WJ, Swanson MS, MacDonald KG, et al. Who would have thought it? An operation proves to be the most effective therapy for adult-onset diabetes mellitus. *Ann Surg* 1995;222(3):339-50; discussion 50-2.

[247] Yusuf S, Hawken S, Ounpuu S, et al. Effect of potentially modifiable risk factors associated with myocardial infarction in 52 countries (the INTERHEART study): case-control study. *Lancet* 2004;364(9438):937-52.

[248] Wong ND, Pio JR, Franklin SS, L'Italien GJ, Kamath TV, Williams GR. Preventing coronary events by optimal control of blood pressure and lipids in patients with the metabolic syndrome. *Am J Cardiol* 2003;91(12):1421-6.

[249] Gaede P, Vedel P, Larsen N, Jensen GV, Parving HH, Pedersen O. Multifactorial intervention and cardiovascular disease in patients with type 2 diabetes. *N Engl J Med* 2003;348(5):383-93.

[250] Eyre H, Kahn R, Robertson RM, et al. Preventing cancer, cardiovascular disease, and diabetes: a common agenda for the American Cancer Society, the American Diabetes Association, and the American Heart Association. *Circulation* 2004;109(25):3244-55.

In: Metabolic Syndrome Research Trends
Editor: Thomas E. Batone, pp. 225-233
ISBN: 978-1-60456-224-8

Chapter IX

Comparing the Definitions of WHO and ATPIII Metabolic Syndrome (MS) in School Children

V. Hirschler[1], C. Aranda[2], G. Maccalini[2], C. Gonzalez[3] and M. Jadzinsky[1]
[1] Durand Hospital, Nutrition, Buenos Aires, Argentina
[2] Durand Hospital, Laboratorio Central, Buenos Aires, Argentina
[3] University Buenos Aires, Farmacologia, Buenos Aires, Argentina

Abstract

Studies indicate that MS starts in children. The purpose was to determine: a) the prevalence of MS among children using ATPIII defined MS and WHO defined MS, as well as b) the agreement between both definitions. We evaluated 478 (221M) school children aged 9.62 years between April and July 2005. Data for BMI, waist circumference (WC), blood pressure (BP), Tanner, OGTT, lipid profile and insulinemia were obtained. The presence of MS was determined using two different criteria: a) analogous to ATPIII (de Ferranti Circulation 110: 2494-97, 2004) and b) analogous to WHO guidelines. WHO guidelines were defined as insulin resistance (>=HOMA-IR III quartile) or fasting glucose >100 mg/dL and at least two of the following criteria: WC 75%ile , BP>95%ile; HDL<5%ile; triglycerides>95%ile , urinary albumin excretion (UAE) III quartile was assessed. Of 478 children examined, 87 (18.2%) were OW (BMI>95%ile, z-BMI=2.0.3), 126 (26%) at risk of OW (BMI>85<95%ile; z-BMI=1.31) and 265 (55.4%) non-OW (BMI<85%ile; z-BMI= -0.03). Two hundred forty-eight (57.6%) were Tanner 1. There was a higher ($p<0.01$) prevalence of WHO-defined MS (10.8%; n=52) than ATPIII-defined MS (5.3%; n=26). However, mean values for HOMA-IR (4.3 vs 3.9), systolic BP (99 vs 97 mmHg), TG (144 vs 158 mg/dl), HDL-C (42 vs 40mg/dl), fasting glucose (89 vs 91mg/dl), and UAE (1.1 vs 1.5mg/l) were not significantly different by either definition. No age or sex differences were found either. Agreement between definitions was poor (Kappa 0.34; 95% CI 0.19-0.48 $p<0.001$). Results indicate that there was a higher prevalence of WHO-defined MS and agreement between both definitions was poor. These differences suggest that the concept of a common MS defined by these two guidelines may be flawed.

Introduction

Childhood obesity has contributed to an increased incidence of type 2 diabetes mellitus and metabolic syndrome (MS) among children. There are a number of risk factors for type 2 diabetes among children and adults associated with overweight. The MS, which predisposes individuals to diabetes and cardiovascular disease had been already described in adults [1]. There is a growing body of evidence on the prevalence of components of the MS among obese children and adolescents [2,3]. This raises great concern about the potential development of not only diabetes but also early stages of cardiovascular disease in childhood [4].

The MS is a clustering of cardiovascular risk factors that include elevated blood pressure, dyslipidemia (high triglycerides and low high-density lipoprotein [HDL] cholesterol), impaired glucose metabolism with insulin resistance, and obesity. This syndrome represents a high-risk state that corresponds to an increased risk of developing type 2 diabetes mellitus and premature cardiovascular disease in adults [5,6]. The MS has now been linked as a comorbid condition associated with the childhood obesity epidemic [7].

The increased prevalence of obesity in the pediatric population has been associated with an increase in the MS. Both the National Cholesterol Education Program Adult Treatment Panel III (ATPIII) [8] and the World Health Organization (WHO) criteria [9] for MS predict cardiovascular disease in adults. Only the WHO criteria require evidence of insulin resistance or abnormality in carbohydrate metabolism.

The aim of this population-based cohort study was to compare frequency, concordance, clinical and laboratory stigmata with those of the established definitions by the National Cholesterol Education Program (ATPIII) and World Health Organization (WHO). in a school cohort of children. The purpose was to determine: a) the prevalence of MS among children using ATPIII defined MS and WHO defined MS, b) the agreement between both definitions.

Participants

The data were collected cross-sectionally from 478 (221M) school children from 5 schools, aged 9.62 years between April and July 2005.The sampling design of the survey was a two-stage probability sample. The first stage was the selection of the schools, and the second stage consisted of an invitation to all the students and their mothers to undergo testing. The overall response rate was 80.2% of mothers and students. There was not a significant difference in the mean age, BMI, sex, and socioeconomic class among all the school children and those who underwent testing. The Tanner stage of 25 children was not assessed because children did not agree to be examined.

Data for BMI, waist circumference (WC), blood pressure, Tanner stage, serum glucose levels, and serum lipids were obtained. Argentinians are an ethnically mixed population, with a high prevalence of Caucasians, a low prevalence of Hispanics and very low prevalence of Africans. Exclusion criteria included: missing BMI information; not in the fasting state for at least 8 hours; known diabetes or other chronic diseases; and the use of medication that alters blood pressure or glucose or lipid metabolism. All subjects were examined by the same physician. The study was approved by the Human Rights Committee of Durand Hospital in Buenos Aires. Each subject and parent gave written informed consent after an explanation of the study and before its initiation.

Height and weight were measured with subjects wearing light clothing and without shoes. Height was measured to the nearest 0.1 cm. with a wall-mounted stadiometer. Weight was measured to the nearest 0.1 kg on a medical balance scale. BMI was calculated as weight in kilograms divided by height in meters squared. Normal weight children were defined as having a BMI $\leq 85^{th}$ percentile. Overweight and obesity were defined as a BMI 85th to 94th and $\geq 95^{th}$ percentile, respectively, for age and sex according to the Centers for Disease Control standards for US children. BMI z-score (BMI-z) was also determined [10].

WC measurement was taken at the level of the umbilicus and recorded to 0.1cm. A non-elastic flexible tape measure was employed with the subject standing without clothing covering the waist area. Because WC varies according to age and sex we standardized values for age and sex by converting them to z scores. Central obesity was defined for children as WC >75 %ile based on 5000 normal Argentinian children (unpublished data) and WC > 88cm for their mothers.

Urinary albumin creatinine ratio (UAC), and urinary albumin excretion (UAE) on a spot urine were recorded. UAE was used instead of UAC as there was a strong association between them (rho 0.9 $p<0.01$). Because the distribution of UAE was skewed the natural logarithm of UAE (median 2.36+/-2.56) was used for analysis. Microlabuminuria was defined as UAE> III quartile.

Three separate blood pressure measurements were recorded by a trained technician using a random-zero sphygmomanometer after the participant was seated at rest for 5 minutes. The averages of the last 2 measurements of systolic and diastolic blood pressures were used. Because normal pediatric blood pressure varies significantly, we used the National Heart, Lung and Blood Institute's recommended cutpoint for age, gender, and height [11].

Children had oral fasting glucose, lipid profile, and insulin assays. Insulin resistance was assessed by homeostasis model assessment (HOMA-IR). HOMA-IR was validated in children and adolescents and was strongly correlated with insulin resistance [12]. The following equation for HOMA-IR was used: fasting insulin (uU/l) x fasting glucose (mmol/l)/22.5 [13,14]. Insulin-resistance was defined as the upper quartile of HOMA-IR. The upper quartile of insulin resistance for all children was >2.54.

Definition of Metabolic Syndrome

Although they share common parameters, the WHO and ATPIII definitions of MS differ significantly. The WHO guidelines defined as insulin resistance (assessed by HOMA-IR> III quartile; 2.54) or fasting glucose $\geq$ 100 mg/dL and at least two of the following criteria: waist circumference >75%ile based on our measurements of normal children, blood pressure(BP) > 95%ile (Task force cut point); HDL <5%ile; triglycerides >95%ile adjusted for age and sex, and urinary albumin excretion (UAE) > III quartile. In contrast, to have ATPIII- defined MS, the presence of 3 of 5 possible risk factors was required, including hypertension, low HDL-C, hypertriglyceridemia, hyperglycemia, or high waist circumference. Risk factor cut-points are those used among adults except in relation to obesity, which was defined by using the waist circumference > 75th percentile.

Table 1. Criteria analogous to ATPIII : ≥3 of the following[3]

High Triglycerides	> 95th percentile for age and sex
HDL	< 5th percentile for age and sex
Fasting glucose	> 100 mg/dL ADA new criteria
WC	>75th percentile for age and sex *
Blood Pressure	> 90th percentile for age sex and height

Table 2. Criteria analogous to WHO: Insulin resistance assessed by HOMA-IR≥ III quartile and/or fasting glucose>100 mg% and 2 of the following criteria

High Triglycerides	> 95th percentile for age and sex
HDL	< 5th percentile for age and sex
WC	>75th percentile for age and sex *
Blood Pressure	> 95th percentile for age sex and height
UAE	> III Quartile adjusted by age and sex

*based on our measurements of 5130 normal children (unpublished data).

Notably, the ATPIII definition does not include a measure of insulin resistance. According to the ATPIII, MS is a precursor to, but does not include, type 2 diabetes mellitus, whereas the WHO criteria consider MS and diabetes to be intersecting diagnostic categories [7, 8, 9].

Results

Of 478 children examined, 87 (18.2%) were OW (BMI>95%ile, z-BMI=2.0.3), 126 (26%) at risk of OW (BMI>85<95%ile; z-BMI=1.31) and 265 (55.4%) non-OW (BMI<85%ile; z-BMI= -0.03). Two hundred forty eight (57.6%) were Tanner 1, 110 (23%) Tanner II, 76 (16%) Tanner III, and 19 (4%) Tanner IV.

The prevalence of Risk Factors for the MS in the sample was: Low HDL 40.1%, waist circumference >75 percentile 25.6%, and high triglycerides 25.2% were common in this sample. Hypertension 2.7%, and hyperglycemia 3.3% were infrequent (Figure 1). There were not significant differences in age or sex between both groups.

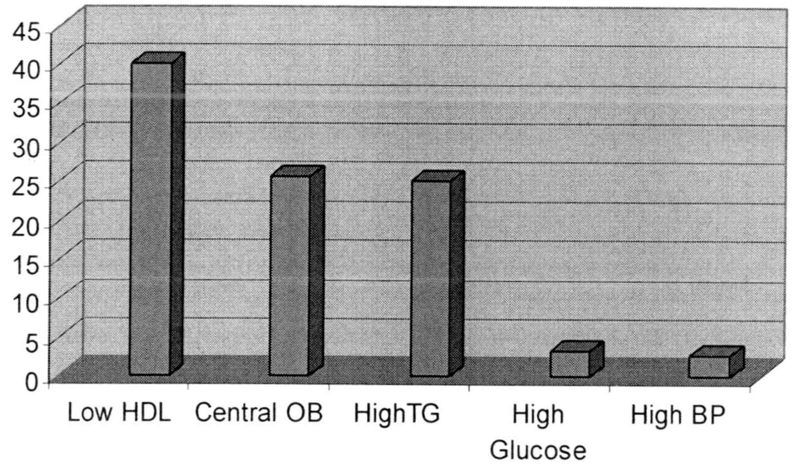

Figure 1.

There was a higher (p<0.01) prevalence of WHO-defined MS (10.8%; n=52) than ATPIII-defined MS (5.3%; n=26). Among OW children the prevalence of WHO-MS was 20.2% and ATPIII-MS was 10.1%. Application of the WHO guidelines classified approximately twice as many children as the ATPIII guidelines.

Clinical and metabolic characteristics of the sample are displayed in Table 3. Mean values for clinical and metabolic features were not significantly different when children were evaluated by either definition. No age or sex differences were found either. Agreement between definitions was poor (Kappa 0.34; 95% CI 0.19-0.48 p<0.001).

Table 3. Comparison of individual risk factors between ATPIII and WHO definitions

	WHO	ATPIII
Prevalence (%) **	10.8	5.3
Gender (M/F) *	19/33	12/14
Z-BMI *	1.2 + 0.9	1.3 + 0.9
Systolic BP (mmHg) *	99.6 + 13.7	96.9 + 16.4
Abuminuria (Median) (mg/l) *	1.1	1.5
HOMA*	4.3 + 2.0	3.9 + 3.0
Triglycerides (mg/dL) *	144.4 + 71.4	158.7 + 80.2
HDL (mg/dL) *	41.9 + 6.1	40.1 + 6.6
Glycemia (mg/dL) *	89.3 + 8.3	90.9 + 10

* Non significant ** P<0.01.

Discussion

Overweight prevalence tripled in children and adolescents aged 6 to 19 years between 1980 and 2002 [15,16]. This study showed that more than 45% of our participants had a BMI at or above the 85th percentile, identifying also a high prevalence of the MS in a population of school children. These are the first findings to apply both the ATPIII adult definition from the 3rd Adult Treatment Panel of the National Cholesterol Education Panel (ATPIII) and the World Health Organization (WHO) adult definition for the MS to a sample of Argentine school children. The Prevalence of WHO defined MS was higher ($p<0.01$) (10.8%) than ATPIII-defined MS (5.3%). Among overweight children the prevalence of WHO-defined MS was 20.2% and ATPIII-defined MS was 10.1%. This means that being overweight doubled the risk of having MS. Given the rising rates of overweight and obesity among children, these data suggest that the prevalence of MS among children will increase unless effective obesity prevention efforts can be implemented for youths.

Two studies contrasted these definitions among adults and found important differences in case identification and prognostic ability [5,17]. Although prevalence of MS was higher when the WHO guidelines were used, the prevalence of MS is this sample of children was much lower than that reported among adults, irrespective of the guideline used to define it. In adults there was a higher prevalence of WHO-defined MS than ATPIII defined MS(17.8% for NCEP and 34.1% for WHO) [18]. Consistent with our study Goodman et al showed that the prevalence of NCEP-defined MS was 4.2% and of WHO-defined MS was 8.4% in adolescents [19], also they did not find sex differences between children with MS.

One step in this process may involve the use of waist circumference measurement in children and adolescents to measure central adiposity. The increase in prevalence of MS parallels the increased prevalence in obesity. Waist circumference is associated with insulin resistance, and has been shown to predict cardiovascular disease and visceral fat better than BMI in adults. Using ATPIII data, we have recently developed optimal waist circumference thresholds for the prediction of risk factor clustering for children from elementary schools. Finding that subjects with high waist circumference values had a greater health risk compared with those with low waist circumference implies that it is important to have a pediatric threshold for sex and age. We have recently found [20] that the optimal waist circumference threshold corresponded to the 71.3th percentile with a sensitivity of 59% and a specificity of 63% for elementary schoolchildren. Waist circumference cutoff values at the 75th percentile, which corresponds to the 71.3th percentile in our sample, could be the ideal threshold values to denote an increased risk. Consistent with our study, de Ferranti et al. [21] described MS in adolescents and considered waist circumference ≥75th percentile as the optimal threshold, which corresponds to the waist circumference of adult males at or above the 72nd percentile (ATPIII). On the other hand, [22] reported sex-, race-, and age-specific waist circumference percentiles in a large representative sample of U.S. youths. In that study, the waist circumference cutoff at the 90th percentile for 13-year-old black girls exceeds the waist circumference value of 88 cm, identified as the cutoff for increased metabolic dysfunction in adult women.

This provides important normative data for practitioners to use to stratify risk in their patients. Waist circumference requires only the removal of clothing around the waist and an inexpensive tape measure made of nonstretchable material [23]. Waist circumference has a low intra-observer and inter-observer error rate, and is usually simple to measure after a short training period [24, 25]. Therefore those children who had waist circumferences on the 75th and 90th percentile for age, and sex were at increased risk for the co-morbidities of hypertension, dyslipidemia, and diabetes. Routine waist circumference measurement in the paediatric population could be clinically useful.

The cross-sectional design of this study precludes any causal inferences and limits assumptions regarding duration for all of the risk factors. The definition used for the MS [7] was devised for older children; and in our study approximately 60% of the children were prepubertal; thus, our findings can only be viewed as MS rates. Moreover, the use of the Adult Treatment Panel III guidelines adapted to adolescents of a unique cutoff value for triglycerides and HDL cholesterol during childhood may lead to misclassification of dyslipidemia [26]. Further longitudinal research will be needed to fully understand the developmental trajectory of MS. Such research will also help clarify whether those who have MS as children have greater risk for type 2 diabetes and cardiovascular disease than those who have MS in their adult years.

Our results indicate that there was a high prevalence of the MS in healthy children between ages 5 and 13 driven mostly by the increase in obesity. There was a higher prevalence of WHO-defined MS than ATPIII –defined MS. These findings indicate that application of the WHO guidelines classified approximately twice as many children as having MS compared to the NCEP guidelines. The classification of MS in children depends strongly on the definition chosen, with MS prevalence estimates higher if insulin is part of the definition and child-specific cut points for metabolic indicators are used. Hyperinsulinaemia and MS are common consequences of childhood obesity. [27]. The agreement between both definitions was poor. These differences suggest that the concept of a common MS defined by these two guidelines may be flawed. The development of a definition of MS applicable to pediatric practice is lacking, highlighting a need for a universal definition of the MS.

References

Reaven GM. Role of insulin in human disease. *Diabetes*. 1988;37 :1595 –1607

Arslanian S, Suprasongsin C. Insulin sensitivity, lipids, and body composition in childhood: is syndrome X present? *J. Clin. Endocrinol. Metab.* 1996;81 :1058 –1062, 7

Weiss R, Dziura J, Burgert T, et al. Obesity and the MS in children and adolescents. *N. Engl. J. Med.* 2004;350 :2362 –2374

Davis C, Kapuku G, Snieder H, Kumar M, Treiber F. Insulin resistance syndrome and left ventricular mass in healthy young people. *Am. J. Med. Sci.* 2002;324 :72 –75

Laaksonen D.E., Lakka H.M., Niskanen L.K., Kaplan G.A., Salonen J.T., Lakka T.A., Metabolic syndrome and development of diabetes mellitus: application and validation of recently suggested definitions of the metabolic syndrome in a prospective cohort study. *Am. J. Epidemiol.* (2002) 156 : pp 1070-1077.

Lakka H.M., Laaksonen D.E., Lakka T.A., Niskanen L.K., Kumpusalo E., Tuomilehto J., The metabolic syndrome and total and cardiovascular disease mortality in middle-aged men. *JAMA*. (2002) 288 : pp 2709-2716.

Cook S., Weitzman M., Auinger P., Nguyen M., Dietz W.H., Prevalence of a metabolic syndrome phenotype in adolescents: findings from the third National Health and Nutrition Examination Survey, 1988-1994. *Arch. Pediatr. Adolesc. Med.* (2003) 157 : pp 821-827.

Executive summary of the third report of The National Cholesterol Education Program (NCEP) Expert panel on detection, evaluation, and treatment of high blood cholesterol in adults (adult treatment panel III). *JAMA*. (2001) 285 : pp 2486-2497.

World Health Organization: Definition, Diagnosis and Classification of Diabetes Mellitus and Its Complications: Report of a WHO Consultation. Geneva, World Health Org., Department of Noncommunicable Disease Surveillance, 1999, p. 31–33.

Kuczmarski R, Ogden C, Guo SS, Grummer-Strawn LM, Flegal KM, Mei Z, Wei R, Curtin LR, Roche AF, Johnson CL .: 2000 CDC growth charts for the United States: methods and development. *Vital Health Stat.* 2002;11:1–190.

National High Blood Pressure Education Working Group on High Blood Pressure in Children and Adolescents. The Fourth Report on the Diagnosis, evaluation and treatment on High Blood Pressure in Children and Adolescents. *Pediatrics;* 2004;114: 555-76.

Young- Hyman D, Schlundt D, Herman L, De Luca F, Counts D. Evaluation of the Insulin Resistance Syndrome in 5 to 10 Year Old Overweight/obese African American Children. *Diabetes Care.* 24: 2001; 1359-2364.

Matthews DR, Hosker JP, Rudenski AS, Naylor BA, Treacher DF, Turner RC. Homeostasis model assessment ;insulin resistance and beta cell function from fasting plasma glucose and insulin concentrations in man. *Diabetologia.* 1985; 28: 412-419.

Mc Auley K, Williams S, Mann J, Walker R,Lewis Barned N, Temple L Duncan A. Diagnosing Insulin Resistance in the General Population. *Diabetes Care.* 2001; 24:460-464.

Flegal KM, Carroll MD, Ogden CL, Johnson CL. Prevalence and trends in obesity among US adults, 1999–2000. *JAMA.* 2002;288:1723–1727.

Hedley AA, Ogden CL, Johnson CL, Carroll MD, Curtin LR, Flegal KM. Prevalence of overweight and obesity among US children, adolescents, and adults, 1999–2002. *JAMA.* 2004;291:2847–2850.

Ford ES, Giles WH. A comparison of the prevalence of the metabolic syndrome using two proposed definitions. *Diabetes Care.* 2003;26:575–581.

Bonora E, Kiechl S, Willeit J, Oberhollenzer F, Egger G, Bonadonna RC, et al. Metabolic syndrome: epidemiology and more extensive phenotypic description: cross-sectional data from the Bruneck Study. *Int. J. Obes. Relat. Metab. Disord.* 2003;27:1283–1289.

Goodman E, Daniels SR, Morrison JA, Huang B, Dolan LM. Contrasting prevalence of and demographic disparities in the World Health Organization and National Cholesterol Education Program Adult Treatment Panel III definitions of metabolic syndrome among adolescents. *J. Pediatr.* 2004 Oct;145(4):445-51.

Hirschler V, Maccallini G, Calcagno M, Aranda C, Jadzinsky M.Waist circumference identifies primary school children with metabolic syndrome abnormalities. *Diabetes Technol. Ther.* 2007 Apr;9(2):149-57.

de Ferranti S, Gauvreau K, Ludwig D, Neufeld EJ, Newburger JW, Rifai N.: Prevalence of the metabolic syndrome in American adolescents. Findings from the Third National Health and Nutrition Examination Survey. *Circulation.* 2004;110:294–297.

Fernandez et al. Fernandez JR, Redden DT, Pietrobelli A, Allison DB: Waist circumference percentiles in nationally representative samples of black, European-American, and Mexican-American children and adolescents. *J. Pediatr.* 2004;145:439–444.

Kahn HS,Imperatore G, Cheng YJ: A population-based comparison of BMI percentiles and waist-to-height ratio for identifying cardiovascular risk in youth *J. Pediatr.* 2005;146:482–488.

Wang J, Thornton JC, Bari S, Williamson B, Gallagher D, Heymsfield SB, Horlick M, Kotler D, Laferrere B, Mayer L, Pi-Sunyer FX, Pierson RN Jr.: Comparisons of waist circumferences measured at 4 sites. *Am. J. Clin. Nutr.* 2003;77:379–384.

McCarthy HD, Jarrett KV, Crawley HF: The development of waist circumference percentiles in British children aged 5.0 to 16.9 y. *Eur. J. Clin. Nutr.* 2001;55:902–907.

Porkka KV, Vilikari JS, Ronnemaa T, Mariniemi J, Akerblom HK: Age and gender specific serum lipid and apolipoprotein fractiles of Finnish children and young adults. The Cardiovascular Risk in Young Finns Study. *Acta Paediatr.* 1994;83:838–848.

Golley RK, Magarey AM, Steinbeck KS, Baur LA, Daniels LA. Comparison of metabolic syndrome prevalence using six different definitions in overweight pre-pubertal children enrolled in a weight management study. *International Journal of Obesity.* 2006 May;30(5):853-60

Index

A

acarbose, 202
acceptance, 195
access, 14, 161
accessibility, 160
accidents, 159
accounting, 7, 41, 42, 66
accumulation, 112, 134, 176, 181
accuracy, 71
acetylcholine, 39, 63
acid, 17, 34, 132, 143, 148, 155, 166, 176, 180, 181, 189, 192, 193, 215, 223
activation, 15, 18, 25, 30, 34, 35, 45, 52, 62, 71, 72, 77, 155, 166, 176, 179, 183
activity level, 160
acylation, 34, 119
adhesion, 33, 46, 106, 114, 126, 172, 175, 176, 179, 188
adipocyte(s), 24, 25, 30, 31, 34, 37, 48, 49, 51, 53, 59, 60, 71, 78, 116, 119, 155, 178, 186, 187, 188, 189
adipocytokines, xi, 5,52, 171, 172, 174, 176, 177, 187
adiponectin, xi, 28, 29, 32, 34, 52, 61, 63, 119, 171, 176, 177, 187
adipose tissue, 5, 15, 24, 25, 28, 29, 30, 31, 34, 46, 48, 49, 50, 54, 71, 78, 83, 106, 112, 114, 118, 123, 155, 156, 165, 166, 174, 175, 176, 177, 178, 185, 186, 187, 195, 196, 205, 210, 215
adiposity, xi, 18, 23, 30, 34, 60, 61, 81, 122, 155, 156, 157, 177, 187, 188, 191, 195, 196, 197, 213, 216, 230
adjustment, 74, 77, 79, 97, 109, 180, 195
administration, 17, 26
adolescence, 194, 214, 216
adolescents, 32, 43, 54, 59, 145, 146, 170, 179, 180, 189, 194, 197, 213, 214, 221, 226, 227, 229, 230, 231, 232
adrenal gland (s), 15, 22
adrenaline, 22
adult population, ix, 3, 121, 140, 194
adulthood, 18, 180, 194, 195, 214
adults, vii, ix, 57, 69, 77, 82, 85, 92, 96, 101, 102, 109, 116, 117, 118, 121, 122, 125, 126, 127, 140, 142, 145, 147, 154, 158, 160, 163, 164, 165, 169, 179, 189, 193, 197, 204, 210, 211, 212, 213, 214, 216, 219, 220, 226, 228, 230, 231, 232, 233
Aedes, 170
aerobic, 127, 128, 156, 158, 159, 166, 204, 220
aerobic exercise, 127, 128, 166, 204, 220
aetiology, 23, 56, 165
affect, 108, 113, 117, 198, 205
Africa, 131
African American, 69, 87, 232
age, xii, 19, 25, 39, 40, 57, 61, 67, 69, 74, 76, 77, 79, 87, 92, 95, 97, 98, 111, 157, 176, 177, 185, 188, 192, 194, 196, 197, 201, 208, 211, 225, 226, 227, 228, 229, 230
ageing, 18, 172
agent, 205, 206, 207
aggregation, 179
aggressiveness, 53
aging, 154
albumin, xi, 4, 67, 76, 78, 79, 87, 91, 184, 186, 193, 194, 225, 227
alcohol, 7, 17, 53, 69, 77, 124, 125, 126, 127, 128, 130, 134, 137
alcohol consumption, 69, 125, 126, 130
alcohol dependence, 17, 53
alcoholism, 7, 22, 46
aldosterone, 23, 24, 47, 71, 73, 83
allele (s), 9, 10, 11, 17, 18, 22, 25, 30, 31, 32, 40, 47 56, 60

alpha-linolenic acid, 143
alternative (s), 7, 12, 26, 28, 34, 42, 90, 102, 113, 115, 162, 210
American Association of Clinical Endocrinologists (AACE), viii, ix, 67, 68, 89, 90, 91, 101, 193, 194
American Cancer Society, 208, 224
American Diabetes Association (ADA), 66, 68, 71, 81, 131, 199, 200, 208,213, 224, 228
American Diabetes Association (ADA), 199
American Heart Association (AHA), x, 60, 81, 90, 101, 119, 121, 123, 139, 140, 141, 142, 143, 146, 149, 184, 199, 200, 203, 208, 209, 218, 220, 224
American Indian (s), 77, 82, 92, 97
amino acid, 17, 27, 56, 166
amputation, 159
Amsterdam, 142
anabolism, 116
anatomy, 86
androgen, 221
angina, 175, 188, 210
Angiotensin, 42, 51, 59, 60
angiotensin converting enzyme, 24, 59, 206
angiotensin II, 9, 24, 39, 47, 54, 55, 71, 72, 78, 83, 190
angiotensin receptor blockers, 206
animal models, 7, 8, 23, 60, 71, 77, 150
animals, 17, 71, 107, 113, 114
anorexia nervosa, 17, 57
ANOVA, 76
antagonists, 8, 22, 23
anterior pituitary, 15
antibody, 29
antigen, 205
antihypertensive drugs, 91, 92
anti-inflammatory, 29, 176, 181
antioxidant (s), 129, 130, 147, 148, 215
aorta, 79
aortic elasticity, viii
apoptosis, 31
appetite, 16, 21, 31, 35, 43, 44, 52, 108, 133, 135, 178, 205
Argentina, 225
argument, 182
ARIC, 77, 79, 85, 148, 188, 195, 214
arithmetic, 192
arrhythmia, 150, 151
arterial hypertension, 142
arterial thickening, 214
arteriosclerosis, 32, 189
artery (ies), x, xi, 79, 80, 85, 140, 143, 148, 153, 155, 164, 183, 187, 191, 192, 195, 210, 212, 214, 215
Asia, 95, 102
aspirin, 181, 184
assessment, 79, 85, 90, 116, 148, 175, 182, 185, 227, 232
association, 107, 114, 173, 179, 180, 185, 186, 189, 192, 195, 196, 210, 216
assumptions, 231
asymptomatic, 74, 164, 195, 214
atherogenesis, 46, 114, 157, 178
atherogenic markers, xi, 171
atherosclerosis, viii, xi, 17, 32, 33, 34, 45, 47, 48, 51, 52, 55, 60, 65, 74, 115, 116, 148, 172, 178, 182, 183, 186, 188, 190, 191, 192, 195, 199, 209, 214
Atherosclerosis Risk in Communities, 77, 79, 85, 87, 148, 184, 211
atherosclerotic plaque, 19, 33, 77
atherosclerotic vascular disease, 184, 185
athleticism, 156, 157
Atkins, x, 110, 118, 122, 129, 135, 136, 137, 138, 146, 147, 201, 218
ATP, 67, 68, 69, 73, 82, 111, 123, 124, 126, 155, 172, 211
ATPIII, vi, viii, xi, 4, 65, 68, 69, 70, 73, 74, 78, 80, 132, 134, 136, 225, 226, 227, 228, 229, 230, 231
attention, vii, xi, 2, 9, 13, 171, 192, 198
attitudes, 170
atypical, 84
Australia, 102, 131
autonomic nervous system, 15
availability, 172, 178
awareness, 79, 126

B

B vitamins, 148
barriers, 156, 159, 161, 163
B-cell, 48
beef, 136
beer, 127
bchavior, 52, 157, 158, 159, 161, 163, 168, 169, 170
Beijing, 94
Belgium, 140, 183
beliefs, 163
beneficial effect, ix, 105, 108, 110, 113, 129, 180, 199, 202, 205, 206, 207, 217
benefits, 110, 113, 115, 117, 139, 144, 148, 149, 200, 203
beta blocker, 51
beverages, 114, 127
bias, 11
binding, 18, 19, 24, 33, 34, 44, 45, 56
biological activity, 175
biological media, 78
biomarker, 109, 186

biomarkers, ix, 105, 107, 108, 111, 113, 114, 115, 117, 165
biopsy, 24
biosynthesis, 22, 39, 47
birth, 7, 17, 20, 51
birth weight, 7, 17, 51
blocks, 18, 134
blood flow, 179, 195, 214
blood pressure (BP), x, xi, 2, 3, 4, 21, 22, 23, 25, 36, 39, 40, 43, 45, 49, 51, 52, 55, 56, 57, 58, 59, 61, 66, 67, 68, 69, 71, 74, 83, 90, 91, 108, 111, 113, 115, 122, 124, 125, 126, 135, 138, 139, 141, 154, 157, 164, 167, 175, 177, 181, 187, 191, 192, 194, 198, 199, 201, 202, 204, 205, 206, 208, 217, 218, 219, 221, 224, 225, 226, 227
blood pressure reduction, 125, 135, 208
blood vessels, 24
blood-brain barrier, 106, 119
bloodstream, 35
body, ix, x, xi, 105, 106, 108, 110, 112, 113, 114, 115, 116, 117, 119, 122, 126, 127, 128, 135, 138, 140, 143, 145, 172, 173, 175, 177, 178, 179, 180, 189, 191, 193, 194, 197, 198, 201, 203, 209, 215, 218, 219, 221
body composition, 165, 221, 231
body fat, 16, 48, 58, 59, 71, 114, 119, 122, 140, 157, 158, 166, 167, 168, 177, 189, 215
body mass index (BMI), xi, 4, 7, 16, 19, 25, 32, 36, 49, 59, 67, 69, 71, 73, 91, 92, 94, 95, 96, 106, 116, 122, 123, 135, 138, 157, 162, 168, 172, 173, 175, , 177, 179, 180, 191, 193, 194, 195, 196, 197, 207, 215, 221, 225, 226, 227, 228, 229, 230, 232
body weight, ix, x, 17, 21, 29, 30, 35, 44, 62, 87, 105, 108, 110, 113, 115, 117, 119, 122, 124, 126, 127, 128, 135, 138, 140, 143, 145, 155, 157, 158, 165, 172, 173, 177, 179, 180, 192, 197, 198, 203, 215, 218, 219, 221
Boeing, 52
bone, 29, 135
bone marrow, 29
Botnia Study, viii, 73, 89, 96, 210
BP, xi, 7, 55, 63, 72, 76, 77, 79, 126, 128, 129, 138, 193, 194, 225, 227, 229
brain, 5, 15, 18, 30, 53, 57, 59, 62, 106, 114, 119
Brazil, 130
BRCA1, 43
breast cancer, 131, 144
British children, 233
British Regional Heart Study, viii, 89
Brussels, 140, 183
bulbs, 21
bulimia, 57

C

calcium, 72, 73, 83, 84, 195
California, 153
caloric intake, 109, 110, 114, 133, 199, 201, 205
caloric restriction, 106, 110, 126, 135, 142, 197, 201, 217
calorie, ix, 109, 121, 125, 130, 142, 146, 157, 180, 196, 199, 201, 202, 205, 217, 218
campaigns, 161
Canada, ix, 121, 122, 131, 133, 135, 139, 140, 141, 144, 146, 196
cancer, 2, 129, 131, 144, 148, 196, 224
candidates, 18
carbohydrate (s), ix, x, 23, 27, 69, 105, 106, 107, 108, 109, 110, 111, 112, 113, 114, 115, 116, 117, 118, 119, 122, 125, 126, 129, 131, 132, 133, 134, 135, 136, 137, 138, 144, 145, 146, 147, 165, 196, 199, 200, 201, 202, 218, 219, 226
carbohydrate metabolism, 226
cardiac arrhythmia, 151
cardiac involvement, 77
cardiac output, 22
cardiac risk, 138, 166, 174
cardiac risk factors, 138, 166, 174
cardiologist, 133
cardiovascular disease (CvD), vii, ix, xi, 2, 3, 6, 19, 21, 32, 39, 43, 45, 49, 57, 60, 67, 68, 73, 77, 79, 84, 85, 90, 99, 100, 101, 102, 103, 114, 117, 118, 121, 139, 140, 141, 147, 148, 149, 150, 165, 171, 173, 174, 175, 178, 180, 181, 182, 184, 186, 189, 196, 197, 209, 211, 212, 213, 219, 220, 222, 223, 224, 226, 230, 231
cardiovascular function, 22, 23, 58
cardiovascular morbidity, viii, 32, 65, 73, 74, 79, 89, 96, 194, 222
cardiovascular risk, viii, ix, xi, 9, 19, 35, 41, 48, 58, 65, 68, 73, 74, 80, 85, 87, 89, 105, 108, 110, 117, 119, 124, 130, 140, 172, 175, 177, 179, 183, 185, 187, 188, 191, 192, 196, 199, 212, 213, 214, 217, 218, 219, 222, 226, 232
carotenoids, 147, 148
casein, 21, 149
castration, 25
catabolism, 108
catalyst, 172
catecholamines, 22, 63, 77, 86
cation, 72, 84
Caucasian (s), 17, 25, 31, 50, 57, 60, 62, 67, 75, 87, 95, 149, 173, 194, 196, 226
causal inference, 231
causality, 7, 12
causation, 12, 47, 173, 174, 182

CDC, 197, 203, 232
cDNA, 9, 18
cell, 5, 19, 33, 39, 44, 49, 52, 72, 77, 106, 114, 175, 176, 186, 223, 232
cell adhesion, 106, 114, 175
cell culture, 77
cell growth, 72
cellular adhesion, 188
central nervous system (CNS), 15, 16, 21, 26, 28, 50, 106, 114, 177, 178
central obesity, 3, 68, 90, 92, 155, 165, 176, 177, 212
cereals, 129, 133
cerebellum, 21
cerebrospinal fluid, 114
certification, 131
channels, 72
chemical, 137
chemical composition, 137
chemoattractants, 33
chemokines, 54, 58, 181, 189, 221
Chicago, 119
childhood, 18, 43, 180, 214, 226, 231
children, xi, 47, 51, 145, 179, 180, 183, 188, 189, 196, 213, 214, 216, 225, 226, 227, 228, 229, 230, 231, 232, 233
China, 89, 95, 102
Chinese, 25, 53, 61, 89, 93, 94, 95, 100, 102, 183
chloride, 127
cholesterol, vii, viii, x, 3, 7, 20, 23, 35, 49, 51, 53, 65, 66, 68, 90, 91, 92, 96, 97, 98, 106, 108, 110, 113, 115, 117, 118, 122, 123, 125, 127, 128, 130, 132, 133, 135, 137, 138, 145, 146, 149, 150, 154, 157, 175, 177, 178, 184, 185, 188, 190, 192, 194, 199, 201, 211, 215, 217, 218, 220, 222, 223, 226, 231
chromosome (s), 8, 20, 30, 32, 36, 40, 42, 44, 46, 47, 48, 50, 52, 57, 59, 60, 63
chronic diseases, 227
cigarette smoking, 124, 189
circadian clock, 63
circadian oscillator, 21
circadian rhythm (s), 21, 52
circadian rhythmicity, 21
circadian timing, 57
circulation, 26, 35, 40, 112, 178
classes, 160, 162
classification, 60, 76, 81, 92, 101, 123, 137, 139, 140, 210, 231
clinical diagnosis, 186
clinical judgment, 194
clinical trials, x, xi, 99, 108, 122, 125, 133, 142, 161, 181, 191, 200, 206
clinicians, 155, 164, 214
cloning, 28, 54, 61, 63
clotting factors, xi, 171, 179
cluster, 174
clustering, 10, 68, 96, 99, 165, 172, 192, 214, 226, 230
coagulation, 20, 179, 189, 205, 210
coagulation factor (s), 20, 205
cocaine, 15, 58
coding, 17
coenzyme, 190, 206
cognitive, 130, 160, 169
cohort, 10, 20, 23, 31, 43, 73, 84, 92, 97, 100, 101, 103, 131, 157, 165, 195, 196, 202, 211, 212, 226, 231
combined effect, 40, 42
commercial, 131, 143, 144
community, 49, 107, 157, 160, 161, 163, 168, 169, 170, 202
competition, 156
complement, 175
complex carbohydrates, 107, 137, 201, 202
complex interactions, 7, 40
complexity, 6, 25, 36, 38, 42
complications, x, 34, 66, 81, 86, 101, 118, 121, 122, 123, 126, 129, 138, 139, 140, 142, 165, 172, 173, 184, 208, 210, 222
components, viii, xi, 5, 6, 13, 16, 21, 22, 23, 26, 33, 36, 54, 69, 74, 76, 77, 78, 79, 90, 92, 95, 96, 97, 98, 113, 123, 125, 130, 155, 157, 158, 165, 177, 178, 179, 180, 181, 191, 192, 193, 195, 196, 198, 199, 201, 202, 205, 206, 208, 211, 226
composite, 12
composition, 106, 108, 118, 119, 124, 131, 132, 137, 138, 165, 172, 174, 180, 201, 215, 221, 231
computation, 172
computer simulations, 60
concentration, viii, 24, 26, 35, 40, 46, 51, 62, 73, 84, 90, 107, 115, 130, 132, 136, 145, 180, 188, 194
conceptualization, 66
concordance, 226
confidence interval (s), 12, 98
confounders, 157, 196
confounding variables, 74
confusion, 107, 182
congestive heart failure, 181
Congress, iv
Connecticut, 105, 119
consensus, 17, 24, 182, 183
consent, 227
conservation, 7, 8
constipation, 136
consumers, 131

consumption, 26, 107, 110, 114, 116, 123, 124, 125, 126, 127, 129, 130, 131, 132, 133, 134, 136, 137, 147, 148, 150, 165
context, 110
contraceptives, 26
control, x, 10, 15, 16, 18, 22, 23, 26, 27, 30, 34, 35, 38, 39, 55, 56, 61, 70, 113, 122, 126, 127, 130, 131, 132, 136, 139, 141, 145, 150, 155, 158, 159, 160, 162, 164, 170, 177, 195, 198, 199, 200, 201, 204, 208, 217, 219, 222, 224
control group, 130, 136, 160, 204
controlled studies, 108
controlled trials, 115, 131, 145, 156, 207, 216, 217, 220
conversion, 23, 53, 113, 143
conversion rate, 113
cooking, 132
copper, 149
corn, 107
coronary arteries, 195
coronary artery disease (CAD), x, xi, 29, 66, 122, 123, 137, 138, 140, 143, 148, 153, 154, 155, 157, 159, 164, 167, 183, 187, 191, 192, 194, 195, 198, 199, 200, 201, 203, 205, 206, 207, 208 210, 212, 214, 215
coronary heart disease (CHD), ix, x, 50, 51, 54, 58, 73, 74, 85, 96, 99, 100, 101, 102, 105, 106, 108, 110, 116, 117, 121, 139, 143, 144, 145, 148, 164, 165, 167, 182, 183, 185, 186, 190, 209, 211, 212, 214, 216, 221, 222
coronary thrombosis, 177, 181
correlation, 10, 107, 113, 175, 177, 179
correlations, 71
cortex, 22
cortisol, 23
costs, 116, 194, 214
counsel, 162
counseling, 144, 158, 160, 161, 162, 163, 169, 170
coupling, 77
covering, 161, 227
craving, 134
C-reactive protein (CRP), xi, 12, 61, 85, 106, 113, 114, 119, 130, 171, 172, 173, 174, 175, 176, 177, 180, 181, 182, 183, 184, 185, 186, 187, 188, 189, 190, 192, 202, 205, 210, 211, 223
creatinine, 4, 67, 91, 194, 227
cross-sectional study, 70, 74, 165
culture, 43
curriculum, 161
CVD, ix, x, 90, 96, 97, 99, 121, 124, 126, 129, 133, 138, 174, 175, 177, 194
cycles, 21
cytokines, ix, xi, 5, 29, 32, 33, 34, 46, 48, 49, 105, 108, 171, 174, 175, 176, 177, 178, 180, 183, 185, 186, 187

D

daily living, 156
dairy, 125, 126, 127, 128, 130, 137, 199
dairy products, 125, 126, 127, 128, 137, 199
damage, 172, 173
data analysis, 61, 194
data base, 92
database, 14, 36, 37, 38, 43
death, vii, 21, 32, 79, 87, 96, 97, 126, 130, 142, 143, 148, 150, 154, 167, 173, 184, 188, 192, 193, 196, 212
death rate, 143, 193
decision-making process, 163
DECODE study, viii, 89, 94, 97, 98
defects, 5, 20, 28, 53, 155, 156
defense, 188
deficiency, 16, 18, 19, 20, 52, 71, 176
deficit, 26, 125, 136, 138, 201, 203
definition, viii, xii, 3, 25, 53, 60, 65, 68, 69, 70, 71, 73, 79, 81, 82, 90, 92, 93, 94, 95, 96, 97, 98, 99, 101, 102, 122, 130, 140, 154, 164, 173, 176, 182, 183, 209, 210, 211, 216, 225, 228, 229, 231
dehydrogenases, 34
demand, 70
density, vii, viii, 11, 20, 65, 66, 90, 91, 106, 117, 118, 124, 126, 134, 143, 145, 148, 154, 175, 178, 184, 185, 192, 194, 218, 226
Department of Agriculture, 200, 218
Department of Health and Human Services, 141, 213, 218
deposition, 71, 177, 178, 195
deposits, 33
derivatives, 181
detection, 10, 47, 54, 118, 186, 211, 231
developed countries, vii, 3, 99
developing countries, 103
diabetes mellitus, xi, 43, 58, 59, 60, 62, 73, 74, 81, 82, 84, 100, 101, 103, 106, 107, 119, 139, 140, 143, 144, 145, 149, 155, 156, 157, 158, 161, 164, 168, 169, 184, 185, 191, 192, 194, 210, 213, 215, 217, 219, 222, 223, 226, 228, 231
diabetic patients, 31, 46, 51, 53, 95, 113, 114, 117, 139, 143, 144, 146, 149, 184, 202, 204, 217
diagnostic criteria, 201
diarrhea, 136
diastolic blood pressure, 18, 25, 91, 92, 111, 125, 204, 227

diet (s), ix, x, 7, 21, 39, 56, 69, 103, 105, 106, 107, 108, 109, 110, 112, 113, 114, 115, 116, 117, 118, 119, 121, 124, 125, 126, 127, 128, 129, 130, 131, 132, 133, 134, 135, 136, 137, 138, 139, 141, 142, 143, 145, 146, 147, 149, 150, 155, 156, 158, 159, 161, 165, 166, 169, 174, 180, 189, 193, 196, 197, 199, 200, 201, 202, 203, 204, 205, 206, 208, 215, 217, 218, 219, 221
dietary factors, ix, 90, 180
dietary fat, 34, 115, 116, 138, 199, 215
dietary fiber, 116, 196, 215
dietary habits, 197
dietary intake, 149, 196, 222
differentiation, 24, 31, 54, 172, 209
digestion, 202
digitalis, 84
dimensionality, 12
dimer, 205
direct action, 28
disabilities, 188
discipline, 8
discordance, 92
disease gene, 11
disequilibrium, 10, 12, 27, 42, 49, 54, 60
disorder, 17, 45, 66, 126, 206
distribution, viii, 9, 58, 59, 70, 71, 74, 90, 110, 122, 140, 166, 215, 221, 227
diuretic, 135
diversity, 18, 90, 161
DNA, 9, 20, 21, 29, 44, 55
dogs, 26, 47, 86
dopamine, 22, 51, 56, 58, 62, 63
dopaminergic, 22, 56
down-regulation, 21, 24, 187
Drosophila, 21, 63
drug therapy, 180, 181, 217
drug treatment, 24, 68, 91, 99
drugs, 8, 34, 91, 181, 206
duration, ix, 74, 76, 105, 108, 134, 158, 162, 168, 199, 201, 231
dyslipidemia (s), vii, ix, x, xi, 1, 5, 23, 61, 79, 92, 98, 99, 105, 108, 109, 112, 123, 135, 171, 172, 173, 174, 175, 177, 179, 181, 187, 191, 192, 209, 210, 221, 223, 226, 230, 231
dysmetabolic syndrome, viii, ix, 3, 65, 90

E

eating, 17, 52, 126, 127, 134, 143
eating disorders, 17
education, viii, 4, 67, 68, 77, 81, 89, 90, 91, 101, 102, 111, 117, 118, 123, 124, 127, 128, 139, 141, 143, 146, 150, 153, 154, 164, 168, 183, 185, 193, 194, 198, 199, 200, 209, 211, 214, 218, 226, 230, 231, 232
egg (s), 125, 130, 134, 136, 137
elasticity, viii, 65, 79
elderly, 6, 23, 43, 55, 95, 102, 147, 149, 157, 160, 161, 163, 169, 212, 221
electron, 164, 195
elementary school, 230
emergence, 180
encoding, 13, 26, 28, 35
endocrine, vii, 2, 5, 13, 15, 28, 34, 35, 36, 37, 38, 40, 44, 51, 52, 56, 61, 78, 187
endocrine glands, 37
endocrine system, vii, 2, 15
endocrinology, 14, 52
Endothelial, 46, 130, 182, 188, 223
endothelial cells, 33, 45, 54, 84, 86, 176, 177
endothelial dysfunction, 19, 84, 86, 143, 176, 179, 182, 183, 184, 185, 186, 187, 189, 195, 219
Endothelin, 73, 86
endothelin-1, 78, 86, 175
endothelium, 33, 55, 79, 172, 174, 175, 181, 190
end-stage renal disease, 187
endurance, 166, 204, 220, 221
energy, ix, 7, 15, 16, 21, 22, 23, 28, 29, 30, 45, 107, 108, 109, 110, 113, 114, 115, 116, 118, 119, 121, 124, 126, 127, 130, 131, 133, 134, 135, 137, 138, 141, 142, 145, 147, 176, 178, 196, 197, 198, 199, 200, 201, 203, 218
enlargement, 20
environment, 6, 7, 38, 40, 42, 159, 168, 178
environmental factors, ix, 2, 6, 8, 36, 70, 121, 198, 192, 210
environmental influences, ix, 6, 121
enzyme (s), 15, 17, 22, 33, 34, 55, 112, 113, 181, 206, 222
enzyme inhibitors, 181, 206
epidemic, viii, ix, x, xi, 65, 69, 103, 116, 121, 153, 154, 155, 171, 189, 193, 196, 208, 213, 218, 226
epidemiologic studies, 23, 174
epidemiology, 8, 9, 10, 25, 46, 54, 58, 209, 210, 232
epinephrine, 40, 62
equipment, 167
essential fatty acids, 187
ester (s), 118, 150, 215
estrogen, 25, 26, 48, 51, 55, 59
Estrogen replacement therapy, 26
ethanol, 187
ethnic diversity, 161
ethnic groups, 29, 68, 92
ethnicity, 67, 69, 91, 194
etiologic factor, 145
etiology, 155, 182

Europe, 68, 92, 133, 218
European, viii, 4, 6, 17, 45, 57, 67, 68, 69, 81, 82, 89, 90, 91, 92, 94, 97, 101, 102, 127, 128, 142, 164, 188, 193, 194, 196, 210, 213, 216, 232
European Group for Study of Insulin Resistance (EGIR), viii, 4, 67, 68, 89, 90, 91, 92, 93, 96, 97, 101, 193, 194, 213
European Youth Heart Study (EYHS), 196, 216
evening, 163
evidence, vii, viii, x, 2, 5, 6, 8, 10, 11, 12, 13, 18, 19, 20, 21, 22, 23, 25, 26, 27, 28, 29, 30, 31, 32, 33, 34, 35, 39, 40, 42, 58, 65, 66, 69, 71, 74, 78, 79, 80, 85, 108, 115, 122, 135, 140, 155, 173, 177, 179, 180, 184, 185, 190, 195, 197, 198, 201, 204, 206, 207, 208, 214, 220, 223, 226
evolution, 9, 85, 146, 147, 218
examinations, 216
excess body weight, 124, 192, 198
excretion, xi, 4, 40, 67, 76, 78, 79, 87, 91, 184, 194, 225, 227
exercise, x, 103, 106, 107, 116, 122, 127, 128, 138, 142, 143, 153, 155, 156, 157, 158, 159, 160, 161, 162, 163, 165, 166, 167, 168, 169, 170, 197, 200, 201, 202, 203, 204, 205, 217, 219, 220, 221
exercise participation, 159
exons, 42
expenditures, 194
experimental design, 61
experts, 107, 198
exposure, 7, 34, 57, 85
expression, 176, 178, 187, 210
extracellular, 33

F

fabric, 99
factor analysis, 100
factor VIII, 179, 188
failure, 5, 123, 172, 181, 207
family, 10, 16, 19, 27, 45, 60, 67, 163, 174, 175, 194, 221
family history, 67, 174, 194, 221
famine, 57, 188
Food and Agriculture Organization (FAO), 131, 144
fasting, xi, xii, 3, 5, 16, 17, 18, 23, 24, 35, 55, 61, 66, 67, 68, 70, 71, 90, 91, 92, 94, 95, 109, 111, 113, 117, 123, 124, 148, 175, 183, 185, 186, 194, 202, 204, 205, 208, 215, 221, 223, 225, 226, 227, 228, 232
Fasting, 4, 7, 67, 109, 154, 228
fasting glucose, xi, 23, 35, 67, 68, 70, 94, 95, 183, 194, 204, 205, 223, 225, 227, 228
fat, x, 5, 13, 16, 19, 21, 22, 24, 28, 30, 44, 45, 46, 50, 70, 71, 108, 109, 110, 113, 114, 115, 116, 117, 118, 119, 121, 122, 124, 126, 127, 128, 129, 130, 132, 133, 134, 135, 136, 137, 138, 140, 141, 143, 146, 147, 149, 150, 155, 156, 157, 158, 166, 167, 168, 176, 177, 178, 186, 188, 189, 196, 197, 199, 200, 201, 202, 203, 205, 215, 218, 219, 221, 230
fat reduction, 146
fats, 129, 130
fatty acid (s), 5, 24, 32, 34, 58, 60, 71, 108, 112, 115, 123, 125, 129, 130, 133, 150, 151, 155, 176, 187, 189, 192, 199, 210, 213, 215, 218
fecal, 149
feedback, 21, 30, 35, 160, 161
females, 25, 70, 194, 197
fertility, 52
fetus, 7
fiber, 110, 114, 116, 130, 144, 145, 149, 165, 196, 201, 202, 215, 218
fibrillation, 150
fibrin, 205
fibrinogen, xi, 20, 33, 44, 99, 171, 173, 174, 179, 184, 186, 188, 192, 205
fibrinolysis, 179, 188, 210
fibroblasts, 62
fibrous cap, 172
fingerprinting, 12
Finland, ix, 89, 90, 209
fish, 127, 130, 134, 136, 150
fish oil, 150
fitness, 126, 160, 166, 167, 168, 196, 197, 198, 215, 216, 220
flexibility, 220
fluctuations, 21
fluid, 114, 181, 207
focus groups, 163
focusing, 2, 77, 130, 197
folate, 149
folic acid, 148
food, ix, 7, 15, 16, 17, 23, 28, 30, 35, 44, 107, 108, 113, 114, 121, 123, 124, 127, 130, 131, 132, 133, 134, 136, 143, 145, 148, 178, 196, 198, 200
Food and Drug Administration, 149
food intake, 15, 16, 17, 23, 28, 30, 35, 44, 114, 145, 178, 200
food products, 148, 196
Ford, 55, 73, 82, 85, 100, 102, 116, 118, 139, 140, 145, 163, 164, 186, 210, 213, 215, 216, 232
frameshift mutation, 16
Framingham Offspring Study, viii, 69, 89, 96, 97, 165, 185, 186, 212, 223
free radical (s), 173
fructose, 107, 108, 112, 114, 116, 119, 143

fruits, 126, 127, 128, 129, 130, 132, 133, 134, 147, 180, 196, 199
fuel, 2, 25

G

gastric, 207
gel, 9
gender, 24, 25, 26, 35, 36, 39, 47, 54, 70, 74, 76, 79, 192, 196, 208, 227, 233
gender differences, 24, 36
gene (s), 2, 6, 7, 8, 9, 10, 12, 13, 14, 16, 17, 18, 19, 20, 21, 22, 23, 24, 25, 26, 27, 28, 29, 30, 32, 34, 35, 36, 38, 39, 40, 42, 43, 44, 45, 46, 47, 48, 49, 50, 51, 52, 53, 54, 55, 56, 57, 58, 59, 60, 61, 62, 63, 83, 118
gene expression, 13, 20, 24, 25, 30, 34, 40, 43, 45, 47, 55, 56, 58, 59, 63, 83
gene mapping, 12
gene promoter, 62
gene silencing, 42
gene targeting, 63
generation, 173
genetic defect, 20
genetic factors, vii, ix, 1, 2, 6, 8, 9, 12, 19, 35, 36, 39, 42, 90, 121
genetic information, 8
genetic linkage, 55
genetic marker, 11
genetic setpoints, vii, 2, 34, 38, 42
genetics, 8, 9, 10, 14, 44, 45, 52, 60, 63, 210
Geneva, 81, 101, 140, 218, 232
genome, 11, 13, 14, 27, 50
genomic regions, 8
genomics, 12, 51, 53
genotype, 7, 25, 29, 30, 31, 32, 34, 46, 55, 56
gestational diabetes, 67, 194
girls, 206, 216, 230
gland, 15, 36, 78
glass, 127
glucagon, 21, 26, 135
glucocorticoid receptor, 62
glucocorticoids, 22, 23
gluconeogenesis, 135
glucose intolerance, viii, 5, 27, 90, 176
glucose metabolism, 5, 18, 26, 29, 114, 119, 206, 207, 226
glucose regulation, 91, 92, 98, 168
glucose tolerance, x, 5, 32, 35, 47, 53, 67, 69, 94, 95, 99, 103, 122, 140, 143, 169, 178, 183, 188, 194, 198, 199, 202, 206, 207, 209, 213, 215, 217, 219, 221, 223
GLUT4, 34, 60, 155, 156, 166
glycogen, 17, 72
glycolysis, 136
glycosylated hemoglobin, 149, 208
goals, 123, 125, 159, 161, 163, 198
gout, 209
government, iv
grades, 76
grains, 126, 127, 130, 180, 199
Greenland, 82, 164, 214
groups, vii, 1, 18, 36, 67, 80, 91, 109, 110, 111, 113, 126, 131, 134, 138, 162, 163, 192, 196, 208, 228
growth factor (s), 18, 19, 20, 21, 33, 35, 36, 45, 46, 47, 48, 50, 52, 53, 55, 58, 72, 77, 78, 86, 232
growth hormone, 18, 21, 35, 36, 46, 53, 55, 58
guidelines, x, xi, 122, 126, 128, 130, 131, 138, 140, 142, 155, 156, 157, 158, 162, 163, 164, 181, 183, 198, 203, 214, 225, 227, 229, 230, 231
gut, 35, 43, 132, 207, 208

H

haemostatic factors, viii, 90
hair follicle, 18
haplotypes, 9, 10, 11, 19, 27, 31, 33, 39, 40, 42, 45, 47, 53, 55, 58
Harvard, 189
health, x, 3, 6, 14, 47, 56, 68, 106, 110, 116, 118, 121, 126, 129, 131, 135, 138, 139, 140, 141, 144, 149, 151, 156, 159, 160, 162, 163, 164, 167, 168, 170, 175, 178, 180, 181, 184, 193, 194, 197, 198, 208, 213, 214, 219, 220, 230
Health and Human Services, 166, 213, 218
health care, 106, 138, 181, 194
health care costs, 194
health care professionals, 138, 181
heart, vii, ix, x, 19, 20, 21, 22, 37, 40, 44, 51, 55, 60, 63, 71, 73, 77, 81, 82, 84, 85, 86, 87, 89, 90, 92, 93, 96, 97, 100, 101, 102, 105, 106, 108, 110, 111, 116, 117, 118, 119, 121, 123, 126, 129, 130, 132, 133, 139, 140, 141, 142, 143, 144, 145, 146, 147, 148, 151, 157, 164, 165, 167, 170, 182, 183, 185, 186, 187, 189, 190, 197, 199, 200, 203, 206, 207, 208, 209, 211, 212, 214, 216, 218, 221, 222, 222, 223, 224, 227
heart disease, vii, ix, x, 19, 73, 105, 106, 108, 110, 111, 116, 117, 118, 121, 126, 130, 133, 139, 143, 144, 145, 147, 148, 151, 164, 165, 167, 182, 183, 185, 186, 190, 209, 211, 212, 214, 216, 218, 221, 222
heart failure, 87, 123, 207
heart rate, 40, 71, 187
heat, 71
height, 74, 75, 76, 77, 122, 193, 227, 228, 232

hemodynamics, 83, 86
hemoglobin, 109, 149, 208
hepatocytes, 30, 31, 59, 113
hepatomegaly, 17
heritability, 6, 7, 36, 59
heterogeneity, 2, 53, 63
heterozygote, 9, 16
Helsinki Heart Study (HHS), 207, 213
high blood cholesterol, 118, 124, 211, 231
high blood pressure, viii, 5, 21, 47, 65, 66, 71, 73, 90, 96, 124, 125, 126, 141
high carbohydrate diets, ix, 105, 107
high density lipoprotein, 106, 118
high fat, ix, 109, 113, 121, 134, 199, 201
high-density lipoprotein (HDL), viii, xi, 3, 4, 7, 17, 35, 66, 67, 68, 69, 70, 90, 91, 92, 96, 106, 107, 108, 109, 110, 111, 113, 115, 124, 132, 135, 137, 154, 157, 177, 178, 192, 194, 199, 200, 201, 204, 205, 207, 220, 222, 223, 225, 226, 227, 228, 229, 231
hip, 17, 32, 58, 61, 67, 91, 92, 94, 95, 123, 193
hippocampus, 21
Hispanic, 69, 112, 118, 207, 211
Hispanic population, 112
Hispanics, 111, 226
HK, 63, 233
homeostasis, 15, 16, 21, 23, 28, 29, 30, 70, 114, 116, 119, 143, 168, 177, 196, 215, 223, 227
homocysteine, 148, 149, 175
homozygote, 16
Hong Kong, 25, 61
Hoorn Study, viii, 87, 89, 97, 101, 149
hormone (s), 2, 5, 13, 15, 18, 19, 21, 22, 23, 25, 26, 27, 28, 29, 30, 32, 34, 35, 36, 43, 49, 51, 52, 60, 72, 78, 119, 178, 186, 207, 208
household income, 69
human genome, 14, 40
hunting, 12
hyperactivity, 57
hypercholesterolemia, 26, 150, 220
hyperglycaemia, viii, 89
hyperglycemia, 21, 27, 61, 66, 69, 70, 112, 172, 173, 179, 227, 228
hyperhomocysteinemia, 149
hyperinsulinemia, 18, 20, 70, 72, 77, 86, 112, 133, 140, 141, 172, 175, 177, 178, 179, 186, 221
hyperlipidemia, 21, 66, 70, 107, 109, 113, 117, 145, 147, 172, 209, 219
hyperlipidemic, ix, 106, 109, 201, 220
hypertension, vii, viii, x, xi, 1, 3, 13, 16, 23, 24, 25, 35, 39, 46, 47, 49, 51, 53, 55, 56, 58, 59, 60, 65, 66, 67, 68, 69, 70, 71, 72, 74, 76, 77, 79, 80, 81, 82, 83, 84, 86, 87, 89, 91, 92, 97, 98, 99, 107, 121, 122, 123, 124, 126, 127, 128, 129, 137, 138, 140, 141, 142, 167, 171, 172, 173, 174, 175, 177, 179, 181, 191, 192, 194, 208, 209, 212, 217, 219, 221, 222, 227, 230
Hypertension, 4, 44, 45, 47, 49, 58, 59, 70, 71, 82, 83, 84, 87, 124, 126, 127, 128, 140, 141, 142, 190, 193, 212, 219, 228
hypertriglyceridemia, 35, 48, 66, 81, 115, 117, 145, 209, 227
hypertrophy, viii, 65, 74, 75, 76, 77, 78, 85, 86, 87, 133
hyperuricaemia, viii, 89
hyperuricemia, 66
hypothalamic-pituitary-adrenal axis, 36
hypothalamus, 18, 21, 28, 35
hypothesis, vii, 2, 5, 7, 10, 18, 38, 40, 42, 49, 50, 155, 172, 182, 184, 195, 206

I

ICAM, 33, 55, 175, 178
identification, vii, xi, 1, 3, 8, 11, 13, 19, 28, 45, 51, 68, 85, 90, 99, 125, 191, 197, 213, 230
IFNγ, 33
image analysis, 9
immune regulation, 178
immune system, 56, 175, 210
immunity, 178
immunization, 178
implantable cardioverter defibrillators, 151
implementation, 80, 208
imprinting, 25
in situ, 24, 115
in utero, 43
in vitro, 21, 23, 32, 55, 78, 86, 115, 144
in vivo, 54, 55, 66, 77, 86, 115, 144
inbreeding, 9
incidence, viii, ix, x, xi, 7, 21, 65, 100, 103, 105, 107, 121, 129, 148, 151, 161, 168, 181, 191, 196, 202, 204, 205, 209, 211, 215, 217, 226
inclusion, 79
independent variable, 74
India, 189
Indian (s), 31, 53, 54, 57, 82
indicators, 231
indices, 32, 44, 47
individualization, 161
induction, 30, 58
infarction, 123, 126, 129, 130, 139, 141, 142, 150, 169, 173, 175, 178, 187, 188, 190, 206, 208, 212, 213, 222, 224
infection, 175
inferences, 8, 9, 231

inflammation, xi, 35, 70, 108, 114, 116, 143, 171, 172, 173, 174, 175, 176, 177, 178, 179, 180, 181, 182, 183, 184, 185, 186, 187, 188, 189, 190, 206, 219, 223
inflammatory, ix, xi, 23, 32, 33, 46, 54, 105, 114, 117, 119, 130, 167, 171, 173, 174, 175, 176, 177, 178, 179, 180, 181, 182, 183, 184, 189, 202, 205, 207, 210, 221
inflammatory disease, 182
inflammatory response, 114, 177, 183
influence, 108, 114, 125, 126, 129, 132, 136, 189, 196, 220
informed consent, 227
ingestion, 107, 116, 146, 196
inheritance, 2
inhibition, 8, 15, 16, 20, 39, 48, 50, 133, 150, 222
inhibitor (s), 24, 32, 34, 47, 72, 176, 181, 188, 190, 192, 202, 205, 260, 222
inhibitory, 84
initiation, 16, 58, 227
injury, 159, 172, 173, 203
insertion, 25, 46, 53, 61
insight, 34
instability, 19
insulin sensitivity, ix, 8, 29, 31, 35, 48, 62, 71, 82, 90, 105, 107, 113, 115, 118, 126, 131, 132, 138, 141, 156, 166, 169, 175, 176, 177, 178, 195, 196, 199, 200, 202, 204, 205, 206, 207, 215, 220
insulin signaling, 155, 156, 166
insulinemia, xi, 225
integration, 12, 198
integrity, 172
intelligence, 2
intensity, 107, 116, 156, 157, 158, 160, 161, 162, 163, 168, 203
interaction (s), 2, 5, 6, 7, 9, 12, 18, 26, 34, 36, 37, 38, 39, 40, 42, 54, 217 118, 139, 188
interest, 107, 129, 178
interferon, 44, 48, 59
interleukin (s), 28, 29, 44, 50, 54, 56, 61, 62, 173, 175, 177, 178, 185, 187, 192, 202, 210
interleukin-1, 175
iInternational Classification of Diseases (ICD), ix, 90
International Diabetes Federation (IDF), viii, 3, 4, 67, 68, 81, 89, 90, 91, 94, 95, 96, 97, 140, 172, 183
internists, 170
interpretation, 10, 110
interval, 20, 40, 74, 126, 142
intervention, ix, x, xi, 99, 103, 106, 109, 110, 113, 114, 115, 122, 123, 124, 127, 130, 131, 136, 143, 154, 155, 156, 157, 158, 159, 160, 161, 162, 163, 168, 169, 170, 191, 195, 197, 201, 202, 204, 207, 208, 217, 224
intima, 33, 77, 85, 172, 195
ischaemic heart disease, 118, 151
Isoflavones, 149
isoforms, 28, 54, 55
isozymes, 23
Italy, 65

J

Jordan, 146, 150
judgment, 194

K

kidney, 13, 21, 22
kinase, 21, 30, 32, 50, 72, 84, 155, 166
kinase activity, 32, 50, 72
King, 21, 46, 49, 52, 140, 160, 169
knowledge, 182
Korea, 93, 95, 102
Kuopio Ischemic Heart Disease Study, viii, 89, 93, 96
Kuwait, 82

L

later life, 7, 18
laws, 2
lead, xi, 7, 30, 33, 72, 73, 95, 112, 114, 137, 158, 176, 177, 178, 191, 197, 202, 208, 231
lean body mass, 71
learning, 163
legumes, 130
leisure, 156, 197, 205
lending, 71
leptin, ix, xi, 8, 16, 24, 28, 31, 36, 45, 46, 48, 52, 53, 60, 61, 71, 78, 83, 86, 87, 105, 114, 119, 171, 176, 178, 188
lesions, 33, 60
leucine, 17, 51
leukocyte (s), 33, 46, 58, 186
life expectancy, 129, 192
lifestyle, vii, ix, x, xi, 7, 57, 68, 80, 99, 103, 115, 121, 123, 124, 126, 127, 131, 137, 147, 153, 154, 155, 158, 160, 161, 163, 164, 166, 167, 168, 169, 172, 174, 180, 189, 191, 193, 194, 196, 197, 198, 202, 204, 208, 214, 215, 217, 220, 221
lifestyle changes, 166, 202, 220, 221
lifetime, 136, 193
ligand (s), 33, 35

likelihood, 12, 74
limitation, 109
linkage, 9, 10, 11, 12, 13, 16, 17, 27, 43, 51, 54, 60
links, 10, 14, 29, 33, 49, 60
linoleic acid, 132, 180, 189
lipase, 34, 113, 118, 187, 205, 220
lipemia, 109, 117, 147
lipid (s), x, xi, 18, 22, 23, 27, 30, 31, 33, 44, 52, 58, 66, 72, 90, 91, 105, 107, 108, 109, 110, 113, 115, 116, 117, 118, 119, 122, 126, 129, 134, 135, 137, 138, 143, 145, 149, 150, 154, 157, 164, 166, 167, 172, 176, 177, 178, 181, 189, 198, 199, 201, 204, 205, 206, 207, 208, 218, 219, 220, 221, 222, 223, 224, 225, 226, 227, 231, 233
lipid metabolism, 18, 22, 23, 30, 31, 72, 134, 166, 222, 227
lipid oxidation, 18
lipid profile, x, xi, 109, 110, 113, 122, 135, 137, 181, 201, 204, 206, 207, 208, 225, 227
lipolysis, 16, 18, 31, 108, 133, 134, 135, 136, 145
lipoprotein (s), vii, viii, 5, 20, 34, 44, 65, 66, 83, 90, 91, 106, 107, 108, 113, 116, 117, 118, 123, 126, 138, 140, 143, 145, 147, 148, 149, 150, 151, 154, 157, 165, 167, 172, 175, 178, 184, 185, 187, 192, 194, 212, 217, 218, 219, 220 226
literature, 10, 11, 14, 18, 20, 22, 25, 35, 38, 48, 188
lithium, 83, 86
liver, 5, 17, 20, 21, 24, 53, 60, 66, 108, 112, 135, 155, 174, 175, 178, 179, 194
liver disease, 112, 194
localization, 10, 44, 48
location, 12, 20
locomotor activity, 52
locus, 10, 18, 27, 32, 39, 43, 44, 46, 50, 55
logistics, 160
longevity, 39, 47, 167
long-term safety, x
Los Angeles, 153
loss of appetite, 135
Louisiana, 191
low carbohydrate diets, ix, 105, 108, 109, 129, 200, 201
low fat diet (s), x, 109, 110, 114, 115, 119, 122, 137, 147, 202, 218
low-density lipoprotein, 55, 143, 175, 184, 185
low-grade inflammation, 180, 184
lung, 21, 22, 117, 139
lycopene, 148
lymphocyte (s), 33, 39, 48

M

macronutrients, 107, 113, 130, 200, 218
macrophages, 33, 172, 175, 176, 177
major histocompatibility complex, 55
males, 25, 49, 55, 70, 111, 193, 230
management, x, 51, 99, 101, 107, 121, 124, 127, 128, 131, 138, 139, 141, 142, 144, 145, 150, 160, 161, 162, 169, 170, 174, 182, 198, 199, 218, 233
manifold, 180
manipulation, 21, 44
mapping, 10, 11, 12, 20, 43, 61
market, 181
mass, 140, 197, 203, 212, 214, 219
mast cell, 17, 45
mast cells, 17, 45
mathematical methods, 13
matrix, 33
MCP, 33, 189, 205, 221
meals, 114, 119, 134, 145, 146
measurement, 90, 123, 173, 176, 227, 230
measures, 123, 165, 178, 180, 196, 198
meat, 127, 130, 134, 149
mechanical stress, 86
media, 77, 85, 195
median, 78, 227
medication, 4, 67, 80, 181, 227
medicine, 2, 9, 10, 51, 63
Mediterranean, 129, 132, 142, 143, 180, 201, 202
medulla, 22, 39, 47, 63
men, 6, 7, 18, 19, 20, 25, 26, 30, 31, 35, 36, 44, 50, 52, 53, 55, 57, 58, 60, 67, 68, 69, 70, 73, 75, 82, 83, 85, 86, 91, 92, 93, 94, 95, 96, 97, 100, 101, 108, 110, 111, 117, 118, 123, 124, 125, 127, 128, 131, 133, 134, 140, 141, 145, 146, 148, 149, 154, 155, 156, 157, 159, 160, 161, 162, 164, 165, 166, 167, 169, 182, 183, 184, 187, 196, 203, 204, 211, 212, 215, 216, 219, 220, 221, 223, 231
menopause, 26
messenger RNA, 44, 45, 47
meta-analysis, 48, 108, 115, 145, 150, 188, 201, 207, 216, 217, 220
metabolic changes, 19, 21
metabolic disorder, vii, 1, 42, 82, 211
metabolic disturbances, x, 107, 122, 155
metabolic dysfunction, 34, 230
metabolism, 15, 18, 21, 22, 23, 24, 25, 27, 28, 30, 34, 35, 43, 52, 56, 66, 71, 72, 84, 107, 108, 114, 116, 119, 134, 136, 143, 145, 150, 155, 166, 176, 206, 207, 212, 217, 222, 226, 227
metabolites, 155
metformin, 103, 168, 204, 205, 206, 217, 221, 222
methodology, 144
methylphenidate, 62
Mexican Americans, 17, 44, 69, 92
Miami, 133

mice, 16, 17, 18, 20, 21, 25, 28, 29, 31, 45, 51, 52, 53, 61, 63, 87, 113, 115, 118, 178
microalbuminuria, viii, 65, 74, 76, 77, 78, 79, 82, 83, 85, 87, 99, 192
microarray, 12
microcirculation, 46
microsatellites, 10, 11
migration, 9, 33, 172, 176
milk, 115
mineralocorticoid, 23
minerals, 129, 135
mining, 12
Minnesota, 170
minorities, 163
mitochondrial, 155, 165
mitogen, 72
mobility, 33
model system, 13
modeling, 208
models, 8, 9, 10, 11, 74, 150, 159, 168
modern society, 196
molecular biology, 8, 10
molecular mechanisms, 42
molecules, ix, 33, 44, 105, 108, 175, 176, 188, 189
monitoring, 125, 181
monkeys, 58
monocyte chemoattractant protein, 205
monocytes, 33
mononuclear cells, 29, 172
monounsaturated fat, 113, 119, 125, 129, 130, 133, 134, 146, 199, 218
Moon, 31, 54
morbidity, xi, 2, 81, 99, 100, 122, 123, 139, 173, 174, 185, 189, 191, 194, 196, 208, 211, 222
mortality, vii, viii, xi, 1, 2, 25, 43, 65, 73, 79, 81, 82, 85, 89, 96, 97, 98, 99, 100, 101, 129, 139, 147, 157, 164, 167, 174, 181, 185, 189, 191, 192, 194, 196, 203, 205, 206, 207, 208, 209, 211, 212, 215, 219, 222, 231
mortality rate, 129
mortality risk, vii, 1
mothers, 226, 227
motivation, 160
mouse model, 20, 44, 63
mRNA, 9, 24, 25, 27, 29, 39, 42, 46, 48, 52, 71
mucosa, 113
multi-ethnic, 43
multivariate, 74, 97, 154
muscle cells, 33, 172, 176
muscle strength, 196, 216
muscles, 21, 112
mutant, 21, 61
mutation (s), 9, 10, 16, 18, 27, 28, 34, 43, 45, 53
myocardial infarction, 21, 49, 73, 85, 123, 126, 129, 130, 139, 141, 142, 150, 169, 173, 175, 178, 187, 188, 190, 206, 208, 212, 213, 222, 224
myocyte (s), 86, 87

N

National Cholesterol Education Program Expert (NCEP), viii, 4, 67, 65, 68, 70, 73, 74, 78, 80, 81, 89, 90, 91, 92, 93, 94, 95, 96, 97, 101, 117, 118, 123, 124, 126, 132, 134, 136, 139, 164, 172, 183, 185, 193, 194, 198, 199, 200, 209, 211, 230, 231
National Health and Nutrition Examination Survey II Mortality Study, viii, 89, 100
National Health Interview Survey, 216
National Institutes of Health (NIH), 122, 123, 124, 125, 136, 139, 140, 183, 200, 203, 213, 214, 219
Native American (s), 62
necrosis, 28, 50, 62, 106, 114, 173, 175, 187, 210
needs, 114, 117
nephropathy, 84, 173, 184
nerve, 17, 24
nervous system, 106, 177
network, vii, 2, 12, 36, 37, 38, 40, 48, 62, 161
neural network (s), 12
neuronal systems, 15
neurons, 15, 48
neuropeptide, 15, 16, 44, 51, 53, 55
neurotransmitters, 22
neutrophils, 54
New York, 53, 61, 146, 147, 218
Newton, 11, 55
nicotine, 39, 43, 63
nitric oxide, 24, 72, 73, 175
non-alcoholic fatty liver, 112, 194
non-institutionalized, 78
nonsense mutation, 16
non-smokers, 123
noradrenaline, 22
norepinephrine, 40, 72, 86
normal children, 227, 228
North America, ix, 121, 123, 124, 139, 200, 203
nuclear receptors, 181
nucleus, 15, 16
nutrients, 126, 196
nutrition, 71, 125, 131, 137, 144, 145, 161
nutritional supplements, 109
nuts, 127, 130, 134, 136, 180

O

Obese, 175, 177, 197

obese patients, x, 24, 56, 122, 125, 142, 146, 197, 198, 199, 201, 202, 205, 221
obesity, vii, viii, ix, x, xi, 1, 3, 4, 5, 6, 7, 10, 11, 13, 16, 17, 18, 19, 21, 22, 23, 24, 25, 27, 28, 29, 30, 31, 32, 34, 35, 38, 44, 46, 47, 48, 49, 50, 51, 52, 53, 56, 57, 58, 59, 60, 61, 62, 65, 66, 68, 69, 70, 71, 72, 79, 81, 83, 86, 87, 90, 91, 94, 95, 98, 99, 102, 105, 107, 108, 109, 111, 112, 114, 115, 116, 117, 118, 119, 121, 122, 123, 124, 125, 126, 129, 131, 133, 135, 138, 139, 140, 141, 142, 145, 146, 147, 153, 154, 155, 157, 163, 164, 165, 166, 171, 172, 173, 174, 175, 176, 177, 178, 180, 181, 183, 185, 186, 187, 188, 189, 191, 192, 193, 194, 195, 196, 197, 198, 199, 205, 207, 208, 209, 210, 211, 212, 213, 214, 215, 216, 217, 218, 219, 221, 226, 227, 228, 230, 231, 232
obesity prevention, 230
observations, 7, 25, 26, 31, 36, 40
obstructive sleep apnea, 207
oil (s), 119, 125, 129, 130, 134, 150, 180
older adults, 85, 160, 169
olfactory, 21
olive, 119, 129, 130, 134, 180
omega-3, 150, 180
orange juice, 136
organ, viii, 28, 51, 52, 65, 74, 79, 80, 82, 187
organizations, viii, 65, 66, 68, 192
Orlistat, 205, 221
Ornish, x, 118, 122, 129, 137, 138, 147, 201, 218
oscillator, 21
Ottawa, 140
outpatients, 149, 217
overeating, 145
overproduction, 176
overweight, viii, ix, 49, 54, 62, 65, 72, 102, 105, 106, 109, 110, 114, 115, 116, 117, 118, 119, 121, 122, 123, 125, 126, 131, 133, 143, 144, 154, 155, 167, 168, 170, 178, 183, 188, 189, 193, 195, 197, 198, 201, 206, 213, 216, 219, 221, 222, 226, 230, 232, 233
oxidation, 110, 111, 113, 133, 135, 148, 149, 176
oxidative stress, xi, 157, 167, 171, 172, 173, 175, 182, 184, 189
oxide, 72, 175
oxygen, 203

P

Pacific, 95, 102
packaging, 112
pancreas, 15, 21, 26, 28, 42, 44, 70, 133, 178
pancreatic, 5, 20, 22, 31, 56, 133, 178, 223
paradox, 167
parameter, 110
Paris, 142, 146, 212
particles, 108, 122, 143
passive, 28, 178
pasta, 134, 136
pathogenesis, vii, ix, xi, 1, 2, 5, 6, 27, 32, 48, 49, 51, 54, 71, 90, 133, 171, 182, 192
pathogenic, 33, 182, 184
pathology, 55, 172, 195
pathophysiology, 5, 36, 46, 62, 83, 139, 165, 172, 178
pathways, vii, 2, 13, 14, 15, 28, 30, 33, 34, 35, 36, 40, 50, 72, 109, 155, 181
pediatric, 179, 226, 227, 230, 231
peptide, 15, 16, 35, 43, 51, 52, 62, 72, 78, 87
Peptide, 18, 84
peptides, 15, 16, 18, 28, 72, 78, 83, 175
percentile, 227, 228, 229, 230
performance, 156, 220
perfusion, 24
peripheral nervous system, 22
peripheral vascular disease, 209
permit, 138, 176
personal, 157, 160, 194
personal history, 157, 194
perspective, 117, 144, 188
PET, 157, 158
phagocytosis, 33
pharmacogenetics, 9
pharmacological, x, 8, 9, 23, 26, 121, 124, 198, 223
pharmacological treatment, x, 121, 223
pharmacotherapy, 216
phenotype, 9, 10, 12, 16, 19, 28, 118, 176, 210, 231
phenotypes, 2, 6, 9, 10, 11, 12, 16, 17, 19, 23, 27, 28, 34, 38, 40, 56, 57, 59, 95
phosphate, 83, 113
phosphorylation, 31
physical activity, x, xi, 7, 99, 126, 153, 154, 155, 156, 157, 158, 159, 160, 161, 162, 163, 167, 168, 169, 170, 177, 180, 189, 191, 196, 197, 198, 199, 203, 205, 208, 215, 216, 217, 218, 220, 221
physical exercise, x, 103, 121, 138, 155, 156, 157, 159, 160, 166, 167, 169, 217
physical fitness, 166, 196
Physicians, 208
physiology, 24, 25, 55, 59
pilot study, 113, 170
pineal gland, 15
pioglitazone, 181, 190, 223
placebo, 202, 204, 205, 221, 222
plant sterols, 150
plaque (s), 33, 148, 172, 173

plasma, viii, ix, 3, 4, 16, 17, 19, 22, 24, 26, 28, 29, 35, 40, 46, 62, 68, 70, 71, 72, 78, 83, 86, 90, 91, 92, 105, 106, 107, 108, 109, 110, 111, 112, 113, 115, 119, 123, 133, 140, 143, 145, 147, 148, 149, 150, 154, 157, 165, 167, 187, 189, 194, 196, 209, 215, 218, 219, 220, 221, 223, 232
plasma levels, 71, 72, 189, 221
plasma membrane, 24
plasminogen, 24, 34, 173, 176, 188, 192, 205
Plasminogen Activator Inhibitor (PAI), xi, 171
plasticity, 39
platelet count, 205
platelets, 21, 44
pleiotropy, 63
polycystic ovary syndrome, 67, 194, 221
polymetabolic syndrome, viii
polymorphism (s), vii, 1, 9, 12, 17, 20, 23, 25, 27, 29, 30, 31, 32, 34, 35, 36, 42, 43, 44, 45, 46, 47, 48, 49, 50, 51, 52, 53, 55, 56, 58, 59, 61, 62, 63, 148
polypeptide, 26
polysaccharides, 131
polyunsaturated fat, 125, 133, 137, 150, 196, 201
polyunsaturated fatty acids, 150
poor, ix, xii, 106, 126, 168, 193, 196, 197, 200, 225, 229, 231
population, viii, ix, 2, 8, 9, 10, 11, 12, 14, 16, 20, 23, 31, 40, 42, 43, 44, 47, 49, 51, 53, 56, 59, 60, 65, 67, 69, 70, 73, 74, 75, 77, 82, 89, 91, 92, 93, 94, 96, 97, 99, 100, 101, 102, 103, 105, 106, 112, 121, 137, 140, 150, 162, 164, 172, 176, 179, 184, 188, 194, 196, 209, 211, 212, 215, 226, 229, 230, 232
population size, 9
pork, 130
portal vein, 26, 112
portfolio, 150
positive correlation, 71
positive relationship, 78
postmenopausal women, 51, 59, 109, 111, 119, 148
potassium, 66, 83
potatoes, 133, 134, 136
poultry, 127, 130, 136
power, 9, 11, 74, 75, 76, 175, 176, 177
precipitation, 181
prediction, 2, 3, 63, 79, 100, 101, 119, 183, 184, 185, 186, 198, 223, 230
predictors, viii, 3, 66, 74, 80, 199
preference, 116
premenopausal, 116, 117, 195
preparation, 113
preschool, 51
pressure, x, xi, 3, 16, 36, 54, 71, 108, 111, 113, 115, 122, 124, 125, 126, 135, 139, 141, 154, 157, 164, 167, 175, 177, 181, 187, 191, 192, 193, 194, 198, 199, 201, 202, 204, 206, 208, 217, 218, 219, 221, 224, 225, 226, 227
prevention, 25, 50, 51, 103, 107, 116, 127, 130, 131, 133, 138, 143, 147, 156, 158, 163, 165, 170, 186, 195, 198, 202, 203, 207, 208, 218, 219, 220, 221, 222, 223, 230
prices, 116
primary school, 47, 232
principle, 196
probability, 226
production, 5, 15, 18, 25, 28, 30, 31, 48, 71, 72, 108, 112, 113, 114, 129, 143, 155, 176, 178
progesterone, 55
prognosis, 43, 123, 131
prognostic value, 79, 174
program, 106, 129, 130, 131, 132, 133, 137, 138, 142, 143, 144, 146, 147, 156, 157, 158, 160, 161, 162, 163, 169, 198, 202, 204, 218, 220
pro-inflammatory, 31, 32, 173, 207
proliferation, 19, 33, 52, 72, 172, 176
promote, ix, 15, 19, 30, 34, 71, 105, 107, 112, 125, 129, 130, 133, 158, 173
promoter, 17, 24, 26, 27, 29, 30, 31, 32, 34, 42, 44, 46, 50, 52, 53, 56, 59, 62
promoter region, 27, 29, 32
propagation, xi, 79, 171
protective factors, vii, 1
protective role, 43
protein, 13, 15, 18, 19, 21, 29, 30, 33, 34, 35, 45, 46, 53, 55, 62, 63, 72, 108, 109, 114, 118, 119, 123, 125, 126, 129, 132, 133, 134, 135, 137, 138, 142, 146, 149, 164, 173, 179, 186, 187, 199, 201, 202, 205, 218, 219
proteinuria, 124
prothrombotic, xi, 33, 70, 171, 179, 181, 192, 205, 207
prototype, 158
psychological well-being, 144
psychosocial factors, 126
public health, viii, 65, 106, 141, 163, 180, 184, 198, 208, 219
pulse (s), 40, 74, 79, 80, 117, 144

Q

QT interval, 126, 142
quality of life, 144
quartile, xi, 91, 92, 194, 225, 227, 228
query, 14
questioning, 68

questionnaire, 159
Quinones, 183

R

race, 48, 173, 188, 230
radiation, 58
random mating, 10
range, vii, 1, 7, 22, 25, 31, 38, 124, 131, 196, 198, 210, 215
reactant (s), 56, 174, 175, 178, 182, 210
receptors, 16, 17, 18, 19, 22, 23, 24, 25, 26, 27, 28, 35, 36, 39, 54, 55, 63, 71, 77, 156, 178, 181
recidivism, 159
recognition, 5, 195, 208
recombination, 10
reconstruction, 12
recurrence, 130
red meat, 127, 130
reduction, x, xi, 12, 20, 23, 28, 99, 108, 109, 110, 113, 114, 115, 118, 119, 122, 123, 124, 125, 126, 127, 128, 130, 133, 135, 138, 139, 146, 147, 153, 155, 156, 157, 158, 161, 162, 167, 170, 175, 191, 198, 199, 200, 201, 202, 204, 205, 206, 207, 208, 218, 220, 222
regional, 166
regression, 74, 110
regression analysis, 110
regulation (s), 13, 15, 17, 25, 29, 34, 35, 36, 40, 44, 47, 49, 52, 54, 55, 59, 61, 107, 108, 114, 133, 134, 135, 145, 168, 178, 187
regulators, 19
rehabilitation, 138, 147
reinforcement, 161
relationship (s), viii, ix, 14, 18, 23, 26, 35, 44, 48, 49, 66, 74, 77, 79, 80, 84, 89, 96, 106, 110, 167, 176, 177, 187, 188, 189, 192, 195, 196, 207
relatives, 92
relaxation, 72, 137
relevance, 26, 133, 145
reliability, 10
renal, viii, 40, 47, 49, 65, 71, 74, 80, 83, 87, 124, 135, 137
renal disease, 74, 137
renal dysfunction, 87, 124
renal function, 83
renin, 23, 24, 26, 45, 47, 48, 49, 59, 60, 71, 72, 77, 78, 83, 86, 179, 181
repair, 172, 179
replacement, 149
representative samples, 232
repression, 60
resistin, xi, 28, 29, 52, 56, 60, 171, 176, 178
resolution, 10, 11, 12, 207, 208
resources, 14, 160, 163
respiratory, 16
responsiveness, 82
restructuring, 130
retention, ix, 72, 77, 106, 207
retinol, 148
retinopathy, viii, 65, 76, 79, 184
Revolutionary, 146
Reynolds, 102
rheology, 173, 179
rheumatoid arthritis, 55
rhythm, 21, 53
rhythmicity, 20
rhythms, 21, 61
rice, 133, 134, 136
risk assessment, 2, 175
risk factors, ix, x, xi, 3, 32, 66, 67, 68, 96, 99, 100, 105, 108, 110, 118, 124, 125, 126, 138, 141, 142, 149, 154, 158, 164, 165, 166, 167, 171, 172, 173, 174, 175, 176, 177, 179, 181, 182, 183, 184, 185, 187, 188, 191, 192, 194, 195, 196, 197, 200, 208, 213, 215, 216, 217, 218, 222, 223, 224, 226, 227, 229, 231
risk profile, 146, 164, 221
RNA, 34
rodent (s), 17, 28, 29, 35
Rome, 144
rosiglitazone, 181, 189, 207, 223

S

safety, x, 122, 150, 201, 218, 221
Salen, 142, 143, 150
salt, 72, 125, 127, 128
sample, 11, 31, 43, 53, 59, 75, 79, 92, 95, 103, 168, 196, 211, 214, 226, 228, 229, 230
sampling, 226
San Antonio Heart Study, viii, 85, 89
sarcoidosis, 60
saturated fat, 108, 110, 113, 114, 123, 125, 126, 127, 128, 129, 133, 134, 135, 149, 199, 201, 202
saturated fatty acids, 123
schizophrenia, 60
Schmid, 170
school, xi, 225, 226, 229, 230, 232
science, 2
scientific community, 3, 42, 107
scores, 175, 195, 227
seafood, 130
search (es), 14, 18, 45, 60, 80
secretion, 18, 24, 25, 27, 39, 40, 43, 56, 59, 86, 108, 112, 113, 114, 116, 119, 129, 135, 177, 178, 187

sedentary behavior, 157
sedentary lifestyle, ix, 67, 90, 121, 164, 172, 174, 194, 214
segregation, 9, 51, 177
selenium, 130
self, ix, 121, 131
self-efficacy, 168
self-monitoring, 170
sensing, 15
sensitivity, ix, 8, 105, 107, 113, 115, 118, 126, 131, 132, 138, 141, 156, 166, 169, 175, 176, 178, 195, 196, 199, 200, 202, 204, 205, 206, 207, 211, 214, 215, 220, 230, 231
series, 112, 140, 159
serine, 31, 155
serum, 17, 24, 29, 43, 46, 48, 51, 52, 58, 60, 62, 97, 109, 114, 115, 116, 117, 129, 130, 135, 145, 149, 150, 151, 156, 173, 187, 200, 202, 205, 215, 219, 221, 226, 233
severity, 74, 164
sex, xii, 22, 25, 36, 40, 69, 76, 92, 96, 98, 188, 225, 226, 227, 228, 229, 230
sex chromosome, 36
sex differences, xii, 36, 225, 229, 230
sex hormones, 22
sexual dimorphism, 36
shellfish, 125
shock, 43
Sibutramine, 205
side effects, 136
signal peptide, 17, 51
signal transduction, 23, 30
signaling, 25, 48, 54, 55, 62, 84, 86, 87, 155, 156, 166, 178
signaling pathway, 48
signaling pathways, 48
signalling, 5, 18, 26, 30, 31, 33, 40
signals, 15, 28, 44, 114
signs, viii, 65, 82, 189
Singapore, 94, 95
single-nucleotide polymorphism, 56
sites, 12, 20, 33, 55, 87, 233
skeletal muscle, 5, 20, 37, 113, 155, 166, 204, 213
skills, 163
skin, 2, 15, 112
sleep apnea, 83, 207
sleep disorders, 21
smokers, 19, 123
smoking, 19, 22, 56, 58, 69, 77, 97, 98, 124, 126, 138, 159, 168, 170, 172, 173, 174, 181, 187, 189
smoking cessation, 138, 159, 170
smooth muscle, 22, 26, 33, 52, 55, 72, 84, 172, 176
social environment, 159
social support, 130
society, 196
sodium, 71, 72, 73, 77, 83, 86, 124, 125, 126, 128, 137, 141, 142, 161, 202, 219
software, 13, 42, 49
soil, 182, 184
South Africa, 131
South Beach diet, x, 122, 129, 133, 134, 135
South Carolina, 171
soybean, 149
species, 8
specificity, 59, 79, 230
spectrum, 22, 178
speed, 79, 157
sphygmomanometer, 227
spinal cord, 159
Sprague-Dawley rats, 24
stabilization, 71
stages, 5, 159, 168, 172, 208, 226
standards, 227
starch, 131, 144
starch polysaccharides, 131
starvation, 7, 115
statin (s), 109, 117, 150, 181, 186, 190, 206, 207
statistics, 10, 12
steroid hormone (s), 23
sterols, 149, 150
stimulus, 77, 133
stochastic, 9
stomach, 35, 52
storage, 28, 133, 176, 178
strain, 28
strategies, 8, 9, 126, 138, 161, 170, 199, 208
stratification, 11, 85
strength, 43, 196, 203, 216, 219, 220
stress, xi, 5, 22, 23, 43, 63, 142, 157, 167, 171, 172, 173, 175, 177, 178, 182, 183, 184, 189
stroke, vii, 21, 73, 85, 96, 97, 100, 126, 164, 213, 223
structural equation model, 183
students, 226
subgroups, 92, 125, 176
substitution, 8, 17, 129
substrates, 26, 27
success rate, 198
sucrose, 108, 132
sugar (s), 108, 112, 116, 126, 127
sulfonylurea, 206
Sun, 63
supervision, 125, 138, 220
suppression, 26, 119
suppressor, 30
suprachiasmatic nucleus, 21, 53

surface area, 74, 75
surface component, 113
Surgeon General, 141, 213
surgery, 24, 198, 199, 207, 208, 217
survival, 7, 190
survivors, 144
susceptibility, 6, 25, 27, 30, 39, 50, 56, 57, 60, 110, 119, 148, 172
susceptibility genes, 6
Swedish Study in Uppsala, viii, 89
sweets, 127, 134
Switzerland, 81, 218
sympathetic nervous system, 24, 63, 71, 73, 83, 86, 177
symptoms, ix, 106
syndrome X, viii, 3, 65, 89, 100, 209
synthesis, 15, 17, 18, 19, 20, 22, 71, 72, 108, 113, 175, 176, 179
systems, 2, 26, 29, 72
systolic blood pressure, 23, 91, 92, 96, 138, 205

T

tachycardia, 150
targets, x, 122, 174
T-cell (s), 33
technician, 227
technology, 26
teens, 113, 194
telephone, 160, 162, 170
temporal, 207
territory, 181
testosterone, 25, 26
Texas, 44, 164
The Zone, x, 122, 134, 137
theory, 9, 30, 47, 62, 106, 160, 169
therapeutic, x, xi, 2, 80, 153, 172, 178, 180, 181, 182, 190, 191, 195, 197, 202, 208
therapeutic approaches, 2
therapeutic interventions, xi, 172, 182, 190
therapeutic lifestyle change (TLC), x
therapy, 25, 26, 59, 74, 76, 109, 117, 125, 126, 131, 141, 142, 150, 154, 180, 181, 186, 190, 198, 199, 203, 217, 222, 223
thiazolidinediones, 34, 50, 189, 206
threshold (s), 3, 35, 40, 68, 216, 230
thrombin, 184
thrombosis, 173, 177, 178, 181, 188
thrombus, 172, 179
thyroid, 52
time, 18, 20, 21, 63, 66, 70, 74, 107, 110, 115, 132, 133, 150, 156, 163, 167, 172, 175, 181, 194, 197, 205, 214, 216, 221
time frame, 107
time periods, 115
tissue Necrosis Factor (TNF), xi, 5, 13, 22, 24, 25, 28, 29, 31, 32, 33, 43, 46, 48, 49, 50, 51, 52, 53, 56, 58, 59, 61, 62, 71, 72, 77, 78, 106, 112, 113, 114, 118, 123, 155, 156, 165, 166, 171, 173, 174, 175, 176, 177, 178, 185, 186, 187, 192, 195, 196, 205, 210, 215
tissue plasminogen activator, 205
tobacco, 40, 177, 193, 196
tofu, 149
total cholesterol, x, 96, 106, 110, 113, 115, 122, 124, 130, 138, 201
total energy, 107, 108, 110, 113, 115, 125, 130, 131, 135, 137
total plasma, 29
Toyota, 45
training, 156, 157, 160, 161, 163, 166, 167, 169, 202, 203, 204, 217, 219, 220, 221, 230
traits, vii, 1, 2, 3, 6, 7, 8, 9, 10, 11, 12, 13, 15, 16, 17, 18, 19, 20, 21, 22, 23, 25, 27, 29, 35, 36, 40, 42, 47, 50, 51, 58, 59, 62, 66, 68
trajectory, 231
transcription, 18, 20, 21, 22, 27, 29, 34, 39, 50, 53, 54
transcripts, 42
transduction, 30
transformation, 52
transgenic, 17, 18, 25, 52, 63
transition, 33
translation, 16, 27
translocation, 156
transmission, 23
transport, 18, 20, 72, 114, 155, 176, 178, 220
trend, 99, 109, 154
trial, 51, 103, 110, 117, 118, 127, 129, 130, 141, 143, 146, 147, 148, 149, 150, 156, 160, 162, 166, 167, 168, 169, 170, 189, 190, 202, 218, 219, 220, 222, 223
triggers, 24
triglyceride, viii, 3, 51, 66, 90, 107, 117, 137, 165, 177, 199, 223
triglycerides, vii, xi, 4, 5, 7, 18, 20, 22, 65, 66, 67, 68, 69, 91, 92, 96, 106, 112, 113, 117, 119, 132, 136, 157, 176, 179, 192, 194, 220, 222, 225, 226, 227, 228, 229, 231
Troglitazone, 207
tumor necrosis factor, xi, 29, 31, 50, 54, 58, 59, 60, 61, 62, 71, 106, 114, 117, 173, 175, 178, 187, 210
tumour, 28, 50, 62
twins, 6, 56, 58, 63
type 1 diabetes, 27, 43

type 2 diabetes, viii, ix, x, xi, 3, 4, 5, 8, 18, 23, 25, 27, 29, 35, 49, 53, 54, 55, 56, 61, 65, 66, 67, 68, 69, 72, 85, 86, 90, 91, 92, 97, 99, 100, 103, 114, 116, 119, 121, 131, 133, 134, 144, 145, 146, 149, 156, 157, 165, 168, 169, 171, 173, 179, 180, 181, 184, 185, 186, 189, 191, 192, 194, 211, 212, 213, 215, 217, 219, 221, 222, 223, 224, 226, 228, 231
tyrosine, 19, 22, 32, 43, 44, 45, 46, 47, 48, 50, 51, 53, 54, 55, 56, 59, 61, 63, 155

U

UK, 1, 20, 36, 57, 119, 196, 206, 222
uniform, 99
United States, 53, 68, 85, 92, 96, 101, 116, 124, 125, 127, 131, 135, 139, 147, 163, 192, 193, 200, 212, 213, 218, 232
unstable angina, 21, 175
urban population, 82
uric acid, 192
urinary albumin, 184, 227
urine, 227
US Department of Health and Human Services, 141
USDA, 200
Utah, 14

V

Valencia, 57
validation, 11, 14, 84, 100, 164, 231
values, xii, 6, 67, 70, 71, 78, 90, 91, 130, 138, 146, 155, 163, 175, 195, 208, 225, 227, 229, 230
variability, 2, 8, 90
variable (s), ix, 11, 35, 42, 44, 87, 106, 123, 138, 165, 167, 188, 214, 221
variance, 213
variation, 2, 6, 7, 8, 12, 13, 14, 16, 18, 23, 27, 28, 29, 30, 31, 34, 35, 38, 40, 42, 44, 47, 49, 54, 60, 173, 187
vascular disease, 84, 148, 180, 184, 185, 217
vasculature, 63, 72
vasoconstriction, 71, 72
vasoconstrictor, 16, 49
vasodilation, 72
vasopressin, 84
vegetable oil, 125
vegetables, 126, 127, 128, 129, 130, 133, 134, 136, 147, 196, 199
vein, 112
velocity, 74, 79, 80
ventricular arrhythmia (s), 151
ventricular fibrillation, 150
ventricular tachycardia, 150
venue, 161
visceral adiposity, 195, 196, 213
viscosity, 173, 205
vitamin E, 148
vitamin K, 179
vitamins, 129, 135, 147, 148
VLDL, viii, 90, 108, 111, 112, 113

W

waist circumference (WC), xi, 4, 25, 31, 58, 67, 68, 73, 77, 91, 94, 95, 106, 111, 112, 113, 122, 123, 126, 127, 140, 154, 155, 164, 172, 175, 193, 194, 200, 214, 216, 225, 226, 227, 228, 230, 233
walking, 156, 157, 159, 160, 161, 165, 167, 169
Washington, 14, 101, 116, 166, 218
wealth, 173, 179
web, 14
websites, 13, 14
weight control, x, 122, 130, 133, 145, 155, 170, 198, 219
weight gain, ix, xi, 15, 50, 71, 107, 113, 114, 121, 134, 165, 170, 173, 178, 181, 191, 195, 197, 198, 199, 200, 203, 207, 222
weight loss, ix, x, xi, 57, 105, 106, 107, 110, 113, 114, 115, 116, 118, 119, 121, 122, 124, 125, 126, 127, 128, 129, 130, 131, 133, 134, 135, 136, 137, 138, 139, 143, 144, 147, 153, 155, 156, 157, 158, 161, 162, 166, 167, 168, 170, 175, 187, 189, 191, 198, 199, 200, 201, 202, 203, 204, 205, 206, 207, 208, 217, 218, 219, 220, 221
weight management, 131, 170, 198, 199, 218, 233
weight reduction, x, 15, 122, 124, 126, 127, 130, 138, 139, 146, 147, 153, 155, 156, 158, 161, 162, 170, 198, 201, 206, 207, 220
Weight Watchers, x, 110, 122, 129, 130, 131, 132, 138, 147, 201, 218
well-being, 144
wellness, 159, 162
wheat, 133
whole grain, 126, 127, 129, 130, 180, 199
wine, 127
women, 6, 7, 24, 25, 26, 32, 35, 36, 50, 55, 57, 58, 61, 67, 68, 69, 70, 73, 75, 82, 85, 91, 92, 93, 94, 95, 96, 97, 101, 109, 110, 111, 113, 114, 115, 116, 117, 119, 123, 124, 125, 127, 128, 131, 134, 140, 142, 143, 144, 145, 147, 148, 154, 155, 156, 157, 158, 159, 160, 161, 162, 164, 165, 167, 168, 169, 177, 185, 186, 187, 188, 195, 196, 197, 198, 204, 206, 207, 210, 211, 212, 213, 215, 216, 217, 218, 219, 221, 223, 230
words, 182

World Health Organisation, 91, 101, 140
(World Health Organization (WHO), vi, viii, xi, 4, 25, 46, 53, 67, 68, 69, 70, 73, 79, 80, 81, 89, 90, 91, 92, 93, 94, 95, 96, 97, 98, 101, 102, 122, 126, 131, 139, 140, 144, 193, 194, 200, 210, 214, 218, 225, 226, 227, 228, 229, 230, 231, 232
World Wide Web, 102
writing, 181

Y

Y chromosome, 36, 39, 45, 47, 49, 51, 58
yogurt, 130, 134
young adults, 87, 165, 189, 233
Young Finns Study, 233
young women, 216, 219

Z

Zone 1, 146